International Conflic

M000187282

This survey provides students with an accessible overview of the logic, evolution, application, and outcomes of four major approaches to the practice of international conflict management:

- traditional peacekeeping;
- peace enforcement and support operations;
- mediation;
- adjudication.

The book aims to provide the student with a fuller understanding of the strengths and weaknesses of these four techniques within the dynamic context of the contemporary security environment, especially in relation to recent and ongoing case studies of inter-state and intra-state conflict. To demonstrate the changing nature of security in the post-Cold War world, the text contrasts this with competing visions of security during the Cold War and earlier periods, and provides numerous points of comparison with the dominant causes, types, strategy, and prosecution of warfare in other eras.

International Conflict Management will be essential reading for all students of conflict management, mediation, peacekeeping, peace and conflict studies, and international security in general.

Michael J. Butler is Assistant Professor at the Department of Government and International Relations, Clark University, USA.

International Conflict Management

Michael J. Butler

Routledge
Taylor & Francis Group

LONDON AND NEW YORK

First published 2009
by Routledge
2 Park Square, Milton Park, Abingdon, Oxon OX14 4RN

Simultaneously published in the USA and Canada
by Routledge
711 Third Avenue, New York, NY 10017

Routledge is an imprint of the Taylor & Francis Group, an informa business

© 2009 Michael J. Butler

Typeset in Times by Wearset Ltd, Boldon, Tyne and Wear

British Library Cataloguing in Publication Data
A catalogue record for this book is available from the British Library

Library of Congress Cataloging-in-Publication Data
Butler, Michael J., 1972–
International conflict management/Michael J. Butler.
p. cm.
Includes bibliographical references.
1. Peacekeeping forces. 2. Conflict management. 3. Peace-building. 4. War –
Prevention. I. Title.
JZ6374.B88 2009
327.1'72 – dc22   2008044651

ISBN10: 0-415-77229-X (hbk)
ISBN10: 0-415-77230-3 (pbk)
ISBN10: 0-203-87915-5 (ebk)

ISBN13: 978-0-415-77229-7 (hbk)
ISBN13: 978-0-415-77230-3 (pbk)
ISBN13: 978-0-203-87915-3 (ebk)

Contents

Illustrations

Boxes

Figures

Maps

Tables

Preface and acknowledgments

> The fact is that we prepare for war like precocious giants, and for peace like retarded pygmies.
>
> Lester B. Pearson

Few can argue that the management of armed conflict is of little consequence; fewer still can make the claim that improving upon the existing track record is unnecessary or, for that matter, undesirable. The main purpose of a book such as this one is not to 'prove' such claims, but rather to synthesize as clearly, succinctly, and objectively as possible the breadth and depth of existing scholarship about what is assuredly a timely and important subject. This is a difficult task given the nature of that subject, which is both profoundly complex and exceedingly dynamic. At the same time, a book such as this must engage with the 'real world,' and seek to highlight areas where even the finest scholarly contributions to the study of security and armed conflict leave us guessing as to how to best manage inter-state and, increasingly, intra-state conflicts – therefore requiring us to confront the failings of such efforts. Out of necessity, then, this book strives for honesty, both in acknowledging and accurately representing the scholarly contributions on which it rests, as well as reflecting the reality that the management of international conflict remains much more art than science.

Above all else, this book was prompted by a curiosity about war, peace, and especially everything inbetween instilled in me at a young age. For that, I owe my parents, who introduced me to the world of books and the life of the mind, and never once questioned the value of either. For sustaining and harnessing that curiosity, I must acknowledge the many wonderful teachers who introduced the supple concept of 'gray' to what might have become a black-and-white mindset. For that, and for them, I shall forever be indebted. In the spirit of coming full circle, I must also thank my students, who continue to keep the flame of curiosity alight. In teaching courses on war, peace, and security at three different universities over nearly a decade, queries both great and small resonating from seminar rooms and lecture halls have shaped my thinking about the concepts and dilemmas dealt with here in innumerable ways.

I would like to specifically recognize those without whom this book would never have come to fruition. I must begin by acknowledging my editor, Andrew Humphrys at Routledge, for his unyielding commitment to this text and his equally unyielding support through the rough patches in its development. The final product certainly bears his imprint. I would also like to offer thanks to those colleagues and friends whom I have consulted along the way, whether for specific insights and feedback or for more general words of advice and encouragement. At the risk of inevitably excluding someone, I specifically would like to thank Alex Bellamy, Mark Boyer, Joe de Rivera, Jeannie Grussendorf, Natalie Hudson, Christopher Knight, Anat Niv-Solomon, and Jean-Sébastien Rioux. Larissa Forster of the University of Zurich helped me greatly in the preparation of the penultimate chapter. I would also be remiss in not acknowledging my many fine colleagues in the Government and International Relations Department at Clark, whose good humor and steadfast commitment to academic rigor and informed discourse make for a terrific work environment. This book also would not have been possible without the generous support of the Francis A. Harrington Public Affairs Fund.

Finally and most importantly I must thank my wonderful family. Anyone who has brought a project such as this to completion knows too well the sacrifices it entails and the demands of those sacrifices on loved ones. For bearing that burden so graciously, I owe a tremendous debt to Ethan, Ben, and especially Melissa. One could never ask for a better and more stimulating partner for this journey. In closing, I dedicate this book to my mother, Eileen, who first introduced me to the library. The rest, as they say, is history. Her untimely passing during its writing served as a constant reminder of the personal grief that so many of those touched by violence and conflict around the world know all too well.

Michael J. Butler
Worcester, MA, USA
October 2008

Acronyms

ACHR	American Convention on Human Rights
ASDT	Associação Social Democrática Timor/Timorese Social Democratic Association
ASEAN	Association of Southeast Asian Nations
AU	African Union
AUC	Autodefensas Unidas de Colombia/United Self-Defense Forces of Colombia
BINUB	UN Integrated Office in Burundi
CIS	Commonwealth of Independent States
CIS-PKF	CIS Peacekeeping Force (Georgia)
CMF	Commonwealth Monitoring Force (Rhodesia/Zimbabwe)
CNRT	Conselho Nacional Da Resitência Timorense/Council of Timorese National Resistance
COW	Correlates of War
CPA	Comprehensive Peace Agreement (Sudan)
CSCE	Conference on Security and Cooperation in Europe
CSS	critical security studies
DFS	Department of Field Support (UN)
DHA	Department of Humanitarian Affairs (UN)
DoP	Declaration of Principles (Sudan)
DPA	Department of Political Affairs (UN)
DPKO	Department of Peacekeeping Operations (UN)
ECHR	European Court of Human Rights
ECJ	European Court of Justice (EU)
ECOMOG	Economic Community of West African States Monitoring Group
ECOWAS	Economic Community of West African States
ECSC	European Coal and Steel Community
EDCs	economically developed countries
ELN	Ejército de Liberación Nacional/National Liberation Army (Colombia)
EOKA	Ethniki Organosis Kyprion Agoniston/National Organization of Cypriot Fighters
EPL	Ejército Popular de Liberación/Popular Liberation Army (Colombia)
EU	European Union
EUFOR	European Union Force (Bosnia-Herzegovina)

FALINTIL	Forças Armadas de Libertação Nacional de Timor Leste/Armed Forces for the National Liberation of East Timor
FARC	Fuerzas Armadas Revolucionarias de Colombia/Revolutionary Armed Forces of Colombia
FRETILIN	Frente Revolucionária do Timor Leste Independente/Revolutionary Front for an Independent East Timor
IACHR	Inter-American Court on Human Rights
IAEA	International Atomic Energy Agency
ICC	International Criminal Court
ICJ	International Court of Justice
ICTR	International Criminal Tribunal for Rwanda
ICTY	International Criminal Tribunal for former Yugoslavia
IDP	internally displaced person
IEMF	Interim Emergency Multinational Force (Democratic Republic of the Congo)
IGAD	Intergovernmental Agency on Development
IGO	international governmental organization
IMPP	Integrated Mission Planning Process
INTERFET	International Force for East Timor
IPKF	Indian Peacekeeping Force (Sri Lanka)
ISAF	International Security Assistance Force (Afghanistan)
ISF	International Stabilisation Force (East Timor)
KFOR	Kosovo Force (NATO)
LDCs	lesser developed countries
LTTE	Liberation Tigers of Tamil Eelam (Sri Lanka)
M-19	Movimiento 19 de Abril/19th of April Movement (Colombia)
MAS	Muerte a Secuestradores (Death to Kidnappers)
MFO	Multinational Force and Observer Group (Sinai)
MID	Militarized Inter-state Disputes
MINUGUA	UN Verification Mission in Guatemala
MINURCA	UN Mission in the Central African Republic
MINURCAT	UN Mission in the Central African Republic and Chad
MINURSO	UN Mission for the Referendum in Western Sahara
MINUSTAH	UN Stabilization Mission in Haiti
MNCs	multinational corporations
MNF-I	Multinational Force I (Lebanon)
MNF-II	Multinational Force II (Lebanon)
MONUA	UN Observer Mission in Angola
MONUC	UN Organization Mission in Democratic Republic of the Congo
NATO	North Atlantic Treaty Organization
NGO	non-governmental organization
NIF	National Islamic Front (Sudan)
NSAs	non-state actors
NSC	National Security Council
OAS	Organization of American States
OAU	Organization for African Unity
OHCHR	UN Office of the High Commission on Human Rights
ONUB	UN Operation in Burundi

ONUC	UN Operation in the Congo
ONUCA	UN Observer Group in Central America
ONUMOZ	UN Operation in Mozambique
ONUSAL	UN Observer Mission in El Salvador
OSCE	Organization for Security and Cooperation in Europe
P-5	Permanent Five (UN Security Council members)
PCA	Permanent Court of Arbitration (the Hague)
PCCs	police contributing countries
PCIJ	Permanent Court of International Justice
PDF	Popular Defense Force (Sudan)
PLO	Palestine Liberation Organization
PMCs	private military contractors
POLRI	Police of the Republic of Indonesia
RAMSI	Regional Assistance Mission to the Solomon Islands
RGO	regional governmental organization
ROE	rules of engagement
RPF	Rwandan Patriotic Front
SA	Strategic Assessment
SADC	Southern African Development Community
SOA	School of the Americas
SPLM/A	Sudan People's Liberation Movement/Army
TAM	Technical Assessment Mission
TCCs	troop contributing countries
TNI	Tentara Nasional Indonesia (Armed Forces of Indonesia)
UAV	unmanned aerial vehicle
UDT	União Democrática Timorense/Timorese Democratic Union
UNAMA	UN Assistance Mission in Afghanistan
UNAMET	UN Mission in East Timor
UNAMIC	UN Advance Mission in Cambodia
UNAMID	African Union–UN Hybrid Operation in Darfur
UNAMIR	UN Assistance Mission for Rwanda
UNAMSIL	UN Mission in Sierra Leone
UNASOG	UN Aouzou Strip Observer Group
UNAVEM I	UN Angola Verification Mission I
UNCI	UN Commission for Indonesia
UNCRO	UN Confidence Restoration Operation (Croatia/Serbia)
UNDOF	UN Disengagement Observer Force (Golan Heights)
UNDP	UN Development Programme
UNEF-I	UN Emergency Force I (Sinai)
UNEF-II	UN Emergency Force II (Sinai)
UNESCO	UN Educational, Scientific, and Cultural Organization
UNFICYP	UN Peacekeeping Force in Cyprus
UNGA	UN General Assembly
UNGOMAP	UN Good Offices Mission in Afghanistan–Pakistan
UNHCR	UN High Commissioner on Human Rights
UNICEF	UN Children's Fund
UNIFIL	UN Interim Force in Lebanon
UNIIMOG	UN Iran–Iraq Military Observer Group

UNIKOM	UN Iraq–Kuwait Observation Mission
UNIOSIL	UN Integrated Office in Sierra Leone
UNIPOM	UN India–Pakistan Observer Mission
UNITAF	Unified Task Force (Somalia)
UNMEE	UN Mission in Ethiopia and Eritrea
UNMIH	UN Mission in Haiti
UNMIK	UN Mission in Kosovo
UNMIL	UN Mission in Liberia
UNMIS	UN Mission in the Sudan
UNMISET	UN Mission of Support in East Timor
UNMIT	UN Integrated Mission in Timor-Leste
UNMOGIP	UN Military Observer Group in India and Pakistan
UNMOP	UN Mission of Observers in Prevlaka
UNMOT	UN Mission of Observers in Tajikistan
UNOCI	UN Operation in Côte d'Ivoire
UNOGIL	UN Observation Group in Lebanon
UNOK	UN Operation in Korea
UNOMIG	UN Observer Mission in Georgia
UNOMIL	UN Observer Mission in Liberia
UNOMSIL	UN Observer Mission in Sierra Leone
UNOMUR	UN Observer Mission in Uganda–Rwanda
UNOSOM-I	UN Operation in Somalia I
UNOSOM-II	UN Operation in Somalia II
UNOTIL	UN Office in Timor-Leste
UNPAs	UN protected areas (Bosnia-Herzegovina)
UNPREDEP	UN Preventative Deployment Force (FRY–Macedonia)
UNPROFOR	UN Protection Force in Bosnia-Herzegovina
UNSC	UN Security Council
UNSCOB	UN Special Committee on the Balkans
UNSF	UN Security Force in West New Guinea
UNTAC	UN Transitional Authority in Cambodia
UNTAET	UN Transitional Administration in East Timor
UNTAG	UN Transition Assistance Group (Namibia)
UNTEA	UN Temporary Executive Authority in West New Guinea
UNTSO	UN Truce Supervision Organization (Middle East)
UNYOM	UN Yemen Observation Mission
WFP	World Food Programme
WMD	weapons of mass destruction
WTO	World Trade Organization

Introduction

What, in a general sense, is this book about? How is it structured? What are the core audiences to whom it is directed? This brief introductory chapter seeks to address these questions as a means of contextualizing this survey of international conflict management.

What is this book about?

In the most basic sense, conflict management refers to any effort by a third party at preventing a conflict from getting worse. It follows from this point of origin that conflict management as an approach presumes that some conflict has already occurred, or is occurring. Conflict management also presumes that said conflict can somehow be contained, controlled, and possibly even ended. In considering each presumption in light of the other, it is fairly evident that conflict management is in equal measure realistic and optimistic, pragmatic and hopeful.

Conflict management is something that is widely used and valid in a variety of contexts. It is not hard to envision how the concept itself, and even some of the approaches to conflict management in the international arena dealt with in this text, might relate to other walks of life. Corporations employ scores of professional conflict managers (often, but not exclusively, in human resources and personnel offices) to cope with conflictual relations among employees, or between employees and customers, clients, the media, or the public at large. To the extent that it rests on the practices of mediation and adjudication, the legal profession can be seen as providing a forum for conflict management. At an individual level, anyone who has attempted to navigate difficult personal or family relationships has engaged in conflict management, probably without even thinking about it.

One who engages in or wishes to employ the practices of conflict management accepts the occurrence, persistence, and recurrence of conflict as a thick and profound strand in the tapestry of social life. Yet at the same time, one who understands and wishes to utilize any of the various approaches to conflict management is able to appreciate the integrity of the whole of that tapestry, and to envision the potential for other strains to be woven into, over, and around the conflict strand so as to maintain that integrity.

Conflict management is something that we, as social actors, engage in on a daily basis. Yet we often do so without much reflection as to what tools of conflict management we are using, and whether they are effective in light of the kinds of conflict we see or are involved in. This lack of reflection is to the detriment of the practice of conflict management. It limits the improvement of available means of conflict management and impairs our collective determination and understanding of what are the best (most effective) approaches for managing any particular case of conflict.

Reflecting on conflict management

It is in that spirit that this book, launched in part at the urging of a significant number of students in both graduate and undergraduate courses dedicated to the study of war and peace, national and international security, and contemporary conflict and conflict management, was conceived. Indeed, if I were to distill one singular and recurring concern from the many animated and lengthy discussions with students in these courses, it would be this: How can the pursuit of security (and in particular attempts to manage international conflict) in the contemporary, post-Cold War environment be updated to reflect the changed realities and dynamics of that environment? In other words, can approaches to conflict management and security provision developed in the strategic environment of the Cold War be updated to effectively respond to the questions and problems those changed realities and dynamics raise?

The centrality of change

A failure to reflect on the nature and workings of international conflict management is particularly detrimental in a fluid and rapidly changing context, such as the contemporary (post-Cold War) international system. To use a hackneyed metaphor drawn from the sporting world, international conflict since the end of the Cold War is a new game, played on a new field with a new opponent (actually, many new opponents) using a new strategy (again, many new strategies), and accordingly raising new challenges and obstacles to 'victory.' The effective management of that 'game' accordingly requires revision of the playbook, which in turn requires us first to ascertain which of the old 'plays' should be thrown out; which could be modified and salvaged; and which might work as they are.

New and fresh thinking about the concept of conflict management and the tried-and-true translations of that concept in light of the changing nature of the conflicts we seek to manage therefore would seem to be the order of the day. However, while many scholars operating within the field of security studies have provided careful appraisals of the extent to which changes in the international system since the end of the Cold War have re-shaped the nature of conflict, less attention has been paid to the effectiveness of various approaches to conflict management in light of those changes. Amidst characterizations of a 'new security environment' that produces 'new wars' – characterizations that will be considered in detail in subsequent chapters – one is left to ask whether the most prominent approaches to conflict management can withstand those changes, and how they might do so.

The need for re-evaluation

In seeking to address this conundrum, this text rests on a fairly straightforward assumption. The changes afoot in the international system, particularly in the security arena, necessitate re-evaluation of our approaches to collective security provision in the form of conflict management. As 'old wars' fought by, for, through, and about the nation-state are increasingly supplanted by 'new wars' with an entirely different set of causes, actors, tactics, and implications (a change discussed at length in the following chapters), it is imperative that students of conflict and security carefully and systematically assess the effectiveness of existing approaches to conflict management in light of those changes.

Not surprisingly, despite the deficit of reflection on the subject, efforts at managing inter-state and intra-state conflict have proceeded apace in recent years. International conflict management has been carried out by a variety of actors, including individual nation-states, collectivities of nation-states, international governmental organizations (IGOs) and regional governmental organizations (RGOs), and increasingly non-governmental organizations (NGOs). Conflict management has been attempted through application of long-standing and fairly conventional approaches (peacekeeping and mediation), and through more extensive elaborations on these approaches (peace enforcement and adjudication). This text confronts the approaches being used, *as they are being used*, and asks whether or not they are well-suited to the task(s) at hand.

A roadmap to this book

As you set out to read this book, you likely find yourself enrolled in any number of courses in the fields of international security, international relations, or perhaps foreign policy analysis or international organization. You might be intensively studying conflict processes, conflict resolution, or peace operations, or engaged in a more general inquiry of security, war, or political violence. Regardless of your specific intellectual concern, the goal of this book is to provide a comprehensive text dealing with multiple approaches to conflict management viewed in a contemporary light.

In seeking to provide readers with a thorough and consistent baseline exploration of contemporary conflict management and its various translations, this book is structured around twin points of emphasis: the changing nature of conflict in the post-Cold War era, and the plethora of approaches to managing conflicts occurring in this changed environment. Whereas many courses and books dealing with these kinds of subjects have traditionally tilted toward the causes of conflict, the aim of this volume is to lend greater consideration to the management of conflict once it has occurred.

The question(s)

The central question facing the reader of this text is the same question that precipitated its writing. It is also a question of fundamental importance to any serious student of inter- and intra-state conflict and its management today. What are the major tools, actors, and approaches that characterize conflict management, and how effective are they in responding to contemporary conflicts? This question, in turn, spawns a series of closely related questions that are also dealt with on a recurring basis throughout the book. Have the major approaches to the management of armed conflict in the contemporary international arena kept pace with the changing nature of conflict itself? Are peacekeeping, mediation, peace enforcement, and adjudication – individually and collectively – viable means of limiting and containing inter- and intra-state conflict? Do they need revision, and if so, in what ways and for what reasons?

The assumptions

These questions in turn are prompted by three core operating assumptions underlying this inquiry. Each is crucial to the orientation and structure of this book, and
therefore demands airing here. The first is my belief that scholars of security studies
have done an inadequate job in cumulating existing knowledge and delivering it in
an accessible way to decision-makers and the public. The problems of the
contemporary security environment are exceedingly complex, and reside in the
'gray' area requiring thoughtful and innovative responses steeped in relevant and
accessible subject matter expertise. For every ill-conceived exercise in pre-emptive
war (which are, after all, easy to recognize and condemn), there have been that
many more situations of failing states, ethnic cleansing campaigns, humanitarian cat-
astrophes, and civil wars posing security challenges potentially deserving of conflict
management. In order to respond appropriately to these challenges, the input of a
robust security studies field that combines conventional knowledge and expertise
with new insights is needed. This book represents an effort at synthesizing those
insights that do exist, and adding some of my own in the hope of lending some
coherence to the message from the academy.

The second operating assumption here is that, in contemporary application, traditional distinctions between 'national security' and 'international security' are becoming
less salient. As globalization has been lain bare in various other areas of political,
social, economic, and cultural activity, so too does it seem that security threats, problems, and solutions are no longer confined by national or state boundaries. Indeed, the
changing nature of contemporary conflict itself (discussed at length in Chapter 2) has
moved warfare far from the Clausewitzian notion of organized militaries pursuing
national interests on the battlefield. As in the case of commerce, crime, pollution, and
various other policy issues, security must be thought of as at least in part a transboundary problem shaped by transnational actors and forces. Contemporary conflicts
are increasingly prosecuted by non-state actors (NSAs) fighting for seemingly every
reason *but* national interest, relying on decentralized combinations of regular, irregular,
and 'fifth column' forces, and drawing on a mix of post-modern and pre-modern tactics,
weapons, and sources of support and inspiration. The ideal of security in a world
shaped by these kinds of conflicts and their protagonists may be just that; but if it is an
ideal to be pursued, doing so through policies and ideas that compartmentalize threats
and responses by traditional 'levels of analysis' would seem counter-productive.

A third (and related) assumption underlying this book pertains to the place of
'the state' in the contemporary security environment. The post-Cold War era is an
era of fundamental change with respect to the role of the state, in all facets of its
activities and roles – not least of these being security and conflict. While nation-
states remain crucial actors in the international system, it is clear that the end of the
Cold War has ushered in a new era in which a variety of NSAs have elbowed their
way to the security table, and in the process have altered not only the rules of international politics that restrict power and influence to the realm of nation-states, but
also those that govern interactions within the global system. Whether this power and
influence is exercised by NSAs seeking to utilize violence to alter (perhaps radically)
those interactions, or by NSAs seeking to contain the use of violence to sustain (or
gently modify) them, it seems evident that states are no longer the sole threat to (or
provider of) security in the global arena.

The objective

Taken together, these three assumptions suggest that this book is launched from a place of respect and concern for the ongoing transformation of the global arena, a transformation with profound implications for efforts toward the management of intra-state and inter-state conflict in the twenty-first century. This transformation, probed and engaged repeatedly throughout the book, undoubtedly requires new thinking about the suitability of prevailing approaches to conflict management and the pursuit of collective security. Accordingly, this text seeks to stimulate new insights about the problems of, and prospects for, conflict management in light of evident changes in the nature and dynamics of conflict in the contemporary international system.

The goal of the book, then, is three-fold: to provide a thorough scholarly accounting of conflict management techniques; to evaluate each of these techniques in relation to the changed and changing nature of conflict and security; and finally, to examine each technique in contemporary application. The book's central premise is decidedly simple. In building out from the widely chronicled changes in contemporary conflict, one is left to confront the question of what, if anything, can be done to effectively manage contemporary conflicts. In service of that purpose, the book is designed to integrate the leading edge of thinking about contemporary conflict with a comprehensive and critical overview of conflict management (past and present).

The aim here is not to offer a new theoretical treatise or analytical dissection of contemporary efforts at conflict management in the international arena. Instead, I have elected to focus on what I believe to be the most salient and important themes and approaches to conflict management, as a means to shed light on the patterns and possibilities for managing and containing conflict in the years to come. I deliberately emphasize key concepts over abstract theory, and rely on empirical evidence rather than explanatory models to illustrate and support my main arguments about the evolution of (primarily intra-state) conflict and the somewhat slower and less complete evolution of attempts at managing such conflicts. As such, this book is intended to address a conspicuous gap in the security studies literature, by extending the 'new wars' literature into the realm of conflict management and peace operations, yet to do so in a way that is as accessible to students as it is relevant to scholars and practitioners.

The challenge(s)

We currently reside in the midst of a global transformation with profound implications for the nature of conflict and security. As a result, adequately addressing the questions outlined in the preceding section requires both the reader and the author to close an intellectual and generational gap in the field of security studies. One must be familiar with the dynamics of traditional approaches to conflict management, such as peacekeeping and some forms and examples of mediation. These traditional approaches are typically defined not only by their operational parameters, but also by the central involvement of states and/or IGOs. These approaches have traditionally provided the building blocks for collective security operations, and remain central and viable options for conflict management.

At the same time, assessing the applicability and utility of these four approaches to conflict management – and in turn, of conflict management as a concept – also requires familiarity with newer approaches. In this category, one can locate such post-Cold War introductions as peace enforcement, as well as revised and expanded efforts at adjudication and mediation involving any combination of multilateral institutions, NGOs, and other NSAs. These approaches have themselves emerged in response to the increasing frequency of intra-state warfare, ethnic and identity conflict, and weak and failing states – and the inability of nation-states and IGOs to adequately manage such conflicts.

This degree of inclusiveness is motivated by an intellectual purpose; incorporating a wider range of techniques (including 'traditional' or state-based ones) allows us to consider and appreciate the design and implementation problems associated with applying traditional approaches to contemporary conflicts which themselves are decidedly *not* state-centric. Furthermore, this broad focus allows readers to examine the ways in which the techniques themselves continue to evolve. For example, approaches customarily defined as 'traditional,' such as mediation, have changed as third parties other than states have become increasingly involved in such activities. Similarly, adjudication today has a significant multilateral component, and has increasingly come to encompass elements of post-conflict reconciliation.

The structure

This book begins with an overview of international conflict management, including an assessment of the origination and evolution of the concept and a chronicling of its various translations, central debates, and core themes (Chapter 1). From this baseline, the book proceeds to a direct consideration of the major changes in both security and conflict that define the contemporary, post-Cold War environment (Chapters 2 and 3). A central theme of this consideration is the emergence and defining features of the concept of 'new wars,' the security environment in which such 'new wars' have emerged, and the problems and puzzles that both the changing nature of conflict and security present to the management of international conflict.

These two conceptual and historical chapters serve as two parts of a coherent whole. Though they each deal with discrete topics and phenomena, taken in sum they aim to illuminate the historical pathway as well as highlight the major defining elements that shape conflict and conflict management in the contemporary global arena. Along the way they illustrate several of the more important recurring themes of this book: namely, that security is a fluid concept, conflict is ever-changing, and that attempts to manage and contain armed violence can be constrained by outmoded intellectual assumptions as well as by more obvious shortcomings in necessary material resources and capabilities.

From this foundation, the main objective of this text (its 'value added,' as an economist might say) is pursued in earnest. The succeeding chapters present a series of four paired conceptual and empirical chapters appraising, in turn, peacekeeping (Chapters 4 and 5), mediation (Chapters 6 and 7), peace enforcement (Chapters 8 and 9), and adjudication (Chapters 10 and 11) as approaches to the management of inter- and intra-state conflict. Each pairing features a topical chapter that carefully documents the origins, underpinnings, issues, and controversies surrounding a particular conflict management approach, including discussion of previous applications of the approach in recent history. This topical chapter is then followed by an empirical companion, presenting a structured and focused case study of the approach in question in application to a recent and/or ongoing case of intra-state conflict.

This paired approach is designed to serve the overriding objective of this book, providing the reader with a comprehensive assessment of the strengths and weaknesses of conflict management both as a concept and in application within the dynamic context of the contemporary security environment and in response to the dynamics and processes of 'new wars.' A key to achieving this goal is the presentation of contemporary (post-Cold War) case studies, which allow (in conjunction with the use of opening vignettes and empirical examples within the topical chapters themselves) for close contemporary examination of the concepts and themes associated with each approach to conflict management.

These are case studies of conflict management behaviors more than events. Each case study provides 'real world' illustrations of peacekeeping, mediation, peace enforcement, and adjudication in recent (and in some cases, ongoing) conflicts, thereby presenting the reader with a data-rich evaluative summary of some of the major conflict management operations of the post-Cold War era. More to the point, they allow the reader not only to examine each 'real world' individual application of conflict management, but also to utilize each case to examine and evaluate the merits of that approach in light of what we know about the nature of contemporary conflict. Finally, the book concludes with a retrospective assessment of 'lessons learned' from the previous consideration of these four approaches to conflict management in contemporary application as well as a brief comment on the possibilities for international conflict management in the future (Chapter 12).

The niche

There is of course nothing inherently new about international conflict management, or for that matter any of the approaches to conflict management examined in this text. Each has an existing track record, and each has generated a significant array of both empirical and theoretical inquiry. Similarly, other (and better) treatments of the changing nature of conflict precede this one. Rather, the niche that this book occupies is as an update to our collective knowledge-base with regard to each of these four major approaches to conflict management, on the basis of these well-chronicled changes in international conflict since the end of the Cold War.

This text provides a conceptual inventory of peacekeeping, mediation, peace enforcement, and adjudication as approaches to international conflict management. Given the centrality of change to conflict processes, it does so in a historically informed way. Each chapter pairing is therefore designed and intended to assess not only the key themes and concepts associated with each conflict management approach, but to appraise those approaches in an evolutionary light so as to ascertain their utility in contemporary application. Such temporal considerations are essential to assessing conflict management as a concept and a set of approaches if we hope to gauge its pros and cons today.

The boundaries

The aforementioned objectives, questions, challenges, and design combine to make this a unique text. It marries the best of the 'new wars' scholarship, emphasizing the changing nature of conflict with a systematic consideration of the major techniques of conflict management, which lends the book a contemporary and applied focus. This marriage requires the reader to possess a basic appreciation of the frequency, intensity, and deadliness of armed conflict in our world today. However, the focus of this book on the qualitative changes evident in contemporary conflict and the ability (or inability) of the predominant approaches to conflict management to account for those changes, rules out any extended discussion of the statistical parameters of armed conflict or in-depth consideration of the causes of war itself. These subjects have been frequently and well-chronicled in other volumes, and the reader is heartily encouraged to consult these sources as a pretext to, or in combination with, this work.

Of its distinguishing features, perhaps the main defining parameter of this book is its pragmatism – appropriate, given the 'middle ground' position occupied by conflict management. This text starts from a point of origin that accepts the pervasive (if not endemic) nature of conflict in the contemporary international system, but also holds out the potential to contain such conflict on a case-by-case basis. As you embark upon this text, then, it is important to recognize that the presentation following this introductory chapter is decidedly shorn of any illusions that the major structural changes currently underway in the international system – including the growing importance of international organizations and NSAs, the rise of both transnational interests and norms, and the decline of the state's monopoly on violence, to name just a few – represent a new dawn of cooperation and peace.

These changes are fully acknowledged, and their significance for conflict and security in the global arena proves a central theme of the book. However, that significance is treated here in relation to how such changes intersect with the continued tendency of people operating in defined and discernable groups to utilize varying levels of organized violence as a means of pursuing some political, social, economic, or cultural end(s). In appraising the utility of conflict management as a means of limiting 'new wars,' this text chooses to emphasize, as the 'new wars' literature does, that much of what is 'new' about the conduct and process of global politics is merely an empty vessel that can be (and most assuredly *is*) employed in the service of death and destruction.

Though emanating from a concern with managing and limiting conflict in the international system, this text clearly lacks the transformative focus and advocacy orientation evident in the fields of conflict resolution and peace studies. Such approaches emphasize a level of social re-engineering subsumed under the heading of peacebuilding that, while likely necessary, has, to date, rarely been attempted and possibly lies beyond the bounds of what seems feasible at the current moment in history. Given this emphasis, it is not altogether surprising that these fields and the scholarship they generate devote relatively little attention (other than scathing critique) to the types of 'traditionalist' approach encompassed under the heading of conflict management.

Such critique is both useful and often valid. However, this book is of a very different orientation, and originates from a very different starting point than one might encounter in the conflict resolution or peace studies literature. Given its twin emphases on analytical summary and empirical evaluation, this text seeks to expose the reader in an unvarnished fashion to the wider and still-evolving debate over the appropriate scope and extent for conflict management in the international community *as it is currently practiced*.

In acknowledging the origins and evolution of these conflict management techniques, this book is not in a position to advance any philosophical argument about approaches to conflict management and peace operations, choosing instead to simply chronicle them in their glory and ignominy (typically, they feature plenty of each). While some approaches to international conflict management do remain quite 'traditional' in their acceptance of the prevailing norms and institutions governing the conduct of international relations, excluding these approaches from one's purview – or labeling them tools of 'negative peace' (Barash and Webel, 2008) seems to obscure rather than illuminate.

At the same time, this text is not intended to serve as a fatalistic chronicle of the ways in which the twenty-first century, like every preceding century before it, portends a solitary, nasty, brutish, and short life for all of us. Nor does this text represent an uncritical acceptance of the concept and practices of international conflict management. In fact, neither could be further from the truth. At its core, conflict management represents a bridge between the 'real' and the 'possible,' as exemplified in the approaches to conflict management examined in this text, and the many empirical examples of their application. This text is likewise intended to serve a bridge-building function. In a narrow (scholarly) sense, this book forges a link between the 'new wars' and conflict management literatures, and between traditional and newer schools operating within the field of security studies. In a wider (applied) sense – and one likely of more concern to most of its readers – this text seeks to connect the evident reality of the persistence and complexity of conflict in our contemporary world with a set of available tools that have most often been employed in the past to contain it.

Suggested reading

Betts, Richard K. 2007. *Conflict After the Cold War: Arguments on Causes of War and Peace*, 3rd edn. New York, NY: Pearson Longman.

Brown, Michael E. (ed.). 1996. *The International Dimensions of Internal Conflict*. Cambridge, MA: MIT Press.

Burton, John and Frank Dukes. 1990. *Conflict: Practices in Management, Settlement and Resolution*. New York, NY: St. Martin's Press.

Nye, Joseph S. 2006. *Understanding International Conflicts: An Introduction to Theory and History*, 6th edn. New York, NY: Pearson Longman.

Steiner, Barry Howard. 2004. *Collective Preventative Diplomacy: A Study in International Conflict Management*. Albany, NY: SUNY Press.

Thompson, W. Scott and Kenneth M. Jensen. 1991. *Approaches to Peace: An Intellectual Map*. Washington, DC: USIP Press.

Zartman, I. William. 2007. *Peacemaking in International Conflict: Methods and Techniques*, revised edn. Washington, DC: USIP Press.

Part I
Continuity and change

1 What is international conflict management?

This chapter provides a cursory review of international conflict management, both as a concept and in application. It begins by introducing a basic operational definition and outlining the historical evolution of conflict management in conjunction with, and as a means for, the provision of collective security. Attention is then directed toward situating the concept in relation to ongoing debates concerning the intellectual position and wider implications of conflict management.

Defining international conflict management

Of all the phenomena ripe for inquiry in the study of international relations, the collective employment of armed violence is undoubtedly the most pervasive and enduring. International conflict is simply a form of social conflict, and bears all the hallmarks thereof. Such conflicts arise from a mutual recognition of competing or incompatible material interests and basic values. Furthermore, most conflicts in the social realm are dynamic rather than static in nature, and evolve in accordance with interactions between and among the aggrieved parties. The particular form of social conflict of concern here (international conflict) is distinguishable from other forms only due to the parties involved. Over the great expanse of human history conflicts have been waged between states, within states, and by NSAs irrespective of states.

Nearly as enduring as conflict are considerations of how third parties can manage, contain, and limit these evolving social conflicts between actors in the international arena. Attempts at conflict management, though not as pervasive (or as widely chronicled) as conflict, are every bit as instrumental and worthy of our attention. This has much to do with the implications of these efforts. Attempts at managing, containing, and limiting the use of armed violence by third parties can have positive, even transformative, outcomes, in the form of order, stability, and even peace. At the same time, ill-conceived, inappropriate, poorly timed, or half-hearted efforts at conflict management can *worsen* a conflict, generating even more danger, destruction, and death for even more people. Given these two possible trajectories, the real-world stakes associated with international conflict management are clearly high.

What is international conflict management?

As the title suggests, this text is expressly concerned with the practice of conflict management in response to contemporary international conflicts. In that particular context, conflict management is best understood as any effort to control or contain an ongoing conflict between politically motivated actors operating at the state or sub-state level, typically through the involvement of a third party (Burton and Dukes, 1990). Conflict management is centrally concerned with making an ongoing conflict less damaging to the parties directly engaged in it. Conflict management also often originates from a concern on the part of a third party with containing the conflict's damaging and destabilizing effects to other semi-involved or non-involved parties (horizontal escalation) as well as containing the conflict's ascent up the ladder of violent goals and implements (vertical escalation). Finally, conflict management operates from the premise that the escalation or intensification of a conflict is not inevitable. Rather, the goal of conflict management is to deny 'victory' to the aggressor(s), or perhaps more accurately, to deny the utility of aggression.

Conflict management approaches are those utilized when the prospects for conflict resolution seem far-off, but the dynamics of the conflict demand that something be done to contain it (Von Hippel and Clarke, 1999). In cases where the escalation or intensification of a conflict seems likely in the absence of any overarching governing authority, third parties can stem the tide of escalation or intensification in numerous ways. At the most general level, third parties employ an array of approaches when seeking to manage international conflicts. Two leading scholars of international conflict management have grouped these approaches into four broad categories (Bercovitch and Regan, 2004). These approaches, defined by a mix of actor objectives and means employed, are:

- *threat-based* (including the use and/or threat of force and other tools to compel other parties);
- *deterrence-based* (including the use and/or threat of force, and various instruments of coercive diplomacy to deter other parties);
- *adjudicatory* (including legal, extra-legal, and normative institutions and approaches to craft, and reach legal settlements with other parties); and
- *accommodationist* (including traditional and non-traditional diplomatic means to broker agreement with other parties).

These categories mirror the ways in which parties to a particular conflict typically approach the dispute at the heart of that conflict. Threat-based and deterrence-based approaches correspond most clearly with the threat and/or use of 'hard' (coercive) power in the pursuit of interest, with the main difference being the objective sought. Adjudicatory approaches rely heavily on the recognition of, and appeal to, a system of norms and rights and a legal architecture arrayed around them. Finally, approaches predicated on accommodation emphasize the utility of 'soft' (persuasive) power as a means to pursue interests. Each of these approaches, whether in relation to conflict or its management, carries with it different ramifications and consequences, entails different cost, demands different resources, and may succeed (or fail) under different circumstances.

What international conflict management is not

The study of international conflict management can be confusing. A chief source of confusion is the imprecision in the lexicon used to describe various mechanisms for dealing with conflict. Terms such as conflict resolution, termination, transformation, and settlement are sometimes used interchangeably with conflict management (and with one another) by commentators and even scholars. These misrepresentations work against an accurate understanding of what conflict management is (and isn't), while also oversimplifying the wide array of concepts and approaches to containing violence – the fundamental and defining objective of conflict management.

Perhaps the most prominent area for imprecision and, as a result, confusion comes with respect to the relationship between conflict management and conflict resolution. As noted above, conflict management refers to the efforts of third parties in concert with disputants to limit the spread or escalation of a conflict, to minimize suffering, and to create an environment for interaction without resorting to violence. As a result, conflict management is entirely distinct from conflict resolution on a basic conceptual plane. Whereas conflict resolution seeks to promote reconciliation at the basic level of a conflict by resolving the underlying grievances at the heart of a particular dispute to the satisfaction of all parties involved, conflict management remains closer to the surface. As such, conflict management is far less ambitious in its objectives than conflict resolution, which seeks to transform the personal values, cultural practices, and social and political rules and institutions sustaining a conflict.

Conflict management practices and practitioners shy away from such far-reaching endeavors, focusing on containing conflict as a precursor to settling a dispute, rather than full-fledged conflict resolution. Conflict management is therefore far more likely to accept the notion that a particular conflict is too complex, deeply embedded, and intractable to be resolved at a particular juncture. The focal point of conflict management efforts thereby become management of the deleterious effects of a conflict rather than resolution of its underlying causes. Accordingly, the objectives of conflict management, while limited, tend to be feasible and widely applicable.

Conflict management and collective security

Outlining the historical trajectory of international conflict management leading up to the contemporary (post-Cold War) period is a somewhat daunting proposition. Conflict management as defined in this book is a relatively new introduction to international political life. Active efforts by third parties to limit inter- and intrastate conflicts and contain their negative effects are largely, though not exclusively, twentieth-century phenomena. That being said, the underlying impetus behind conflict management is the pursuit of collective security, which has a longer track record worth investigating in order to gain purchase on the emergence of international conflict management (see Box 1.1).

Box 1.1 What is collective security?

Collective security is based on three core ideas: first, that armed aggression is an unacceptable form of international political behavior; second, that an act of aggression directed against any one member in good standing in the international system should be construed as a breach of security and an act of aggression directed against all parties; and third, that the provision of security (including the prevention and reversal of acts of aggression) is the duty of all actors in the international system. To this end, as Baylis (2001: 264) points out:

collective security involves a recognition by states that (1) they must renounce the use of military force to alter the status quo, and agree instead to settle their disputes peacefully; (2) they must broaden their conception of the national interest to take account of the interests of the international community as a whole; and (3) they must overcome the fear which dominates world politics and learn to trust one another.

The communitarian strain at the heart of collective security is what distinguishes collective security systems from alliances. Whereas the latter are usually precipitated by a common external threat, they remain self-regarding in both interest and action. Collective security systems, on the other hand, are defined by shared and other-regarding interests and actions, particularly regarding the obligation of all to join in a collective response to aggression and other threats to security.

Conflict management and collective security share a common point of origin in the preservation and observance of certain norms governing the behavior and interactions among states and other actors on the world stage. The most notable of these shared norms is the undesirability of using armed conflict as a means for settling disputes, as well as the appeal of collective responses to limit threats to security and order posed by armed conflict. Given the extent to which the tools of conflict management have been utilized as a means to the end of collective security today, it is worth reviewing the origins and evolution of collective security and its nexus with conflict management at several crucial junctures in history.

Early antecedents

The impetus to manage conflicts and limit their effects is evident even in the tentative collective security arrangements of antiquity. Ancient China was home to some mixed experiments in cooperative leagues of independent states in the seventh and sixth centuries BC, in which limiting warfare and its deleterious effects was a primary objective; the dissolution of these proved a precursor to a long period of bitter warfare. Elements of collective security and conflict management were also present in the Pan-Hellenist leagues of classical Greece. From their origins as military alliances born of convenience, these arrangements evolved to a point where the most powerful actors were entrusted with the responsibility for the maintenance of order, in return for some executive powers and privileges conferred by weaker members of the coalition.

While amassing ever-increasing sums of wealth and power was undoubtedly the chief objective, it is also clear that imperial Rome (as well as some of its chief subordinate units) undertook policing and enforcement action against disloyal subject nations as well as against external enemies in order to maintain *Pax Romana*. Later, the institutionalized alliances of Renaissance Italy (crafted by the ruling *reggimento* of Venice, Florence, Bologna, Perugia, Siena, and others beginning in 1415), like the League of Venice (1495) and the wider Holy League arranged by Pope Pius V (1571) that followed, provided mechanisms for harnessing armed conflict for the purposes of the collective (in the latter two cases, for defense against outside enemies) while otherwise attempting to limit its use.

The Concert of Europe

One of the most successful and enduring efforts at creating an inter-state system for the provision of collective security was the Concert of Europe. Strictly speaking, the Concert of Europe describes a period of non-war between the great powers of Europe that entailed from 1815 to 1854. However, the Concert of Europe's significance and legacy were much broader, as it helped undergird a prevailing order in Europe that persisted for the most part until the Franco-Prussian war of 1870–1871 and the outbreak of World War I in 1914. Said order was defined by a notable and unusually broad conception of self-interest among the great powers, translated primarily into a shared commitment to upholding that order, at least within the immediate (European) theater.

The Concert itself traced its origins to the wake of the Treaties of Westphalia (1648), which cemented the political and legal primacy of the state, and set into motion the wheels of a state-based order predicated on a hierarchy of power and reserving the right of armed force to *raison d'etat* ('reason of state'). Like the Roman empire, the primary incentive of the Concert's architects (the leading powers of Europe at the outset of the nineteenth century) was the preservation of order so as to allow for the pursuit of self-interest, principally exploitative pursuits outside the continent. Nonetheless, a number of ad hoc enforcement operations designed to contain potential conflicts and other destabilizing events and practices were undertaken by the European great powers, whether singly or jointly. This included campaigns against slave traders and pirates, as well as missions designed to stabilize and pacify peripheral areas such as the Balkans, Lebanon, and Cyprus throughout the nineteenth and early twentieth centuries.

The League of Nations

World War I shattered the Concert of Europe both in theory as well as reality, underscoring the problems inherent in basing even the most limited of collective security ventures solely on the self-interest of great powers. One of the most important problems posed by such an arrangement was the under-provision of conflict management in the face of flagrant acts of aggression that undermined international peace and security. Simply, conflict management efforts were only provided when they conferred advantages on one or more of the great powers, and typically in relation to weaker actors. With organized violence remaining a prominent and unrestricted tool of statecraft for use by the dominant actors in the Concert, it was hardly a surprise when the entire system collapsed amidst imperial rivalry and alliance obligations.

The first institutionalized attempt at constructing a collective security system predicated on international conflict management came in the form of the League of Nations in 1919. The massive devastation of World War I served as a chief pretext to the founding of the League, but so too did recognition that the alliance structures canvassing Europe in the years leading up to the war were insufficient for limiting the outbreak, recurrence, or destructive results of conflict so as to preserve any kind of stable and peaceable order. The League sought to remedy this situation by broadening its membership (and by extension, the commitment to conflict management) beyond Europe's borders.

At this juncture in history, with the introduction of Wilson's Fourteen Points following The Hague conventions of 1899 and 1907, the idea that conflict could be managed and its effects limited was ascendant. Accordingly, the practice of conflict management was ascribed to the League of Nations as a core function. This is evident in examining the League's Covenant, which went so far as to embrace even an early take on peace enforcement (among other approaches to managing conflict) by specifying the possibility of using military force on behalf of the League to uphold the provisions of the Covenant (Article 16.2). Among these provisions were declarations establishing peace and security as a concern to all members of the League (Article 11.1), and defining an act of war by any member of the League as an act of war against all (Article 16.1).

In the early days of the League, it carried out its collective security responsibilities rather effectively, albeit through more limited applications of conflict management. Prominent illustrations include the peacekeeping/policing role granted to deployments of forces to the Saar valley, the 'free city' of Danzig, and Upper Silesia. As any student of world history knows, the emergence of more significant challenges to the collective security and conflict management capabilities of the League paved the way for the organization's undoing. Especially noteworthy in this regard was the League's ineffectual responses to Japan's invasion of Manchuria in 1931, and Italy's attack on Ethiopia in 1935 – two cases where conflict management in some form might have made a difference, but was absent due to a lack of political will and available resources.

'Collective conflict management'

At the heart of the League of Nation's failings as a collective security organization was the principle of unanimity which prevailed over every vote and decision contemplated by the organization. This principle undermined the ability of the League to provide for collective security through timely and effective responses to international conflict. As a result, the architects of the League's successor, the United Nations, were convinced that a more streamlined and centralized institutional structure was essential to the newfound organization's effectiveness in maintaining international peace and security.

To this end, two potential remedies were pursued. The first was the decision to design the UN around two chambers (a General Assembly and a Security Council), with matters of peace and security referred to the latter, smaller body, itself invested with the authority to determine actionable situations as well as the appropriate action (in Chapter VII of the UN Charter). The second 'fix' was prompted by a desire to embed within the institution the notion of 'big power responsibility,' deemed necessary to avoid a repeat of the abdication of responsibility for collective security by the League's strongest actors (Britain and France) in the 1930s. The resulting accommodation was the ascription of permanent membership, along with unilateral veto power, to the five major allied powers (the United States, Britain, France, the Soviet Union, and China), in an attempt to bind these states to the organization's collective security function (Claude, 1984).

As its emergence during the allied war-time conferences suggests, the central purpose of the UN upon its founding in San Francisco in 1945 was to advance collective security and maintain international peace. Despite the best efforts of the victorious great powers to centralize the means for implementing collective security in their own hands on the Security Council, however, the breakdown of great power cooperation that was part and parcel of the emergence of the Cold War limited the Security Council's ability to provide for collective security. The constraints imposed upon the organization by bipolarity instead prompted the UN to place greater emphasis on the more limited goal of conflict management, through practices such as peacekeeping and mediation (Karns and Mingst, 1998).

Collective security and conflict management were also at least indirect concerns of an array of RGOs established after the founding of the UN. Such organizations have included the Congress of Europe (1948), the Organization of American States (OAS) (1951), the European Community, now the European Union (EU) (1958), the Organization for African Unity (OAU), now the African Union (AU) (1963), the Association of Southeast Asian Nations (ASEAN) (1967), the Conference on Security and Cooperation in Europe (CSCE), now the Organization for Security and Cooperation in Europe (OSCE) (1973), and a host of others. Collectively, these organizations have shared (and continue to share) a concern with reducing what Alker *et al.* (1980) called 'collective insecurity dilemmas' and the armed conflicts they produce.

Though falling far short of obtaining sufficient authority to control and limit the use of armed force by member-states, these and other international and regional organizations (and their progeny) placed a premium on concerted collective action as the most desirable method for managing, if not preventing, armed conflict throughout the Cold War era and beyond. While they can not (and do not seek to) transcend the pursuit of national interests by states, such organizations are explicitly intended to provide forums and avenues for realizing those interests by non-violent means. To that end, despite the proliferation of armed conflict throughout the Cold War period, these organizations are considered by some leading scholars of cooperation as representative of a nascent international regime of 'collective conflict management' emergent during the Cold War era (Haas, 1983).

As subsequent chapters will show, conflict management is hardly the exclusive domain of the UN or other IGOs or RGOs. States, state-based coalitions, transnational organizations, and even individuals have also contributed prominently to the development of a nascent conflict management regime since the end of World War II. Yet at the same time, these institutions have clearly played a major role, establishing activities and practices designed to facilitate communication and clarify issues between and among parties to a conflict, leading and conducting fact-finding and observer missions, overseeing and supervising cease-fires and other agreements, offering 'good offices,' substantive mediation, and adjudication, interposing peace-keeping forces, and so forth. As Robert Butterworth (1978: 196) has described them, all of these practices, regardless of the agent(s) carrying them out, have in common an 'aim of reducing the intensity and frequency of serious security disputes and/or the systemic consequences of such conflicts.' This is itself a close approximation of the definition of conflict management, and serves as confirmation of the link between the emergence and development of conflict management and centuries of effort toward the provision of collective security.

Mapping the conceptual field

Having established at least in a rudimentary sense what international conflict management is, as well as its historical association with collective security, it is worth outlining the conceptual field in which conflict management and its various translations reside. Providing a definition of conflict management and situating it in historical terms are necessary, but not sufficient, conditions for operationalizing the concept. It is also crucial to think about what demarcates conflict management relative to other possible approaches to providing peace and security, as well how to distinguish various applications of conflict management from one another.

This chapter offers a characterization of international conflict management as a pragmatic and centrist approach to limiting conflict's negative effects. This characterization is based on the fact that, as a general rule, conflict management accepts the prevailing security landscape arrayed around states, power, and interests, while also seeking to shave off the rough edges that stem from the intersection of these forces. Given this defining trait of international conflict management, it seems sensible to appropriate some of the key features of that landscape when seeking to contextualize conflict management.

What distinguishes the practice of conflict management is its relationship to the essential conditions of sovereignty and force. Though other considerations are important, situating conflict management and its translations relative to each of these essential conditions allows for a more nuanced and complete portrayal of the management of international conflict. Two factors in particular stand out: how much (or little) regard is paid to state sovereignty, and how great (or small) a role is reserved for the use or threat of coercion. Figure 1.1 provides a conceptual map of

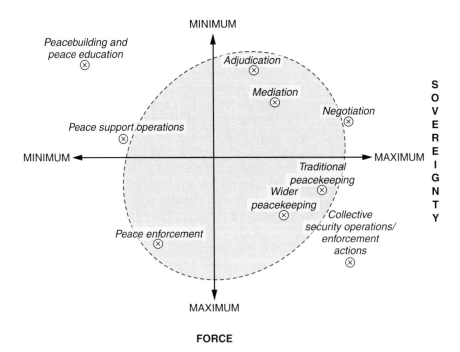

Figure 1.1 Conflict management: plotting the points.

the conflict management landscape, including several of its major translations, and for contextual purposes, other types of peace operations that fall outside the bounds of conflict management as established here. The twin axes in this matrix, used to sort the various approaches, are the aforementioned 'essential conditions' of sovereignty and force; each is introduced as a continuum, ranging from minimum to maximum with respect to relevance or importance.

In thinking about conflict management in the aggregate, there is a threshold effect with regard to each of these conditions. At its very core, international conflict management pays at least some heed to state sovereignty, and ascribes at least some utility to power and coercion as (at a minimum) a background variable. However, too great or little emphasis on either sovereignty or force would locate a behavior outside the bounds of conflict management, leaving it better defined as statecraft or conflict resolution (respectively). That is not to say, of course, that conflict management does not allow for variation within its parameters. Yet by the very definition of the concept, all approaches to conflict management are formulated at least in the shadow of such considerations – as reflected in the shadowed area in Figure 1.1, defining the bounds of conflict management.

On the basis of this claim, it seems clear that those approaches located within the upper-left quadrant of Figure 1.1, in which both state sovereignty and force are minimally relevant if at all, are hardly reflective of conflict management. This is self-evident in the case of peacebuilding/peace education efforts, whose transformative emphasis mark them as exercises in conflict resolution rather than management. Multifaceted peace support operations do come somewhat closer to conflict management, due to the fact that they often incorporate approaches such as wider peacekeeping or mediation – which are strongly influenced by considerations of sovereignty and force – within their purview. Yet at the same time these multiple facets include exercises in statebuilding, civil society promotion, peace education, and economic development which have little relation to force and which may in fact proceed without paying much heed to state sovereignty, and may even seek to weaken it.

Most of those operations seeking to curb violence and elicit peace that fall within the other three quadrants of Figure 1.1 do comport with the concept of conflict management as advanced here. At the same time, they differ by varying degrees in their regard for the sanctity of state sovereignty and the utility of force. Of these two 'essential conditions,' the greater degree of variation comes with respect to the place of force. As many prominent conflict management approaches unfold without much relationship to the use, or even threat, of force (mediation and adjudication) as depend heavily on its measured application (traditional and wider peacekeeping). Again, one can view these approaches as points along a continuum, in this case of force. This continuum extends from those efforts at conflict management that are best understood as restrained and internationally sanctioned applications of collective military force to contain or curtail conflicts (traditional and wider peacekeeping), to third-party judgments by an (purportedly) impartial adjudicatory body that are steeped in the legal process and institutions, and lack much of a coercive component. In converging toward the middle, conflict management practices such as mediation in some cases rely on the threat or possibility of force as a backdrop to non-violent diplomatic activity.

Again, the case can be made that too great of an emphasis on either state sovereignty or force renders practices seemingly similar to conflict management as 'something else.' For example, negotiation falls just outside the bounds of conflict management, given that it typically occurs without the involvement of a third party. This is itself a reflection of the centrality of state sovereignty to negotiation, which defines it as an exercise in statecraft rather than conflict management per se. Also falling outside the bounds of conflict management are those exercises in collectively sanctioned warfare dubbed 'enforcement actions.' Again, as depicted here, the heavy emphasis both on state sovereignty and especially military force distinguishes enforcement actions such as the UN Operation in Korea (UNOK) and Operation Desert Shield/Desert Storm in the Persian Gulf as exercises in statecraft hitched to a collective security mandate, rather than pure translations of conflict management (though the importance and conceptual proximity of enforcement actions to peace enforcement merits revisiting this distinction in later chapters).

Unlike the wide variation with respect to the emphasis on force, the vast majority of conflict management approaches genuflect to the inviolability of state sovereignty. The notable exception to this rule is the decidedly ambitious and unconventional approach to conflict management dubbed 'peace enforcement.' Defined both by an embrace of assertive military force and a diminution of the importance of state sovereignty as a prerequisite for employing that military force, peace enforcement is undoubtedly the most controversial of all translations of conflict management. Peace enforcement aside, the degree of conformity with the prevailing political, legal, and normative construct of state sovereignty that defines the concept and practice of conflict management is what makes it both an excessively practical and pragmatic approach as well as a frequent target for critique from across the theoretical expanse of international relations.

Debating international conflict management

The relatively narrow scope of international conflict management makes it a pragmatic and widely applicable concept in the contemporary international arena. It does not challenge the (current) centrality of sovereignty as an organizing principle in the international system, or the persistence of organized collective violence as a means to which actors in that system will sometimes resort when seeking to settle disputes in their favor. As noted above, conflict management instead seeks to manage that use of violence when it occurs, so as to limit its damaging effects.

This pragmatism hardly renders the concept or its approaches immune from controversy, however. Much of the debate surrounding international conflict management turns on its place relative to the larger theoretical debate in international relations. In general, where do attempts by third parties to manage conflict fall on the spectrum of IR theory, and its dissenting positions on the importance of states, the centrality of power and interests, the applicability of force, and related themes?

Reflecting an intermediary position between theoretical and ideological poles, the concept of conflict management and the four applications of it considered in detail in this book – peacekeeping, mediation, peace enforcement, and adjudication – can be and often are cast as both dangerously ambitious and hopelessly insufficient. These ontological positions are derived from very different notions of the place of the state, power, and interests in the international system, and are informed by, and associated with, several of the major theoretical camps in the international relations field today.

The realist critique

Those viewing conflict and security from a traditional realist standpoint are generally opposed to most conflict management ventures. Because efforts to manage international conflict often involve actors other than states, and almost always are undertaken for reasons other than the pursuit of national interests, conflict management is itself inconsistent with the basic building blocks of realist theory. Not surprisingly, realists tend to characterize efforts at conflict management as adventures in liberal internationalism, and emblematic of the 'do-something' ambitiousness that often underwrites said adventures. From this perspective, efforts at managing inter- or intra-state conflict typically result in the squandering of resources on attempts to manage a situation that is more often than not unmanageable, if not worsening the conflict by introducing further complexity in the form of outside parties.

Most realists also hold a disdainful view of conflict management given its potential to undermine the prevailing order extant in the international system. At its core, the notion of managing international conflict challenges, and potentially subverts, the fundamental notion of self-help anarchy on which that order rests. Approaches to conflict management such as peacekeeping, mediation, peace enforcement, and adjudication hold out the prospect that power and authority may entail to actors other than states. These approaches also afford those actors the ability, and perhaps even the right, to exercise that power to govern conflict between and among actors in that system. Considering these two attributes of conflict management in concert, one can see where it might be interpreted by realists as in some sense threatening to the primary legal position of the nation-state, the normative concept of state sovereignty, and especially to the unbridled exercise of power on which relations between states rests.

Alternative positions

From the opposite end of the theoretical spectrum, conflict management faces withering criticism not because it encroaches on the realm of states, interests, threats, and power, but because it is overly reliant on them. In the view of Kantian cosmopolitanism, critical theory, and the fields and practices of conflict resolution and peace studies, conflict management is exceedingly traditional and short-sighted. From this point of origin, the argument holds that conflict management is likely to fall short not because it is overly adventurous, but because it is overly conservative in both method and objective.

Undoubtedly, the major approaches to conflict management appraised in this book – peacekeeping, mediation, peace enforcement, and adjudication – rely in whole, or in part, on states or state-based international organizations and processes. They also undeniably focus on settling disputes rather than resolving conflicts, thereby retaining a process rather than actor orientation in seeking to solve rather than transform conflicts. Conflict management tends to approach even limited institutional and political reform with trepidation, while avoiding broader efforts at recalibrating the prevailing norms and values of conflict-prone societies.

As a result, conflict management approaches are at best ambivalent toward (if not opposed to) the notion of building a robust normative and institutional architecture for global governance, or attempting to recast the normative and institutional architecture of conflict-prone societies. In accepting the prevailing political, social, economic, and cultural conditions of a conflict setting more or less as they are, and attempting to utilize existing actors and processes to fashion settlements within those contexts, it is also easy to see where those advocating either new or radically different approaches to, and ways of thinking about, the provision of security in the international system would be dissatisfied with the traditionalism of conflict management.

Seeking middle ground

Though higher-order ontological and epistemological debates undoubtedly have their place within the academy, they too often frustrate students with a more policy-oriented mindset, as well as practitioners in the field, two audiences who hunger for concepts they can apply and empirical cases they can apply them to. These are audiences which scholars captivated by grand theoretical debates (myself included) sometimes overlook.

This broad-based assessment of conflict management in the contemporary international system seeks to serve as a remedy of sorts to this frustration. In a nod to Aristotle's golden mean, the worthiness of conflict management stems in no small part from the very characteristic that subjects it to debate and criticism from competing theoretical positions and their advocates – namely, its unrelenting centrism. Conflict management accepts the reality that the collective use of violence is a persistent feature of a world in which power and interests remain paramount, and in which a universal set of governing norms and/or laws remains elusive. At the same time, it seeks to tame and limit those conflicts, using techniques such as peacekeeping, mediation, peace enforcement, and adjudication to attempt to minimize the damage they impose on both combatants and bystanders.

Accordingly, conflict management as a concept is devoid of the moral skepticism and fatalism of the realist conception of unrestrained anarchy, as well as the ideological fervor and heavily normative position of the extreme idealist or critical positions. Likewise, conflict management in its various translations is applicable to the pursuit of security, regardless of whether security is conceived of as a systemic condition, the sole province of states, or a basic concern of the individual. It lies somewhere in the breach between raw power and naked self-interest on the one hand, and socio-psychological and cultural transformation and reconciliation on the other.

The intermediary position of conflict management – and, to a lesser extent, this analytical survey of it – serves an important practical purpose, bridging the intellectual divides evident in the security studies field today. The need for such a bridge is evident, given the degree to which policy debates over how to respond to the changing nature of contemporary conflicts and the security challenges they engender is influenced by the prevailing academic discourse, and vice versa (Freedman, 1998). Beyond many other areas of academic inquiry (perhaps with the chief exception of economics), scholars in the security studies field have long occupied a place of prominence as policy advisers, influential critics, and important sources of ideas. They have enjoined in spirited debate and shaped and advanced policy through 'thinktanks' such as the Brookings Institution or Chatham House; descended from the ivory tower to contribute to public service in the realm of security, defense, and foreign policy; and even, as in the cases of a prominent few, such as Henry Kissinger, Zbigniew Bruzinski, Jeannie Kirkpatrick, or Condoleezza Rice, ascended to the rarefied air of high-level positions in government. Further, security studies experts are employed by the UN, the OSCE, the International Atomic Energy Agency (IAEA), and numerous other international organizations with a security and/or conflict management function in a wide variety of policy and planning capacities.

Providing such thoughtful and critical insight, advice, and expertise has long been an essential ideal and function of the scholarly community, as translated through the Platonic conception of the 'responsibility of the expert' (Kuklick, 2006). Yet to the degree that purely theoretical differences over the essential workings of international relations or the appropriate referent for security concerns consume the field, practitioners of security studies will find it difficult to weave together and apply the important contributions of mainstream scholarship and the relevant insights of the leading edge in a way that meets the need to respond to ever-changing realities.

Conversely, a systematic appraisal of the pragmatic practice of conflict management, in the form of a review of what most often has been done to respond to inter- and intra-state conflict, and especially an assessment of the effectiveness of these efforts in light of the changing nature of contemporary conflict, speaks more directly to this need. Intellectual debate and the advance and refinement of contesting discourses are crucial to the development of security studies, or indeed any intellectual field. Yet equally crucial is the presentation of cumulated and relevant knowledge in an accessible and useful fashion for public consumption and, potentially, social gain. Accordingly, it is out of a desire to speak to those who wish to learn more about the subject of conflict management and how it might be applied to the management and resolution of *actual* conflicts in the contemporary international arena that this book emanates.

Study questions

1 What are the main elements and approaches that define international conflict management?
2 How does conflict management differ from conflict resolution?
3 What is collective security? In what ways has its evolution shaped conflict management, and vice versa?
4 What are the two essential conditions that distinguish conflict management from other approaches to peace? How do these conditions also distinguish different translations of conflict management from one another?
5 What is the basis of the realist critique of international conflict management? What about the liberal, critical, and pacifist critiques?

Suggested reading

Alagappa, Muthiah and Takashi Inoguchi. 1999. *International Security Management and the United Nations.* New York, NY/Tokyo: United Nations University Press.
Bennett, Andrew and Joseph Lepgold. 1993. 'Reinventing Collective Security after the Cold War and Gulf Conflict,' *Political Science Quarterly*, 108 (2): 213–237.
Bercovitch, Jacob and Richard Jackson. 1997. *International Conflict: A Chronological*

Encyclopedia of Conflicts and their Management, 1945–1995. Washington, DC: Congressional Quarterly.

Bercovitch, Jacob and Patrick Regan. 2004. 'Mediation and International Conflict Management: A Review and Analysis,' in Zeev Maoz, Alex Mintz, T. Clifton Morgan, Glenn Palmer, and Richard J. Stoll (eds.) *Multiple Paths to Knowledge in International Relations*. Lanham, MD: Lexington, pp. 249–272.

Claude, Inis. 1984. *Swords Into Plowshares: The Problems and Progress of International Organization*. New York, NY: Random House.

Crocker, Chester, A., Fen Osler Hampson, and Pamela Aall (eds.). 2007. *Leashing the Dogs of War: Conflict Management in a Divided World*. Washington, DC: USIP Press.

Haas, Ernst B. 1993. 'Collective Conflict Management: Evidence for a New World Order?' in Thomas G. Weiss (ed.) *Collective Security in a Changing World*. Boulder, CO: Lynne Reinner.

Matthews, Robert O., Arthur G. Rubinoff, and Janice Gross Stein. 1989. *International Conflict and Conflict Management: Readings in World Politics*. Scarborough, ON: Prentice Hall.

Princen, Thomas. 1992. *Intermediaries in International Conflict*. Princeton, NJ: Princeton University Press.

Ramsbotham, Oliver, Tom Woodhouse, and Hugh Miall. 2005. *Contemporary Conflict Resolution: The Prevention, Management and Transformation of Deadly Conflicts*, 2nd edn. London: Polity.

Thompson, Kenneth W. 1968. 'Collective Security,' in *International Encyclopedia of the Social Sciences*. New York, NY: Macmillan.

2   The changing nature of security

This chapter chronicles the changing nature of security from a conceptual and theoretical standpoint. Beginning with an elaboration of the defining features of security in the traditional (realist) view, the chapter also catalogs the 'broadening and deepening' of the concept of security over the past quarter-century, outlining the essential characteristics of the so-called 'new security environment' and its implications for contemporary conflict.

The traditional (realist) view

Much has been said about the changing landscape of international relations. These changes have particularly affected the pursuit of collective security and attempts to manage the threats to security posed by inter-state and intra-state conflict. The extensity and intensity of these changes have reached the point that many scholars of security studies now characterize them as reflections of a 'new security environment' resting on new rules, actors, and threats.

The introduction of this term signals an effort to supplant the traditional approach to security, which emphasized states, interests, and power – emphases derived almost entirely from realist theory. Realism is the oldest intellectual position in international relations; in actuality, it is a deceptively complex theory with numerous elaborations and translations beyond the scope of this discussion. Given its roots in a Machiavellian appreciation for power, a Hobbesian pessimism regarding human nature, and a Clausewitzian belief in the notion of war as the continuation of politics by other means, realism is the progenitor of the field of security studies (Crawford, 1991). This assertion is born out by the prevalence of three key realist propositions in the security studies field since its emergence after World War II:

1   The state, as the central unit in international relations, is the central reference point for security.
2   Armed conflict between states over competing interests constitute the major and recurring threat to security.
3   Material capabilities and especially military force represent the main currency by which security can be provided or threatened.

Realism's place in defining the security studies field is related at least in part to the key assumptions and concepts spawned by that theory, items which remain central not only to the realist ontology but to the security studies field itself.

The centrality of the state

Since the rise to prominence of state sovereignty in accordance with the Treaties of Westphalia in 1648, security has been more or less equated with the nation-state. This association attained an almost dogmatic orthodoxy in the inter-war period, with E.H. Carr's *The Twenty Years Crisis ...* (1939) proving a seminal contribution in that regard. Accordingly, the emergence of a security studies field in the twentieth century was chiefly out of a concern with the preservation of state sovereignty as entailed in the pursuit of 'national security.' As Sheehan puts it:

> during the long domination of international relations by realism [approximately from the late 1930s to the late 1970s], the working definition of security was a strictly limited one, which saw its nature as being concerned with military power, and the subject of these concerns as being the state.
>
> (2005: 5)

Self-help anarchy

Another central assumption of realism is the notion that the international system is structured by, and operates in accordance with, the particular logic of self-help anarchy. Unlike the lay tendency to equate anarchy with 'no order,' the realist use of anarchy refers to a particular *kind* of order. Absent any central governing authority in the international system, states exist in a self-help relationship with one another. As such, realists contend that states can and will do whatever they must to survive and, further, to pursue their interests – up to, and frequently including, resort to armed conflict.

The relationship between states and the anarchical order in which they operate varies in accordance with variations on realist theory. Classical realists conceive of anarchy as a by-product of state behavior and interaction, while structural or 'neo' realists invert the causal arrow, viewing anarchy as an independent condition that impinges upon and structures the behavior and interaction of states. Despite these differences, the common thread is the crucial role that power, force, threat, and by extension armed conflict, plays in an international system without rules and institutions that can effectively govern the actions of states.

The security dilemma

An international system that turns on the logic of self-help anarchy is a system that is inherently volatile and insecure. One by-product of this volatility and insecurity is the recurring dynamic of the security dilemma. Often (but not exclusively) applied to binary interactions between states, the security dilemma provides a crucial account for the unfolding of arms races and even direct armed clashes between and among states. A particular focal point driving the dynamic is the paramount influence of (mis)perception and (mis)information within an anarchical system, as well as the subjective nature of security threats in general (Jervis, 1976, 1978).

The dilemma at the heart of the security dilemma is that actions intended to enhance security are, in the end, likely to breed only greater insecurity. Because states are locked into self-help relationships with one another, they can and do take

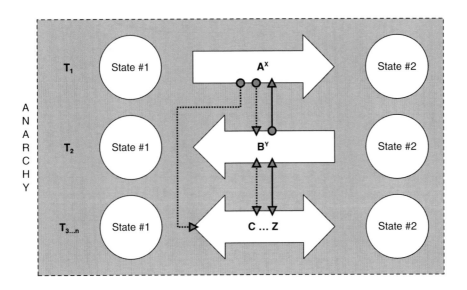

- **Step 1**: given anarchy at starting point T_1, State #1 decides to adopt action A, as a means of protecting security interest X. This action (say, the procuring of a new weapons system, or the crafting of a bilateral defense accord) may be a response to some specific action or behavior of another state or states, or it may be entirely self-regarding. In either case, action A is a product of the self-help anarchy with which State #1, like all other states, must contend.

- **Step 2**: regardless of the actual intent of State #1's actions, State #2 (again, given anarchy) necessarily *perceives* action A to be a threat to its own security interest Y. Therefore, in responding to the perceived threat of action A and out of a desire to protect its own interest Y, State #2 adopts action B – an action clearly structured as a response to action A.

- **Step 3**: reacting to the reaction of action B by State #2, State #1 retaliates to its own heightened sense of threat, at which point the dynamic reaches a point of self-sustaining escalation (actions C … Z) until termination of T_n.

Figure 2.1 The security dilemma.

what they deem to be necessary measures for the protection and advancement of their security in an insecure world. At the same time, the absence of robust mechanisms for moderated interaction means that states are more or less opaque, leaving decision-makers unsure of one another's intentions – and therefore often threatened by one another's actions. The workings of the security dilemma can easily be understood by applying the essential conditions of anarchy to a simplified two-way interaction (see Figure 2.1). The outcomes of security dilemmas are rivalries, arms races, and potentially, war – all prompted as much by *subjective* perceptions of threat as by *objective* threats.

The balance of power

The balance of power is also central to the realist conception of security. In the words of the modern translator of classical realism, Hans Morgenthau:

> The aspiration for power on the part of several nations, each trying to maintain or overthrow the status quo, leads of necessity to a configuration that is called the balance of power, and to policies that aim at preserving it.
>
> (1948: 173)

Structural realists are no less concerned with the balance of power; in fact, given their emphasis on the constraints imposed on states by anarchy, they often privilege the balance of power in their accounts of how anarchy works. The difference lies in divergent understandings of how and why a balance-of-power arrangement emerges. Classical realists such as Morgenthau contend that states consciously seek out partners to balance against adversaries and the threats they present (see Box 2.1). Conversely, neo-realists argue that a balance-of-power arrangement is a structural artifact produced by the striving for dominance of states; in other words, it is not something that states intentionally create, but instead results from efforts to attain supremacy.

Box 2.1 Morgenthau's 'six principles of political realism'

From a post-World War II conviction that heedless idealism was a central cause of World War I and World War II, the German émigré Hans Morgenthau launched a paradigm shift in the study of international relations. His seminal works *Scientific Man Versus Power Politics* (1946) and *Politics Among Nations: The Struggle for Power and Peace* (1948) established the parameters for realist international theory. Exceedingly dubious about linking the prospect for world order and peace to the allegedly limitless capacity of human reason and scientific progress, as idealists had long advocated, Morgenthau formulated what he called the 'six principles of political realism' as a rejoinder. In doing so, he advanced not only the defining criteria of realist theory, but the basis for the conduct of much of post-World War II statecraft. Morgenthau's six principles of political realism, in abridged form, state:

1   Politics, like society in general, is governed by objective laws that have their roots in human nature which is itself unchanging: therefore it is possible to develop a rational theory that reflects these objective laws.

2   The main signpost of political realism is the concept of interest defined in terms of power which infuses rational order into the subject matter of politics. Political realism stresses the rational, objective, and unemotional.

3   Realism assumes that interest defined as power is an objective category which is universally valid but not with a meaning that is fixed once and for all. Power is the control of man over man.

4   Political realism is aware of the moral significance of political action; it is also aware of the tension between moral command and the requirements of successful political action.

5   Political realism refuses to identify the moral aspirations of a particular nation with the moral laws that govern the universe. It is the concept of interest defined in terms of power that saves us from the moral excess and political folly.

6   The political realist maintains the autonomy of the political sphere. He asks 'How does this policy affect the power of the nation?' A man who was nothing but 'political man' would be a beast, for he would be completely lacking in moral restraints. In order to develop an autonomous theory of political behavior, 'political man' must be abstracted from other aspects of human nature.

The larger point with respect to the realist approach to security is that armed conflict is seen as a valid and useful instrument for achieving and defending a balance-of-power arrangement. Given its realist origins, it is important to remember that the goal of balance-of-power or balance-of-threat arrangements is not peace, but maintenance of the status quo and prevention of the domination of the system by any one state or alliance (Walt, 1985, 1987).

The deficiencies of realism

From the vantage point of its critics, realism's unwavering emphasis on the state renders the theory unable to account for or formulate an effective response to emerging security and related challenges which do not 'fit' with, or cannot be accommodated through, the state (Brown, 1998). Critiques of the realist conception of international security have focused not only on the central position of the state, but also an associated ontology that equates security with material capabilities (particularly organized military force) and emphasizes the maintenance of order through the machinations of statecraft. The assertion that maintaining order and stability through forceful means is the primary imperative shaping the behavior of actors in the international system has proven especially problematic for assessing the behaviors of actors who may be threatened by and/or opposed to that status quo, or those whose actions do not relate to or correspond in any way with the order it produces (Katzenstein, 1996).

An additional deficiency of the realist approach to contemporary security problems stems from its evolution and unique applications during the Cold War. Brought on by the perceived necessity of 'winning' the Cold War by imbuing strategy and policy with the contributions of leading intellectuals (such as Bernard Brodie, Herman Kahn, Thomas Schelling, and the like), the basic tenets of *realpolitik* were brought to bear on the pressing security threats of the time. However, many of those threats were spatially and temporally bound, and linked to the peculiar and unprecedented dynamic of a bipolar rivalry between two military and economic superpowers that produced them.

Security under fire

Change is not a topic that the security studies field by and large embraces readily. As a result, until fairly recently much of the security studies literature has operated in accordance with the preceding description of the traditional understanding of international conflict as a phenomenon driven primarily, if not exclusively, by states and their coherent and decisive pursuit and/or defense of national interests through the material capabilities (especially, but not solely, military force) at their disposal. In this way, the security studies field has traditionally emphasized the study of conflicts fought by, for, and through 'the state' and its interests, and gravitated toward examining and even promoting approaches to conflict management and collective security that are similarly rooted in the state and interest-based calculations. Whether in assuming rationality in motivation or materialism in means and ends, traditional and mainstream approaches to security studies clearly originate from a position that power serves the pursuit of interests, and interests dictate the use of power.

Broadening and deepening

The primacy of realism notwithstanding, the Cold War era in particular bore witness to the beginnings of a discernable transformation in the prevailing meaning of security along multiple dimensions (Booth, 1997). The foremost example of this was a shift in the central focus for security concerns evident in the evolution from 'strategic' to 'security' studies, as well as a migration of referent point from 'national' to 'international' security by the 1970s (Freedman, 1998). Such shifts betrayed an emerging dissatisfaction with the exceedingly narrow conception of security prevalent at that time. This dissatisfaction reached a critical mass in the form of a number of significant contributions to the scholarly literature and policy debate over the nature of security in the early 1980s (UN, 1980; Ullman, 1983).

With the fading of the military and ideological confrontation between the superpowers that defined the Cold War, security was subjected to even greater critical scrutiny. Much of the impetus for this scrutiny came from the inroads made by critical theory into the social sciences in general and the security field in particular by the 1980s. In many cases these reformulations of security were explicitly advanced as responses to the ontological and epistemological question raised by the Copenhagen School – namely, why some issues get 'securitized' and receive priority treatment by states and international organizations, while others with crucial security implications do not (see Box 2.2). This critical turn triggered both a broadening and deepening of security, prompted by an increased recognition of interdependence and the non-military security threats it produces.

Box 2.2 The Copenhagen School and securitization

For the nearly 20 years (1985–2004) of its existence, the Copenhagen Peace Research Institute (COPRI) provided a home base of sorts for one of the leading strains of security studies revisionism, dubbed the 'Copenhagen School.' Advancing a number of theoretically informed yet empirically oriented collaborative studies of security, the Copenhagen School, in conjunction with COPRI, sought to develop and test new concepts in light of the post-Cold War transformation of European and global security (Huysmans, 1998: 483–484).

One of the most prominent and lasting of these innovations was the effort to define and examine the process of 'securitization.' Securitization was defined as a discursive process by which agents in a position of decision-making power determine what issues get defined as security issues and receive extensive public attention and governmental redress (and which do not). The concept of securitization helped foster a broadened 'sectoral' approach in which multiple realms of security conerns (military, political, social, economic, environmental, etc.) were introduced as a means of defining, analyzing, and responding to differing security threats (for illustrations of the Copenhagen School, see Wæver, 1995; Buzan *et al.*, 1998; Buzan and Wæver, 2003).

A proliferation of ethnic conflict, humanitarian disaster, and general social disorder in Somalia, Bosnia, Rwanda, and beyond in the early-to-mid-1990s also proved crucial to furthering the challenge to traditional definitions of security. Such events prompted clarion calls from the so-called 'Aberystwyth School' and other devotees of critical security studies (CSS) for emphasizing the security of the individual rather than the state (see Box 2.3). One direct outcome of such calls was the emergence of a human security agenda fashioned largely by NGOs and embraced to varying degrees in the halls of the UN and by governments in Canada and Scandinavia. Taken together, these and other inroads in the critical investigation of security have produced a dizzying array of reformulations of the concept, as well as radically different policy prescriptions for providing it.

Box 2.3 Critical security studies and the Aberystwyth School

Another prominent point of departure in the security studies field is the turn to CSS, led by scholars such as Keith Krause, Michael Williams, Ken Booth, and Richard Wyn Jones. These and other scholars working under the CSS banner drew from such diverse points of origin as the earliest applications of critical theory to IR (such as Robert Cox's appropriation of historical materialism), the post-positivism of the Frankfurt School, and the 'dissidence' of North American scholars such as R.B.J. Walker and Richard K. Ashley.

The main concern of CSS has been to expose the statist and militarist assumptions of traditional security studies, and especially the degree to which these assumptions direct scholarly attention to a particular and limited range of questions at the expense of a vast expanse of security-related issues and concerns. A further extension of CSS, led by the so-called 'Aberystwyth School,' has developed a research program around what it considers the logical next step for security in the twenty-first century: namely, the recasting of security studies (and policies) to emphasize the security of the individual, measured by human emancipation (significant examples of CSS include: Booth, 1991, 2005; Krause and Williams, 1996, 1997; Wyn Jones, 1996, 2001; Sheehan, 2005).

The perils of pluralism

Critical approaches to security of various stripes have helped to shed light on the reciprocal links between a variety of political, social, economic, cultural, and natural (as well as military) factors and security. In the process, such critiques have expanded the parameters of what are considered security threats or concerns. Yet as with any attempt at launching a paradigm shift, the discussion of a 'new security environment' prompted by these changes has as much potential to obscure as to clarify. Whether for good or ill, the pluralism of a broadened and non-traditional approach to security has the effect of undermining what was previously a coherent and parsimonious understanding of security (Walt, 1991; Booth, 1997).

For some, the move toward a 'hyphenated security,' linking security with the environment, migration, health, and so forth, can infuse non-military policy problems with a degree of militarization and confrontation that is needless and counterproductive (Deudney, 1990; Huysmans, 1995). Others view the broadening of security as a response to inevitability, given the traditionally close association between 'security' and 'the state' in concert with the overwhelming array of challenges to the state today (Walker, 1997). Still others contend that retaining a prominent place for states even in updated considerations of security is self-limiting (Shaw, 1994).

The plethora of deeply divergent and broadly critical approaches to the study of security makes it increasingly difficult to define a security studies field without excluding one or another contribution. Further troubling is the potential for a loss of rigor in the rush to redefine security studies. While the strongest examples of this effort have helped to identify the security dimensions of natural resource, health, and migration issues (among others), it is crucial that these issues not be defined entirely in relation to their security implications at the expense of other (economic, social, ecological) facets of the challenges they pose. For example, while climate change has spawned numerous security-related challenges (with more to come), to define climate change solely or even primarily as a security challenge would be to overlook its biologic, climatologic, economic, and historic dimensions.

To the extent that the revision of security in both conceptual and policy terms is intended to address the deficiencies and insufficiency of the traditional approach to security and its realist underpinnings, it is a crucial and necessary endeavor. At the same time, a half-century (or more) of domination of the field of security studies by realism should not be construed as providing cause for jettisoning the important contributions produced during that era – in other words, to throw out the proverbial baby with the bath water. Broadening and deepening should not prompt deconstruction, but rather synthesis and expansion. While the security studies field needs to expand its parameters to include the new threats and challenges posed by resource scarcity, disease, or gender inequality (to name a few), and to ask the question of what constitutes a security threat (and why), it should not do so at the expense of continuing to advance the frontiers of knowledge with respect to the security threats posed by armed conflict – whether those conflicts take place between, among, within, or without regard to states.

Debating the security referent

Irrespective of the particular actors, issues, or other factors that may characterize an armed conflict, it is security (rather than justice, reconciliation, retribution, or some other end) that is the overriding objective of any serious efforts by third parties at containing international conflict. As a result, establishing a firm grasp on how security is construed within the narrow purview of international conflict and its management is essential. Establishing this grasp is more difficult than one might initially think, even in the security studies field.

Security is the epitome of what the prominent social theorist W.B. Gallie referred to as an 'essentially contested concept' (Gallie, 1956). Accordingly, one must accept that security is a relative, ambiguous, fluid, and subjective condition. The UN, which after all has as its chief purpose the maintenance of international peace and security, has yet to even define the concept! In the most general and basic sense, security refers to a condition of being (or perceiving to be) protected from loss, risk, or harm. One finds at the heart of security an aversion to, along with a desire to avoid, threatened or actual injury of one form or another to one's person, property, loved ones, and other markers of general well-being. Beyond that, security as a condition and a concept has a dizzying array of applications, which vary by time, space, and especially reference point.

The preceding discussion notwithstanding, the most prominent point of departure among beholders of security studies today is the debate over the referent object – the unit or actor that is the centerpiece of one's concern when thinking about security. While largely a theoretical debate, differences in referent object are important in practical terms. What one chooses to prioritize plays an essential role in establishing how security is defined, what the chief threat(s) to security is (are), and how threats posed by conflict can be managed and contained.

System as referent

The appreciation of security from a systemic perspective requires a 'big-picture' holistic view based on the idea that security is an all-encompassing condition that applies, is provided, or is undermined in relation to the structure of the international system (the distribution of power prevailing within the system) at any given point in time. Those of a more pessimistic orientation, referred to as structural realists, emphasize that security is a fleeting condition that is systematically underprovided, and where it does entail is a by-product of the power and capabilities of the units in the system acting to defend themselves and their interests (Waltz, 1979). Conversely, those of a more optimistic leaning, sometimes dubbed neo-liberal institutionalists, contend that security can (and will, in time) be understood as a collective good with benefits accruing to all, making its maintenance and provision through established institutions and practices an increasingly likely proposition (Keohane, 1989; Keohane and Nye, 2001).

Differences of theoretical orientation aside, the common point of origin here is that security should be thought of as a condition that entails or is compromised at the broadest level of the international system. As a result, the units of the system – mostly states, but also potentially non-state or sub-state actors – are of secondary importance in comparison to the larger system in which they are embedded, and which exists as a separate (if related) entity operating according to its own dynamics. Accordingly, the security of the United States, and threats to that security, have wider ripple effects that impact other actors across the globe – as does the security of Norway, Nigeria, Nicaragua, or Nepal (to varying extents).

Nearly all those who approach security from a systemic vantage point emphasize this relational aspect of security. One common outgrowth of thinking about security as a systemic proposition is an appreciation for, and emphasis on, sustaining and extending order between and among the actors in the system. Therefore, those who consider the international system to be the reference point for thinking about security tend to emphasize collective or even global security, and by extension the need to locate and marshal the appropriate means for managing threats to that order entailing from inter-state and intra-state conflicts and their effects. Despite that shared concern and the common reference point for thinking about security that produces it, significant differences (prompted, again, by differing theoretical orientations) over what those means are, what agents ought to employ them, when and in what cases they should be employed, and other related questions prevail.

State as referent

Using the state as the reference point in considerations of security significantly narrows one's analytical focus, if not the importance of the stakes involved, to traditional considerations of national security. Each state is understood to have its own particularistic and unique interests and imperatives that determine, and impinge upon, its own security. These interests and imperatives are known to states and their leaders, who act rationally to process the information and assess the capabilities at their disposal to maximize that security.

Importantly, the security of the sovereign state is not bound up with or dependent upon the security of other states. Rather, security is a good that sovereign states can, do, and in the strongest variant of this perspective, *must* provide for themselves. Likewise, threats are posed to (and by) states and their security interests in an independent fashion, irrespective of the threats or interests concerning other states. Ripple effects are cast aside, with *direct* consequences and implications – for the security of the United States, or Norway, Nigeria, Nicaragua, or Nepal, *independent of one another* – the main object of concern.

In some ways this approach presents a mirror image of the systemic perspective; the source of concern is not the security of the system as an independent proposition, but rather the enhancement of the security of the components of that system. Where a systemic approach views security as a macro-level condition that, when evident, flows 'down' to the system's units (states), state-level approaches reverse the causal arrow and contend that security in the international system can only entail as a by-product of the security of states in the system; in other words, security and order are only possible when states are free to seek, and successfully attain, their own security and to uphold that order.

Using the state as one's referent for thinking about security naturally leads to an emphasis on the security needs of, and threats to, individual nation-states. This emphasis in turn places the unit of the state and the concept of state sovereignty at the forefront of the security agenda. As a result, the security concerns of sub-state constituents, other states, or the international system are necessarily diminished in relative importance. With security understood as something provided by and for 'the state,' occasions for third-party involvements to manage conflicts tend to be relatively infrequent. Where conflict management is needed, it may be to ensure or uphold the security of a state whose sovereignty or existence may be unduly threatened, or to quell a conflict that has evolved beyond the capacity of states to control, undermining their security in the process.

Individual as referent

An understanding of security as a concept that derives its meaning from the prevailing structure of the international system, or from 'the state' aside and apart from other actors in the global arena, sustains an intellectual distance between the concept and the human beings who are, presumably, the central object of concern. As a result of this distance, those who advocate appreciation of security from the position of the individual contend that the security plight of human beings is often lost amidst the abstractions of systemic and state-level approaches to security (see Box 2.4).

Box 2.4 The human security agenda

Perhaps the most prominent example of an individualistic approach to the concept of security is that of human security. This approach, which rose to prominence in the mid-1990s (though with older antecedents), was borne of a concern with a fuller and more adequate accounting for human well-being and economic development concerns under the heading of security studies (Hettne and Söderbaum, 2005; Duffield, 1999). Advocates of a human security approach define economic well-being and inequality, public health, environmental quality, political empowerment, and a variety of other measures as first and foremost security concerns – particularly to the degree to which they impact what the Nobel Prize-winning economist Amartya Sen refers to as the 'capabilities' and 'functionings' of the individual.

This individual-oriented approach to security is often referred to as the human security agenda, reflecting the degree to which it is directly concerned with policy advocacy. Given the role that NGOs and development agencies played in the emergence and evolution of human security, this seems an accurate portrayal. The degree of emphasis on individual well-being and economic opportunity and security embedded within the human security agenda render it consonant with the broadening of security studies described in this chapter. At the same time, human security has been challenged for its vagueness and imprecision, which in the view of at least one leading authority on the subject leaves it with little ability to provide policy-makers or academics with an effective guide for what falls within the realm of security, and what lies outside it (Paris, 2001).

If security can be characterized as a relative, ambiguous, subjective, and fluid concept in general, this characterization holds most true with regard to the security of individuals. In part this is due to the relatively more expansive and diverse array of threats to the security of individuals that exist, in comparison to states or the international system. Humanitarian suffering, crimes against humanity, torture, ethnic cleansing and genocide – all are threats to the well-being of individuals and groups that an individualistic approach to security (and law, for that matter) must, by necessity, be concerned with.

Generally speaking, threats to the security of the individual are of a social nature; like the systemic approach to security (and unlike the statist one), the referent in this perspective on security is not viewed in isolation from the larger environment in which it exists. Threats to individual security therefore tend to fall into four main categories: physical (threats leading to pain, injury, ailment, or death); economic (threats to property, economic opportunity, or material resources); political (denial of civil rights, restriction on political participation or liberties); and status (threat to one's place within the social order).

What does it mean to say that individual security is affected by social threats? Consider, for example, that the factors that impinge upon one individual's security usually impinge upon the security of numerous others as well; an outbreak of disease, the existence of a burglar in a one's neighborhood, or a policy of 'ethnic cleansing' declared by a government against a national group are all effective examples. Further, the diminution of one person's security will often diminish others' security as well. Threats to individual security also vary greatly by time and space; for instance, facing a threat to one's security posed by ethnic violence directed against one's person was more likely in Bosnia-Herzegovina in 1994 than in 2004; likewise, it has been and remains more likely to face such a security threat in Bosnia-Herzegovina than in Canada. Finally, efforts to prioritize threats to one's individual security, and to effectively respond to them, are often beyond the means and capabilities of the individual affected; one is unlikely to be able to prevent or treat a disease, catch a burglar, or defend oneself against an ethnic cleansing campaign without some kind of outside help.

The shifting and nebulous character of security when viewed in relation to the individual makes the application of conflict management exceedingly difficult. With so many objects of concern, and so many potential security threats to consider, this approach to thinking about security presents many, varied, and messy dilemmas, widening the scope for possible action in the process. Indeed, it stands to some extent as the obverse to the more parsimonious considerations of security with the system or the state as the referent – approaches which narrowed, rather than broadened, the range of potential circumstances where conflict management might be appropriate.

The 'new security environment'

An understanding of the broadening and deepening of security as a concept, as well as the debates over the appropriate referent for security concerns, are each in their own way crucial for comprehending the contemporary security landscape and the conflicts that characterize it. The remainder of this chapter seeks to highlight the practical implications of a revised approach to security studies for the present concern of this book with international conflict management. The major contributions of contemporary security studies are synthesized through discussion of the origins of the 'new security environment,' the new and closely interrelated rules, actors, and threats defining it, and the significance of these rules, actors, and threats for contemporary armed conflict.

Origins

Not so long ago, a claim that the provision, maintenance, and fundamental nature of security in the international arena has changed would have been the sole province of a small number of critical scholars and intrepid journalists. However, in the turbulent post-Cold War period, this claim has gone mainstream. This characterization is difficult to dispute given the prominence of the 'new security environment' as a point of reference in such disparate pockets of officialdom as UN Educational, Scientific and Cultural Organization (UNESCO) policy reports, position papers produced by US War Colleges, and even keynote addresses by North Atlantic Treaty Organization (NATO) military commanders. A small cadre of residual Cold Warriors aside, the vast majority of scholars and practitioners with a concern for, and appreciation of, international security have come to accept (however begrudgingly) the changing nature of security threats and responses, as well as the often volatile and unpredictable nature of these changes.

End of the Cold War

Seismic geopolitical disruptions such as that represented by the collapse of the Soviet Union are certainly central features on the changing landscape of international security. Without a doubt, the end of a half-century of military, political, and ideological struggle between the superpowers radically recast the structure of the international system. Though clearly the bipolar system was no more, the degree and speed of the transformation that began with the reforms of Gorbachev in the mid-1980s, the fall of the Berlin Wall in 1989, and the collapse of the USSR in 1991 left scholars at a loss to provide a singular account of the international security environment in the Cold War's immediate wake.

Differing interpretations of the larger significance for international security of the end of the Cold War ranged from proclamations of the 'end of history' (Fukuyama, 1989), Cold War nostalgia and concern for a new multipolar balance of power arrayed around the United States, Europe, and Japan (Mearsheimer, 1990), and dire predictions of an impending and all-encompassing 'clash of civilizations' (Huntington, 1996). The major (and perhaps only) common theme in these and numerous other attempts at offering an informed forecast of the future was that dramatic changes were at work. In a twist on George H.W. Bush's much celebrated assertion of the emergence of a 'New World Order' in conjunction with the international community's response to security challenges in the Persian Gulf and Somalia, one leading scholar of international conflict management referred to the post-Cold War period as one of 'new world disorder' (Zartman, 2008). In this widely accepted view of the contemporary security landscape, the end of the Cold War triggered and/or revealed a plethora of new and/or previously overlooked security threats and challenges. Included among these challenges was the increasing frequency of intra-state wars (many triggered by identity rather than traditional national interests), threatened proliferation of weapons of mass destruction (WMD), the actual and rampant spread of light arms, the rise in both failing and predatory states, and so forth.

The 9/11 effect

Many observers (especially in the United States) have elected to equate the transformation of contemporary security with the rise to the fore of transnational terrorism in the aftermath of the September 11, 2001 attacks on the World Trade Center and the Pentagon. Though continuous assertions that '9/11 changed everything' are themselves rather trite, certainly 9/11 has had an appreciable effect on the ways in which security is defined and pursued. Perhaps most importantly from the standpoint of considerations of a 'new security environment,' 9/11 illuminated for the first time for a mass audience (again, particularly in the United States) the importance of the rising tide of NSAs and transnational forces and processes within the security realm.

The high profile nature of the 9/11 attacks, as well as the major policy shifts in the United States in response to them, have elevated the tactics, organizational design, and ideology of transnational terrorist groups such as al-Qaeda to an unprecedented level of prominence. This heightened concern with terrorism has also revealed new and complex motives for engaging in armed conflict, as well as new means and methods of doing so, which underpin not only transnational terrorism but a wide range of contemporary security threats and challenges.

The salience of transnational terrorism notwithstanding, the concept of a 'new security environment,' and the changing nature of security and conflict it refers to, speaks to something much more fundamental and far-reaching than the perpetration of attacks by al-Qaeda or its affiliates and subsidiaries. Indeed, while it can certainly be said that the changes at the heart of the aforementioned 'new security environment' encompass transnational terrorism, so too do they include within their purview ethnic conflict, state failure, genocide, ecological and natural resource wars, and numerous other security threats and challenges (C.A.S.E. Collective, 2006; Matthews, 1989). In that sense, events such as 9/11 or the end of the Cold War should be understood as reflections rather than causes of a deeper and more pronounced transformation in the international system.

Defining features

The transformation to a 'new security environment' has been a rather gradual process, with origins stemming back decades. It is reflected not only in the transnational terrorist attacks on the World Trade Center and the Pentagon, but by protracted territorial disputes in the Caucasus, violent struggles over self-determination in southeast Asia, explosions of genocidal violence amidst civil war in sub-Saharan Africa, or violent clashes involving paramilitary and government forces in Latin America. The extent to which these defining characteristics – new rules, new actors, new threats – have reshaped and continue to reshape the contemporary security landscape, in doing so triggering the conflicts that so often imperil that security, renders them worthy of consideration here.

New rules: state sovereignty in decline

As discussed above, state sovereignty played a dominant role within the traditional approach to security. This characterization is borne out in the degree to which actionable security threats were almost exclusively associated with forceful threats to, or violations of, the political, legal, and/or territorial sovereignty of one or more states. At the same time, from the response side, the decision to respond to security threats by states (either individually or collectively) was traditionally predicated on the existence of such a threat to or violation of sovereignty as a, or even the, crucial precondition for action.

This precondition remains valid today, as even a cursory glance at the UN Charter indicates. In the event, such a precondition was or is satisfied, identification of the appropriate response has often been predicated by an overriding concern with preserving or restoring the sovereignty of the threatened state, without dramatically unseating the local, regional, and international order – and the primacy of state sovereignty within that order – in the process. State sovereignty has customarily enjoyed such a prominent position within security and conflict management that this traditionalist approach has been dubbed the 'Westphalian' conception of security (see Box 2.5).

Box 2.5 Sovereignty and security at a crossroads

As is reflected in this chapter, much of the current debate over security turns either directly or indirectly on divergent views of the utility of the state, and in particular the importance of retaining state sovereignty as a central organizing tenet of international relations. Bellamy *et al.* (2004) offer a useful dichotomy for thinking about this divergence, and its crucial implications for the study and pursuit of collective security in the post-Cold War era. This dichotomy, along with its normative underpinnings, logical trajectory, and key assumptions and implications, is summarized in the table below.

Collective security – *Westphalian conception*	*Collective security –* *post-Westphalian conception*
Normative basis: – state sovereignty – right to non-interference – centrality of power/order	*Normative basis:* – liberal values and institutions as guarantors of peace – centrality of markets, rights – sovereignty as responsibility
Trajectory: – preservation of inter-state order begets ... – free trade and inter-state coop, begets ... – democracy and liberalism, begets ... global peace	*Trajectory:* – liberal states (internal character) begets ... – liberal international relations, begets ... – inter-state cooperation, begets ... – global peace

Assumptions/implications:
– state sovereignty retains customary
  political and legal centrality
– security at state-level, provided
  collectively via states
– UN peace ops should target
  inter-state conflicts
– states move *gradually* toward liberal
  institutions and political culture
	Assumptions/implications:
	– state sovereignty both reformed
	  (sovereignty = responsibility) *and*
	  declining
	– security at global or individual level
	– UN peace ops should target intra-state as
	  well as inter-state conflicts
	– liberal institutions and political culture
	  should be cultivated in the short run
	  (through peace operations, statebuilding)

Certainly the state itself remains an important actor that should not be lost in a rushed embrace of a post-Westphalian conception of security. Yet in seeking to understand the complex dynamics of contemporary world politics and in particular the dynamics most affecting conflict and conflict management today, one must acknowledge that the central place of state sovereignty is no longer uncontested. As will be discussed in the following chapter, basic empirical data suggests that armed conflicts, as well as responses to them, are each decreasingly likely to be linked to or shaped by state sovereignty. Likewise, since many of the concepts spawned by the traditional approach to security studies chronicled above are derivative of state sovereignty (e.g., anarchy, the security dilemma, balancing), it behooves us to consider whether and to what degree they retain relevance for application to security dynamics where state sovereignty is less immediately relevant.

New actors: the impact of NSAs

A particular target of nearly all efforts to reformulate contemporary security studies is the singular emphasis of realist theory on militarized interactions between competing states striving to advance national interests as the main, if not only, source for concern. This emphasis is itself a by-product of the theory's essential precept that the state is the central, if not sole, important actor in international politics (Baldwin, 1997). The statist orientation of realism and its deliberate emphasis on power, order, and competing interests rendered the theory highly useful for describing security threats and proscribing security responses in a Cold War world in which these factors were predominant.

Constructs like deterrence, containment, and 'flexible response' undoubtedly provided the key intellectual firmament for the difficult balancing act necessitated by nuclear bipolarity. However, given the central importance of social inequality, gender inequity, poverty and relative deprivation, resource scarcity and environmental degradation, crime, health, external and internal migration, and the like within the 'new security environment,' the utility of such constructs for contemporary security application remains something of an open question. In a world where the source, target, and delivery of a security threat may be only tangentially related to a state, its interests, or its military capabilities, a cognitive lens that places primary emphasis on those factors seems inadequate.

Partly as a function of the diminished role of the state relative to the changing parameters of security, it is clear that the end of the Cold War has ushered in a new era in which states have been elbowed aside by a variety of NSAs. Since the end of the Cold War, the degree to which NSAs, including multinational corporations (MNCs), NGOs, transnational terrorist networks, paramilitaries, private military contractors (PMCs), policy thinktanks, peace advocates, and the like have altered the long-standing rules of international politics reserving power and influence to the realm of nation-states should not be underestimated. This 'party-crashing' by NSAs has dramatically (and quickly) altered the status quo in the global system, as anyone with even a cursory familiarity with contemporary world politics is likely well aware.

Consider, for instance, the intrusion of the World Trade Organization (WTO) into high-level disputes between the United States and the EU over steel tariffs; the direct involvement of the NGO umbrella Coalition for an International Criminal Court in the negotiations shaping the Rome Statute and the International Criminal Court (ICC); the crucial role of remittances from migratory workers to the economies of many developing countries; or the hugely significant role of one Spanish judge (Baltasar Garzon) in bringing former Chilean dictator Augusto Pinochet to justice. These and untold numbers of similar examples point to two crucial dimensions of structural change with great implications for contemporary security: one, the rise to the fore of NSAs as sources of both collective security threats and responses; and two, the potential that NSAs in either capacity may foster and perpetuate a weakening of state capacity in the security realm.

New threats: the 'dark side' of interdependence

Suppositions of a 'new security environment' are dependent not only on changing rules and new actors, but also a recognition of new (or, more accurately, previously overlooked) sources of insecurity. At an abstract level, these sources of insecurity can be understood as unintended outcomes or, in microeconomic terms, 'negative externalities' produced by the complex interdependence animating the current era of globalization. The degree to which the end of the Cold War revealed and furthered interdependence, in the process underwriting the penetration of state borders and integration of the 'internal' and 'external' realms of politics, economics, and society, should not be underestimated.

The benefits of such interdependence are many and oft-celebrated (Keohane and Nye, 2001; Friedman, 2007). Yet at the same time, the depth and expanse of networked interactions between and among societies and individuals is not without its hazards. Most notable among these is the increased sensitivity and vulnerability of an ever-greater number of actors to an increasingly wide range of security threats (Baldwin, 1980). To a very real extent, globalization can be said to be the main impetus driving the emergence of a new security environment.

Certainly the political, social, economic, cultural, and ideational processes of globalization, as well as the backlash against these processes, pose a very real security challenge, in the form of a boiling over of frustrations about the transformations wrought by these processes into violence. Yet it is not just a turn to violence within, between, or across societies by globalization's 'discontents' that is important here. The increasing intensity and extensity of global interdependence has also created a degree of densely networked and weakly governed interconnectedness in commerce, transport, energy and natural resources, migration, and information technology that has raised both the profile and stakes of activities within these issue areas, wiping away the 'high' and 'low' politics dichotomy commonplace in a previous generation.

Whether in the rise of transnational terrorism, potential global epidemics such as HIV/AIDS or avian flu, multiple and competing organized crime networks, the proliferation of WMD as well as the free and easy exchange of conventional arms, or a variety of other developments, the new security environment provides an account of what might be considered the 'dark side' of interdependence. At the core of the issue is the degree to which economic underdevelopment is linked to political instability and volatility and, in turn, violent conflict – and the degree to which the field of security studies is coming to acknowledge and account for the notion of security serving as a precondition for political and economic development, and of political and economic development as a crucial sustaining force for security.

One useful launching point for thinking about this 'dark side' in the broader and deeper sense intended by revisionist security studies – while still retaining a focus on armed conflict – is the 'five sectors' approach introduced by Barry Buzan (1991). Developed to provide a multi-sectoral account of security, Buzan's menu allows for thorough appraisal of the effort to 'securitize' a wider range of phenomena in response to what he dubbed the 'rising density' of globalization. Whether one's security referent is international, national, or individual, Buzan contends security concerns can be located in one (or sometimes more) of five sectors:

- *military security*: concerns produced by the reciprocal interaction of the armed offensive and defensive capabilities and/or perceptions of states and their leaders;
- *political security*: concerns produced in relation to the organization stability (or instability) of states, governing systems, and ideologies;
- *economic security*: concerns generated by limited or unequal access to economic resources (including financial capital and markets) needed to sustain an acceptable level of social welfare;

- *societal security*: concerns triggered by either excessive adherence *or* real/perceived threats to traditional patterns of language, culture, religious and national identity, custom;
- *environmental security*: concerns prompted by threats to the local, regional, or global ecosystem and the natural resource base on which human life depends.

As this schema suggests, while military security is no longer equated with security per se, it retains a high degree of importance – both in its own right and in its interactions with other types of security threats and challenges. This latter point is especially crucial; one of the strengths of Buzan's multi-sectoral approach is the extent to which it not only illustrates distinct categories of security problems apart from military security, but also suggests a significant degree of overlap between and among sectors. In this way we can see where, for example, an environmental security concern (e.g., a sudden decline in arable land) might trigger a military security concern (e.g., the outbreak of armed conflict over land rights and access), or vice versa (where, for instance, an ongoing civil war might reduce the availability of or access to arable land).

While this schema is not all-encompassing, it does offer a basic conceptual roadmap for appreciation of the attempt to broaden and deepen the concept of security in the contemporary era. A notable omission, of course, is the more radical styling of post-modernists, embodied in fundamental challenges to the socially constituted 'realities' at the heart of mainstream approaches to security studies, including concepts such as anarchy and the state. From the standpoint of the centrist and pragmatic concern of international conflict management, the decision to retain rather than reject an important role for the unit of the state and the logic of anarchy provides a helpful bridge between the traditional and revisionist approaches to security studies. For instance, the persistent absence of any effective central governing authority in the international system – and even, in some quarters, the decline of central authority at the state level – makes anarchy seem as potentially relevant for consideration in the 'new security environment' as in the old (see Box 2.6).

Box 2.6 'The Coming Anarchy'

In 1994, journalist Robert Kaplan intentionally disrupted the myopic self-congratulation of the immediate post-Cold War 'victory' (in the West, at least) through publication of a seminal essay entitled 'The Coming Anarchy' (subtitle: 'How Scarcity, Crime, Overpopulation, Tribalism, and Disease are Rapidly Destroying the Social Fabric of our Planet'). Using the violence and chaos of Cote d'Ivoire and Sierra Leone as a launching point, Kaplan unraveled a broad, complex, and prescient argument about the chief sources of contemporary conflict and instability, and their global implications.

Greatly informed by the revisionist security studies literature of the time (which he openly acknowledged throughout the essay), Kaplan's chief contention in the essay was that a range of demographic, environmental, and social stressors, fueled largely by poverty and inequality, were seriously undermining political, economic, and social systems across the globe. As a result, the quest for survival was playing out in rampant violence, crime, lawlessness, and disorder, as an increasing number of states proved insufficient, unable, or unwilling respondents to the challenges posed by disease, overpopulation, migration and refugee flows, or providers of even basic public goods to their populations. The 'coming anarchy,' Kaplan warned, would be a world torn asunder by such chaos, with states and borders declining in both influence and capacity as private security firms, drug cartels, mass migrations, and various transnational forces and actors filled the void and reshaped the global security context – with potentially massive and widespread ramifications.

The 'new security environment' and conflict management

Acting from an intellectual, normative, and policy perspective at odds with the basic tenets of realism, a burgeoning number of advocates for the redefinition of the prevailing security agenda have sought to direct the spotlight in new and disparate directions. Such a diverse and multifaceted alternative to the tradition-bound emphasis of realist conceptions of security on states, military power, and national interests is in many ways a welcome development in light of the significant structural changes underway in the international system.

At the same time, of course, this imperviousness runs both ways. Much of this innovation mentioned in passing above has been shrouded in jargon, lacking in empirical grounding, and in some cases downright (and needlessly) confrontational. When 'critical' approaches to security studies openly and intentionally eschew conventional concepts and assumptions solely to prove a point rather than to advance a line of inquiry, they tend to obscure rather than illuminate – to much the same degree that traditionalists who steadfastly refuse to look past states and interests tread an already well-worn path.

What about the 'new security environment' chronicled here is important for an appraisal of international conflict management? The main significance of the changes outlined in this chapter stems from the ways in which the transformation of security threats and challenges has paved the way for an accompanying transformation in the prosecution of armed conflict. The interrelated emergence of new rules, new actors, and new threats within the contemporary security landscape profiled here has played a crucial role in the emergence of 'new wars' and the causes, actors, support mechanisms, and rules by which they operate – topics to be considered in detail in the next chapter.

Study questions

1   What is the basis for the traditional approach to security studies? On what key concepts and core assumptions does it rest?
2   What precipitated the move to 'broaden' and 'deepen' security studies, beginning in the 1980s? What are some of the leading examples of these efforts, and what have they produced?
3   What are the three main reference points for security extant in the security studies field today? How does conflict management vary in relation to these referents?
4   What were the origins of the 'new security environment'? What are its crucial defining features?

Suggested reading

Baldwin, David A. 1997. 'The Concept of Security,' *Review of International Studies*, 23 (1): 5–26.

Booth, Ken. 1991. *New Thinking About Strategy and International Security*. London: Harper-Collins.

Buzan, Barry. 1991. *People, States, and Fear: The National Security Problem in International Relations*, 2nd edn. Boulder, CO: Lynne Rienner.

Freedman, Lawrence. 1998. 'International Security: Changing Targets,' *Foreign Policy*, 110: 48–63.

Homer-Dixon, Thomas. 1999. *Environment, Scarcity, and Violence*. Princeton, NJ: Princeton University Press.

Kaplan, Robert D. 1994. 'The Coming Anarchy,' *Atlantic Monthly*, 273 (2): 44–76.

Krause, Keith and Michael C. Williams (eds.). 1997. *Critical Security Studies*. Minneapolis, MN: University of Minnesota Press.

Matthews, Jessica Tuchman. 1989. 'Redefining Security,' *Foreign Affairs*, 68 (2): 162–177.

Morgenthau, Hans J. 1948. *Politics Among Nations: The Struggle for Power and Peace*. New York, NY: Alfred A. Knopf.

Paris, Roland. 2001. 'Human Security: Paradigm Shift or Hot Air?' *International Security*, 26 (2): 87–102.

Sheehan, Michael. 2005. *International Security: An Analytical Survey*. Boulder, CO: Lynne Rienner.

Ullman, Richard. 1983. 'Redefining Security,' *International Security*, 8 (1): 129–153.

Walt, Stephen. 1991. 'The Renaissance of Security Studies,' *International Studies Quarterly*, 35 (2): 211–239.

Waltz, Kenneth N. 1979. *Theory of International Politics*. Reading, MA: Addison-Wesley.

3   The challenges of 'new wars'

This chapter seeks to capture the prevailing characteristics of contemporary conflict. The chapter begins with a brief presentation of war as a concept, followed by an empirical snapshot of conflict patterns in the post-Cold War era. A main focus is the conceptual distinction between 'new' and 'old' wars and a comparison of the causes, strategies, tactics, objectives, and support mechanisms that define each abstract typology.

War as a concept

For all his many contributions to strategic thought and the study of warfare, the famous Prussian military strategist Carl von Clausewitz is probably best known for his oft-cited dictum that 'war is the continuation of political intercourse, with the addition of other means' (Clausewitz, 1976: 605). Perhaps the best confirmation of this statement is that, like politics, war is as old as humanity itself. Though difficult to quantify and subject to varying definitional criteria, numerous sound estimates point to the occurrence of at least 14,000 wars throughout recorded history, killing over three billion people (Sheehan, 2008). Though major defining moments in international politics have come and passed along the way, war has proven a singularly devastating constant.

Defining and measuring war

In what seems to be a recurring theme in security studies, war (like security) does not possess a single widely accepted definition. Despite war's historical omnipresence and our continually improving means of studying it (from both a quantitative and qualitative vantage point), war remains a fluid concept. Certainly, the behavioral turn in social science beginning in the 1950s, epitomized by the founding of the *Journal of Conflict Resolution* in 1957, has enhanced our understanding of the patterns and dynamics of war. At the same time, neither the behavioral nor subsequent post-behavioral approaches have produced a uniform definition around which study of the phenomenon can be oriented.

This is undoubtedly due at least in part to the competing theoretical assumptions that underwrite these data collections and establish their selection criteria. Definitions of war proliferate in lockstep with the various datasets crafted and methodologies employed to analyze them. Such definitions tend to differ in relation to one or more of the following factors: the actors included as combatants; the actions that 'count' as war, and/or the causes or issues precipitating the armed violence. Among some of the major examples, Singer and Small's Correlates of War (COW) Project originating at the University of Michigan in the early 1960s traditionally focused on inter-state wars, defined as 'conflicts involving at least one member of the inter-state system on each side of the war … [and] resulting in a total of 1,000 or more battle deaths'; those with fewer casualties fell under the heading of 'armed conflict' (Singer and Small, 1972). Richardson took a distinctly opposed tack, building his dataset around the somewhat nebulous unit of 'deadly quarrels.' Included within this purview was 'anything which caused death to humans … the term includes murders, banditries, mutinies, insurrections, and wars small and large' (Richardson, 1960).

More recent endeavors have sought to navigate the expanse between the narrow focus of Singer and Small and the broad net cast by Richardson. Among the more notable examples, the Militarized Interstate Dispute (MID) dataset (an extension of the COW project) examines conflicts between states with fewer than 1,000 deaths, featuring some use of military force (Ghosn *et al.*, 2004). The University of Uppsala's Conflict Data Project (UCDP) has also sought to forge a path between specificity and generality. Expanded to include the period since 1946 through a collaborative effort with the Centre for the Study of Civil War (CSCW) at the International Peace Research Institute, Oslo (PRIO), the UCDP/PRIO data rests on the concept of 'armed conflict.' This refers to 'prolonged combat between the military forces of two or more governments, or of one government and at least one organized armed group,' a set of criteria which allows for an expanded consideration of both inter- and intra-state wars.

Additional examples of prominent efforts at systematizing the study of armed conflict exist. Some, like the International Crisis Behavior (ICB) Project and its associated dataset (based at the University of Maryland) spurn the definitional morass by focusing on a distinct unit of analysis (crisis, rather than war) altogether (Brecher and Wilkenfeld, 2000). Others, such as the Minorities at Risk Project (housed at the Center for International Development and Conflict Management (CIDCM), also at Maryland), incorporate a concern with armed force, including terrorism and guerrilla war, as a component of a larger interest in various forms of political behavior employed by political minorities (Minorities at Risk Project, 2005). Additionally, the plethora of conflict studies which reject the assumptions and methodologies of behavioralism offer competing alternatives, none of which broadly resonate (Heldt, 1999).

As with security, war must be studied within the limits of persistent contestation over its very essence. Yet as the prolific range of conflict studies indicates, it is possible to do so, provided one explicitly operationalizes the concept in a fashion consistent with their immediate concerns. Accordingly, I draw from a definition proffered by Quincy Wright well over a generation ago, of war as 'a conflict among political groups, especially sovereign states, carried on by armed forces of considerable magnitude, for a considerable period of time' (Wright, 1968: 453). War construed in this way refers to a form of conflict in which violence is both central and enduring, the political goal or goals are evident, and states are likely to be involved in some capacity, though not exclusively or even centrally. This definition seems equally applicable for contemporary and historical analysis, as it includes several crucial elements evident in all definitions of war, while leaving openings for variation by degree.

The persistence of war

The collective pursuit of organized armed violence to some defined end has proven a recurring feature of international society since the codification of the rules and practices of a state-based system in the Treaties of Westphalia (1648). War has maintained its viability in the face of numerous supposed portents of its demise. Examples of such portents include (but are not limited to) the dawn of the Enlightenment and the birth of popular sovereignty in the latter half of the eighteenth century, the founding of the Concert of Europe in the aftermath of Napoleon's defeat in 1815, and the convening of a series of peace conferences beginning in the late nineteenth century (such as The Hague Conferences of 1899 and 1907).

The twentieth century featured the most extensive and substantial indication of war's allegedly approaching obsolescence (Mueller, 1989). In this vein, one can point to the formation of not one, but two, international organizations (the League of Nations in 1919, the UN in 1946) as well as numerous NGOs dedicated to the pursuit of peace. Further evidence includes the establishment of the so-called 'North American security community' (epitomized by the founding of NATO in 1949, and the entire European integration process beginning in the early 1950s), as well as multiple successive 'waves' of democratization expanding the liberal 'zone of peace' and supporting assertions of the 'iron law' of the democratic peace (Doyle, 1983a; Levy, 1988).

Despite these purported challenges from pacific values and institutions, warfare has endured. The persistence of warfare even after the sudden and welcome demise of the Cold War has rendered anticipations of a more pacific 'new world order' a distant memory. Indeed, extensive proliferation of armed conflict unleashed in the immediate aftermath of the transformative events of 1989 and 1991 quickly exposed the fallacy of triumphal proclamations of the 'end of history.' Since 1990, almost four million people have died in wars (90 percent of them civilians), while over 18 million people world-wide have left their homes as a direct result of conflict (Sheehan, 2005).

Box 3.1 The 'zone of peace'

One of the most fertile areas in international relations research is the study of the so-called 'democratic peace.' Within this literature, a crucial contribution was Michael Doyle's two-part essay *Kant, Liberal Legacies, and Foreign Affairs* (1983a, 1983b). As Doyle noted in that essay, modern liberalism contains two dueling strains – pacifism, and imperialism. On the former score, Doyle pointed to what he and others have since dubbed a 'zone of peace' in which liberal states enjoy decidedly and increasingly pacific relations with one another. This zone, which the philosopher Immanuel Kant forecast in his *Perpetual Peace* (1795) as a 'pacific union' began to be established among liberal societies in the eighteenth century, expanding steadily since. Borne out in two centuries lacking major war between liberal states, the 'zone of peace' has spawned the democratic peace thesis – as well as a litany of theoretical and empirical studies to confirm, refine, and challenge the thesis that the norms and institutions of democratic societies prevent them from warring with one another.

Empirical trends in armed conflict

The changing nature and pursuit of security has brought with it significant quantitative and qualitative changes in armed conflict in recent decades. Over the past half-century changes are evident both in the broad patterns of conflict occurrence as well as in the prevailing dynamics of conflict prosecution. While the distinct concern of this book with the application and challenges of contemporary conflict management rules out an elaborate discussion of the statistical parameters of armed conflict itself, it is important to possess at least a basic understanding of the patterns of contemporary conflict in order to gauge the challenges facing the management of those conflicts.

Incidence

Armed conflict of all types increased by a factor of three during the period 1960–1992 (Human Security Centre, 2008). However, two key factors animating these increases – the struggle against colonialism and Cold War bipolarity – no longer exist. The unraveling of the bipolar order in particular brought about the resolution of numerous longstanding civil conflicts around the world (including those in Namibia, Angola, and Cambodia) that had been fueled by the zero-sum clientelism of superpower rivalry. The end of the Cold War was also followed by a largely peaceful (if challenging) democratic transition concentrated mainly in the former Soviet bloc, for the most part dampening conflicts involving these states and republics.

These developments have had a restraining effect on armed conflict. Indeed, empirical data suggests that both the aggregate number of armed conflicts and the incidence of new armed conflicts are declining, especially in the latter instance (see Figure 3.1). These patterns are strongest with respect to inter-state wars (Harbom and Wallensteen, 2007). In 2007, for the fourth consecutive year, no new inter-state

Figure 3.1 Number of armed conflicts by type, 1946–2006 (source: Uppsala Conflict Data Program, UCDP Database: www.ucdp.uu.se/database, Uppsala University, 2008).

war was recorded. In fact, since 1990 only four active conflicts have been classified as inter-state wars: The Persian Gulf War (1990–1991) and its aftermath; Eritrea–Ethiopia (1998–2000); India–Pakistan (1997–2003); and Iraq versus the United States and its allies (2003).

The diminishing likelihood of inter-state war since the end of the Cold War is part of a pronounced historical trend. This trend is not only evident in the Uppsala/PRIO armed conflict dataset cited here, but is also reflected in other research on political violence (Marshall and Gurr, 2005; Mueller, 2004; Holsti, 1996). The significance of this decline is magnified when one considers that the number of states in the international system has greatly increased since the end of the Cold War; since 1990 we continue to witness fewer wars occurring despite the existence of more states to engage in them. Finally, at the same time that the incidence of new inter-state wars and armed conflicts has decreased, the likelihood of conflict termination has increased. These trends translate to fewer ongoing conflicts than at any time since the early 1950s (Eck *et al.*, 2008).

Type

Figure 3.1 also reveals another interesting trend in aggregate conflict patterns. While inter-state wars are steeply in decline, armed conflicts occurring since the end of the Cold War are increasingly likely to take place within the boundaries of one state. A total of 30 of the 33 major armed conflicts recorded since 1998 have been intra-state in nature (Stepanova, 2008). However, two qualifications are in order. While the number of internal conflicts occurring since 1990 make up an overwhelming proportion of all armed conflicts, the total number of major intra-state armed conflicts active today is roughly equivalent to that which prevailed during the late 1960s and again during the mid-1980s (Hegre, 2004; Lacina, 2004). This finding is consistent with the trajectory dating to the end of World War II (Fearon and Laitin, 2003). Indeed, while a brief peak did ensue in the immediate aftermath of the Cold War, resulting from conflicts in the Balkans and the Caucasus associated with the dissolution of the USSR, since the mid-1990s a slight decline in the incidence of internal armed conflicts has occurred. As a result, the trend toward a reduction in the incidence of armed conflict over time holds for both inter-state and intra-state conflicts, albeit to varying degrees.

Intensity

Measuring intensity when studying armed conflict is a tricky business; one would be hard pressed to imagine any armed conflict that is not intense. Still, one would not likely equate the intensity of the US invasion of Granada in 1983 with that of World War II or the Vietnam War. Studying aggregate patterns of armed conflict in a systematic fashion therefore requires introduction of measures to ascertain such relative differences in intensity. One such measure that has been used is that of battle-deaths. Although they do not necessarily account for all deaths (especially civilian deaths) related to armed conflict, battle-deaths are in steep decline since the end of the Cold War (Lacina *et al.*, 2006; Mack, 2005). This decline is evident whether considering battle-deaths in aggregate terms (Figure 3.2) or by distinctions based on whether total battle-deaths in a discrete armed conflict exceed 1,000 (Figure 3.3).

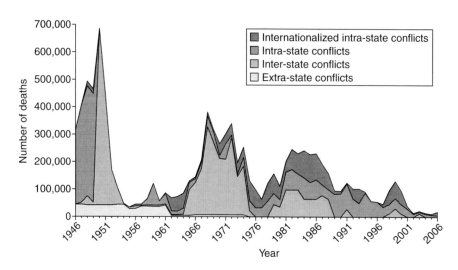

Figure 3.2 Battle-deaths worldwide, 1946–2006 (source: Uppsala Conflict Data Program, UCDP Database: www.ucdp.uu.se/database, Uppsala University, 2008).

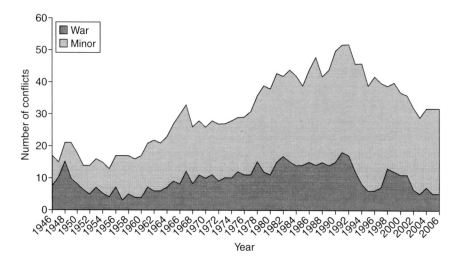

Figure 3.3 Conflicts by intensity and year, 1946–2006 (source: Uppsala Conflict Data Program/International Peace Research Institute-Oslo; UCDP Database: www.ucdp.uu.se/database, Uppsala University, 2008).

In comparing these two portrayals of intensity, similar themes evident in the earlier considerations of incidence and type resonate. Consistent with the fact that the vast majority of armed conflicts since the end of the Cold War are intra-state in nature, it is not surprising that intra-state conflicts also account for most of the battle-deaths during that same period. At the same time, battle-deaths, like armed conflict in general, are in sharp decline. This decline translates to a related finding that the bulk of armed conflicts since the end of World War II, and especially since the end of the Cold War, are 'low intensity' (meaning they feature fewer than 1,000 battle-deaths). It also holds in aggregate terms for all internal armed conflicts, and when averaged by civil conflict.

The changing character of warfare

Quantitative assessments of armed conflict reveal a mixed picture of warfare as a phenomenon in decline, yet still vitally important. While trends in the incidence, type, and intensity of armed conflict all point downward, the data is hardly robust enough to support proclamations of the dawn of perpetual peace (or anything close to it). Indeed, the fact that more than half of all armed conflicts since the end of World War II have been or remain active in the post-Cold War period (116 out of 226) offers sufficient proof of the persistence and salience of conflict in the contemporary era (Eriksson and Wallensteen, 2004).

Appraisals of the qualitative dynamics of conflict after the Cold War are less equivocal in advancing the case for change. At the same time that a so-called 'third wave' of democratization was cresting and proxy wars throughout the former Third World were coming to an end, a sudden and somewhat surprising upsurge in new and intensely violent civil (intra-state) conflicts in the Balkans, the Caucasus, and Africa occurred, in the process commanding the attention of scholars, policy-makers, and the mass media. From the standpoint of numerous assessments of the qualitative nature of these and other similar conflicts, the vast majority of these conflicts are said to conform with a 'new pattern of conflict' defined by 'challenges to existing state authority' rather than territory or other conventional national interests (Wallensteen and Axell, 1995: 345).

Conflict in context: 'old' and 'new' wars

The similarity of the changes evident in many post-Cold War conflicts has prompted a new school of thought about warfare. The chief rationale for this departure was a belief that the evolution of contemporary armed conflict, as documented above, was largely unexplained by 'standard theoretical devices of international politics' (Holsti, 1996: 25). With major inter-state wars declining in frequency and intensity, and low-intensity, internal, and often intractable conflicts driven by identity and fueled by scarcity rising to the fore, prevailing conceptualizations of warfare were deemed insufficient tools for analysis.

As scholars ranging from Clausewitz to Kaldor concur, warfare is an inherently social endeavor that reflects, and is a reflection of, wider social forms and institutional arrangements prevailing at any particular time and place. By the late 1990s a number of scholars of conflict and security studies responded to perceived changes in the structure and arrangements of international society by introducing the conceptual device of 'new wars.' Of course, introducing such a concept necessarily begs the question of what came before.

'Old wars'

Origins and logic

In the view of the 'new war' thesis, 'old wars' originated in a specific place and era (Western Europe from the sixteenth to nineteenth century) defined by a complete social metamorphosis associated with the emergence of modernity. Among other things, this metamorphosis transformed war from a feudal endeavor to a thoroughly modern one. Whereas armed conflict was formerly a contest of honor and skill as well as a display of power, launched by vassals at the behest of monarchs and waged through the proxy of knights and mercenaries, the forces of modernity brought armed conflict under the complete and total control of the state. As such, war has proven to be a chief political instrument utilized by states dating to the establishment of the state as the primary unit of political organization by the Treaties of Westphalia.

The historical evolution of the state to a position as the primary unit of political organization in the international system is closely intertwined with the evolution of modern warfare. This representation is borne out when considering the key developments in the evolution of 'old' warfare, and the central position of the state in those developments. Included among these are: the formation of professional standing armies to wage war; the creation of public sector finance and the establishment of permanent systems of taxation to fund those armies and their military campaigns; the introduction of the convention of *raison d'etat* as a central, even sufficient, justification for said wars; and the promulgation (and occasional enforcement) of secularized rules to govern the conduct of war. These are all characteristics of 'old' or 'modern' warfare (evident in such widely chronicled conflicts as World War I) that we take for granted today, but which did not exist prior to establishment and consolidation of the modern state (see Box 3.2).

Box 3.2 Modernity and the basis of 'old wars'

In the view of most 'new war' theorists, the prevailing characteristics of 'old wars' (such as their prosecution via standing armies, the funding through public revenue streams, and so forth) are linked to other, broader social transitions considered pivotal in the transition to 'modern' society. The creation of separate realms along these axes was a defining element of modernization, as such distinctions were largely unknown prior to the emergence of the state. Furthermore, their conflation and erosion are key claims at the heart of 'new war' theorizing. Included among these key distinctions are:

- *Public/private*, or the idea of a public (state-controlled) and private sector with distinct and mutually exclusive activities such as warfare (in the former case) and religious worship (in the latter).
- *Internal/external*, or the idea of separate and distinct social and political activities at the internal (domestic) and external (international) level.
- *Economic/political*, or the distinction between economic and political activity or, more simply, the realms of government and commerce.
- *Civil/military*, or the separation of civil and military affairs and authority, with the latter answering to the former.
- *Civility/barbarism*, or the idea that some acts and forms of behavior are socially acceptable in a civil society governed by the rule of law, while others are non-normative and suggestive of uncivilized depravity.

- *Soldiers/non-combatants*, in concert with the creation of professional standing armies, the idea that the prosecution of war (and its associated costs and responsibilities) is the sole province of the professional soldier, a trained and equipped agent of the state; all others fall in the realm of non-combatants, ranging from innocents (civilians) or criminals (unsanctioned and unlawful combatants).
- *War/peace*, or the basic and previously alien concept that states of war and peace were mutually exclusive and distinguishable from one another.

With respect to 'old wars,' the key institution shaping and defining warfare was the state. In fact, in the view of 'new war' theorists, the relationship between the state and war is so extensive (and mutually reinforcing) that 'old wars' are represented as primarily Westphalian endeavors fought by, through, and for the state. In seeking to advance a conceptual distinction from wars of this type, 'new war' theorists have been forced to acknowledge and contend with the social theory that undergirds this conventional view of war. Among the primary targets of 'new war' advocates were nineteenth-century typologies of warfare advanced by Carl von Clausewitz, and of the state advanced by Max Weber.

Clausewitz on war

The noted theorist of war Bernard Brodie once said that *On War* (written between 1816 and 1830, and published posthumously in 1832) was 'not simply the greatest, but the only truly great book on war' (in Clausewitz, 1976: 53). Whatever the merits of this claim, it is clear that the Prussian military strategist Carl von Clausewitz has contributed greatly to our appreciation of warfare and strategy, so much so that 'new war' theorists frequently refer to 'old' wars as Clausewitzian. Two general and interrelated themes of *On War* have proven particularly instrumental, not only for conventional understandings of war, but also as a springboard for much of the 'new war' revisionism. These themes relate to Clausewitz's claims regarding the essential political character of war, as well as his views on the very nature of warfare itself.

Given the centrality of violence in the formation and evolution of the modern state, it is not hard to envision how war evolved to represent the type of Clausewitzian policy instrument referenced at the outset of this chapter. Indeed, he insisted that 'the only source of war is politics,' and further that 'if war is part of policy, then policy will determine its character' (Clausewitz, 1976: 605–606). In Clausewitz's contingent logic, the political objective determines the military objective, which establishes the ends to be utilized in service of these objectives. This sequence poses two essential and related challenges for the conduct of war; first, the need to cope with the 'friction' imposed by practical and strategic constraints by identifying the appropriate means of warfare for attaining the particular ends sought, and second (and more importantly), the need to reconcile sometimes contradictory political and military ends.

Clausewitz was unequivocal in asserting that while the particular objective(s) of war vary by situation, the purpose of war is always to impose one's will on the adversary – in other words, to compel one's adversary to submit. This was consistent with his view that the nature of war has an objective facet ('abstract war'); i.e., war possesses some qualities that are common across time and space. Conversely, Clausewitz was equally convinced that the nature of war possessed a second, relative, facet ('real war') meaning that the prosecution of war always varies in conjunction with the political end(s) to which it is linked. These facets can be reconciled when considering, for example, how the purpose of compelling submission can be fulfilled in a variety of ways (ranging from absolute destruction to conditional surrender) depending on the political objectives driving the war.

Clausewitz himself reconciled these perspectives on war through introduction of the conceptual device of the 'remarkable trinity' (see Figure 3.4). In seeking to account for the seeming paradox that war is both constant and contingent, he argued that the subjective facet of war (real war) is driven by the volatile mix of passion, chance and creativity, and reason. Since war is shaped by the intersection of forces such as enmity, strategy, and policy objectives, Clausewitz argued, one can see where the actual prosecution of war can vary greatly with the tension between and among these types of factors motivating and sometimes altering that prosecution.

Though Clausewitz himself stopped short of doing so, many scholars have extended the remarkable trinity of passion, chance/creativity, and reason to provide an account for war as a phenomenon caught between the aligned, and sometimes competing, forces of the people, the army, and the government (van Creveld, 1991). Clausewitz did in fact grant that these were the three categories of agents which war concerned, and that they did more or less correspond with those three aspects of the trinity. As a result, the triangular relationship between and among the public, the military, and the government captured by the remarkable trinity is often cited as Clausewitz's main contribution to the study of modern war.

Weber and the state

The prominent nineteenth-century sociologist Max Weber posited that the defining feature of the modern state, and indeed a major wellspring of its power and authority, was its possession of a monopoly on the legitimate employment of organized violence. With the legitimacy of the state contingent on the notion that it is the state and only the state that possesses the right to employ violence both domestically and on the world stage, one can see (as Weber did) the construction of a mutually dependent relationship between organized violence and the state. Internally, such a

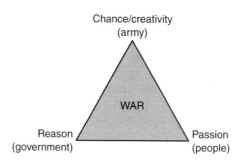

Figure 3.4 Clausewitz's 'remarkable trinity'.

monopoly underwrote the very authority of the state, as violence could be (and was) used to thwart potential internal challenges to ruling elites, while simultaneously allowing for any such challenges to be framed by agents of the state as inherently illegitimate.

The central importance of violence in the process of fashioning the modern state and establishing its central position both in domestic society and in the international system is evident and has been well-chronicled (Mann, 1993). The Weberian monopoly, once asserted and (at least mostly) achieved at the domestic level, helps consolidate state power and eliminate potential challenges both to actual states and to the abstract concept of the state itself. Violence can be used to crush dissent or avert potential challenges to the government. At the same time, such a monopoly also contains an important external dimension. Possessing sole and unchallenged (or mostly unchallenged) authority to utilize organized violence similarly permits the state to employ violence to defend national interests and advance national objectives relative to other states, or even to divert attention from domestic problems by initiating armed conflict with 'enemies.' By virtue of possessing this monopoly, individual states are able to secure their interests and protect their sovereignty while also advancing the central position of the state as the most legitimate and important actor on the world stage.

'New wars'

Origins and logic

The archetype of the Clausewitzian 'old' war held that wars were the product of rational calculation. Political leaders utilized the tools of the state over which they presided (professional standing armies and national economies of scale) to deploy overwhelming force against similarly organized opponents in a contest over some discernable national interest(s). At the heart of the 'new wars' perspective is the assertion that the social relations underpinning this understanding of warfare have fundamentally changed since the end of the Cold War (Kaldor, 1999).

The logic of the Clausewitzian/Weberian typology of 'old' war has been almost entirely dismissed by 'new war' theorists. Both in deference and contrast to Clausewitz, contemporary conflicts have been characterized as 'wars of the third kind' – successors to the limited war of eighteenth- and nineteenth-century statecraft, and the total war of the twentieth-century world wars (Rice, 1988). They have also been referred to as 'internal conflicts' (Brown, 1996), 'new wars' (Kaldor, 1999), 'small wars' (Harding, 1994), 'protracted social conflicts' (Azar, 1990), and so forth. Regardless of the terminology employed to describe them, this emerging view of contemporary conflict coalesces around three general propositions: conflict is increasingly likely to be carried out by actors other than states, for causes other than traditional national interests, and by means and tactics other than those associated with regular, professionalized standing armies.

'New war' theorizing holds that the 'key distinctions' at the heart of modern society around which the modern state was organized and warfare prosecuted have been deeply eroded, if not negated (Shaw, 1999). In 'new wars' occurring in such disparate arenas as Bosnia-Herzegovina, Nagorny-Karabakh, Sierra Leone, and Colombia (to name a few), armed conflict is advanced without much regard for separation between internal and external political and social realms, public and private goods and activities, civilian and military authority, or even between states of 'war' and 'peace' (Münkler, 2004). 'New wars' are understood to be identity-fueled and chaotically disorganized conflicts, waged by a range of official and irregular combatants and sustained by remittances, organized crime, and transnational networks moving money, arms, and people.

Globalization as catalyst

Why are 'new wars' happening now? 'New war' theorizing rests on the assumption that globalization is an all-encompassing transformative process. While the 'new wars' scholarship recognizes that globalization is not something that began in 1990, there is a decided emphasis on the intensity and extensity of the current wave of globalization and the acceleration of these dynamics with the decline of bipolarity as the catalyst for 'new wars.' 'New war' theorists point to globalization as a phenomenon that has radically recast nearly all forms of social relations and interactions, including war.

In the 'new war' perspective, armed conflict can naturally be lumped in with the increasingly unfettered flow of goods, services, and capital, mass migration, transboundary problems such as pollution and disease, and so forth as phenomena that have become 'globalized,' both in their workings and implications. This recasting has triggered a well-documented backlash against the agents, forces, and processes of economic, political, and cultural globalization. Such a backlash has been characterized along various divides such as *Jihad* v. *McWorld* (Barber, 1996), a 'clash of civilizations' (Huntington, 1996), or 'globalization and its discontents' (Stiglitz, 2002). Regardless of one's favored cognitive lens or individual perspective, it is important to recognize that globalization's simultaneously integrative and fragmentary tendencies, its tendency to produce and reinforce significant economic disparities, and the prevalence of negative perceptions of the phenomenon are all crucial animating aspects of 'new wars.'

The crisis of the state

New war theorists contend that globalization triggers two simultaneous and interrelated 'crises.' The first of these stems from the increasing inability of states to control their internal and external relations. This diminished control leaves the state (and especially weak states) struggling to contend with the causes, dynamics, and implications of transnationalism in the realm of collective violence as well as in the realms of commerce, health, migration, and the environment. The extension of globalization to include the decision to employ collective violence, as well as the actual prosecution of armed conflict, not only undermines the capacity but also threatens the primacy of the state itself. With armed conflict no longer the sole province of the state, the state's unquestioned monopoly on the use of organized violence is itself eroded by 'new wars.'

As products of complex interdependence, 'new wars' are thought to pose an existential crisis to the modern state. At the same time that an increasing number of states have proven unable to cope with the negative effects of the disruptive, polarizing, and seemingly haphazard processes of globalization, these processes have come to be seen as threats by millions of individuals. Furthermore, the spillover of globalization into the realm of collective violence poses a real, direct, and enhanced threat to the security of individuals. At the very juncture when state capacity is most pivotal – in the midst of the chaotic violence and lawlessness of 'new wars' – the inefficacy, particularly of weak states, is apparent. The Weberian 'monopoly' is compromised not only by the inability of states to contend with globalizing forces, but by their deficiencies in security provision.

The crisis of identity

At the same time, 'new wars' are thought to produce a second crisis of identity, fueled by the particularistic identity politics that serve as the main sources of 'new wars.' In 'old' and 'new' wars alike, the manipulation of group identity by elites is important, as is the resonance of group identity within the populace. Taken together, these factors are crucial to the process of creating and sustaining a climate whereby the use of violence in relation to a real or perceived grievance is seen as acceptable, if not desirable. 'Old wars' were fought largely for abstract conceptions of the national interest, with mass mobilization occurring through broad-based and inclusive appeals rooted either in overarching national identities, or general ideological principles and positions (liberalism, socialism, fascism, etc.). The two totalizing world wars of the early twentieth century represent the apex of such mobilization, as the rationale for unrestricted warfare was overwhelmingly embraced by mass audiences.

Conversely, what sets 'new wars' apart with respect to identity is the degree to which they are fought for causes that are indistinguishable from the particularistic identity used to mobilize the combatants; the reason for making war therefore becomes making war. 'New wars' are at base violent contests between inclusive and exclusive notions of social organization, prompted by the social-psychological distinctions of 'in-group' and 'out-group' arrayed around ethnic, religious, linguistic, or other cognitive signifiers (Druckman, 1994). These distinctions are often rooted in deep-seated historical and cultural grievances (whether real or imagined), grievances sustained through a mix of exaltation (of the in-group's honor, past, and traditions), demonization (of the out-group's motives and actions), and the manufacturing of an omnipresent threat (Stein, 2001). Such identities are usually historically derived and therefore have broader and more sustained appeal in the face of challenges to the nation-state, particularly given the degree of romanticized myth-making associated with them. This transference of the locus of identity from nation-state to sub-state group lies at the very heart of 'new wars.'

The extent to which the twin crises of the state and identity are not only related but mutually reinforcing within the 'new wars' literature should not be overlooked. With the capacity of all states (and particularly weak states) exposed by globalization, national cohesion and personal fealty to the state declines, which in turn further undermines state capacity and, by extension, cohesion and loyalty. In such a context, it is natural that individuals would look to other sources for both security and identity reinforcement. In this way, ethnic, religious, or other 'primordial' identities serve as appealing replacements for national identity, a source of identity closely associated with the state whose capacity is in decline.

Waging 'new wars'

In 'new wars', the basic calculus of warfare in terms of strategy and tactics is transformed. That is not to say that 'new wars' lack a political dimension; far from it. Indeed, 'new wars' are associated with an effort by sub-state groups (with transnational support networks) to contest, hijack, or weaken the authority of the state; further, they are often prosecuted to obtain and secure territorial advantage. However, in strategic terms the employment of violence in 'new wars' veers drastically from the pursuit of traditional political or military objectives.

Ultimately, 'new wars' are those advanced and shaped by the desire to sow and reap the gains of fear and hatred on which particularistic identity politics turn. Combatants engaged in 'new wars' are singularly unified in the pursuit of political power and economic gain, and roundly dismissive of unifying ideologies, restraints on the use of force, or concerns with perceived political legitimacy. Rather than a tool to advance the national interest, in 'new wars' violence is both the means to an end, and an end unto itself. As a result, 'new wars' often feature the application of what seems from the outside as senseless brutality as well as rampant war profiteering as intentional political tactics.

The chief point of departure for 'new wars' is that the interests pursued by the combatants and the source of mobilization are one and the same; namely, the defense and advancement of one's own group relative to the much-demonized 'other.' This is established and maintained through the selective and targeted administration of violence to expel or eliminate any challengers, particularly those of the out-group(s). In 'new wars,' population displacement, massacres, widespread and systematic human rights violations, and criminal activity are transformed from ancillary outcomes to deliberate strategies.

Technology is a relatively insignificant part of the 'new war' equation. Personal communication devices (especially cell phones) as well as mass media (radio and television) are widely used to coordinate activities and perpetuate fear and divisiveness. Yet in terms of the actual application of violence, the flood of light arms unleashed with the privatization of arms production after the end of the Cold War, in combination with large residual arms caches from the proxy struggles of the Cold War era, generally suffice. In some cases, makeshift and rudimentary implements (such as machetes, the weapon of choice in the Rwandan genocide) are employed in low-intensity, but extremely bloody, spasms of internecine warfare.

The violent spasms of 'new wars' are carried out by a combination of paramilitaries, mercenaries, organized crime syndicates, and various other irregular forces in place of the standing, professionalized, hierarchically organized armies of the state. These front-line combatants straddle and intentionally blur the distinction between combatants and non-combatants – both as a result of their own murky status as well as their favored targets. Indeed, the object of 'new war' violence is typically not the corresponding irregular forces of other competing groups but civilians (Snow, 1996). As a result, rules governing the conduct of war embodied in various international treaties and conventions (such as the Geneva Conventions) are repeatedly and egregiously violated. In the process, core distinctions at the heart of modern society and 'old wars' – between combatants and non-combatants, and civility and barbarism – are stretched to the point of irrelevance.

Sustaining 'new wars'

Given the extensity of physical destruction and the weakness of state institutions in most theaters of 'new war,' unregulated social behavior is the rule rather than the exception. Violence, lawlessness, and economic insecurity are rampant and public goods practically non-existent. Such circumstances promote the adaptability and opportunism of shadowy and violent criminal networks, utilizing their structures to equal measure in the pursuit of war booty and the conduct of organized criminal activity on the one hand, and the prosecution of internecine warfare on the other. Kaldor (1999) describes this increasingly prevalent scenario within 'new wars' as the 'globalized war economy.' This is a form of economic organization and activity that is especially well-suited in societies defined by economic scarcity and inequality (Berdal, 2003).

Arms production and trade has become globalized, as has organized crime, whether connected to brokering arms transfers or providing other goods and services convertible into revenue streams for sustaining and expanding armed conflicts. Those revenues, combined with remittances drawn from transnational communities of exiles and other supporters, are easy to launder and even easier to transfer within a largely deregulated global financial system. At the same time, the basis of 'new wars' in clashing identities serves as a natural animus for recruiting, fundraising, and propagandizing all along such networks, in various 'cells' located in far-flung locales wherever émigré and refugee communities with strong kin loyalties flourish. Combatants are drawn from all quarters of the globe, and are relatively easy to recruit and move into and out of conflict zones using the channels of transnational (oftentimes diasporic) networks (Jung, 2003).

The multiplicity of actors involved in 'new wars' (whether states, remnants of states, local political elites, paramilitaries, mercenaries, or otherwise) share a dependence on the perpetuation of violence for both political and economic reasons. 'Old wars' are highly regulated and planned endeavors, closely approximating the Fordist model of complex, highly organized, and sequential production. As endeavors of the state, they also feature rigid vertical bureaucratic hierarchies evident both in their political and military authority structures. Conversely, 'new wars' more closely approximate the flattened and flexible horizontal structure of the network, an organizational arrangement long prominent in the informal (illicit) economy but also increasingly prevalent in innovative areas of economic activity such as the technology sector (Powell, 1990).

Critiques

The 'new war' concept is not without its critics. Much of the criticism turns on two significant deficiencies in the thesis: one, that 'new wars' are not appreciably new, and two, that the phenomenon that 'new war' theorists describe is not consistent with the concept of war in any tangible sense (Gray, 2005; Newman, 2004; Henderson and Singer, 2002; Kalyvas, 2001). Other scholars have utilized empirical analysis to challenge the trends asserted by 'new war' theorists, especially claims regarding increases in the targeting of civilians as well as population displacement (Kalyvas, 2001; Lacina, 2006; Lacina *et al.* 2006; Lacina and Gleditsch, 2005; Mack, 2005). The validity of these critiques is underwritten by the failure of those advancing the 'new war' distinction to produce structured and focused comparisons of contemporary conflict with conflict from other historical eras.

Most of the 'new war' literature has been, and remains, concerned with abstract theorizing about the nature of contemporary conflict, relying on isolated case studies for evidence. 'Old wars' are left in the realm of the abstract, in the process overlooking some aspects of (especially pre-Westphalian) wars which are remarkably similar to what is evident today (Hall *et al.*, 2006). Whatever the merits to the claim of 'newness,' the 'new wars' literature in concert with the effort to broaden and deepen security studies (as chronicled in Chapter 2), does shed light on a number of changes in the contemporary international system with particular relevance for conflict management.

Study questions

1   Why is an agreed-upon definition of war elusive? What are some central and recurring elements in the most prominent definitions?
2   What trends are evident in the incidence, type, and intensity of armed conflict today? What accounts for these trends?
3   What are the key distinctions of modernity, and how do they relate to the organization and conduct of 'old' and 'new' wars?
4   What were the main contributions of Clausewitz and Weber to the typology of 'old wars?'
5   What is the catalyst and sustaining force for 'new wars?' What two crises did it spawn?

Suggested reading

Azar, Edward E. 1990. *The Management of Protracted Social Conflict: Theory and Cases.* Aldershot: Dartmouth.
Brown, Michael (ed.). 1996. *The International Dimensions of Internal Conflict.* Cambridge, MA: MIT Press.
Clausewitz, Carl von. 1976. *On War* (edited and translated by M. Howard and P. Paret). Princeton, NJ: Princeton University Press.
Druckman, Daniel. 1994. 'Nationalism, Patriotism, and Group Loyalty: A Social Psychological Perspective,' *Mershon International Studies Review*, 38 (1): 43–68.
Harbom, Lotta and Peter Wallensteen. 2007. 'Armed Conflict 1989–2006,' *Journal of Peace Research*, 44 (5): 623–634.
Holsti, Kalevi J. 1996. *The State, War, and the State of War.* Cambridge: Cambridge University Press.
Kaldor, Mary. 1999. *New and Old Wars: Organized Violence in a Global Era.* Stanford, CA: Stanford University Press.
Mueller, John. 2004. *The Remnants of War.* Ithaca, NY: Cornell University Press.
Münkler, Herfried. 2004. *The New Wars.* Cambridge: Polity.
Stein, Janice Gross. 2001. 'Image, Identity, and the Resolution of Violent Conflict,' in C.A. Crocker, F.O. Hampson, and P. Aall (eds.), *Turbulent Peace: The Challenges of Managing International Conflict.* Washington, DC: United States Institute of Peace Press, pp. 189–208.

Part II
Concepts and application

4   Peacekeeping

This chapter chronicles peacekeeping from its origins in tentative efforts at collective security provision, through its embedding in the multidimensional peace operations of the twenty-first century. The chapter begins with a profile of one of the first and most prominent examples of traditional peacekeeping – the UN Peacekeeping Force in Cyprus (UNFICYP). It then turns to consideration of peacekeeping as a concept, why, when, and how peacekeeping is provided, and the major debates surrounding it.

Peacekeeping in brief: insights from UNFICYP

On 21 December 1963, long-simmering tensions between Greek and Turkish communities on the island of Cyprus boiled over into inter-communal violence. This violence triggered the rupture of the tenuous power-sharing arrangement that defined the Republic of Cyprus for the first three years of its existence. It also paved the way for four decades of a peacekeeping presence under the mandate of the UNFICYP.

Roots of the conflict

The UN peacekeeping operation in Cyprus is perhaps the best-chronicled peacekeeping operation of all time (Ker-Lindsey, 2006; Talman, 2002; Mirbagheri, 1998; Birgisson, 1993; Theodorides, 1982; Coufoudakis, 1976). The roots of the civil war that spawned that operation are equally as well documented. A large island located at the far eastern end of the Mediterranean, the population at the time of the founding of the independent Republic of Cyprus (in August 1960) was approximately 700,000 (80 percent Greek, 18 percent Turkish); today the total population approaches 850,000, with the demographic proportions of Greeks and Turks remaining roughly the same. Despite the island's proximity to Turkey, the population has historically enjoyed strong cultural, political, and economic ties with Greece.

Imperial rule and enosis

Links between Cyprus and Greece have persisted over the centuries, intensifying with the incorporation of both entities into the Ottoman Empire in the sixteenth century. Ottoman imperial strategy over the next three centuries unintentionally contributed to this dynamic. Turkish reliance on local religious elites affiliated with the Greek Orthodox Church to administer the territory encouraged pan-Hellenist sentiment in both Cyprus and Greece. Such sentiment gained full political expression in the concept of '*enosis*' (union) in the late nineteenth century, a concept that emerged in conjunction with the transfer of Cyprus from Ottoman to British rule in 1878.

Repeated efforts by the British to sever the connection between political and religious authority on the island sparked a backlash among the Greek Cypriot community. Several decades of British rule saw *enosis* become the central organizing tenet of (Greek) Cypriot political life. The intensification of nationalist sentiment culminated in the establishment of the EOKA (Ethniki Organosis Kyprion Agoniston, or National Organization of Cypriot Fighters) under the command of Colonel George Grivas in 1955, ushering in a violent campaign for national liberation against the British colonialists. The insurrection's challenge led to a set of negotiated agreements between the United Kingdom, Greece, and Turkey, establishing the Republic of Cyprus on 16 August 1960.

The Republic of Cyprus

The Zurich agreements produced four significant documents: A Treaty of Establishment, a Treaty of Guarantee, a Treaty of Alliance, and a Constitution. The first two documents (signed by Greece, Turkey, Cyprus, and the United Kingdom) were intended to bind all four actors to the establishment of the Republic and to the common defense of its independence, while the third (signed by Greece, Turkey, and Cyprus) was designed to defuse inter-communal tensions and external encouragement of them. Finally, the Constitution attempted to balance the interests of both the Greek and Turkish communities by establishing a consociational power-sharing arrangement, including the allocation of executive and cabinet offices, fixed proportions of legislative seats, and veto power in rough proportion to the demographics of the population.

This institutionalized power-sharing arrangement could not overcome the mutual distrust between the two political communities in Cyprus, as well as the sustained appeal of *enosis* within the Greek community. In late November 1963, the Republic's President, Archbishop Makarios, proposed a series of constitutional amendments intended to eliminate the earmarks for Turkish Cypriots within the political system under the guise of promoting national unity. The rejection of the Makarios proposal by Turkish Cypriot leaders prompted the outbreak of violence in Nicosia and outlying areas on 21 December 1963.

The civil war

At the outset of the conflict, the numerically superior Greek community enjoyed the upper hand. Nearly 25,000 Turkish Cypriots (about one-fifth of the Turkish Cypriot population) fled for heavily fortified enclaves in the north and east of the island. In response to a looming civil war, and seeking to stem a likely refugee crisis, Turkey (who had already deployed a military contingent to aid Turkish Cypriots) threatened a full-scale invasion of the island. Acting in accordance with the Treaty of Guarantee, on 24 December 1963 the governments of Greece, Turkey, and the

United Kingdom agreed to assemble a peacekeeping force from military contingents already present on the island, placed under British command. The government of Cyprus consented to the arrangement, and a truce was fashioned along with the so-called 'Green Line' running through Nicosia.

Despite the efforts of the governments of Greece, Turkey, and the United Kingdom to fashion a truce and a peacekeeping force to monitor it, armed attacks carried out by factions on each side escalated throughout early 1964. On 15 February 1964, the United Kingdom and the Republic of Cyprus requested urgent action by the Security Council. At the behest of UN Secretary General U Thant, negotiations to create an independent peacekeeping force began. On 4 March 1964, the Security Council unanimously adopted Resolution 186, establishing the UNFICYP.

UNFICYP – mandate and mission

The UNFICYP became fully operational on 27 March 1964, and was complemented (on 14 April 1964) by a civilian police unit (UNCIVPOL). According to its original mandate, UNFICYP was deployed 'to prevent a recurrence of the fighting and, as necessary, to contribute to the maintenance and restoration of law and order and a return to normal conditions.' Consistent with the *ethos* of traditional peacekeeping, the UN force was primarily dedicated to separation of the warring parties. It was assumed that diplomatic efforts to address the grievances between the Greek and Turkish communities would follow in conjunction with the pacification of Cyprus by UNFICYP, though this was not a central focus of the operation's mandate.

By the late spring of 1964, in accordance with the cease-fire, a distinct territorial separation of Greek and Turkish Cypriots was established for the first time. The Turkish Cypriot community established an 'autonomous civil administration' to oversee the enclaves that had emerged in the early days of the war. These enclaves, accounting for approximately 3 percent of the island's landmass, eventually wound up containing almost the entire Turkish Cypriot population, while the remainder of the island's territory was ceded to the Greek-controlled government of the Republic of Cyprus. This territorial demarcation was fully accepted by the UN, with UNFICYP forces critical to its administration and maintenance for a decade thereafter.

The 1974 coup

At the instigation of the military dictatorship in Athens, on 15 July 1974 a *coup d'etat* displacing the government of Archbishop Makarios was launched by Greek Cypriot operatives committed to *enosis*. Five days later Turkish military forces intervened, with Ankara citing the Treaty of Guarantee and the Treaty of Alliance as legal justification. The direct clashes between Turkish troops and the Greek Cypriot National Guard were extensive. Turkish forces advanced steadily, occupying much of the northern part of the island. Within days nearly 180,000 Greek Cypriots had fled southward, with about 40,000 Turkish Cypriots migrating toward new Turkish enclaves in the north; amidst the tumult, the military regime established by the coup quickly collapsed.

At the request of the interim government, as well as UN Secretary-General Kurt Waldheim, the Security Council convened on 16 and 19 July 1974 and issued calls for a cease-fire; these were finally heeded on 24 July. The foreign ministers of Greece, Turkey, and the United Kingdom convened in Geneva on 25–30 July to establish a security arrangement to be administered by UNFICYP forces. With talks stalemated, violence erupted again on 14 August 1974, prompting further Turkish advances. With the final cessation of hostilities on 16 August, Turkey controlled approximately 40 percent of the island (in the north), which was subsequently turned over to Turkish Cypriot control.

Partition and stalemate

In the wake of the 1974 cease-fire, Cyprus was effectively partitioned. In an arrangement that persists today, two de facto cease-fire lines corresponding with the Turkish and Greek Cypriot National Guard positions (extending approximately 180 km across the island) were established. These cease-fire lines remain separated by a buffer zone ranging in width from 20 m in central Nicosia to 7 km in rural areas, comprising 3 percent of the island's territory.

UN operations have been further complicated by the assertion of greater autonomy by the Turkish Cypriot community since the events of 1974. Beginning with the proclamation in February 1975 of a 'Turkish Federated State of Cyprus' and continuing through the November 1983 declaration of the independent state of the 'Turkish Republic of Northern Cyprus,' UNFICYP has been forced to engage and interact with both political entities in Cyprus. Despite the invalidation of these actions on the part of the Turkish community by the UN Security Council (UNSC), UNFICYP has operated primarily as an inter-state peacekeeping force since 1974, administering the cease-fire lines and attending to a variety of security, law enforcement, and humanitarian tasks as the political situation in Cyprus remains predominantly defined by stalemate.

What is peacekeeping?

Conceptual imprecision

Fewer terms in international security and conflict management are more frequently misapplied than 'peacekeeping.' The term has been used to refer to disparate and even dissimilar events, from the deployment of UN forces to the Sinai in 1956 (to defuse the Suez crisis), to the US invasion of Granada in 1983, to the extended and multifaceted deployments to Kosovo and East Timor beginning in 1999. As Diehl (1994) points out, if 'peacekeeping' is used in reference to any effort by third parties to terminate an armed conflict then systematic efforts at theory-building suffer, and the essence of peacekeeping becomes hopelessly obscured. At the same time, the significant differences between peacekeeping and other forms of conflict management are also lost.

This characterization is borne out when one considers the credibility-straining range of use of the term in recent years. 'Peacekeeping' has been used to refer to coercive military actions designed to punish aggressors (such as Operation Desert Storm in the Persian Gulf), mixed operations with both stabilization and war-fighting components (such as the International Security Assistance Force (ISAF) deployment in Afghanistan), and nakedly self-interested military interventions (such as the US-led Operation Iraqi Freedom). Using the term in reference to operations where peace is assuredly not the first objective (or an objective at all) seems to directly challenge if not contradict any basic notions of peace or efforts to 'keep' it. In addition, while the fast-and-loose use of the term has significant implications for the study of peacekeeping, it is also important from a policy standpoint, as a poor grasp of the *concept* may contribute to misuse of the *practice* (Rieff, 1994).

While the terminological imprecision associated with peacekeeping is particularly evident in political circles and media coverage, it is not limited to those realms. While most scholars of peacekeeping seem to operate within a common frame of reference, using the term to refer to international efforts built around operations to promote the termination of armed conflict and/or the resolution of their underlying disputes, significant and sometimes contradictory variants exist (see Box 4.1). Some analyses of peacekeeping seem to embrace this imprecision, implying that it is an ad hoc technique of conflict management best studied through descriptive profiles of individual applications (Gordon and Toase, 2001). This scenario is not helped by the fact that the UN, which is perhaps best known by the public for its essential role in providing and promoting peacekeeping, also lacks an established definition of peacekeeping.

Box 4.1 Prominent definitions of peacekeeping

International Peace Academy: The prevention, containment, moderation, and termination of hostilities, through the medium of a peaceful third-party intervention, organized and directly internationally, using multinational forces of soldiers, police, and civilians to restore and maintain peace.

Diehl (1994): peacekeeping is … the imposition of neutral and lightly armed interposition forces following a cessation of armed hostilities, and with the permission of the state on whose territory these forces are deployed, in order to discourage a renewal of military conflict and promote an environment under which the underlying dispute can be resolved.

Durch (1993): Peacekeeping missions may involve … uncovering the facts of a conflict; monitoring of border or buffer zones after armistice agreements have been signed; verification of agreed-upon force disengagements or withdrawals; supervision of the disarming and demobilization of local forces; maintaining of security conditions essential to the conduct of elections; and even the temporary, transitional administration of countries.

Goulding (1993): Field operations established by the United Nations with the consent of the parties concerned, to help control and resolve conflicts between them, under UN command and control, at the expense collectively of the member states, and with military and other personnel and equipment provided voluntarily by them, acting impartially between the parties and using force to the minimum extent necessary.

Heldt and Wallensteen (2005): A peacekeeping operation is defined as a third-party state intervention that involves the deployment of military troops and/or military observers and/or civilian police in a target state; is, according to the mandate (as specified in multilateral agreements, peace agreements, or resolutions of the UN or regional organizations), established for the purpose of separating conflict parties, monitoring cease-fires, maintaining buffer zones, and taking responsibility for the security situation (among other things) between formerly, potentially, or presently warring parties; and adopts a neutral stance toward the conflict parties, but is not necessarily impartial toward their behavior.

United Nations, DPKO (2008): Peacekeeping is a technique designed to preserve the peace, however fragile, where fighting has been halted, and to assist in implementing agreements achieved by the peacemakers. Over the years, peacekeeping has evolved from a primarily military model of observing cease-fires and the separation of forces after inter-state wars, to incorporate a complex model of many elements – military, police, and civilian – working together to help lay the foundations for sustainable peace.

Defining features

Perhaps the best way to specify the essence of peacekeeping is to identify its major defining attributes. As a form of third-party intervention in conflict, peacekeeping has certain features in common with collective security and peace operations, most notably a reliance on military forces provided by nation-states. Yet as the historical evolution and application of peacekeeping discussed at length in this chapter will show, the practice of peacekeeping as a form of conflict management is defined by a set of unique and interrelated attributes that clearly distinguish it from other endeavors linked to the pursuit of security and peace.

A wide variety of activities can be plausibly characterized as peacekeeping tasks, including but not limited to observation, fact-finding, monitoring cease-fires, and interposition. Peacekeeping forces are typically assigned to carry out mandated responsibilities (specified in multilateral agreements, peace agreements, or resolutions of the UN or regional organizations) to monitor cease-fires, maintain buffer zones, and otherwise facilitate security.

Non-enforcement

Like both standard third-party military interventions and collective security and enforcement actions, peacekeeping operations involve the introduction of armed military personnel into zones of conflict. Unlike either of these forms of conflict behavior, peacekeeping operations deploy armed military (as well as civilian police) personnel in a non-coercive posture. Peacekeeping operations differ dramatically from traditional military operations which seek to deter or defeat opponents, seizing territory and other key strategic assets in the process. Peacekeeping is not designed to use deadly force to coerce or compel submission. In fact, peacekeepers enjoy a neutral position relative to the parties to the conflict, and occupy territory or secure strategic targets only to the extent that doing so contributes to their success as an interposition force or 'buffer.'

Peacekeeping operations enjoy some overlap with collective security operations or enforcement actions. Peacekeeping shares with these types of actions a long-term objective of restoring order in settings gripped by conflict. However, unlike collective security operations and enforcement actions, peacekeeping forces are not tasked with forcibly restoring that order or arresting or altering the conflict. Unlike collective security or enforcement actions (or traditional military intervention) peacekeeping forces are usually deployed *after* armed violence has been halted, underscoring their non-coercive dimension.

Limited force/self-defense

Following on from the non-coercive character of peacekeeping operations is the reality that peacekeeping forces, while potentially numerous, are always lightly armed. The typical peacekeeper possesses no more than a rifle and/or small arms, and the typical peacekeeping deployment is arrayed around the use of equipment for transport and logistics (such as helicopters and armored personnel carriers) rather than those better suited for offensive action (such as tanks, fighter planes, and aircraft carriers). The lightly armed character of peacekeepers is less a by-product of resource deficiencies than a reflection of the essence of what peacekeeping is and what it seeks to achieve.

Because peacekeeping operations are decidedly non-traditional military operations, lacking an offensive intent or strategic aspirations, they do not require significant or extensive levels of armaments. That is not to say that peacekeeping forces are unarmed or insufficiently armed. The degree to which peacekeepers are armed and equipped is consistent with their need to exercise their right to self-defense, and to possess a visible and credible deterrent capability, but does not go beyond that. Since peacekeeping forces are frequently involved in monitoring cease-fires, patrolling demilitarized zones, and other similar actions, this capability is crucial. Equally crucial is that peacekeeping forces are not armed to a level where they pose a threat to the parties to the conflict or the population at-large.

Consent/neutrality

Another crucial aspect of peacekeeping missions is that they are contingent on securing permission from the government(s) of the host state or states where they will be deployed. This condition means that peacekeepers require the consent of warring parties before they can be interposed into a conflict. This is wholly unique to peacekeeping, and is emblematic of the central role occupied by state sovereignty in peacekeeping. For both political and legal reasons, peacekeeping has been and remains fundamentally oriented around upholding state sovereignty and defending the principle of non-interference; therefore, obtaining consent from the warring parties is an essential condition of any peacekeeping operation.

The centrality of consent is closely related to other defining aspects of peacekeeping. Peacekeeping is a wholly reactive activity that occurs after conflicts abate. It is also a military operation strictly delimited by its rules of engagement (ROE) and low levels of force and armaments. Given these factors, it stands to reason that securing consent from the warring parties is crucial to the success of peacekeeping operations. Consent allows for the peacekeeping deployment to calibrate its mission and means on the basis of the authority extended to it by the warring parties. Further, by virtue of recognizing and reinforcing the authority of the warring parties, the peacekeeping deployment is established as a non-threatening entity which does not seek to gain military or strategic advantage relative to any or all of the parties to the conflict. This in turn allows the peacekeeping operation to proceed without precipitating attacks from the armed forces of one or more of the parties to the conflict (especially important given the lightly armed character of peacekeeping forces).

Impartiality

The neutral nature of the character, activities, and composition of peacekeeping operations also distinguishes them from other forms of conflict management. In order to be consistent with the essence of peacekeeping, a peacekeeping operation must avoid assigning responsibility for the conflict to any specific party or parties. Peacekeeping deployments can be and often are launched with resolutions and statements sharply condemning the conflict in question and the behavior of one or more parties to it. However, for peacekeeping to be effective (in particular applications, and as a form of international conflict management in general) it must be directed at containing the behavior of the parties rather than focusing on their underlying intentions or grievances.

This requirement of impartiality applies both for strategic and political reasons. Within any particular peacekeeping deployment, it is imperative that the behavior of peacekeepers be impartial so as to avoid lending strategic or tactical advantage to any specific party in the conflict. Avoiding partiality is not only a defining feature of peacekeeping, then, but an essential condition for successfully carrying out the mandated responsibilities of individual operations. From a political standpoint, the practice of peacekeeping as a tool of international conflict management is wholly dependent on maintaining the view in the international system that peacekeepers (especially, but not exclusively, those provided through UN auspices) are impartial.

This dependence on impartiality translates to the composition of peacekeeping forces as well. Since the forces and funds committed to peacekeeping operations come from nation-states, impartial behavior within a conflict setting is not only a theoretical imperative but a practical one. Any state contributing its forces or funds to a peacekeeping operation might at some later juncture be involved in a conflict in which peacekeepers are deployed, and therefore as a condition for supporting the present effort requires assurance that peacekeepers will not be used partially. In actuality, most peacekeeping contingents are made up of forces from generally non-aligned states which accentuates and helps uphold the condition of impartiality.

Precursors to peacekeeping

In assessing the historical trajectory of peacekeeping as an approach to conflict management, activities bearing some resemblance to peacekeeping date back decades, if not centuries. The origins of peacekeeping can be located amidst nascent efforts at maintaining collective security, including the establishment of the League of Venice in fifteenth-century Renaissance Italy, the wider Holy League arranged by Pope Pius V in the 1570s, and especially the Concert of Europe (fashioned at the Congress of Vienna in 1815).

The Concert of Europe and 'proto-peacekeeping'

The Concert system was formally established by the Treaty of Paris, which assigned responsibility for maintaining order in the aftermath of the Napoleonic wars to the Quadruple Alliance of Austria-Hungary, Britain, Prussia, and Russia. This arrangement spawned several proto-peacekeeping operations, even as the Concert broke down in the latter half of the nineteenth century (Mangone, 1954). Most of these operations fell under the heading of 'expeditionary operations' designed to stabilize conflict zones of interest to European colonial powers (such as the British occupation of Cyprus in 1878), or multinational operations against piracy.

Much of this early wave of proto-peacekeeping operations in the late nineteenth century bore only a passing resemblance to contemporary peacekeeping in terms of mandate responsibilities. The closest approximations were a series of commitments by the major Concert powers (plus a rehabilitated France) to the Balkans after the Congress of Berlin in 1878. Convened to address security problems and human rights abuses rampant amidst the decline of the Ottoman Empire, the Berlin congress produced a series of collective operations, including deployment of a 20,000-member international force to Crete by Britain, France, Austria-Hungary, Germany, Italy, and Russia to avert a clash between Greece and Turkey over the Ottoman-held territory (Schmidl, 2000). Other early analogues, including the commissioning of an international force to safeguard Albanian sovereignty in 1913 and, outside of the European theater, the deployment of a multilateral force including US, British, French, German, Austrian, Italian, Japanese, and Russian contingents (operating under separate command) to rescue European legations in the 1900 Boxer Rebellion in China.

The League of Nations experiment

As joint military actions undertaken by sovereign authorities in the pursuit of collective security goals, the deployment of international forces to the Balkans and China in the waning days of the nineteenth century could be construed as rudimentary attempts at peacekeeping (Ikenberry, 2001). At the same time, the coercive and self-interested thrusts of these efforts and the absence of any meaningful and institutionalized intergovernmental coordination prevent them from being characterized as true peacekeeping efforts. It was not until the first concrete effort at the intergovernmental coordination of security and conflict management that anything resembling contemporary peacekeeping emerged.

Legal authority

The end of World War I led directly to the creation of the first membership-based international organization with the primary purpose of ensuring international peace and security through coordination and collective action – the League of Nations. Founded in 1919, the League of Nations was the embodiment of the vision expressed in Woodrow Wilson's famous 'Fourteen Points' address of January 1918, particularly the call for 'a general association of nations … formed under specific covenants for the purpose of affording mutual guarantees of political independence and territorial integrity to great and small states alike.'

The earliest efforts at drafting the League's Covenant featured a proposal by France to execute military sanction of breaches of the peace through use of a standing international force. Though rejected by the US and British delegations, Articles 10 and 16 of the Covenant, which emerged to delineate the purpose and responsibilities of the League (and especially the Council, its chief security organ) with respect to maintaining collective security, did provide for direct action:

Article 10

The Members of the League undertake to respect and preserve as against external aggression the territorial integrity and existing political independence of all Members of the League.

Article 16

Should any Member resort to war … it shall be deemed to have committed an act of war against all Members…. It shall be the duty of the Council in such case to recommend to the several Governments concerned what effective military, naval, or air force the Members of the League shall severally contribute to the forces used to protect the covenants of the League.

The explicit activities of the League with respect to its self-imposed security responsibilities were to remain ad hoc and reactive in nature. No explicit provisions to undertake truly joint operations with established and internationalized military forces were made in the League's Covenant, and responses of a non-military nature were afforded great emphasis (Rosner, 1965).

Precedents

The deficiencies inherent in these features of the League's constitution were exposed by the organization's failure to act effectively in response to Japan's occupation of Manchuria in 1931 and Italy's invasion of Ethiopia in 1935. Despite these well-documented failings, the League did pave the way for the emergence of peacekeeping as a form of conflict management – mostly in its pioneering use of observer and inquiry or 'fact-finding' missions. The League established a propensity for undertaking fact-finding missions and administration efforts in conjunction with substantial policing and security contingents.

The immediate post-war aftermath spawned a robust agenda for the League, mainly with respect to administering the terms of the Treaty of Versailles and settling disputes which the Treaty did not directly address. Prominent early examples of League action include the deployment of two Allied battalions to the strategic port of Danzig (1918–1920), and over 15,000 British, French, and Italian troops to Upper Silesia (1920–1922). Perhaps the most prominent action came in conjunction with the international administration of the Saar basin as stipulated in the Treaty of Versailles. That administration (which lasted over a decade) featured the interposition of British, Italian, Swedish, and Dutch forces under a joint commander appointed by the League itself, perhaps the first example of an international peace observer force (Diehl, 1994).

As the League evolved, so too did the nature of the disputes in which it was involved. Throughout the 1920s the League became involved in a greater number and range of disputes with little direct relationship to World War I or the terms of its settlement. Instead, many of these involvements rested on the mediation of hostile disputes between new or small states often over competing territorial claims. Observer and policing forces were more difficult to assemble given the increased complexity and risk associated with conflict management in such disputes. When such deployments did occur, as in the dispute between Poland and Lithuania over Vilna (1920–1922), the Albanian sovereignty crisis (1921–1923), and the Greco-Bulgarian dispute (1925), they were underwhelming. The League's deployment to Vilna constituted of only 1,500 troops (none from Council member-states), while both the Albanian and Greco-Bulgarian crises featured only small observer missions.

Peacekeeping: a narrative history

It is beyond contention that the establishment of peacekeeping as a tool of conflict management, as well as the doctrines guiding and the discourse surrounding it, can all be traced to the founding of the UN. Indeed, over the past six decades, peacekeeping has evolved in lockstep with the evolution of the UN, and has been shaped within the context of more than 60 UN peace operations launched since 1948.

The legacy of the League

The failings of the League of Nations were prominent in the minds of the architects of its successor organization. Most were attributed to the League's inability to act with certainty, utilize the resources available to it, and maintain and draw upon an inclusive membership with respect to its collective security responsibilities (Kupchan and Kupchan, 1991). The framers of the UN sought to avoid these problems by emphasizing the principle of 'great-power responsibility' and institutionalizing it in Security Council membership and voting procedures (see Box 4.2). Particularly noteworthy in this respect was the ascribing of a veto to the five permanent members of the Security Council, as well as stipulating majority rather than unanimity voting requirements.

Box 4.2 The principle of great-power responsibility

Throughout much of its history, the practice of peacekeeping has been closely associated with the principle of great-power responsibility. Itself a product of the concept and pursuit of collective security, this principle rests on the conviction that order in the international system (and, as a potential by-product, peace) cannot be maintained without the commitment of the great powers. The full extension of this conviction is that it confers upon the great powers (whoever they might be at any point in time) a special duty to maintain order and to bear most of the burden for providing the conditions which might sustain peace, through whatever means available and/or necessary.

The principle of great-power responsibility has long resonated in calls for and attempts at developing collective security systems. Most of these attempts, such as the League of Nations, have lacked a formal institutionalization of the principle. As a result, the architects of the UN created a Security Council in which the victorious great powers after World War II would occupy permanent seats and through which they would wield unlimited veto powers. Over time, this approach has proven sub-optimal both for reasons of application and design. Critics of the principle of great-power responsibility have seized upon the disproportionate powers and influence afforded to the great powers in the UN system as reasons for the paralysis that often grips the UN when seeking to carry out its peace and security obligations. Conversely, supporters of the idea have countered with arguments for Security Council reforms to expand the ranks of the great powers (and, accordingly, the responsibility for maintaining peace and security). Still others have argued for the creation of a more decentralized approach to collective security structure that would continue to revolve around the principle, but would see the responsibilities associated with maintaining security and keeping peace delegated to the major power(s) in each geographic region of the world (Morris and McCoubrey, 1999).

Within the narrower purview of peacekeeping, the experience of the League of Nations demonstrated that a reliance on fact-finding missions, paired with policing or security deployments, was both overly reactive and cumbersome. At the same time, the tentative first steps toward peacekeeping undertaken by the League established a number of important precedents which provided a baseline for thinking about the new organization's security and peace operations. As the League experience showed, peace and security operations were likely to be most successful when undertaken in cases where direct military hostilities were not evident, or had abated. Likewise, the prospects for such efforts were enhanced when they did not involve the major powers, given the increased perception of neutrality and impartiality this afforded. Finally, obtaining the consent and compliance of the parties to the conflict was also clearly important, as was the utility of using the deployment as an interposition force to establish or preserve buffer zones and lines of demarcation and demilitarization (James, 1990).

Legal authority

The main provisions of the UN Charter stipulating the authority for conflict management for the most part parallel those in the League of Nations Covenant. For example, Chapter VI ('Pacific Settlement of Disputes') outlines and elaborates upon a number of non-coercive mechanisms for dispute mediation, adjudication, and resolution, in the process establishing the broad authority and means by which the UN is to proceed. At the same time, the UN Charter is far more explicit about the authority of the UN to pursue additional action should these approaches fail, and in stipulating what those alternatives are. These additional provisions, largely contained in Chapter VII ('Actions with Respect to the Peace, Breaches to the Peace, and Acts of Aggression'), include coercive instruments such as economic sanctions as well as military force as stipulated in Article 42: 'The Security Council may take such action by air, sea, or land forces as may be necessary to maintain or restore international peace and security.'

The UN Charter also sought to resolve the capacity problems that had plagued the League. Chapter VII, Articles 43 and 47 are especially remarkable in their calls for the provision of armed forces from member-states as and when necessary to assist the organization in carrying out its mandated responsibility to maintain international peace and security (as stipulated in Article 1(1) of the Charter), as well as the creation of a UN Military Staff Committee to command them. While these articles stop short of creating a standing UN military force, the emphasis on operations involving military force as well as on establishing a unified UN command for them opened the door for peacekeeping operations as presently understood.

Precursor operations

Despite the twin points of emphasis contained within Chapter VII of the UN Charter, peacekeeping operations did not occur immediately, or even often, in the organization's early years. The UN's first decade was mostly defined by a continuation and extension of the League's penchant for observer missions. Such missions included the commission of UN forces to investigate foreign intervention in the Greek civil war (UN Special Committee on the Balkans (UNSCOB)); to monitor compliance with the armistice ending the first Arab–Israeli War (UN Truce Supervision Organization (UNTSO)); to support the transfer of sovereignty from the Dutch colonial administration to newly independent Indonesia (UN Commission for Indonesia (UNCI)); and to monitor compliance with the Indo-Pakistani cease-fire in Kashmir (UN Military Observer Group in India and Pakistan (UNMOGIP)). Each of these operations featured small deployments, with functions falling short of traditional peacekeeping (UN, 1996). Ultimately it was the failure of one of these observer missions (the heavily circumscribed UNTSO) to adequately contain hostility and violence in the Middle East that opened the door for the first true peacekeeping operation (the UN Emergency Force (UNEF-I)) as well as the concept of peacekeeping as it is understood today.

The golden age of peacekeeping

UNEF-I and the dawn of peacekeeping

As a condition of its post-colonial transition, in June 1956 Britain acted on a long-overdue pledge to transfer administration of the Suez Canal to the Egyptian government. This transfer came at a time of great volatility in the Middle East. Israeli and Egyptian military forces had engaged in direct military hostilities in Gaza in August 1955, with an Israeli assault on the Golan Heights also occurring in November of that year. With pan-Arab nationalism arguably at its peak, Egyptian President Gamal Abdel Nasser decided to nationalize the critical waterway on 26 July 1956.

Nasser's decision provided the final necessary spark for the Suez Crisis. Prompted by significant economic interests, Britain and France denounced the Egyptian nationalization and tacitly encouraged the Israeli invasion of Egypt on 29 October. With the United States and the Soviet Union favoring a diplomatic solution, they strongly condemned the Israeli attack, as well as outside provocations by Britain and France. Paralysis in the Security Council triggered by the confluence of Cold War alignments and the legacy of colonialism resulted in referral of the matter to the UN General Assembly (UNGA). Over a period of several days in early November 1956, Secretary-General Dag Hammarskjöld and Canadian foreign minister (and UN architect) Lester Pearson worked with the UNGA to devise an alternative approach (Urquhart, 1994).

Upon declaring objectives in UNGA Resolution 997 (which called for an immediate cease-fire, withdrawal of forces, and re-opening of the Suez Canal), in UNGA

Resolution 998 the UNGA accepted the Secretary-General's recommendation for creation of a 'UN force large enough to keep these borders at peace while a political settlement is being worked out.' Rejecting appeals for a Korea-style enforcement action (especially given the degree to which the great powers were already enmeshed in the affair), Hammarskjöld's recommendation to the UNGA was defined by a pragmatic acceptance of the geopolitical realities of the time, including the relative dependence of the UN on its member-states in carrying out its peace and security responsibilities. Hammarskjöld, Pearson, and the UNGA worked at breakneck pace over a span of days to define the parameters of UNEF-I (deployed on 15 November 1956), and by extension, the practice of peacekeeping (see Box 4.3).

Box 4.3 The UNEF-I precedent

The exceedingly dangerous security situation during the Suez Crisis was perhaps only matched by the sensitive political context surrounding that crisis. In seeking to manage both the security and political dimensions of the crisis, UN Secretary-General Dag Hammarskjöld sought to craft a new alternative for carrying out the UN mandate for maintaining international peace and security within the prevailing structural parameters of the international system. The result was the establishment, through UNGA Resolution 1000, of UNEF-I. UNEF-I was crafted in accordance with a set of conditions that wound up shaping all peacekeeping operations for the next four decades:

- *command*: deployments launched at the behest and under the direction of the Secretary-General, and under the command of a neutral officer;
- *force composition*: UNEF-I forces were not to include troop contributions from major powers;
- *rules of engagement*: UNEF-I was commissioned as a strictly neutral force, not to alter the military balance or to participate in hostile actions other than for the purposes of self-defense;
- *deployment*: UNEF-I was deployed as an interposition force, to provide a physical barrier between parties to the conflict;
- *mandate*: UNEF-I was presented with two primary responsibilities: monitoring the cease-fire and supervising withdrawal of all forces.

Peacekeeping after UNEF-I

The success of UNEF-I (which endured until the outbreak of the Six Day War in 1967) in delivering on its mandate responsibilities rendered it a model for subsequent operations. Hammarskjöld strongly touted the achievements of UNEF-I, promoting peacekeeping not only as a tool for the management of violent conflict, but also as a means for advancing the larger agenda of 'preventative diplomacy.' In the flush of immediate success after UNEF-I, peacekeeping was considered a key implement by which the UN might serve as a neutral third party – managing conflicts with wider geopolitical ramifications and, in the process, helping avert a direct clash between the superpowers. Accordingly, peacekeeping was transformed into the public face of the UN.

Several operations consistent with prominent definitions of the concept were launched between the initiation of UNEF-I in 1956 and the end of the Cold War (see Table 4.1); a number of these remain active today (see Table 4.3). The high-

Table 4.1 Completed UN peacekeeping operations, 1956–1990

Mission	Initiation/ termination	Mandate	Initial authorized deployment (approx.)
UN Emergency Force (UNEF I)	1956/1967	Interposition force between Israel and Egypt in the Sinai	6,100
UN Observation Group in Lebanon (UNOGIL)	1958/1958	Monitor movement of arms and military forces	600
UN Operation in the Congo (ONUC)	1960/1964	Assist Congolese government in restoration of order and security*	20,000
UN Security Force in West New Guinea (UNSF)	1962/1963	Assist UNTEA in advance of transfer of sovereignty to Indonesia	1,500
UN Yemen Observation Mission (UNYOM)	1963/1964	Monitor movement of arms and military forces into Yemen	200
UN India–Pakistan Observer Mission (UNIPOM)	1965/1966	Monitor ceasefire	100
UN Emergency Force II (UNEF II)	1974/1979	Interposition force between Israel and Egypt in the Sinai	7,000
UN Good Offices Mission in Afghanistan–Pakistan (UNGOMAP)	1988/1990	Monitoring Afghanistan–Pakistan border; oversee withdrawal of Soviet forces; assist in refugee repatriation	50
UN Transition Assistance Group (UNTAG)	1989/1990	Interposition force monitoring cessation of hostilities; supervise disarmament and withdrawal of forces; maintain border security; assist with civil society tasks	8,000

Sources: DPKO, 2008; Bellamy *et al.*, 2004.

Notes
* Though launched and defined by the UN as a peacekeeping operation, ONUC conforms with the 'peace enforcement' definition advanced three decades after the mission (see Chapter 8)

Table 4.2 Completed UN peacekeeping operations since 1990

Mission	Initiation/ termination	Mandate	Initial authorized deployment (approx.)
UN Angola Verification Mission I (UNAVEM I)	1988/1991	Verify withdrawal of foreign military personnel	70
UN Iran–Iraq Military Observer Group (UNIIMOG)	1988/1991	Verify ceasefire and withdrawal of forces	400
UN Observer Group in Central America (ONUCA)	1989/1992	Verify compliance with peace accords	1,100
UN Advance Mission in Cambodia (UNAMIC)	1991/1992	Monitor ceasefire	1,500
UN Transitional Authority in Cambodia (UNTAC)	1992/1993	Implement political settlement and conduct elections	22,000
UN Operation in Somalia I (UNOSOM I)	1992/1993	Facilitate delivery of humanitarian aid	4,300
UN Operation in Mozambique (ONUMOZ)	1992/1994	Monitor ceasefire and force withdrawals; humanitarian aid; assist in implementing General Peace Agreement	8,500
UN Observer Mission Uganda–Rwanda (UNOMUR)	1993/1994	Monitor border	80
UN Aouzou Strip Observer Group (UNASOG)	1994/1994	Monitor withdrawal of Libyan forces from Chad	15
UN Observer Mission in El Salvador (ONUSAL)	1991/1995	Verify and assist in implementing peace agreements	1,300
UN Protection Force in Bosnia-Herzegovina (UNPROFOR)	1992/1995	Monitor ceasefires; assist humanitarian relief efforts; protect civilians	38,000
UN Assistance Mission for Rwanda (UNAMIR)	1993/1996	Monitor compliance with Arusha Accords	6,000
UN Mission in Haiti (UNMIH)	1993/1996	Implementation and oversight of Governor's Island Agreement	1,500
UN Confidence Restoration Operation (UNCRO)	1995/1996	Monitor ceasefires between Croatia and Serbia; humanitarian assistance	7,000
UN Observer Mission in Liberia (UNOMIL)	1993/1997	Implement peace agreements; uphold ceasefire; support humanitarian relief efforts; observe and verify elections	350
UN Verification Mission in Guatemala (MINUGUA)	1997/1997	Oversee ceasefire; assist in institutional reforms	200
UN Preventative Deployment Force (UNPREDEP)	1995/1999	Monitor developments along border areas of Yugoslav Republic of Macedonia	1,100
UN Observer Mission in Angola (MONUA)	1997/1999	Assist in implementation of peace agreement; promotion of national reconciliation	3,500

Mission	Dates	Mandate	Strength
UN Observer Mission in Sierra Leone (UNOMSIL)	1998/1999	Monitor security situation; oversee demobilization and disarmament	200
UN Mission of Observers in Tajikistan (UNMOT)	1994/2000	Monitor and assist in implementation of ceasefire	100
UN Mission in the Central African Republic (MINURCA)	1998/2000	Maintain and enhance stability; oversee disarmament; assist in policing; support elections	1,400
UN Mission of Observers in Prevlaka (UNMOP)	1996/2002	Demilitarization and demobilization in disputed Prevlaka province	30
UN Mission in Sierra Leone (UNAMSIL)	1999/2005	Monitor ceasefire; assist in security provision; disarmament/demobilization; humanitarian aid; election supervision	17,500
UN Operation in Burundi (ONUB)	2004/2006	Monitor ceasefire; provide security assistance; ensure compliance with Arusha Agreement	5,600

Sources: DPKO, 2008; Bellamy *et al.*, 2004.

Notes
This listing features only operations corresponding with the defining features of peacekeeping outlined here (consent, impartiality, non-enforcement, etc.) and featuring a discernable military component. Operations with an explicit 'peace enforcement' dimension (including those possessing full Chapter VII authority) or those focused predominantly on policing, civil society reform, or peacebuilding and lacking a military contingent are not included.

water mark of peacekeeping during the Cold War was the early 1960s, which featured major deployments in the Congo, New Guinea, and Cyprus, among others (UN, 1996). Each was precedent-setting: the UN Operation in the Congo (ONUC) was the first peace enforcement operation; UNSF/UNTEA the first joint peacekeeping/trusteeship arrangement; and UNFICYP one of the longest-running peacekeeping missions.

The post-Cold War era

The dramatic structural changes in the international system wrought by the end of the Cold War (chronicled in previous chapters with respect to security and conflict) had a significant effect on peacekeeping as well. Indeed, some leading scholars of peace operations have referred to the effects of the end of the Cold War on peacekeeping as a 'triple transformation,' defined by quantitative, qualitative, and normative changes (Bellamy *et al.*, 2004). As the term implies, the changing political and security context in which peacekeeping was enmeshed brought different forms of pressure to bear on peacekeeping that became more common at the end of the Cold War.

More peacekeeping operations were launched between 1989 and 1993 than during the entire Cold War period. This was a function both of an increasing demand for peacekeeping operations and an increased ability of the UN to supply them – both direct by-products of the removal of the structural constraint of bipolarity. At the same time, the nature of peacekeeping was also undergoing transformation. New tasks and combinations of tasks (such as providing humanitarian aid, civil reconstruction, training civil servants, etc.) were incorporated into peacekeeping operations. These new activities stretched the concept in new directions ('wider' or 'multidimensional' peacekeeping) and precipitated the introduction of new concepts and terms (peace enforcement, peace support) to accommodate new responsibilities (O'Neill and Rees, 2005).

Multidimensional peacekeeping

The aforementioned triple transformation in the early 1990s sparked a renaissance of peacekeeping; over two dozen operations have been commissioned and completed since the end of the Cold War alone (see Table 4.3). Peacekeeping was seen within and outside UN circles as an all-purpose fix for the proliferation of conflicts and security concerns. Accordingly, peacekeeping was used more often and in previously unthinkable circumstances, with successive operations granted increasingly wider mandate responsibilities to engage in tasks such as disarmament, the conduct of elections, the implementation of peace agreements, and the delivery of humanitarian aid. This expansion of peacekeeping spawned what the Department of Peacekeeping Operations (DPKO) has since come to refer to as 'multidimensional' operations.

The diverse range of tasks subsumed under the heading of multidimensional peacekeeping has fueled calls for new forms of peace operations to supplant even this expanded variant of peacekeeping and its residual basis in consent, impartiality, and non-coercion. It was in this climate that UN Secretary-General Boutros Boutros-Ghali published his landmark report *An Agenda for Peace* (1992b).

Acknowledging the successful legacy of traditional peacekeeping as well as the increasing breadth of peacekeeping's range, Boutros-Ghali sought to expand the role and capacity for UN peace operations in response to a changing security landscape, juxtaposing traditional peacekeeping with the types of endeavors a revamped UN might need to undertake in future conflict management operations, when consent was likely to be difficult to obtain, impartiality difficult to sustain, and non-coercive ROE potentially limiting.

The current landscape

At the dawn of the twenty-first century, recognition of the potential for violence and humanitarian emergencies to spread outward from zones of conflict, along with a somewhat more favorable political climate toward peace operations (not only at UN headquarters, but in a number of key states) produced new attitudes about, and new approaches to, peace operations (see Box 4.4). A sustained demand for international conflict management was punctuated by several key events as the 1990s drew to a close. The transition to independence in East Timor, the descent of the Democratic Republic of Congo and Sierra Leone into civil war, and the aftermath of ethnic violence in Kosovo demanded new and multifaceted commitments from the UN, regional organizations, and/or pivotal states.

Box 4.4 Annan, Brahimi, and the resurgence of peacekeeping

A crucial factor in the upsurge of peace operations at the end of the 1990s was the arrival of new political leadership at the top of the UN organization, in the person of new Secretary-General Kofi Annan. Annan's vision neatly dovetailed with a contemporaneous upsurge in activism by several 'pivotal states' (such as the United Kingdom, Australia, and the United States), reflected in their extensive involvement in enforcement actions in Sierra Leone, East Timor, and Kosovo (respectively). This return of peace operations to favor was prominently codified in an independent review of UN peace operations chaired by diplomat Lakhdar Brahimi. The so-called 'Brahimi report' produced by this review frankly addressed the failings of the previous decade while making the case for more expansive peace operations with greater authority than traditional peacekeeping. Not surprisingly, the Brahimi report provided the foundation for a number of active multidimensional peace operations, including the UN Mission in Liberia (UNMIL), the UN Operation in Côte d'Ivoire (UNOCI), the UN Mission in the Sudan (UNMIS), and the UN Stabilization Mission in Haiti (MINUSTAH). These operations, many possessing Chapter VII authority, are defined by attempts at creating a stable and secure environment while simultaneously promoting the rule of law, human rights, and economic and political reform.

The increased involvement of pivotal states, as well as regional organizations, in conflict management, along with reform efforts at the UN level (including the 'Peace Operations 2010' review and the associated publication of a 'Capstone Doctrine' *United Nations Peacekeeping Operations: Principles and Guidelines*) have undoubtedly salvaged peace operations (see Figure 4.1). Since 1995 the number of 'blue helmets' deployed have increased by an average of 12 percent annually, while the total peacekeeping budget during that period has grown by an annual average of 17 percent (DPKO, 2008).

Table 4.3 Active UN peace operations (ca. March 2008)

Mission	Date initiated	Mandate	Initial authorized deployment (approx.)
UN Truce Supervision Organization (UNTSO)	1948	Monitor compliance with general armistice in the Middle East	350
UN Military Observer Group in India and Pakistan (UNMOGIP)	1949	Monitor compliance with terms of India–Pakistan ceasefire in Kashmir	100
UN Force in Cyprus (UNFICYP)	1964	Maintaining order and stability (pre-1974); patrol and monitor ceasefire zone (post-1974)	1,300
UN Disengagement Observer Force (UNDOF)	1974	Interposition force between Israel and Syria in Golan Heights	1,200
UN Interim Force in Lebanon (UNIFIL)	1978	Interposition force between Israel and Lebanon	3,300
UN Iraq–Kuwait Observation Mission (UNIKOM)	1991	Monitor Kuwait–Iraq border	1,100
UN Mission for the Referendum in Western Sahara (MINURSO)	1991	Monitor ceasefire; organize and conduct referendum	200
UN Observer Mission in Georgia (UNOMIG)	1993	Oversee separation of forces; monitor ceasefire; supervise CIS-PKF	400
UN Interim Administration Mission in Kosovo (UNMIK)	1999	provide transitional administration; establish and oversee development of democratic institutions; provide humanitarian assistance; aid in economic reconstruction and development	3,500
UN Organization Mission in the Democratic Republic of the Congo (MONUC)	1999	Forcible implementation of ceasefire agreement; monitoring and reporting violations of ceasefire; disarmament, demobilization, repatriation, resettlement, and reintegration; organization of credible elections	16,500
UN Mission in Ethiopia and Eritrea (UNMEE)	2000	Monitor cessation of hostilities; ensure observance of security commitments agreed by the parties; monitor and verify redeployment of Ethiopian and Eritrean forces and temporary security zone; chair military coordination commission; coordinate and provide humanitarian and technical assistance (later revised to include de-mining and logistical support for Boundary Commission)	4,200

Mission	Year	Mandate	
UN Assistance Mission in Afghanistan (UNAMA)	2002	Coordinate international support to Afghan Government; strengthen cooperation with ISAF; provide political outreach and good offices to Afghan-led reconciliation programs; support efforts to improve governance and rule of law; coordinate and facilitate delivery of humanitarian aid; monitor and protect human rights; support electoral process through the Afghan Independent Electoral Commission; support regional efforts toward Afghan stability and prosperity	1,300
UN Mission in Liberia (UNMIL)	2003	Multiplicity of tasks related to support for implementation of ceasefire agreement; protection of UN staff and civilians; provision of humanitarian and human rights assistance; support for security sector reform; implementation of peace process	15,000
UN Operation in Côte d'Ivoire (UNOCI)	2004	Monitoring cessation of hostilities and movements of armed groups and combatants; disarmament, demobilization, reintegration, repatriation and resettlement; operations identifying the population and registering voters; promoting security sector reform; protection of UN personnel and civilians; monitoring arms embargo; support for humanitarian aid and reform and redeployment of government institutions; support for open, free, and fair elections; assistance in protection of human rights; provision of public information; maintenance of law and order (later revised to include coordination of efforts by French-led peace enforcement mission)	6,500
UN Stabilization Mission in Haiti (MINUSTAH)	2004	Support transitional Government in providing secure environment, disarmament, demobilization, and reintegration; reform of police and corrections systems, and restoring and maintaining the rule of law; protect UN personnel and civilians; support constitutional and political process and foster democratic governance and institutional development; assist in national dialogue and reconciliation; assist in organizing, monitoring, and carrying out free and fair elections and promoting good governance; monitor and support human rights, including status of refugees and displaced persons; coordinate with OAS and CARICOM	8,000

continued

Table 4.3 continued

Mission	Date initiated	Mandate	Initial authorized deployment (approx.)
UN Mission in the Sudan (UNMIS)	2005	Support implementation of Comprehensive Peace Agreement; facilitate voluntary return of refugees and displaced persons; provide de-mining assistance; contribute to efforts to protect and promote human rights in Sudan	10,000
UN Integrated Office in Sierra Leone (UNIOSIL)	2006	Assist government of Sierra Leone in: enhancing capacity of state institutions, providing services, accelerating poverty reduction and economic growth, enabling private investment and efforts to combat HIV/AIDS, establishing a national human rights commission, promoting good governance and transparency, organizing free, fair, and credible elections, and strengthening police and security sectors; promoting a culture of peace and dialogue through public information; developing initiatives for the protection of youth, women, and children; report on security situation; coordinate with UN missions and offices on regional security and human rights issues in West Africa; coordinate with Special Court for Sierra Leone	300
UN Integrated Mission in Timor-Leste (UNMIT)	2006	Support Government in consolidating stability, enhancing a culture of democratic governance, and facilitating political dialogue to bring about a process of national reconciliation; support all aspects of electoral process; ensure restoration and maintenance of public security and contribute to police and security sector reform; monitor and build institutional capacity in areas of justice and human rights; facilitate provision of relief and recovery assistance; assist in justice and reconciliation process, including investigation of human rights violations committed in 1999; cooperate and coordinate with all UN agencies and international partners in peacebuilding; mainstream gender perspectives and those of children and youth in all aspects of the Mission; protect UN personnel and civilians	1,800

UN Integrated Office in Burundi (BINUB)	2007	Monitor ceasefire and illegal arms transfers and report/ investigate violations; disarmament, demobilization, reintegration; provide secure conditions for provision of humanitarian aid; facilitate voluntary return of refugees and internally displaced persons; contribute to electoral process stipulated in Arusha Agreement; protect civilians and UN personnel; provide advice and assistance to transitional Government in monitoring borders, institutional reforms, electoral activities, promotion of human rights	5,650
African Union–UN Hybrid Operation in Darfur (UNAMID)	2007	Monitor and observe compliance with various ceasefire agreements signed since 2004; support implementation of the Darfur Peace Agreement; protect UN personnel and equipment and civilians; provide conditions necessary for delivery of humanitarian assistance throughout Darfur; assist and participate in political process and support AU–UN joint mediation efforts; promote conditions for economic reconstruction and development; promote return of refugees and internally displaced persons; contribute to promotion and protection of human rights and fundamental freedoms in Darfur; assist in promotion of rule of law and good governance; monitor and report on security situation at Sudan's external borders	26,000
UN Mission in the Central African Republic and Chad (MINURCAT)	2007	Select, train, advise and support humanitarian security force in Chad; liaise with the national army, police forces, national guard, and judicial authorities in Chad and Central African Republic to promote secure environment; support efforts toward relocating refugee camps along Chad/CAR border; liaise with national and regional governing institutions and other UN agencies to exchange information on threats to humanitarian actions in region; contribute to monitoring, promotion, and protection of human rights with attention to gender-based violence and use of children by armed groups; support efforts at strengthening capacity of state institutions and civil society in Chad and CAR; coordinate efforts with European Union security force	350

Sources: DPKO, 2008; Bellamy *et al.*, 2004.

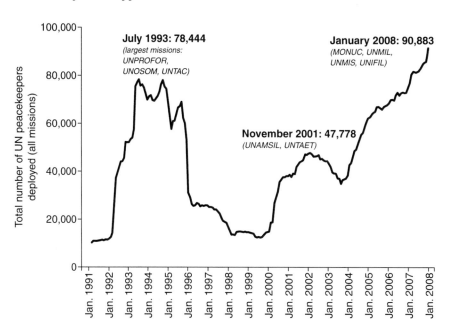

Figure 4.1 The trajectory of UN peace operations, 1991–2008 (source: UN DPKO).

At the same time, the continued evolution toward multidimensional operations with significant peacebuilding, peace support, and governance and administration dimensions has supplanted traditional peacekeeping from its previous lofty perch (Wells, 2008). This is borne out in considering the list of active UN peacekeeping operations, as well as the evolution of their mandates (Table 4.3). The bulk of traditional peacekeeping operations currently active are holdovers from the Cold War, with only two (the UN Observer Mission in Georgia (UNOMIG) and the UN Mission in Ethiopia and Eritrea (UNMEE)) commissioned since the early 1990s.

How peacekeeping works

The broad spectrum of peacekeeping includes both UN-led and non-UN operations of an increasingly diverse qualitative character. With that said, the birth and evolution of the concept of peacekeeping is closely intertwined with the UN, and the vast majority of peacekeeping operations (traditional or multidimensional) have been undertaken either directly by the UN or with UN authorization. Currently, the UN DPKO oversees nearly 110,000 troops deployed on four continents (DPKO, 2008). As such, the profile of the mechanics of peacekeeping presented here is largely predicated on peacekeeping operations undertaken under UN auspices.

Why peacekeeping?

The question of why peacekeeping occurs at all (as distinct from when it occurs, or how it proceeds) is a difficult one to answer. Clearly, many if not all peacekeeping operations are launched with an overriding intention of stabilizing a conflict zone, protecting civilians, and averting humanitarian disaster. However, the provision of peacekeeping is not solely determined by these factors, and these conditions sometimes occur, or persist, without eliciting a peacekeeping response. Furthermore, such considerations can (and increasingly do) prompt other types of conflict management responses. So the question persists – why peacekeeping?

One way of thinking about why peacekeeping is supplied in a particular source of conflict is to consider how it is initiated; or, more precisely, who is requesting peacekeeping. Empirical assessments of the historical record of peacekeeping show that the vast majority of peacekeeping operations originate in one of three ways: at the behest of the UNSC, at the request of a local source (typically a party to the conflict), or through a brokered request involving the UN, a local source, and an additional party or parties. These studies reveal a rough distribution in concert with these three sources of peacekeeping as 25 percent UNSC initiative; 25 percent local request for action; and 50 percent brokered request (Durch, 1993: 16). Whether as an initiator, mediator, tool of last resort, the UN plays an instrumental role in the provision of peacekeeping.

Another element in explaining why peacekeeping occurs is to consider its ultimate function as a form of international conflict management. As the discussion above indicates, peacekeeping has emerged and evolved out of a perceived need on the part of the international community to provide an appropriate interim measure for stabilizing zones of conflict and assisting in the transition to a post-conflict settlement. This is illustrated by the frequency with which especially traditional peacekeeping deployments are associated with overseeing cease-fires, disarmament and demilitarization, verifying agreements between conflict parties, and interposing military forces as a buffer and confidence-building measure.

When peacekeeping?

The custodial role of the UN

Peacekeeping represents an effort to capitalize on the emergence of a mutually hurting stalemate; i.e., a juncture of the conflict where the cost of continuing armed hostilities to the parties themselves exceeds any potential gains. The emergence of a mutually hurting stalemate makes the introduction of an outside party to support the cessation of conflict an appealing prospect to the parties, thereby paving the way for peacekeeping to occur. Peacekeeping (especially in its traditional iteration) does not seek to impose a cessation of conflict, or craft a settlement. Instead, it is best understood as a facilitating mechanism residing in the breach between the two, seeking to provide the conditions in which the former might be sustained and the latter promoted.

Any member-state, regional group, or the UN administration (Secretariat) itself can approach the UN's 15-member Security Council to request a peacekeeping mission. At the most basic level, however, peacekeeping occurs in the vast majority of cases when the UN says so. Chiefly this is due to the fact that while peacekeeping can be supplied by other actors, in a *de jure* sense, international law maintains that it is only the UN that can authorize these activities – what was dubbed over a generation ago as the UN's 'custodial role' for peace and security (see Box 4.5). Provided the basic conditions described above exist, a carefully drafted first resolution will be subjected to Security Council vote. This resolution states that the Council agrees in principle to the mission, and asks the Secretary-General to submit a detailed plan together with a rough cost estimate.

Box 4.5 The UN's custodial role

Inis Claude's introduction of the concept of a 'custodial role' for the UN in the early 1960s speaks of the extent to which its caretaker status in the realm of international peace and security is associated with peacekeeping, which was then at its apex. It is generally the prerogative of the Security Council to determine when and where a peacekeeping operation undertaken directly under UN auspices or with Security Council authorization should be deployed. This means that the first crucial step in the provision of peacekeeping is the Security Council's determination of whether such an action is warranted.

Among the necessary (but hardly sufficient) criteria for such consideration are:

- Does continuation of the situation endanger or constitute a threat to international peace and security?
- Does a cease-fire exist, or have the parties to the conflict otherwise committed themselves to, at a minimum, an abatement of the conflict, if not a political settlement?
- Do clear political goals exist, and can they be reflected in the mandate for a peacekeeping operation?
- Can a precise operational mandate be formulated? Is it likely to be supported within the UNSC, the DPKO, and among the member-states?
- Can the safety and security of UN personnel be reasonably ensured?

Political context

At the same time, any portrayal of peacekeeping as something that occurs entirely at the determination of the UN is flawed. Given the state-centric (Westphalian) nature of traditional peacekeeping, the political context surrounding both the immediate conflict and the debate over what (if anything) to do about it is a crucial intervening variable between determination of an 'actionable' situation and the assembly and deployment of a peacekeeping force. The prevailing political dynamics and the ability (or inability) of potential peacekeepers to navigate them while maintaining open and effective consultations with involved parties has a great deal to do with the formulation of a clear, appropriate, and widely supported mandate. That condition in turn has great bearing on whether sufficient commitments of military and police forces from troop-contributing or police-contributing countries (TCCs and PCCs in UN parlance) and funding streams can be secured for the operation.

Peacekeeping operations have always required at least tacit support from the great powers, at a minimum to prevent them from being blocked in the Security Council (or its equivalent in non-UN bodies). The power of veto enjoyed by the five permanent members (China, France, Russia, the United Kingdom, and the United States) as a result of the enshrinement of the principle of great-power responsibility means that simple majority alone is not sufficient for a mission to proceed. With the end of the Cold War and the increased direct involvement of major powers in peacekeeping and other forms of peace operations (as pivotal states or through RGOs), 'buy-in' from these states is more crucial than ever before.

At the same time, the end of the Cold War has not altered the imperative of receiving direct support from the parties to the conflict, from historical supporters of peacekeeping such as Canada, the Scandinavian countries, and Ireland, and from today's leading TCCs and PCCs (including Bangladesh, India, Pakistan, Nepal, and Jordan). The turn toward multidimensional operations has further magnified the importance of the political context, as the UN's recent emphasis on an integrated approach (embodied by the Integrated Mission Planning Process, or IMPP) for attracting support from all parties affected by or associated with such operations reflects.

How is peacekeeping supplied?

In the event that most, if not all, of the minimal criteria for a peacekeeping operation apply, and the political context is favorable to a peacekeeping deployment, the likelihood that peacekeeping will even be considered feasible is greatly enhanced. In addition to the Security Council and the various categories of concerned member-states (great powers, middle powers, and local parties), the UN Secretariat also plays a pivotal role – particularly in investigating and determining the parameters for action.

Investigation and authorization

The role of the Secretariat, working in concert with the Security Council, is magnified once the political hurdles embodied in the 'why peacekeeping?' and 'when peacekeeping?' questions are surmounted. The Secretariat is a crucial player both in investigating the situation at hand, as well as weighing the possible courses of action. One primary mechanism used in the consultative and investigative stage is a Strategic Assessment (SA). SAs are advanced at the discretion of the Secretary-General. In general, they consist of full analysis of the situation in consultation with parties to the conflict, concerned member-states, potential TCCs and PCCs, RGOs, and IGOs.

Following initiation or completion of an SA, a Technical Assessment Mission (TAM) will be deployed to the zone of conflict to assess the security, humanitarian, and political situation on the ground and to gauge the likely implications and effectiveness of a peacekeeping operation. The Secretary-General's office combines the findings and recommendations of the SA and the TAM, as well as any additional testimony, briefings, expert analysis, and other input into a report to the Security Council. The Secretary-General's report includes recommendations for possible action – including, in the event a peacekeeping operation is determined to be warranted, recommendations for size, resource allocation, and mandate authority. This report becomes the basis for Security Council deliberation and (potentially) authorization through a second resolution approving all or part of the Secretary-General's recommendation.

Organizational capacity

Upon issuing a resolution authorizing deployment of a peacekeeping operation, as well as the terms of the mandate under which that operation will proceed, the key questions concerning peacekeeping become largely administrative. The highly politicized debates over whether and when to deploy a peacekeeping mission certainly do not abate, particularly given the status of the UN and other peacekeeping authorities as intergovernmental organizations prone to internal discord. Yet at the same time, new issues related to the staffing, funding, and implementation and oversight of peacekeeping missions rise to the fore and take up much of the attention of those in the DPKO or its equivalent in non-UN settings.

Box 4.6 The Department of Peacekeeping Operations

While the Secretariat works in consultation with the Security Council to determine whether a peacekeeping operation is warranted, it is the responsibility of the UN DPKO to coordinate, implement, and oversee such operations once they have been authorized. Until the late 1980s, UN peacekeeping operations were coordinated in a fairly ad hoc manner, through the UN Office of Special Political Affairs (an office headed by notables such as Brian Urquhart and Marrack Goulding). This changed with the creation of the DPKO by Secretary-General Boutros-Ghali in 1992, as a part of his wider reforms of peace operations in conjunction with the *Agenda for Peace.*

According to its mission statement, the DPKO is primarily tasked with providing 'political and executive direction' to UN peacekeeping operations, while maintaining 'contact with the Security Council, troop and financial contributors, and parties to the conflict.' The DPKO was originally organized around two chief components (the Office of Operations and the Office of Mission Support), with a number of smaller offices providing guidance on military, policing, and other relevant issues. However, the DKPO was significantly overhauled as part of the 'Peace Operations 2010' review initiated by DPKO Under-Secretary General Jean-Marie Guéhenno in 2005. The chief product of this overhaul was the creation of a new administrative structure in June 2007, with the establishment of the Office of Military Affairs, the creation of an Office of Rule of Law and Security, and the introduction of a new, and separate, Department of Field Support – reforms intended to reflect the current activities and priorities of UN peace operations.

PERSONNEL

Generally speaking, when a new operation is commissioned the Secretariat approaches diplomatic missions at UN Headquarters with specific, if informal, requests for force contributions. These requests are then sent to member-state governments, who after deliberating on the matter reply favorably or otherwise, including additional conditions regarding the proposed contribution. If the terms of the reply are generally consistent with the original request from the Secretariat, a formal request is issued – a procedure which allows 'loss of face' for the UN in the event the request is rejected by one or more member-states.

The Secretary-General identifies and authorizes the Force Commander only *after* the force is voted into being and assembled. Operations themselves are directed, supervised, and supported on a day-to-day basis by the DPKO (in consultation with the newly established Department of Field Support in the case of multidimensional operations). Ultimately, it falls to UN member-states to contribute not only troops and police, but also supplies and equipment for the UN force as well as the transportation, coordination, and logistical support needed for the deployment and its subsequent operations. On the civilian side, more staffing comes from the DPKO, associated UN units (such as the Department of Political Affairs), and other affiliated agencies (such as the UN High Commissioner on Human Rights (UNHCR) and the UN Development Programme (UNDP)). Still, member-states often loan public sector administrative personnel to UN operations on an as-needed basis. As of March 2008, 118 countries contributed either military or police; the leading contributors are developing countries, with Pakistan the largest single contributor (see Figure 4.2).

Because participation in UN peacekeeping operations is voluntary, the training, preparation, equipment levels, and motives of national contingents vary greatly. Though some degree of prestige is associated with the contribution of forces to peacekeeping operations, other incentives come into play, particularly since the pay scale used by the UN for uniformed personnel attached to its operations (roughly US$1,000/person/month, plus additional expenses) far exceeds what many developing countries allocate to their own national militaries. Combined with the disproportionate number of forces drawn from poorer countries, this dynamic has led to characterizations of peacekeeping as a revenue source for lesser developed countries (LDCs) rather than a demonstration of the international community's commitment to maintaining peace and security (Berman and Sams, 2000).

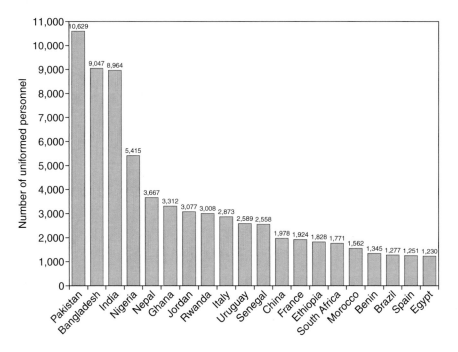

Figure 4.2 Force contributions to UN peacekeeping, 2008 (in thousands) (source: UN DPKO).

FUNDING

Beginning in the mid-1960s (as a result of the suspension of payment by France and the USSR in protest of the escalation of ONUC), a separate budget for peacekeeping funded through special assessments was introduced. Rates for these assessments are graduated in accordance with the economic standing of member-states; at present, levies on the Permanent-5 (P-5) countries are 22 percent higher than regular UN dues; non-P-5 developed countries equal to those dues; and developing countries contribute at reduced levels (see Figure 4.3). More recently, individual operations have been assigned 'special accounts' with discrete budgets.

The approved UN peacekeeping budget for the 2007–2008 fiscal year was approximately US$6.8 billion (DPKO, 2008). Although this figure represents only about 0.5 percent of global military spending (estimated at US$1,232 billion in 2006), peacekeeping nonetheless represents a significant financial outlay. The costs of peacekeeping vary widely by operation, typically as a function of the size of the deployment, the ratio of military to civilians within that deployment, and the transportation and logistical equipment needed (see Table 4.4).

Contemporary issues and debates

Resource and capacity shortfalls

The lack of political will that hamstrings peacekeeping missions has been a central focus of efforts to reform UN peacekeeping in recent years, but continues to impede

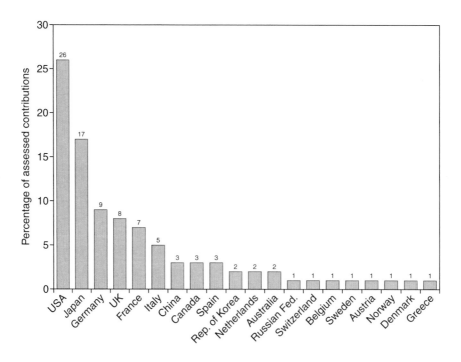

Figure 4.3 Financial contributions to UN peacekeeping, 2008 (source: UN DPKO).

Table 4.4 Budget projections for active UN operations, 2007–2008

Operation	Area of deployment	Current year budget projection (in US$)
MINURSO	Western Sahara	46,471,700
MINUSTAH	Haiti	561,344,900
MONUC	Democratic Republic of the Congo	1,166,721,000
UNDOF	Israel–Syria border	41,586,600
UNFICYP	Cyprus	48,847,500
UNIFIL	Lebanon	748,204,600
UNMEE	Ethiopia–Eritrea	118,988,700
UNMIK	Kosovo	220,897,200
UNMIL	Liberia	721,723,000
UNMIS	Sudan	887,332,000
UNMIT	Timor-Leste	160,589,900
UNOCI	Côte d'Ivoire	493,698,400
UNOMIG	Georgia	36,708,200
Total		**5,253,113,700**

Source: UN DPKO.

the effectiveness of deployments. This problem in large part stems from the structure of the UN and of the international system itself. With the state-centric, self-help condition of anarchy reverberating even within the realm of peacekeeping, the provision of necessary personnel even to missions with clear mandates is a slow and arduous process. As a result, each individual UN operation (whether a peacekeeping operation or otherwise) must be assembled in an ad hoc fashion, largely through the goodwill contributions of national military forces and civilian police units of the member-states.

Given the ad hoc nature of the process of assembling and deploying a peacekeeping force, lead-time and coordination have proven to be critical limiting factors in many operations. These problems are magnified when a mission is deployed with a complex mandate: if the risks associated with a deployment are seen as inordinately high; or if tensions between national military contingents and their commanders and the UN Force Commander exist. Furthermore, while UN allocations to uniformed personnel attached to UN missions of approximately US$1,000/person/month are generous relative to the pay scales of many national military budgets, the total UN payout (including additional payments in excess of that figure) generally covers less than half of the actual cost of keeping troops in the field (Durch, 1993). As a result, contributing states are typically forced to absorb the remainder of the cost of the actual deployment.

An additional reflection of the insufficient political will for peacekeeping (as well as its underlying structural origins) is that peacekeeping operations have been and remain chronically underfunded. Although technically paying peacekeeping assessments is a legal obligation of every signatory to the UN Charter, in actuality member-states are often negligent in paying assessments. The UN has little recourse to compel them to do so; while Article 19 authorizes sanctions for non-payment (up to and including suspension of voting privileges in the UNGA), in actuality such sanction is difficult to apply.

Indeed, non-payment of peacekeeping assessments has frequently been used by member-states as leverage in efforts to promote UN reforms. The latter cause has been cited as one factor in the chronic recurrence of shortfalls in US contributions since the mid-1980s. While these shortfalls have been partially offset by 'voluntary movements' (increases in contributions) from countries supportive of UN peacekeeping as well as an effort to 'catch up' by the United States in recent years, the cumulative budgetary effects are significant. Furthermore, the United States is not alone in falling into arrears; for the current budget year outstanding contributions to peacekeeping total approximately US$1.76 billion, amounting to roughly 25 percent of the size of the aggregate peacekeeping budget (DPKO, 2008).

New sources of peacekeeping

While the vast majority of all peacekeeping operations both during and since the Cold War have been carried out under UN auspices, peacekeeping is not solely limited to the UN. Numerous examples of peacekeeping operations advanced by actors other than the UN exist, dating to the Cold War era. In fact, the first wave of non-UN peacekeeping operations came about as a direct reaction to the encroachment of the bipolar stalemate into the peacekeeping realm (Thakur and Schnabel, 2001). With the transformation of the Cold War largely into a proxy struggle by the late 1960s, the ever-present dueling vetoes of the Security Council took on added frequency and significance. Accordingly, the UN's ability and willingness to authorize new operations diminished, even as the demand for peacekeeping remained evident. In response, peacekeeping operations began to emanate from other sources, including the Commonwealth Monitoring Force (CMF) overseeing the transition from Rhodesia to Zimbabwe (1979–1980), the Multinational Force and Observer Group (MFO) deployed to the Sinai (1982–present), the two Multinational Force deployments to Beirut (MNF-I, 1982; MNF-II, 1982–1984), and the Indian Peacekeeping Force (IPKF) deployed to Sri Lanka 1987–1990 (Heldt, 2008).

The number of peace operations involving actors other than the UN has significantly increased since the end of the Cold War. Some of these operations are of a mixed character, involving the UN and other intergovernmental institutions or pivotal states. On the former score, examples include the simultaneous but parallel UN and NATO efforts in Afghanistan (UNAMA/ISAF) and Kosovo (UNMIK/KFOR), or truly joint efforts such as the UN–AU Hybrid Operation in Darfur (UNAMID). Of the latter, high-profile illustrations include collaborations between the UN and Australia (UNMIT/ISF) in East Timor and the outsourcing of peacekeeping responsibilities to Russia (CIS-PKF) by the UN (UNOMIG) in Georgia. Still other operations carried out by non-UN actors do not feature UN involvement at all, including the deployment of the EU's EUFOR in Bosnia-Herzegovina or the Russian-led Commonwealth of Independent States (CIS) border force in Tajikistan.

In large part the diversification in the sources of peacekeeping is a by-product of reforms undertaken during the tenure of Secretary-General Annan, particularly the promotion of strategies of regionalism and outsourcing (Morrison, 1999). These strategies have facilitated increases in the involvement of RGOs and PMCs in peace operations of all types. Along with this increased involvement by actors other than the UN comes the challenge of coordinating and overseeing their activities. As a result, the UN is increasingly forced to take on a supervisory role, while also grappling with the challenge of cultivating the legitimacy of non-UN operations to secure the buy-in of the parties and others in the affected society (Karns and Mingst, 2001).

Changing norms and practices

Perhaps the central debate concerning peacekeeping today concerns the appropriate goals and practices of peace operations and, by extension, their normative underpinnings. Peacekeeping in its traditional guise places a premium on the associated norms of state sovereignty and non-interference, and is oriented around the triad of consent, impartiality, and non-coercive ROE. Yet as this chapter has noted, the end of the Cold War has prompted significant advocacy for a post-Westphalian approach to security and conflict management. With this advocacy has come increasingly frequent calls (sometimes from UN circles) for using peacekeeping to liberalize the political and economic systems of post-conflict societies, as well as for development of tools of conflict management and resolution free from the dictates of state sovereignty (Rikhye, 2000).

Such calls have shaped not only the multidimensional operations undertaken by the UN over the past several years, but also those launched by the EU, the OSCE, the Economic Community of West African States (ECOWAS), the AU, and the CIS. Yet as these and other examples have shown, such expansive and multifaceted forms of peace operations face the same challenges of capacity and resource shortfalls that have long constrained traditional peacekeeping operations. Additionally, their respective emphasis on liberal reforms and coercive force sullies the legal and political basis for such operations. Given the convergence of these factors, much of the debate over peace operations turns on the trade-offs between a practicable if limited tool of conflict management (traditional peacekeeping) and its potentially more appropriate, but also costlier, riskier, and more controversial alternatives (multidimensional peacekeeping and peace enforcement).

Study questions

1   What does the experience of the UNFICYP say about peacekeeping as a form of conflict management? What precedents (if any) did it establish for later operations?

2   What are the main defining features of peacekeeping? In what ways are they unique?

3   In what ways did early attempts at peacekeeping by the League of Nations (as well as precursors to the League) shape the doctrine and scope of traditional peacekeeping under UN auspices?

4   Is traditional peacekeeping a relic of the Cold War? Why or why not?

5   How are peacekeeping operations born? Do you think the process is effective or cumbersome? In what ways might the provision of peacekeeping be improved?

6   Does the emergence of 'multidimensional' or 'wider' peacekeeping make traditional peacekeeping irrelevant?

Suggested reading

Bellamy, Alex J., Paul Williams, and Stuart Griffin. 2004. *Understanding Peacekeeping.* London: Polity.

Diehl, Paul F. 1994. *International Peacekeeping.* Baltimore, MD: Johns Hopkins University Press.

Durch, William J. (ed.). 1993. *The Evolution of UN Peacekeeping: Case Studies and Comparative Analysis.* New York, NY: St. Martin's Press.

Heldt, Birger and Peter Wallensteen. 2005. *Peacekeeping Operations: Global Patterns of Intervention and Success, 1948–2004.* Research Report no. 2. Stockholm: Folke Bernadotte Academy.

James, Alan. 1990. *Peacekeeping in International Politics.* New York, NY: St. Martin's Press.

Thakur, Ramesh and Albrecht Schnabel (eds.). 2001. *United Nations Peacekeeping Operations: Ad Hoc Missions, Permanent Engagement.* Tokyo: United Nations University Press.

United Nations, Department of Peacekeeping Operations (DPKO). 2008. *United Nations Peacekeeping Operations: Principles and Guidelines.* New York, NY: United Nations.

Wells, Alan. 2008. *International Peacekeeping: The Yearbook of International Peace Operations*, vol. 13. Leiden: Brill.

5 A study in peacekeeping
UNOMIG in Georgia

This chapter features a case study of UNOMIG. Deployed to the contested region of Abkhazia in 1993, this operation illustrates the difficulties in applying a peacekeeping force with a traditional mandate to a complex and multifaceted contemporary conflict driven by ethno-nationalist identity, defined by political fragmentation, and shaped by outside interference.

With the emergence of multidimensional peacekeeping and other forms of conflict management, so-called 'traditional' peacekeeping deployments oriented around monitoring cease-fires and observing the behavior of combatants are becoming increasingly rare. One notable exception to this post-Cold War trend is UNOMIG. First commissioned to monitor a cease-fire between the newly independent Republic of Georgia and the separatist region of Abkhazia in 1993, UNOMIG serves as a telling example of the application of traditional peacekeeping in a complex conflict driven by clashing ethno-nationalist identities and exacerbated by political fragmentation and the interference of self-interested regional powers.

Background and context

Ethno-nationalism

The Republic of Georgia is an ethnically mixed state in the profoundly heterogeneous Caucasus region. Linguistic and religious differences are pervasive within and across the states of the region. Within the boundaries of Georgia, approximately 70 percent of people identify themselves as of Georgian descent, with the next largest ethnicities Armenian (8 percent), and Russian (6 percent). Ossets make up 3 percent and Abkhaz less than 2 percent of the total population (MacFarlane *et al.*, 1996).

The Soviet era

The scenario of inter-ethnic tensions prevailing within Georgia is a familiar one within the former USSR (Goldenberg, 1994). The conflict between the central authority in Tbilisi and the autonomous republic of Abkhazia (strategically located on the Black Sea in northwest Georgia) prompting the deployment of UNOMIG in 1993 has roots predating the collapse of the USSR and Georgian independence. As a condition of its 1925 constitution, Abkhazia enjoyed union republic status in the USSR. With the incorporation of Abkhazia into Georgia in the 1930s, a series of policies were instituted to promote Georgian immigration so as to alter the ethnic balance. By the 1970s, the ethnic Abkhaz population declined from approximately 28 percent to 17 percent (Slider, 1985).

The Abkhaz awakening

In response to this shift, in 1978 the Abkhaz autonomous republic petitioned Moscow for separation from Georgia. Though the petition was denied and a new constitution reaffirming Abkhazia's status within Georgia was drafted, this marked the beginning of a period of increased nationalism persisting throughout the 1980s. This increased nationalism coincided with larger changes to the Soviet system. Designed to aid in the governance of several non-Russian republics with restive populations, the Soviet nationalities policy introduced in the 1970s instead strengthened ethno-national identity (Suny, 1988).

The nature of Soviet federalism also provided a political receptacle for burgeoning national identities among both majority and minority populations. The extension of greater autonomy to republics and sub-republican *oblasts* afforded to even relatively small national minorities such as the Abkhaz the institutional basis from which to exercise and consolidate power (Hunter, 1994). The promotion of national identity in concert with the decentralized federal structure fostered increasing dissidence within several of Georgia's ethnic minorities, particularly in South Ossetia and Abkhazia.

The collapse of the USSR

Political reforms associated with *glasnost* and *perestroika*, as well as economic dislocation and hardships, facilitated the transfer of allegiance from Soviet communism to ethno-nationalism. Government officials throughout the USSR were unprepared to cope with the dislocations associated with a transition away from a centrally planned economy as well as reform of the steeply hierarchical Soviet bureaucracy. These problems were evident in Tbilisi, and radiated out to the various regional and local authorities within Georgia. With the crumbling Soviet state leaving an ideological as well as political vacuum, ethno-national identities (and grievances) in Georgia rose to the fore.

The rise of Gamsakhurdia

The rise of a political culture defined by hyper-nationalism in Georgia (and throughout the former USSR) rewarded extremism and promoted power struggles both between and within national communities. Real and perceived threats to minority groups increased as nationalist-populist movements gained political traction; in Georgia, these threats from the majority Georgian population were met in kind by escalating nationalism and calls for secession in Abkhazia and South Ossetia. In turn, with mounting rebellions posing internal security crises, the attention of the central government to policy and administration waned.

This dynamic of ethno-nationalist rivalry and political crisis defined Georgian political life by the late 1980s. The rising tide of Georgian nationalism embodied in

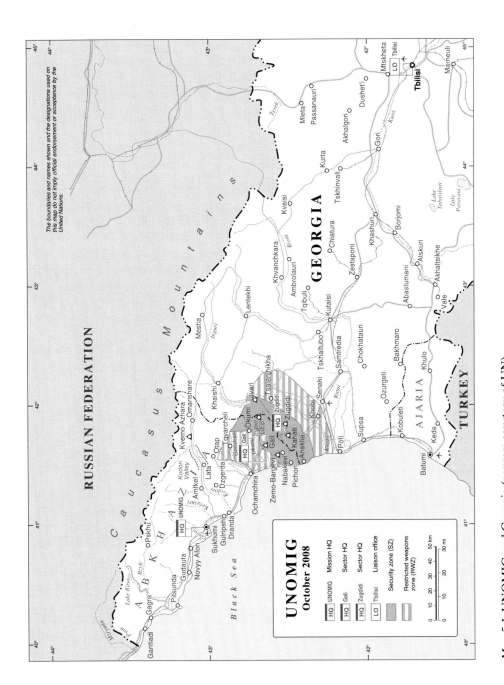

Map 5.1 UNOMIG and Georgia (source: courtesy of UN).

Zviad Gamsakhurdia's Round Table/Free Georgia coalition prompted reaction in Abkhazia. When Abkhaz authorities refused to accept the prefect appointed by Gamsakhurdia (who assumed the position of Chairman of the Parliament in October 1990), and subsequently elected to participate in a referendum on the future of the USSR in March 1991, the erosion of Georgian government control in Abkhazia was evident. Seeking to deliver a rebuke to Georgian nationalism as well as to expand Abkhaz autonomy through cultivating closer relations with the Russian Republic, the vote came out overwhelmingly (98.4 percent) in favor of preserving the union (Lynch, 2006).

The South Ossetia precedent

Mounting tensions between Tbilisi and Abkhaz authorities notwithstanding, the parallel escalation of ethno-national tensions in the South Ossetian Autonomous Oblast commanded most of the Georgian government's immediate attention. The political confrontation in South Ossetia began in earnest with the effective declaration of independence and the electoral victory of Round Table/Free Georgia in March 1990. In response to these developments, and seeking to unify with North Ossetia in neighboring Russia, the South Ossetian Soviet declared the founding of a 'South Ossetian Soviet Democratic Republic' in October 1990. Though this act was immediately annulled by the Supreme Soviet of Georgia, elections for the breakaway republic's Supreme Soviet were held in December 1990; the convention of the body triggered the full abrogation of South Ossetia's autonomy by Gamsakhurdia on 11 December. In response, violence erupted and persisted until mid-1992, with a mix of official forces and local militias loyal to the Ossets and Georgians killing over 1,000 people and spawning massive outflows of Georgian refugees to Georgia and Ossets to North Ossetia.

The conflict in Abkhazia

The catalyst

The uneasy relationship between Tbilisi and the Abkhaz government in Sukhumi unraveled in the summer of 1992, at roughly the same time that a cease-fire in South Ossetia was reached. This was due in large part to the increasing instability within Georgia as a result of the sudden overthrow of Gamsakhurdia in late 1991. With his supporters mounting an insurrection against the military council governing Georgia in the western Georgian region of Mingrelia in the early spring of 1992, Abkhaz territory (particularly the neighboring Gali region) was used for sanctuary by pro-Gamsakhurdia elements.

Not surprisingly, the Georgian government's interest in internal affairs in Abkhazia increased in response to these events, even as former Soviet foreign minister Eduard Shevardnadze returned to Georgia as head of state in March 1992. The need to deny sanctuary to the anti-government forces, along with an interest in securing critical infrastructure (such as the rail link to Russia), were key strategic factors. However, it was the decision by the Abkhaz Supreme Soviet to annul the 1978 Constitution and declare its intent to secede from Georgia that provided the political catalyst for Georgian military intervention into Abkhazia in August 1992 (MacFarlane *et al.*, 1996). Emboldened by a lack of resistance, Georgian defense minister (and director of the National Guard) Tengiz Kitovani ordered a full advance of the Georgian force to Sukhami to bring the secessionist Abkhaz government to heel (Dale, 1993). In response, the Abkhaz Supreme Soviet relocated to Gudauta while Tbilisi issued a decree dissolving that body and establishing Georgian military rule in Abkhazia.

Civil war

Civil war erupted in Abkhazia in August 1992. Although a tentative cease-fire was reached within a month, it was quickly violated by both parties. Abkhaz forces backed by combat volunteers raised by the 'Confederation of Mountain Peoples of the Caucasus' (as well as Russian support and weaponry) established control in northwest Abkhazia by mid-October 1992, and launched a counter-offensive on Sukhumi the following spring. The failure of this assault on Sukhumi along with the stabilization of the Georgian government created a climate favorable for negotiations. These negotiations produced a comprehensive cease-fire agreement (the Sochi Accord) on 27 July 1993.

The Sochi Accord

Mediated by Russia, the terms of the Sochi Accord included full withdrawal of Georgian forces from Abkhazia and the encampment of Abkhaz forces under Russian supervision. It was backed by the advance deployment of UNOMIG (authorized in September 1993) in its first iteration. However, Georgia's complicity with the terms of the agreement exposed the heavily Georgian southern and eastern regions of Abkhazia. Seizing the opportunity, in mid-September 1993 Abkhaz forces renewed hostilities, capturing Sukhumi and most of Abkhazia to the border with Georgia within days (Fuller, 1994).

The sudden success of Abkhaz forces initiated another refugee crisis in the fall of 1993. An estimated 250,000 persons were displaced, with streams of Georgians fleeing south and east into Mingrelia (UN, 1994; Norwegian Refugee Council, 1995). A UN fact-finding mission dispatched by the Secretary-General in October reported that both Georgian government forces and Abkhaz forces, as well as irregulars and civilians cooperating with them, were responsible for massive human rights violations. The Abkhaz offensive also had the effect of reigniting the conflict in Georgia proper, as Gamsakhurdia supporters sought to trade on the perceived vulnerability of the Shevardnadze government.

Russian intervention

With Tbilisi alleging Abkhaz support, by mid-October 1993 pro-Gamsakhurdia forces seized control of all the major towns in Mingrelia and were on the brink of a major assault on Tbilisi. Operating in an unfamiliar region where the populace was supportive of the rebellion, government forces seemed poised for mutiny. Facing this possibility, Shevardnadze requested an emergency meeting with Russian President Boris Yeltsin, conceding to long-standing Russian pressure to join the CIS as well as to establishment of four Russian military bases at strategic locales within Georgia.

Shevardnadze's decision activated the CIS's Collective Security Treaty obligating members to provide mutual aid to any member if attacked (Lynch, 2004). Russian forces assisted Georgia in putting down the insurgency within a matter of weeks, while leaving thousands of forces positioned along the Inguri River. Russia then inserted itself as a mediator over the winter of 1993–1994, helping to fashion a comprehensive cease-fire (the Agreement on a Ceasefire and Separation of Forces, also known as the Moscow Agreement) underwritten by a 3,000 member CIS interposition force (CIS-PKF) consisting of a predominantly Russian deployment along the Inguri River. In sum, the two-year Abkhaz conflict caused an estimated 10,000 deaths, displacing somewhere between 200,000 and 300,000 people (Shenfield, 1995).

Timeline: the conflict in Abkhazia	
June 1988	Publication of the 'Abkhaz Letter' from 60 Abkhaz intellectuals to Mikhail Gorbachev requesting creation of the Abkhaz Soviet Socialist Republic.
March 1989	30,000 Abkhaz sign the independence petition; Abkhaz Popular Forum issues an appeal to Mikhail Gorbachev demanding union republic status for Abkhazia.
9 April 1989	Popular nationalist riot in Tbilisi; 21 demonstrators killed by Soviet forces.
14 May 1989	Georgian Council of Ministers announces the creation of Tbilisi State University branch of Abkhaz State University (for Georgians) in Sukhumi.
15–18 July 1989	Riots erupt in Sukhumi over the status of Abkhazia and the possible Tbilisi State University branch; 17 killed, martial law declared.
25–26 August 1989	First Congress of Peoples of the Caucasus is held in Sukhumi, bringing together representatives of the Abkhaz, Abaz, Adygei, Ingush, Kabardin, Cherkess, and Chechen populations. The decision is made to create Assembly of Mountain Peoples of the Caucasus.
March 1990	Georgia declares sovereignty; Round Table/Free Georgia wins elections to Georgian Supreme Soviet.
31 May 1990	The Assembly of Mountain Peoples of the Caucasus in Sukhumi Georgia release Abkhazia
25 August 1990	Supreme Soviet of the Abkhaz Autonomous Soviet Socialist Republic (ASSR) adopts 'Declaration on the state sovereignty of the Abkhaz Soviet Socialist Republic.'
26 August 1990	The Presidium of the Supreme Soviet of the Republic of Georgia pronounces the actions of Supreme Soviet of the Abkhaz ASSR illegal.
October 1990	Zviad Gamsakhurdia is elected as Chairman of the Georgian Parliament.
11–12 December 1990	Georgia annuls South Ossetian autonomy and declares state of emergency.
9 April 1991	Georgia declares independence from the USSR.
26 May 1991	Gamsakhurdia is elected President of Georgia.
9 July 1991	New law allocates 28 of 65 (43 percent) of seats in Supreme Soviet to Abkhaz population.

8 December 1991	The USSR transfers sovereignty to constituent republics and ceases to exist.
22 December 1991	Beginning of the two-week coup in Tbilisi; Gamsakhurdia is replaced by the Military Council.
January 1992	South Ossetia holds a referendum on joining the Russian Federation; 99 percent vote in favor.
January–March 1992	Government forces battle with Gamsakhurdia supporters in Western Georgia.
February 1992	A Georgian military offensive in South Ossetia is launched.
March 1992	Eduard Shevardnadze returns to Georgia as head of state (Chairman of State Council).
24 June 1992	Yeltsin and Shevardnadze agree on regulation of conflict in South Ossetia.
23–25 July 1992	Abkhaz Supreme Soviet annuls the 1978 Constitution of the Republic of Abkhazia (restoring 1925 Constitution) and declares its intent to secede from Georgia; Georgian Supreme Soviet declares decision null and void.
4 August 1992	Georgia enters the UN.
11 August 1992	Georgian forces enter Abkhazia; general mobilization follows.
18 August 1992	The Georgian National Guard assaults Abkhaz Parliament.
22 August 1992	Confederation of Mountain Peoples of the Caucasus calls for volunteers to assist Abkhazia.
11 October 1992	Shevardnadze is elected chairman of Parliament.
14 December 1992	A missile from Georgian-held territory destroys a Russian helicopter evacuating Russian refugees from Tvarkcheli.
December 1992	The OSCE sends a resident mission to monitor both the South Ossetian and Abkhaz situations.
18 January 1993	Georgia shoots down a Russian helicopter returning from a relief flight to Tvarkcheli.
22 February 1993	Russian Air Force Su-25 bomb Sukhumi.
19 March 1993	Georgian forces shoot down Russian Air Force Su-27.
May 1993	The Secretary-General deploys a special UN envoy to negotiations over Abkhazia.
27 July 1993	The Sochi Accord finalizes cease-fire in Abkhazia.
24 August 1993	UNSC Resolution 858 establishes UNOMIG to verify compliance with 27 July cease-fire.
August–September 1993	Abkhaz attack and capture Sukhumi; Georgian forces are expelled from Abkhazia.
October 1993	Georgia joins the CIS.
30 November 1993	Negotiations toward comprehensive political settlement begin.
19 December 1993	Abkhaz and Georgia exchange prisoners of war.
11–12 January 1994	Second round of Georgia–Abkhaz negotiations on political settlement.
February 1994	Georgia and Russia sign bilateral treaty of cooperation.
February–March 1994	Third round of Georgia–Abkhaz negotiations takes place.
4 April 1994	Four-party framework agreement on internally displaced person (IDP) repatriation and political settlement is reached.
14 May 1994	Quadripartite Accord on cease-fire, separation of forces, and insertion of CIS-PKF is established.

21 July 1994	UNOMIG mandate is expanded.
26 November 1994	Abkhazia adopts a new constitution as sovereign state.
March 1995	The Georgian–Russian accord on military cooperation is signed.
January 1996	CIS heads of state impose economic sanctions and arms embargo on Abkhazia.
May–July 1998	Renewed fighting in the Gali region between ethnic Georgians and Abkhaz militia groups occurs.
October 1999	Abkhaz authorities conduct national referendum on independence; overwhelming vote in favor prompts declaration of independence which remains unrecognized by the international community.
March 2001	New Georgia–Abkhaz pledge to refrain from use of force in dispute is made.
October 2001	There are clashes in Abkhazia between Abkhaz troops and Georgian paramilitaries allegedly backed by fighters from the North Caucasus. Russia accuses Georgia of harboring Chechen rebels.
2002	Russia begins offering citizenship to residents of self-proclaimed republic of Abkhazia.
November 2003	Georgian President Shevardnadze is ousted in the bloodless Rose Revolution; reform-minded Mikhail Saakashvili is elected President of Georgia in January 2004.
January 2005	New (unrecognized) presidential elections are held in Abkhazia; Sergei Bagapsh declared winner after brokering deal with new Russian-backed vice president Raul Khadzhimba.
February 2005	Georgian President Saakashvili unveils proposals on autonomy within Georgia for South Ossetia, offering similar proposals to Abkhazia if Georgian refugees are offered right of return.
July 2006	The Georgian Parliament demands withdrawal of Russian peacekeepers from South Ossetia and Abkhazia, calling for them to be replaced by international forces. Georgia announces plan to establish Abkhazia government-in-exile in Pankisi Gorge.
September–October 2006	Russia/Georgia relations deteriorate. A Georgian military helicopter carrying the defense minister is fired on over South Ossetia; Georgia detains Russian officers on espionage charges; Russia imposes sanctions on Georgia, cutting transit links and expelling hundreds of Georgians. Numerous diplomatic rows ensue over the next two years
March 2008	The Abkhaz political authority asks UN to recognize its independence.
April 2008	Russia announces plans to increase ties with Abkhazia and South Ossetia; Tbilisi accuses Moscow of 'de facto annexation.'
May 2008	Russia sends 300 unarmed troops to Abkhazia for 'railway repairs.' Georgia accuses Russia of planning military intervention.
June 2008	Abkhazia severs contact with the Georgian government, accusing Tbilisi of orchestrating recent attacks in Abkhaz territory.

| 7–9 August 2008 | Exchanges of fire between South Ossetian separatists and Georgian forces sparks Georgian military assault on South Ossetia; Russian troops intervene the next day, striking targets in Georgia and triggering an ongoing international crisis. Pro-Russian Abkhaz forces open a second front with military assaults on Georgian-held Kodori Valley. |

Sources: BBC, 2008; UN, 2007a; Lynch, 2006; MacFarlane *et al.*, 1996.

UNOMIG and peacekeeping in Georgia

Tentative beginnings

The 15-year history of UN peacekeeping operations in Georgia emerged out of a series of incremental and decidedly reactive commitments. The initial involvement of the UN in response to the Abkhaz conflict came around the time of the first tentative cease-fire, through creation of a resident mission consisting of UNHCR and UNDP personnel to Tbilisi in November 1992. Notably, this commitment was officially portrayed as an act in support of the fragile Georgian independence, rather than a direct response to the separatist conflicts in Abkhazia and/or South Ossetia.

In response to looming humanitarian crises associated with these conflicts, the UN established an Inter-Agency Humanitarian Assessment Mission under the Department of Humanitarian Affairs in January 1993, followed by dispatch of a UN Special Envoy in May. At the same time, throughout 1992 and early 1993, the Secretariat continually rebuffed entreaties by the Georgian government (partly as a hedge against Russian interference) for deployment of a UN peacekeeping force. While UN reluctance was ostensibly due to a lack of ripeness, it was also a product of political sensitivities related to Russian involvement as well as pre-existing and extensive UN commitments in the Balkans, Somalia, and elsewhere.

UNOMIG, v.1

The Inter-Agency Mission coordinated the bulk of UN activities in Georgia until the establishment of a second cease-fire in conjunction with the terms of the Sochi Accord in July 1993. With this demonstration of a mutually hurting stalemate by the parties, the Secretary-General proposed deployment of a vanguard of military observers to help verify compliance with the cease-fire, with this advance deployment to be subsumed within any potential successor force. The UNSC agreed to the Secretariat's proposal, and an advance deployment of ten observers arrived in Abkhazia on 8 August 1993.

Initial mandate

With the advance force participating in regular patrols in and around Sukhami, and reporting positively on the status of the cease-fire, the Security Council established UNOMIG via UNSC Resolution 858 (24 August 1993). In its first iteration

UNOMIG was an exceedingly limited operation. UNOMIG's initial mandate charged its 88 lightly armed military observers only with verifying compliance with the terms of the cease-fire contained within the Sochi Accord, and reporting any violations to the Secretary-General (UN, 2007a). The operation was completely invalidated when that agreement was violated weeks later, and UNOMIG proved a non-factor in the face of the Abkhaz capture of Sukhami and subsequent advance to the Inguri River.

Following the breakdown of the cease-fire, UNOMIG was suspended at its existing force levels of four military observers and four civilian staff in Sukhumi, one military observer in Tbilisi, and seven military observers out-of-area in the Russian city of Sochi. UNOMIG was preserved during this period with an interim mandate provided in UNSC Resolution 881 (4 November 1993) to maintain contacts between and among the parties and the Russian force, and to monitor and report on developments relevant to the Special Envoy's efforts at promoting a comprehensive political settlement (UN, 2007a).

Political breakthrough

By the winter of 1993–1994, the breakthrough in Russian–Georgian cooperation transformed the conflict, again putting the Abkhaz on the defensive. As a result, the UN Special Envoy's role morphed into that of mediator in negotiations involving the parties as well as Russia and the OSCE. Multiparty negotiations conducted under the good offices of the Special Envoy yielded the Quadripartite Accord (finalized in May 1994), which included not only a cease-fire, but also specific provisions for the repatriation of refugees and IDPs as well as a declaration outlining the preliminary terms for a political settlement to include provisions for an eventual referendum on the political status of Abkhazia.

Expanding UNOMIG

Despite its presence and involvement in Georgia, the UN steadfastly worked to avoid an elaborate security-related role in Georgia prior to the signing of the Quadripartite Accord. However, general compliance with the Agreement on a Cease-fire and Separation of Forces contained within that Accord provided the impetus for increased UN involvement through an expanded mandate for UNOMIG. The terms of this expanded mandate enumerated in UNSC Resolution 937 (21 July 1994) were also largely driven by events.

Revised mandate

The Quadripartite Accord extended consent from the parties to a Russian-led CIS peacekeeping force as well as an expanded mandate for UNOMIG. While the Security Council was still debating the scope and authority for a revised UNOMIG, in the case of the CIS force the Accord merely granted formal authority to the Russian forces already deployed along the Inguri River. With the UN forced to accommodate itself to this 'ground truth,' Resolution 937 increased UNOMIG troop levels from 88 to 136 (UN, 2007a). The expanded mandate for the revamped deployment included the following responsibilities:

- To monitor and verify the implementation by the parties of the Agreement on a Cease-fire and Separation of Forces signed in Moscow on 14 May 1994.
- To observe the operation of the peacekeeping force of the CIS within the framework of the implementation of the Agreement.
- To verify, through observation and patrolling, that troops of the parties do not remain in or re-enter the security zone and that heavy military equipment does not remain or is not reintroduced in the security or restricted weapons zone.
- To monitor the storage areas for heavy military equipment withdrawn from the security zone and the restricted weapons zone in cooperation with the CIS-PKF as appropriate.
- To monitor the withdrawal of troops of the Republic of Georgia from the Kodori Valley to places beyond the boundaries of Abkhazia, Republic of Georgia.
- To patrol regularly the Kodori Valley.
- To investigate, at the request of either party or the CIS-PKF or on its own initiative, reported or alleged violations of the Agreement and to attempt to resolve or contribute to the resolution of such incidents.
- To report regularly to the Secretary-General within its mandate, in particular on the implementation of the Agreement, any violations and their investigation by UNOMIG, as well as other relevant developments.
- To maintain close contacts with both parties to the conflict and to cooperate with the CIS-PKF and, by its presence, to contribute to conditions conducive to safe and orderly return of refugees and displaced persons.

Implementation and coordination

Over the summer of 1994, UNOMIG forces were deployed in three contested sectors (Gali, Zugdidi, and Sukhumi) along the Inguri River, as well as in permanently staffed sites in villages throughout the Kodori Valley. The competing requirements contained within UNOMIG's mandate presented the operation's commanders with major challenges. These challenges were further compounded by the fact that UNOMIG's responsibilities were varied and in some cases competing, and were to be carried out in a context in which multiple outside actors were involved.

Within the first few months of the UNOMIG deployment, a division of labor emerged which has more or less persisted to the present. This arrangement was facilitated by the crucial fact that all of the external parties agreed to the basic components of the political settlement enumerated in the Quadripartite Agreement: the need to maintain Georgian territorial integrity, the freedom of refugees and displaced persons to return to their homes, and the goal of preserving significant autonomy for the Abkhaz population (Marks, 1995). At the same time, effective coordination between UNOMIG and the array of other external actors involved in the peace process has proven elusive.

CIS-PKF RESPONSIBILITIES

The immediate tasks associated with monitoring the cease-fire were assigned to the CIS-PKF, through a special Protocol to the Moscow Agreement governing the activities of the CIS force. That Protocol specified that the primary responsibility of the CIS-PKF was to maintain the cease-fire and to see that it is scrupulously observed while also supervising disengagement and the Georgian withdrawal from the Kodori Valley, and implementation of the Agreement's provisions regarding the security and restricted weapons zones (Shashenkov, 1995). Finally, in a provision with a major bearing on resettlement, the Protocol stated that CIS-PKF presence should 'promote the safe return of refugees and displaced persons, especially to the Gali District' (UN, 2007a). The initial force deployment was a full allotment of 3,000 troops, drawn largely from Russian units already based in Abkhazia. These forces were rapidly redeployed from an existing mission, and as a result were neither equipped nor trained for the operation (Lynch, 1998). The initial deployment was gradually reduced to somewhere between 1,100 and 1,800 troops, rotated to include Russian forces trained for peacekeeping (CPIS, 1995).

UNOMIG RESPONSIBILITIES

In accordance with the mandate established by UNSC Resolution 937, UNOMIG was tasked with supporting the CIS-PKF efforts toward monitoring the cease-fire. At the same time, the expansion of that mandate required UNOMIG to assume the traditional custodial role of the UN through supervision of the Russian force. The terms of that supervision were initially established by the parties to the cease-fire agreement contained within the Quadripartite Accord, affirmed in Resolution 937. Those terms required renewal of the CIS force's mandate by the Security Council every six months, an arrangement also followed with respect to UNOMIG since 1994. Over the duration of the deployment, problems in the interactions between UNOMIG and CIS-PKF have occurred. These problems largely stem from the encroachment of Russian national interest into the activities of the peacekeeping force, as well as to conflicting conceptions of peacekeeping in UN and Russian circles (MacFarlane and Schnabel, 1995).

OTHER INVOLVED ACTORS

Continuing negotiations concerning an elusive political settlement to the Abkhaz conflict have remained the domain of UN mediators (beginning with the Special Envoy, later supplanted with appointment of a Special Representative to the Secretary-General). Other key contributors to ongoing negotiations include the OSCE, as well as representatives of the Russian Federation and the rest of the Friends of the Secretary-General group (France, Germany, the United Kingdom, the United States, and Ukraine) which meets repeatedly with UN representatives in Geneva. In 2005 a 'New Friends' group (consisting of Bulgaria, the Czech Republic, Estonia, Latvia, Lithuania, Moldova, Poland, Romania, and Sweden) was formed to lobby for involvement from non-UN sources such as NATO and the EU (Lynch, 2006). Russia and the OSCE have carried out other distinct roles as well; Russian delegates in maintaining bilateral relations with both Abkhaz and Georgian authorities; and the OSCE in monitoring human rights conditions. Finally, an extensive number of other UN agencies (the World Food Programme (WFP), UNDP, the UN Children's Fund (UNICEF), and the Department of Humanitarian Affairs (DHA)) have remained active in delivering humanitarian assistance and development aid (Marks, 1995).

The evolution of UNOMIG

As UNOMIG evolved, it gradually expanded its remit into areas beyond the immediate purview of the oversight of the parties to the conflict and the CIS-PKF force. For example, out of an interest in rebuilding the shattered physical infrastructure, by the late 1990s UNOMIG incorporated an engineering and construction dimension. In combination with this effort, UNOMIG began to provide technical advice and logistical assistance to projects of potential benefit to both the Georgian and Abkhaz sides.

Perhaps the major catalyst in UNOMIG's evolution is the rampant criminality in Abkhazia and throughout Georgia. With the diminished state authority of the post-Soviet era exacerbated by the dynamics of 'new wars' in Abkhazia and elsewhere in the Caucasus, lawlessness and crime became a major destabilizing force with direct negative implications for the repatriation of refugees and IDPs and the overall security situation (Chufrin, 2001). These implications triggered significant changes in the UN presence in Georgia, particularly with respect to human rights and law enforcement.

Humanitarian situation and human rights

The international community has been consistently concerned with the human rights situation in Georgia, particularly (but not exclusively) with respect to refugee repatriation. While this concern is an expressed component of UNOMIG's mandate, it was not one that UNOMIG's relatively small deployment of military observers has proven particularly well-suited, or inclined to address. Similarly, whereas the expectation was that the CIS-PKF would assist UNOMIG in the return of refugees (particularly the nearly 250,000 Georgians displaced to Mingrelia), the Russian force was neither trained for, nor disposed to, such endeavors (Chopra and Weiss, 1995). As a result, UNOMIG provided little direct assistance to humanitarian agencies, instead remaining closely affixed to a narrow interpretation of its mandate. This scenario culminated in the March 1995 murder of 20 Georgian civilians by Abkhaz militia patrolling for spontaneous returnees to Gali, reportedly in the presence of CIS and UNOMIG forces (MacFarlane *et al.*, 1996).

In response to the weak performance of UNOMIG on the humanitarian and human rights aspects of its mandate, the UN established the Office for the Protection and Promotion of Human Rights in Abkhazia through UNSC Resolution 1077 (22 October 1996). Jointly staffed by representatives of the Office of the High Commission for Human Rights (OHCHR) and the OSCE, the Human Rights Office was attached administratively to UNOMIG, reporting directly to the UNOMIG Head of Mission on human rights conditions and the status of refugees. Despite this formally institutionalized relationship, interactions between UNOMIG and UNHCR have proven stilted and oftentimes acrimonious.

Lawlessness and policing

By the latter part of the 1990s, occasional restrictions on the movement and activities of UNOMIG forces by the parties to the conflict were supplanted by more serious incidents jeopardizing the safety and security of UN personnel. These incidents were almost exclusively by-products of the high level of criminal activity, as well as the inability and/or unwillingness of Abkhaz and Georgian law enforcement to respond to the problem (Phillips, 2004). Prior to the Rose Revolution in 2003, Georgia was 'less a country than a loose association of fiefs' (*The Economist*, 2003). Thanks to the permissive climate fostered by the Shevardnadze government, the Kodori Valley and the Pankisi Gorge (where Georgian withdrawal was incomplete) became no-go zones in which organized crime and paramilitary groups operated with impunity.

Beginning with the ambush of a UNOMIG bus in Sukhumi in September 1998, and a furtive grenade assault on a new UN office in Zugdidi on 27 September 1999, a series of increasingly brazen attacks on the homes of international and local staff and UN installations morphed into a systematic campaign of abductions, concentrated primarily in the Gali region and the Kodori Valley. This campaign included the kidnapping of seven UNOMIG personnel in October 1999, two UNOMIG observers on 17 January 2000, two military observers, one interpreter and two representatives of an NGO on 1 June 2000, and two UNOMIG military observers on 10 December 2000. In all cases the hostages were returned unharmed within a few days; the latter episode led to the suspension of UNOMIG patrols in the Kodori Valley in early 2001.

Upon resumption of those patrols, an additional abduction of two UNOMIG military observers, one UNOMIG medic and a Georgian interpreter on 5 June by an unidentified armed group in conjunction with an armed assault on a UNOMIG patrol vehicle in Gali ten days later brought the matter to a head. Following the safe release of the hostages on 11 June, the Secretary-General's strong condemnation of the 5 June incident and the continuing impunity for criminal actions against UNOMIG personnel prompted the UN to act. Pursuant to recommendations formulated by a security assessment mission in late 2002 on improving the internal security situation, the Secretary-General recommended the addition of a civilian policing component to UNOMIG. This recommendation was endorsed in UNSC Resolution 1494 (30 July 2003), in which the Security Council authorized that

> a UN police component of 20 officers be added to UNOMIG, to strengthen its capacity to carry out its mandate and in particular contribute to the creation of conditions conducive to the safe and dignified return of internally displaced persons and refugees.
>
> (UN, 2007a)

The outcome

A 'frozen' conflict?

By most accounts, UNOMIG's stabilizing effect has created improved conditions for the operation of aid agencies, while promoting greater recognition of and adherence to international human rights norms (MacFarlane *et al.*, 1996). The distribution of UNOMIG personnel outside of the troubled Kodori Valley and Gali regions has also had a key confidence-building effect in the general population. However, despite the presence of CIS peacekeepers and UNOMIG observers (reaffirmed biannually by UNSC resolutions since 1994), repeated violations of the cease-fire have occurred. A series of high-profile military clashes involving the parties as well as Russian forces in the Kodori Valley (October 2001), the Kodori Gorge (July 2006), and in the downing of two unmanned aerial vehicles (UAVs) over Abkhaz airspace (March/April 2008) clearly tested the fragile calm maintained by UNOMIG ground and air patrols (Nichols, 2008).

The combination of these factors has led to characterizations of the situation in Abkhazia as a 'frozen conflict' (Lynch, 2006). The conflict in Abkhazia has clearly thawed to a degree as a result of the direct military clash between Georgia and Russia over South Ossetia in early August 2008. While large-scale military hostilities have yet to occur in Abkhazia proper since the implementation of the revised UNOMIG mandate in 1994, Abkhaz forces did strike the Kodori Valley during the August 2008 crisis while Russian forces (both regulars and 'peacekeepers') routinely used Abkhaz territory for staging assaults on Georgian targets.

Abkhazia's unsettled political future

The litany of military incidents and turmoil over Abkhazia is clearly a by-product of the unsettled legal, political, and territorial status of the region (Lynch, 2004). Three UN Secretary-Generals (Boutros-Ghali, Annan, and now Ban Ki-moon), assorted Special Representatives, and the Friends of the Secretary-General have committed extensive political capital to crafting a comprehensive political settlement. Despite this ongoing effort, issues such as the political fate of Abkhazia and the return of refugees and IDPs remain unsettled. This problem stems in part from the deliberate ambiguity in Georgia's constitution regarding territorial arrangements between the central government and regional entities, not to mention Abkhazia's 1999 declaration of independence, recognized (along with South Ossetia's) by Russia in the aftermath of the August 2008 conflict.

An apparent breakthrough agreement between Russia and Georgia prioritizing the issues of economic cooperation, IDP and refugee return, and political settlement in the spring of 2003 caused some grounds for optimism. Abkhaz reservations about the political component stalled any further major diplomatic initiatives. At the heart of the issue is the continuing opposition of the Abkhaz authorities to the terms of the 'Basic Principles on the Distribution of Competencies between Tbilisi and Sukhumi' document (introduced by the Special Representative and endorsed as a framework agreement by the Secretary-General in 2002). The spring 2008 rejection by Abkhaz authorities of Georgia's offer guaranteeing international recognition of Abkhazia's autonomy, establishing quotas for Abkhaz representation in Georgia's political institutions, creating a special economic zone in the Gali region, and further internationalizing the peace process affirms the intractability of the issue (Nichols, 2008).

Ongoing humanitarian problems

UNOMIG has proven ineffective in the delivery of humanitarian assistance as well as in monitoring and protecting human rights. With tasks such as refugee repatriation falling outside the purview of traditional peacekeeping, UNOMIG transferred the responsibility for the humanitarian component of its mandate to UNHCR representatives, even foregoing efforts to interpose itself between militias and IDPs. UNHCR personnel have argued that this passive approach has failed to ensure the minimum stability necessary for the effective provision of humanitarian assistance.

The chief result of these poor inter-agency relations is the persistence of a troubling humanitarian situation. UN aid agencies and NGOs continue to struggle to meet the food and medical needs of the most vulnerable segments of the population, while human rights are frequently violated in contested areas such as the Gali region. Despite ongoing UN (and OSCE) sponsored efforts to monitor the situation and repatriate refugees, individual security is jeopardized by weak UN oversight and insufficient provisions on the part of both Georgian and Abkhaz authorities to fully guarantee human rights to refugees and minorities.

Lessons learned

The limits of peacekeeping

This profile of UNOMIG illustrates two crucial overriding themes with respect to peacekeeping. The first is the limitations of traditional operations in relation to many contemporary conflicts. Missions such as UNOMIG, which are highly constrained by the triad of consent, impartiality, and non-coercion, may be unable to effectively manage intra-state contests for political power driven by competing ethno-nationalist identities and exacerbated by external interference from states and NSAs. The tendency of such conflicts to create significant humanitarian problems and to feature egregious human rights violations only further underscores these limitations.

UNOMIG exemplifies the profound disconnection between the extensive humanitarian challenges associated with 'new wars' and the uncertainty within the DPKO about how (or even whether) to respond to them. This uncertainty manifests itself in an evident shortfall both in the necessary capacity and will to undertake the tasks associated with such challenges. The divide between peacekeeping and humanitarian tasks was particularly pronounced in the Abkhaz case. At the same time, the reality that peacekeeping is an endeavor that is almost wholly distinct from negotiations toward a political settlement has not been lost on the parties to the conflict. UNOMIG's limitations have created morale problems, while delegitimizing the operation in the eyes of the host population it was designed to assist; as one UNOMIG officer noted, 'we are the dog that barks but has no bite' (quoted in MacFarlane *et al.*, 1996).

The perils of outsourcing

The expansion of UNOMIG's mandate in July 1994 transferred legal sanction, as well as the responsibility for the bulk of the day-to-day responsibilities for peacekeeping in and around Abkhazia, to the Russian dominated CIS-PKF. First given voice in *An Agenda for Peace*, the reliance on non-UN sources to carry out peace operations remains a key strategy designed to capitalize on political will, where and when it materializes, and to cope with endemic resource shortfalls plaguing the DPKO. This act, which coincided with contemporaneous calls for increasing the capacity and political will of UN member-states for peace operations, has proven to be a major miscalculation given the involvement of Russian 'peacekeepers' in the August 2008 conflict.

Command-and-control problems

Outsourcing peacekeeping to pivotal states and regional organizations likely facilitates the provision of operations that otherwise may not materialize due to a scarcity of resources or political will at the UN. At the same time, UNOMIG serves as a profound cautionary tale illustrating the perils of the strategy. While oversight of the CIS-PKF is consistent with the UN's customary exercise of a custodial role for maintaining peace and security, it also speaks to the ambivalence of an outsourcing dictated by 'ground truth' (in this case, the prior presence of Russian forces as well as Georgia's strategic location in the post-Soviet 'near abroad') rather than any concrete policy directive.

As the UNOMIG case shows, outsourcing peacekeeping transfers the aforementioned problems stemming from the misalignment between traditional peacekeeping and contemporary conflicts to a non-UN source rather than addressing them. It also comes with an attendant cost in the form of a diminished command-and-control authority for the UN. While UNOMIG was re-purposed to oversee the activities of CIS-PKF, it lacked much ability to control the behavior of the Russian peacekeepers. The impotence of UNOMIG combined with a weak central command structure for the CIS force created a significant lack of accountability, with widespread reports of corruption, looting of homes and aid depots, and human rights violations by the Russian force (Gelashvili, 2001).

Impartiality concerns

The UNOMIG experience also raises questions about the feasibility of outsourcing peacekeeping to regional hegemons who may have interests apart from keeping the peace. The Russian involvement in Abkhazia has been driven from its inception by a larger strategic interest in restoring dominion over the strategically vital Caucasus region, with incorporating South Ossetia and subduing the uprising in nearby Chechnya being closely related goals. Moscow has continuously sought to blunt Georgian resistance to Russia's 'near abroad' strategy, embodied in efforts at liberal reforms and overtures to the West on various security and energy partnerships. Vladimir Putin's election to the presidency in 1999 only intensified Russia's manipulation of Abkhaz separatism, triggering corresponding reactions from Georgia's leaders, particularly after the 2003 Rose Revolution (Fairbanks, 2004).

The biggest casualty of Russia's mixed motives in Georgia from a peacekeeping perspective is impartiality, a crucial component of the triad that defines traditional peacekeeping. Extreme examples include reports of Russian battalions assigned to peacekeeping duty after fighting alongside Abkhaz separatists (Kakabadze, 1997). Mirroring shifts in the larger political context, Russia initially tilted toward the Abkhaz side, transferring weaponry to Abkhaz militias, using air power against Georgian targets, and unevenly enforcing the July 1993 Sochi Accord cease-fire. Upon Shevardnadze's momentous concessions of October 1993, Russia reversed course, using military force to help Georgia put down the insurrection in Mingrelia and to impose a military blockade to pressure Abkhaz authorities into concessions at the negotiation table in 1994.

The Putin years have been marked by a pronounced shift back to the Abkhaz side, triggered largely by Moscow's allegations of Georgian complicity in the use of the Pankisi Valley as a base of operations by Chechen rebels and foreign fighters

(Berman, 2005). This concern led Russia to renege on earlier promises to close its military bases in Georgia, while also prompting various directives designed to promote more and deeper government-to-government ties with the Abkhaz authority. These directives include Russia's withdrawal from CIS sanctions and an offer of Russian citizenship to the Abkhaz (Socor, 2006). More recently, Russia threatened to extend diplomatic recognition to Abkhazia, following international recognition of Kosovo (UN, 2007b).

On the basis of Russia's lack of impartiality, in November 2005 the Georgian parliament issued a resolution characterizing the CIS-PKF as a national security threat. A subsequent government investigation concluded that the CIS-PKF did not meaningfully contribute to peace in Abkhazia and led the Georgian legislature to pass a resolution in July 2006 for internationalization of the peacekeeping force. Whether problems can be rectified through reforms such as the UN's new emphasis on integrated missions and coordination with security partners remains to be seen. Nevertheless, it seems safe to say that the long-dubious credibility and effectiveness of the CIS-PKF has taken a fatal blow with the documented involvement of Russian peacekeepers in offensive military actions against Georgian forces in both South Ossetia and Georgia in August 2008. This blatant and egregious violation of the basic tenets of peacekeeping, occurring with little effective response from UNOMIG personnel, has seemingly sounded the death knell for both Russian peacekeeping in Abkhazia, and UNOMIG itself.

Study questions

1   What role does historical context, and in particular the Soviet legacy, continue to play in the conflict in Abkhazia? How does this legacy influence the UN role?

2   When and why was UNOMIG established? How was its mandate expanded? What were the main implications of doing so?

3   What have been the main outcomes of UNOMIG? Are these outcomes products of the design and mandate of the operation, or are they results of the dynamics of the conflict in Abkhazia?

4   On balance, would you characterize UNOMIG as a successful operation? Why or why not?

5   What does this case study suggest are the main limitations facing peacekeeping in contemporary conflicts driven by ethnonationalism and contested state authority?

6   What are the major problems associated with the outsourcing of peacekeeping operations to pivotal states and regional organizations?

Suggested reading

Chopra, Jarat and Thomas G. Weiss. 1995. 'Prospects for Containing Conflict in the Former Second World,' *Security Studies*, 4 (3): 552–583.

Chufrin, Gennady (ed.). 2001. *The Security of the Caspian Sea Region.* Oxford: Oxford University Press.

Lynch, Dov. 2004. *Engaging Eurasia's Separatist States.* Washington, DC: USIP.

Lynch, Dov. 2006. *Why Georgia Matters*, Chaillot Paper no. 86. Paris: ISS.

Marks, Edward. 1995. 'Dynamics of Peacekeeping in Georgia,' *Strategic Forum*, 45.

6   Mediation

Using the 1978 Camp David summit as a springboard, this chapter explores the use and evolution of mediation as a tool of conflict management. Major themes include the diversification of actors, approaches, strategies, and motives incorporated under the broad heading of international conflict mediation. The final portion of the chapter explores in detail the issues and debates surrounding the use of mediation in contemporary (largely intra-state) conflicts.

Mediation in brief: insights from Camp David

One of the most prominent examples of mediation as an instrument of conflict management remains the mediation of the Middle East conflict by US President Jimmy Carter in 1978–1979. This mediation effort culminated in a landmark 1979 peace treaty between Egypt and Israel, in the process making Egypt the first Arab country to officially recognize Israel's right to exist. Carter's efforts toward mediation over 13 days at the presidential retreat at Camp David, Maryland in September 1978 (efforts that produced the landmark Camp David Accords) remain illustrative from the standpoint of the consideration of mediation as a form of contemporary conflict management.

Backdrop to Camp David

Upon election to the presidency, Carter had taken up the Middle East peace process as a central objective of his foreign policy agenda. As such, he had met and interacted with Menachem Begin (then Israel's Prime Minister) and Anwar Sadat (then Egypt's President) on numerous occasions. While Carter found Sadat friendly and engaging, and judged him to be committed to a substantive accord, Carter considered Begin an inflexible hard-liner, and more resistant to necessary concessions than much of the remainder of the Israeli diplomatic corps and the Israeli public at large.

Not satisfied with personal observations gleaned from previous summitry, as the Camp David talks approached Carter asked his National Security Council (NSC) staff to prepare psychological profiles of Begin and Sadat. Based on the information contained within these profiles, in concert with joint talks in Carter's private cabin that frequently escalated to shouting matches during their first three days at the retreat, Carter concluded that continued direct interactions between the leaders (as he and his staff had initially planned) would only lead to deeper entrenchment of their positions and, ultimately, stalemate. A different tack – one in which the Egyptian and Israeli delegates were kept apart, with Carter traversing the space between them – was pursued.

Setting and strategy

In many ways, Camp David was a perfect environment for such deeply antagonistic leaders to meet. A relatively small and isolated retreat, it ensured occasions for cultivated and managed interaction in venues such as the swimming pool, the tennis court, or the film room. Attire was informal, as befitting a retreat in such a bucolic setting. Perhaps most critically (and implausibly from our current, media-saturated vantage point), the world's press were excluded, with White House press secretary Jody Powell the only source of public information (and a rather tight-lipped one at that). The informal interface between Begin, Sadat, Carter, and their aides around the compound helped to reduce some of the immense psychological and personal barriers between the delegations.

At the same time, Carter himself worked relentlessly with each leader and his staff independently over an intense period of ten days. The negotiations thus took on an indirect character, with Carter as mediator performing an on-site variation of shuttle diplomacy, and even resorting on numerous occasions to personal appeals to both the Egyptian and the Israeli delegations to prevent their departure from Camp David (and the collapse of the talks). As a single draft document began to emerge, Carter redoubled his mediation efforts, laboring with each leader separately to revise, re-draft, and amend yet again a workable framework for the peace treaty that would ultimately come six months later.

Reframing intractable issues

A further anecdote from Camp David underscores the importance of the wide-ranging and sometimes unpredictable factors that are essential to successful mediation. Asked years later to describe a turning point in the negotiations, Carter presented the issue of Israeli settlements in the Sinai and the West Bank (a familiar issue that continues to flummox the efforts of Condoleezza Rice, Tony Blair, and other Middle East mediators). The settlements in question were previously established by Israel on highly strategic territory obtained through military victory in the 1967 Six Day War. Upon election as Prime Minister, Begin – a hard-line conservative who had helped found the Likud party, and a former leader of Irgun – took a sworn oath that he would never allow the settlements to be dismantled. On day ten of the talks, as a result of the inclusion of this issue in the draft accord, Begin withdrew from Camp David, brushing aside Carter's entreaties to remain.

Before he left, Carter (acting on the advice of his personal secretary) elected to sign eight photographs of Begin, along with Carter and Sadat, taken at Camp David for Begin's grandchildren. Carter addressed his autographs personally to each of them and delivered the pictures to Begin's cabin. According to Carter, Begin was deeply moved by Carter's gesture, and shortly thereafter informed Carter that he wished to resume negotiations (Carter, 1982). Eventually a compromise on the issue of settlements was struck: consideration of the settlements would be restricted to those on the Sinai only, with the Knesset (Israel's parliament) granted the opportunity to vote on the matter. The Knesset subsequently approved dismantling all Israeli settlements in the Sinai – thereby salvaging the Egyptian–Israeli peace treaty.

As the brief vignette above illustrates, the Camp David experience highlights the importance of advance preparation, the communication process, context, flexibility, and even basic appeals to emotion and sentiment to the successful mediation of a high-level, high-stakes international dispute. Is it any wonder then that the mediation of international conflict is so difficult an endeavor – or so fascinating an enterprise?

What is mediation?

Defining mediation

Mediation is a nearly ubiquitous phenomenon in modern life. Indeed, one of the wellsprings of fiction, film, and television drama – the legal profession – is a prime embodiment of mediation in the real world. Lawyers serve as mediators between their clients and the legal code (not to mention between their clients and the judge sworn to uphold that code). Mediation is also prominent in the business sector, particularly with regard to the negotiation and enforcement of contracts. Anyone who is familiar with labor disputes, for instance, is probably aware of the role and importance of mediators in forestalling, averting, or ending strikes and lockouts; it is hard to imagine the process of establishing a collective bargaining arrangement occurring without the involvement of mediators.

Additionally, mediation is a key, if often overlooked, function of governments. In the view of social contract theorists such as Thomas Hobbes and John Locke, the mediation of disputes between citizens is one of the most important tasks of (representative) government. Whether it be high-profile land disputes between aboriginal peoples and federal governments (such as in the United States, Canada, and Australia in recent years), or a simmering dispute between neighbors over the location of a fence that involves local police and county surveyors, mediation is a service that governments provide – ideally before such conflicts escalate and trigger widespread disorder or even violence.

Mediation is also a principal component of international relations. Even in conflicts (such as those in Sierra Leone or East Timor) that are more closely associated with other forms of conflict management, mediation has been attempted. As a form of intra-state conflict management, mediation is most likely to occur when a conflict is protracted, the parties are at an impasse, neither party is prepared to absorb further costs or escalate the dispute, and both parties are ready to engage in dialogue and welcome mediation (Bercovitch, 1984).

Before embarking on an empirical analysis of mediation as a form of intra-state conflict management, one must elaborate a workable definition of what the term refers to in that context. As Wilkenfeld *et al.* (2005: 1) note in one recent study, intervention by a mediator in the context of intra-state conflicts is best understood as a 'necessary step to help parties move beyond profound disagreements as well as mutual mistrust and resentment.' This is consistent with the majority of definitions advanced in the study of mediation as a form of international political behavior.

A generation ago, in two notable studies of intermediaries in the strategic interactions of principal parties in world politics, Oran Young (1967, 1972) referred to mediation in much the same sense, as efforts by 'third parties attempting to facilitate a settlement of the issues at stake among the original players and the actions third parties take to achieve this objective' (Young, 1972: 52). As two of the most prominent experts on conflict mediation (I. William Zartman and Saadia Touval) aptly summarize:

> Mediation is a form of third-party intervention in a conflict. It differs from other forms of third-party intervention in conflicts in that it is not based on the direct use of force and it is not aimed at helping one of the participants to win. Its purpose is to bring the conflict to a settlement that is acceptable to both sides and consistent with the third party's interests.... Mediation is best thought of as a mode of negotiation in which a third party helps the parties find a solution that they cannot find by themselves.
>
> (Zartman and Touval, 2007: 437–438)

The efforts of scholars dedicated to conceptual clarification of mediation as a form of conflict management allow us to identify and isolate certain features that distinguish mediation from other forms of conflict management behavior.

Mediation must involve third parties

By definition, mediation involves one (or more) actors that are not privy to the original dispute in efforts to manage and potentially resolve that dispute. By doing so, these actors bring their own interests and agendas into the dispute, interests and agendas that demand attention and typically alter the prevailing dynamic of any dispute by making its resolution a core interest of the mediating party or parties (as noted above). The introduction of one or more third parties and their agendas can actually further complicate things. Yet at the same time the infusion of mediators may bring new energies and ideas to a conflict management process that is stalemated, or to a conflict that seemingly defies management.

One can return to the vignette that opened this chapter for further illustration of either (or, more accurately, both) possibilities. The degree to which President Carter hitched his Administration's entire foreign policy to a breakthrough between Egypt and Israel raised the stakes for the principals as well as the United States. In undertaking this bold gambit, Carter's effort re-fashioned the Middle East dispute into a central item on the US foreign policy agenda, which in turn placed resolution of that dispute (as reflected in an Egypt–Israeli peace treaty, at least) squarely within the US national interest (NIDR, 1992).

The intense, hands-on effort that followed certainly broadened, and in some ways further complicated, an already complex relationship between Egypt and Israel; it laid bare previous US policies in the Middle East, as well as perceptions that these policies (including the provision of military and economic aid) had to that point tilted heavily toward Israel, to the detriment of Egypt and the other Arab states, thereby opening a host of new historical grievances between the principals. Yet certainly these higher stakes and more intensive efforts were essential to compel two intransigent adversaries toward a workable peace accord.

Mediation is non-violent

The second defining feature of mediation with respect to its use in the management of intra-state conflict is the absence of the application of violence or physical force by the mediator. This is crucial to the very essence of mediation. As Bercovitch *et al.* (1991: 8) define it, mediation is 'a process of conflict management where disputants seek the assistance of, or accept an offer of help from, an individual, group, state, or organization to settle their conflict or resolve their differences *without resorting to physical force*' (emphasis added).

Given the prevailing dynamic of international anarchy which, depending on one's view of global politics, makes a resort to violence possible, likely, or wise, mediation must rely on something other than the direct use of force in order to distinguish itself from other, more coercive, forms of political behavior.

Box 6.1 Gandhi as mediator

Mohandas K. Gandhi (1869–1948) is well-known as a spiritual and political leader who played a key role in India's independence movement, as well as in establishing the philosophy of non-violence. His marriage of non-violence to activism and dialogue in seeking to resolve various social, political, economic, and cultural conflicts also distinguishes him as a mediator – a role that he was undoubtedly first exposed to in his legal training and practice.

Mediators are (technically) impartial

The third defining aspect of mediation is impartiality. Impartiality in this context is defined by three features. The first is that the activities of a mediator must be driven by a desire to secure an outcome that is acceptable to both sides of the dispute. Second, and on a related note, this outcome is not tantamount to granting 'victory' to one side by tilting the formal outcome in its favor. Finally, as the term suggests, impartiality requires that the mediator possess a genuine and overriding interest in managing and even resolving the conflict – meaning that this interest must take precedence over any other (self-regarding) interest(s) attached to mediation, such as heightened prestige or securing strategic advantage.

Impartiality is important for more than its own sake; it is a central tenet of mediation, and particularly the successful mediation of intra-state conflicts. This is not because impartiality is or seems just or virtuous, but because it prompts and sustains the trust building that is central to effective mediation. Recall that one recurring theme in the definitions of mediation introduced above is the contribution of mediators to facilitating solutions to disputes that the parties themselves either cannot, or will not.

Such consensus-building seems particularly difficult in the long, difficult, and complex intra-state conflicts often referred to as 'new wars.' Whatever disputes or differences are significant enough to precipitate a resort to armed violence are likely to be deep-seated and difficult to overcome. Yet to the extent that mediation offers at least a possibility of doing so – whether in Nicaragua, Nagorny-Karabakh, or Northern Ireland – it is due to the fact that the outside party (or parties) are not bound by or beholden to the disputes or differences that prompted and sustained the conflict.

Mediation: a narrative history

Mediation in history

Mediation has long been a tool employed in attempts to manage or limit conflict in the international arena. Thucydides' famous *History of the Peloponnesian War* remains one of the core texts for consideration of international security and conflict, particularly from a theoretical perspective. It details, among other things, the degree to which the ancient Greek city-states resorted to mediation to avoid military conflict. Imperial Rome used mediation, particularly during the later phases of its empire as it faced challenges from the Visigoths, Vandals, and Moors. The combination of post-Reformation challenges to religious authority, the upwelling of humanism during the Renaissance and the fragmented political landscape of Western Europe in particular also led to an increased need for, and supply of, mediation.

This fragmentation was at the same time altered and institutionalized in the two parallel Treaties of Westphalia (1648). In paving the way for a self-help anarchical system arrayed around nation-states, the Treaties of Westphalia produced the conditions for perpetual conflict. In the absence of a strong and coherent body of international law to mitigate those conditions, it was mediation (along with other forms of diplomacy) that filled the void. Three great and linked conflagrations straddling each side of the dawn of the twentieth century (the Franco-Prussian War of 1870–1871, World War I, and World War II) presented many varied and sobering lessons for humanity in this regard. The successively heightened intensity and extensity of each of these major wars highlighted the need for working mechanisms for collective security and effective diplomacy, as the prematurely idealistic calls for peace such as those sounded at the landmark Hague Conferences of 1899 and 1907 and, later, the failure of the League of Nations reinforced.

Mediation during the Cold War

Given these developments, it is not surprising that the 60-plus years since the end of World War II have featured a rather dramatic increase in the demand for, and supply of, third-party conflict mediation. Consider, for instance, that in cases of international crisis alone (only one kind of international dispute), 84 percent (135 out of 161) of all offers and/or incidences of mediation since 1918 have occurred since 1945 (Brecher and Wilkenfeld, 2000). By another scholar's count, 255 of 310 inter- or intra-state conflicts occurring between 1945 and 1975 featured some form of official mediation (Princen, 1992).

Bipolarity and mediation

This demand for mediation has been sustained across the many equally dramatic changes in the nature and structure of international politics since 1945 (Crocker *et al.*, 2001). Among the most notable of these changes from the standpoint of mediation was the creation of the UN organization (whose Secretary-General was originally envisioned as a 'world moderator' by Franklin D. Roosevelt, among others). Furthermore, the bipolarity of the Cold War era provided a natural setting for mediation to flourish, particularly during several direct and high-stakes crises involving the superpowers and their allies and client states.

As the material and ideological struggle between the United States and USSR stabilized with the advent of *détente* in the mid-1960s, numerous conflicts of varying intensity and strategic significance (often instigated by each superpower's predilection for 'proxy wars') surfaced. These conflicts provided numerous opportunities for mediation during the Cold War. While some of these mediation efforts were made by the superpowers themselves (the United States in the Middle East after 1948; the USSR between India and Pakistan in the 1960s), others were led by regional or former colonial powers (Kenya in territorial disputes between Nigeria and Cameroon in the 1970s and 1980s; the United Kingdom in the Rhodesia–Zimbabwe dispute of the late 1970s).

International organization

Also pressed into service during the Cold War was the relatively new machinery of the UN, along with a sampling of RGOs (the UN in the Falklands/Malvinas conflict of 1981–1982; the Arab League in the various Yemeni conflicts of the 1970s and 1980s; the Organization of African Unity in the various conflicts over the Ogaden region between Ethiopia and Somalia; the OAS in the Nicaragua–United States disputes of the 1980s). Mediation was also frequently provided by so-called 'middle powers' (Canada in the Suez crisis of 1956; Algeria in the Iran hostage crisis of 1979–1981; Morocco in Libya's mass expulsion of Tunisians in 1985) as well as, in some instances, NSAs (the Society of Friends in the Angolan civil war; Pope John Paul II in the 1978–1979 Beagle Channel dispute).

Mediation after the Cold War

The changes in security and conflict since the end of the Cold War have been well-documented throughout this book. With respect to international mediation, the shift from the strategy and organization of 'proxy wars' to the various identity-based and de-rationalized conflicts lumped under the heading of 'new wars' has sustained, if not increased, the necessity of mediation – while simultaneously making effective mediation that much more difficult. Violent and bloody internecine conflicts in Haiti, Somalia, Bosnia, Rwanda, Kosovo, East Timor, Sudan, Liberia, Sierra Leone, and so forth have generated more interest both in the societies involved – as well as throughout the international community – in mediation as a means of fostering lasting negotiated settlements. Yet at the same time, the complex nature of the disputes involved, in concert with the primordial hatreds and resentments that often permeate these disputes, makes mediation daunting – a subject to which we will return in greater detail below.

Given the complexity of many post-Cold War conflicts, as well as the level and intensity of violence associated with them, the range of actors prepared to intervene as mediators is remarkable. Inter- as well as intra-state conflict mediation since the end of the Cold War has come from both expected (e.g., the United States in Bosnia and the Middle East; the UN in the Red Sea Islands dispute between Yemen and Eritrea) and unexpected (e.g., Tanzania in the Great Lakes conflicts; Djibouti in the Ethiopia–Eritrea War) sources. Newer sources of mediation, such as RGOs, NGOs, and private individuals have become especially prominent given changes not only in the nature of the conflicts themselves, but as a result of the proliferation and intrusion of such actors into the traditionally state-dominated arena of international security and law. In a contemporary light, then, conflict mediation tends to come from actors falling under one of three categories.

Individuals

Media treatments of mediation often seize upon and equate mediation with 'shuttle diplomacy.' In this way, reports of a single (usually high-ranking and prominent) individual, laboring against long odds toward the settlement of some intractable conflict with the sanction of his or her government, tend to predominate (think: nightly news reports of Condoleezza Rice's trips to the various capitals of the Middle East). While this variant on mediation remains prominent, in many cases mediation by individuals is carried out by persons without an official, government-sanctioned role, and thus do not represent his or her country. This type of mediation is one variant of so-called 'track two diplomacy' (efforts at fostering diplomatic agreement by informal intermediaries from non-governmental, humanitarian, or religious institutions, academia, peace institutes and think tanks, and so forth).

In some cases, these individuals may actually insert themselves into a conflict setting as a mediator against the wishes of their home government. In recent years, both former US president Jimmy Carter (in trips to Haiti, Cuba, and North Korea), as well as the prominent US civil rights advocate Jesse Jackson (see Box 6.2), have engaged in these kinds of unsolicited and unsanctioned mediation initiatives. Individual mediators may hold different beliefs, values, and attitudes than do emissaries of governments. These differences may further complicate the dispute by sending mixed signals to the protagonists about the interests, intentions, and domestic politics of the country from which the non-official mediator hails. Yet such differences may also grant non-official mediators flexibility and creativity in crafting workable solutions. With the exception of prominent individuals such as Carter and Jackson, individual mediation, like other forms of 'track two diplomacy,' is typically conducted away from the media spotlight, which may create a space for productive dialogue.

Box 6.2 Jesse Jackson and the Taliban

During the brief period between the 9/11 terrorist attacks and the initiation of Operation Enduring Freedom by a US-led coalition in Afghanistan in October 2001, another lower-profile stand-off occurred – over the possibility of veteran civil rights leader the Reverend Jesse Jackson serving as a private mediator between the US government and the Taliban regime then controlling approximately 90 percent of Afghanistan. The origin of the prospective mediation effort by Jackson in late September 2001 remains unclear. Jackson himself contended that he was contacted by Taliban representatives to serve as an intermediary to forestall what appeared to be a certain military assault by the United States. The Islamic fundamentalist regime insisted that 'friends' or associates of Jackson had contacted them about a meeting in Pakistan. Also unclear was the focus of the possible mediation effort. Jackson himself vacillated between a mission aimed at the release of several detained aid workers and a more expansive effort to avert military hostilities and persuade the Taliban leadership to turn Osama bin Laden over to the International Court of Justice (ICJ) (against the wishes of the Bush Administration).

What is decidedly clearer is the hostile reaction of the Bush Administration to the possibility of Jackson serving as a mediator to the looming conflict, seen at a minimum as an unwanted distraction, if not a direct challenge to the authority of the US government by a private citizen during wartime. When questioned about the possibility of Jackson becoming involved as a mediator, Deputy Secretary of State Richard Armitage tersely replied, 'I wouldn't, but of course it's not my decision,' while then-White House Press Secretary Michael McCurry called the potential mediation nothing more than a 'delay tactic by the Taliban.' Further, the fact that the offer/solicitation of Jackson's mediation skills came on the heels of a personal scandal, and after withering criticism of his position as a civil rights leader, triggered suspicion among some regarding Jackson's motives.

Jackson had served as a private mediator (also against the explicit wishes of the US government) on numerous previous occasions, persuading former Syrian leader Hafez al-Assad to release a US pilot shot down over Lebanon in the early 1980s, securing the release of hostages from Kuwait and Iraq during Operation Desert Shield/Storm in 1990–1991, and freeing three captured US soldiers from Yugoslav custody in Belgrade in 1999 during the war over Kosovo. On this occasion, however, Jackson's own diminished public profile and the complex and tumultuous nature of the looming conflict worked against mediation. Ultimately, after consulting with former president Bill Clinton, UN Secretary-General Kofi Annan, former civil rights leader and politician Andrew Young, and Secretary of State Colin Powell, Jackson announced publicly on 28 September that while committed to the need for negotiations led by religious leaders, he saw too little promise in the Taliban's position to consider mediation feasible. A little over a week later, on 7 October, Operation Enduring Freedom began.

Nation-states

The international system is currently comprised of over 190 member-states, each differing according to interests, regime type, capabilities and resources, and the like. The main common thread binding states together, however, is that each must cope to one degree or another with the realities imposed by an anarchical international environment. As has been discussed above, this anarchy imposes a set of conditions on international life that generates conflict, and by extension, opportunities for mediation. Not surprisingly, then, states continue to benefit from, and remain a key source of, conflict mediation.

The chief determinant of whether a state will engage in mediation activities is not the capabilities or relative power assets of the potential mediator, but rather the degree to which a particular conflict is understood to affect that actor. Indeed, mediation by states tends to occur most often in conflicts that either directly or indirectly impinge upon the interests of the third party (or parties), or in conflicts that occur in geographical proximity to a third party (or parties). In this way, as we have seen, mediation can come as easily from Morocco or Kenya as from the United States or Russia.

When a state decides to attempt mediation, it usually does so because its decision-makers perceive the conflict as presenting a genuine threat to regional or international peace and stability, one with direct implications and ramifications for the mediating state. As with other efforts at conflict management by outside parties, mediation tends to be dictated by some measure of self-interest – though in rare cases mediation may be provided by states that place a premium on international mediation, regardless of whether they are directly affected by the conflict (see Box 6.3).

Box 6.3 The Oslo Accords

As outlined by Jan Egeland (the country's Secretary of State at the time), Norway structured its approach to the mediation of the Middle East conflict in the early and mid-1990s around a 'back channel' approach – taking great pains to facilitate negotiations between Israel and the Palestine Liberation Organization (PLO) (which ultimately led to the signing of a 'Declaration of Principles on Interim Self-Government Arrangements,' also known as the Oslo Accords) without publicity. Norway's decision to mediate was largely dictated by the stalemate that had set in; according to Egeland, the Norwegian government was optimistic about its prospects for successful mediation relative to the United States as a result of three main factors:

1   Norway's relatively small foreign policy bureaucracy, which allowed for creativity in facilitation, quick implementation of decisions, and the ability to limit access to information about the process to the media and the public.
2   The narrower scope and range of commitments and interests that defined Norway's foreign policy agenda, which made that agenda coherent and, accordingly, thrust Middle East mediation to the forefront of that agenda.
3   Norway's position in the international system was decidedly independent; it was (and remains) outside the EU, a somewhat ambivalent NATO member, and home to numerous peace institutes.

Egeland also identified several lessons learned from Norway's mediation of the Middle East conflict. These include:

1   the importance of maintaining secrecy;
2   the need to directly confront actors whose expressed intentions contradict their actions at the peace table;
3   the reality that intra-party differences intensify when agreements take shape;
4   asymmetries in power between the parties may 'tilt' an agreement in one direction or another against the best efforts of the mediator (who may be blamed);
5   the essentiality of treating the parties equally;
6   the inconsistencies between international and domestic public opinion with respect to successfully mediated agreements – regardless of their significance or how they are received on the world stage, compromises usually reduce the standing of leaders with their domestic constituencies.

From 'Norway's Back-channel Success Story,' *Negotiation Newsletter*, Spring/Summer 1995: 1–11.

The level of commitment to mediation exhibited by a state tends to increase the prospects for successful mediation. Despite the encroachments of various NSAs and international organizations, states remain the single most cohesive and authoritative actor in international relations. Those that choose to mediate a conflict can often bring to bear a measure of resources, clout, and attention that other types of actors cannot. In addition to having more tangible, material resources at their disposal, states are often better positioned to mobilize their resources in service of mediation efforts, and to act swiftly and decisively.

NSAs

The increased complexity and variation defining contemporary conflict demonstrates that neither individual mediators nor states alone can provide conflict mediation whenever and wherever it is needed. Beyond the question of sheer resources, the intense, protracted, and seemingly intractable nature of many intra-state conflicts requires a level of sustained, flexible, and sophisticated mediation that may not be forthcoming from resource-constrained individuals, or from bureaucratically complex and self-interested states.

A variety of IGOs, RGOs, and NGOs have to some extent filled this void. Many NSAs serving as mediators have some degree of familiarity with the formal practices of conflict resolution, and attempt to facilitate the mediation of conflicts accordingly (sometimes in conjunction with states or officially sanctioned individuals). The tilt toward NSAs as sources of mediation includes institutions and organizations whose main focus lies in transformative efforts aimed at peacebuilding, as well as those prompted by a more narrow interest in problem-solving so as to contain and stabilize conflicts.

Regardless of its intent, mediation by NSAs since the end of the Cold War has been undertaken by a variety of NGOs, whether of a religious (the Quakers; the Mennonite Church; the Plowshares Institute; the Community of Sant'Egidio; the International Network of Engaged Buddhists); humanitarian (the International Committee of the Red Cross; the Center for Humanitarian Mediation; Oxfam) bent; peace centers and thinktanks (the Carter Center; the Centre for Humanitarian Dialogue); RGOs (ECOWAS; OSCE; AU) or IGOs (most notably, the UN (see Box 6.4)).

Box 6.4 UN mediation

Mediation undertaken by the UN organization generally involves the political skills and resources of the UN Secretary-General, as well as his or her representatives. In diplomatic parlance, UN mediation is exercised through what is referred to as the 'good offices' of the Secretary-General. UN mediation under the good offices of the Secretary-General unfolds in a similar fashion to other third-party mediation efforts; the parties to the conflict seek, and are free to accept or reject, the assistance of the UN in managing or resolving the conflict at hand. In accordance with the Charter, UN mediation can take place in any of the following contexts: prior to a conflict (preventative diplomacy); during a conflict (peacemaking); after a conflict (to implement agreements); or in conjunction with other peacebuilding efforts.

Unlike most other mediation efforts, UN mediation brings with it a specifically defined mandate. Among other things, this mandate provides that the UN Secretary-General and/or his or her envoys can and must meet and listen to all parties to the conflict; consult all relevant parties for ideas about how to effectively resolve the conflict; and propose ideas and solutions to facilitate an effective resolution. When parties seek out UN mediation, they are also required to accept this mandate – meaning that they agree to cooperate with the UN mediator, and that they agree that the mediator's efforts are made in good faith. Despite this considerable step, as in other cases, settlements produced through UN mediation are not binding (unless the UNSC passes resolutions to enforce them). The implementation, and ultimate success, of the mediation relies as in all cases on the commitment of the parties themselves to make the agreement 'stick.'

(Adapted from Honeyman and Yawanarajah, 2003)

How mediation works

The mediation process

Mediation is a process in which a third party assists in resolving a dispute between two or more other parties who agree to subject themselves to that mediation. The mediator's tasks are simple in conceptual terms, and at the same time extremely difficult in practice. Among other things, mediators facilitate communication between parties to a conflict or dispute, assist (to varying degrees) the parties in focusing on the major issues at the heart of the dispute, and generate or help generate options that meet the interests or needs of all relevant parties in an effort to resolve the conflict. This requires mediators to take a significant role in defining (or redefining) the relationship, agenda, and issues at the heart of the dispute, to promote communication and search for common ground between the protagonists, and to facilitate fair, equitable, and effective solutions that will be accepted by the parties themselves (Honeyman and Yawanarajah, 2003).

Though the strategies, motives, approaches, and even types of mediators vary widely, in practice most attempts at mediating intra-state conflicts unfold in a similar fashion. Indeed, several major studies of conflict mediation of all types have focused on describing the steps defining that process and cataloging the roles undertaken by mediators throughout it, to great effect (Moore, 2003; Zartman and Touval, 1985). This process is outlined in Figure 6.1.

Mediation strategies

What strategies do mediators employ in attempting to turn oftentimes intractable conflicts into manageable ones? Mediators in inter-state conflicts generally follow one of three unique (though not mutually exclusive, and sometimes overlapping) strategies (Bercovitch, 2004).

Communication-facilitation strategies

Communication-facilitation strategies are characteristic of low-level mediation, meaning that the mediator acts in a fairly passive role. Such mediation strategies are solely devoted to providing information to, and facilitating cooperation among, the parties. While rather limited, mediation strategies of this type do fulfill an important function. Given the complex, recurrent, and intractable nature of many contemporary conflicts, parties typically lack direct channels of communication, possess different conceptions of what the issues at stake are, and do not have the opportunity or willingness to explore mutually advantageous outcomes of their own volition. A mediator facilitating dialogue and communication under such circumstances, even if this translates into simply transmitting information between parties, is at a minimum providing a prerequisite for effective conflict management. This was in fact a key component of Norway's mediation leading up to the Oslo Accords (discussed in Box 6.3).

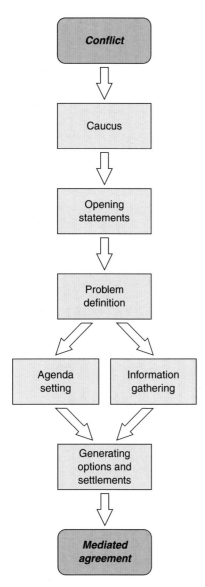

Caucus: mediator holds private and confidential sessions in advance with both parties to brainstorm, expose underlying tensions, and identify areas of common ground.

Opening statements: mediator outlines the role of participants, defines protocol, establishes timeframe, and recaps understanding of the pressing issues. This stage allows the mediator to establish impartiality and maximize information exchange using active listening, paraphrasing and restatement, probing, or clarifying questions. Parties may also issue opening statements, typically concerning procedural rather than substantive issues.

Problem definition: mediator grants each side the opportunity to publicly identify major areas of concern, providing additional information to the mediator as to each party's views. The mediator may decide on the order of discussion, as well as whether conflicts are interest- or value-based (and ways of reframing issues, if the latter).

Agenda setting: mediator leads parties in developing an agenda, either in a sequential, ad hoc, alternating, or simultaneous ('packaged') fashion. Mediator expertise, along with sensitivity to cultural and social dynamics, should dictate the formation of the agenda.

Information gathering: mediator uses open-ended questioning, summarization, and other facilitative techniques to simultaneously gather information about the parties' interests (hidden and explicit) and to build rapport. The mediator encourages each side to acknowledge the other's interests, incorporating both parties' interests into a joint problem statement.

Generating options and settlements: methods for developing acceptable options vary, usually involving mediator-led brainstorming. Parties are led to generate a range of options, addressing either specific issues or general principles. Parties may ratify the status quo, develop objective standards, consider settlement agreements from other similar disputes, or identify linked issues. Mediators must also introduce timetables and implementation considerations.

Settlements typically involve positional and interest-based bargaining, and may be reached by drafting and redrafting a single settlement proposal, agreeing on a decision-making procedure for the future, bringing in outside consultants, or through other means. Stronger agreements are substantive, comprehensive, permanent, detailed, non-conditional, and binding; procedural, partial, provisional, abstract, contingent, or non-binding settlements tend to be weaker.

Figure 6.1 The mediation process.

Procedural strategies

Procedural strategies involve efforts by the mediator to exert control and influence over matters of process such as agenda formulation, timetables, media access, and the overall tenor of the meetings themselves. This requires power, as well as creativity in introducing ways to remove obstacles and circumvent constraints to progress. President Carter's actions at Camp David, as highlighted in the opening vignette of this chapter, serve as an excellent example of a procedural strategy employed by a mediator. Such strategies are especially important when protagonists have had little or no opportunity to interact in any setting other than the battlefield, as was true of Israel and Egypt prior to Camp David. The application of a procedural strategy by a multinational delegation played a profound part in jumpstarting the Northern Ireland peace process in the late 1990s (see Box 6.5).

Box 6.5 Flexible mediation: George Mitchell and Northern Ireland, 1997–1998

Despite the best efforts of negotiators during the 1980s, and again in the early 1990s, the longstanding conflict between (Catholic) nationalists/republicans and (Protestant) unionists over the status of Northern Ireland, renewed in intensity since the onset of 'the Troubles' in the late 1960s, was clearly at an impasse by the mid-1990s. Increased attention from the United Kingdom (and to a lesser extent the United States) by the 1980s – culminating in the 1985 Anglo-Irish Agreement – as well as shifting venues for follow-up negotiations dealing with implementation to include Belfast, Dublin, and London, had failed to alter this dynamic. Most of the various republican and unionist paramilitaries remained outside the process, a factor that even the internal republican dialogue between SDLP leader John Hume and Sinn Fein's Gerry Adams could not alter.

Such was the environment that former US Senator George Mitchell entered as a mediator, charged with finding a way to disarm the paramilitaries as a step toward integrating them into a broader peace process. The June 1997 election of a Labour government in the United Kingdom, followed by a new IRA cease-fire, quickly rendered this approach moot. Mitchell pragmatically tabled calls for disarmament, instead requiring (and getting) all parties to agree to the principles of non-violence he outlined. Mitchell was suddenly thrust into a communicative-facilitative position, as the chair of the first truly inclusive talks over Northern Ireland; for the first time, Sinn Fein and the mainstream Unionist parties (the Ulster Democratic Party and the Progressive Unionist Party) were full and joint participants.

The inclusion of these political actors, with links to the major paramilitaries, increased the chances that any potential settlement could be more comprehensive and potentially bring an end to sectarian violence in Northern Ireland. At the same time, this inclusiveness translated into a wider array of viewpoints and attitudes gaining expression, making compromise difficult. By the fall of 1997, Mitchell faced an interminably slow process defined by antagonism and suspicion. It was at this stage that he made a shrewd and ultimately effective decision to shift from a communicative-facilitative strategy to a procedural one, electing to disaggregate agenda items by party and subject.

The agenda was separated into three strands; strand one, concerning power-sharing structures within Northern Ireland, involved the Northern Irish political parties and the United Kingdom; strand two, concerning the relationship between the two parts of Ireland, also brought in the Irish Republic; strand three, focusing on a new British–Irish treaty, involved only the Irish and British governments, with other parties as observers. The three strands ran concurrently, each with an independent chair; regular progress reports to full plenary sessions were issued. With progress again ground to a halt, in part by the emergence of new paramilitary splinter groups opposed to the cease-fire and negotiations, Mitchell's ability to employ different mediation strategies was again put to the test in early 1998. It was at this stage of the proceedings that Mitchell chose to shift toward a directive strategy. Mitchell's embrace of a directive strategy culminated in the establishment of a final deadline of 9 April. Presented as an ultimatum, the feverish intensity that followed this deadline – and Mitchell's adept use of multiple mediation strategies at the appropriate junctures of the process – secured the Good Friday Agreement.

(Adapted from Bloomfield, 1998)

Directive strategies

Directive strategies constitute the most robust and intense form of mediation, and typically take over when a mediator perceives a settlement to be within reach. A mediator who employs a directive strategy attempts to shape the content and nature of that settlement, through utilizing 'carrots' (material incentives and promises of support) and 'sticks' (threats of sanctions or diplomatic rebuke) in an effort to secure each party's commitment to the emergent settlement. Directive strategies are essential to the successful mediation of intractable conflicts, allowing the mediator to break the cycle of violence and change the mindset and values of the parties through inducement and/or coercion. A not insignificant aspect of the Camp David Accord (particularly given its continued impact on the politics of the Middle East) was President Carter's switch to a directive strategy in the form of offering billions of dollars in economic and military aid on an annual basis in return for Israeli and Egyptian agreement.

Motives of mediators

With regard to contemporary conflict, the motives of mediators vary in conjunction with the variation in the sources of mediation itself.

Nation-states

States use mediation as a foreign policy instrument, with the national interest residing front-and-center in their decisions to mediate a conflict; humanitarian impulses, to the extent they play a factor in such decisions, are typically secondary (see Box 6.6). These interests differ, of course, with respect to the attributes and capabilities of the state in question (Zartman, 1995; Touval, 1992, 1982). Great powers are drawn to mediation, given the wider range and extent of their interests and commitments, as well as the proportionately greater risks they face from a conflict that threatens to destabilize a region or the international system in its entirety. Mediation also offers major powers the ability to consolidate or extend their influence and prestige; the reality that the United States has been the most frequent and active mediator since 1945 bears this assertion out (Touval, 1992). On the other hand, some scholars view the involvement of one or more major powers as mediators as an indicator that the mediation effort will likely prove unsuccessful, with the interests of major powers inevitably overwhelming any sincere desire to manage the conflict (Bercovitch, 2004).

Box 6.6 Russia and Nagorny-Karabakh

Nagorny-Karabakh is a region of approximately 1,700 square miles, located inside the former Soviet republic of Azerbaijan (Betts, 1999). Although the region shares no official common border with Armenia, its population as currently constituted is approximately 75 percent ethnic Armenian. Both Armenia and Azerbaijan have long sought control of Nagorny-Karabakh, a joust only intensified in 1921 when Josef Stalin established Nagorny-Karabakh as an autonomous *oblast* in Azerbaijan. Over Armenian protest, that arrangement remained the status quo until the disintegration of the USSR in 1991, which brought simultaneous declarations of independence from Azerbaijan,

Armenia, and Nagorny-Karabakh itself – and the outbreak of a conflict culminating in over 30,000 dead and one million displaced (International Crisis Group, 2004).

With the dispute internationalized after the demise of the USSR, the involvement of external actors in the conflict was possible. Perhaps most notable among the attempts at mediation were those by the Russian Federation. Beginning with the formation of the 'Minsk Group' by the OSCE in 1992 (a group which also included Armenia, Azerbaijan, the United States, France, Italy, Turkey, Germany, Czechoslovakia, Sweden, and a representative of Nagorny-Karabakh), and continuing through the '3+1 initiative' (also involving Turkey and the United States), Russia has been directly involved in every public and private stage of multiparty mediation since, including arranging a cease-fire (in conjunction with the OSCE) in May 1994.

Russia's intensive involvement as a mediator in Nagorny-Karabakh was borne of interests that have been magnified in importance in recent years. Chief among these are: (a) the need to secure a favorable settlement so as to set a precedent for other potential 'nationalities' questions that may arise in the Caucasus and the former Soviet republics; (b) the desire for stability in the region given the geostrategic implications associated with the vast energy reserves in the Caspian basin and ongoing efforts to extract those resources; and (c) the perceived need to counter the influence of Turkey and Iran while also stemming the rising tide of Islamic fundamentalism in the region. Yet while these significant and varied interests explain Russia's commitment to mediating the dispute, they also convey the degree to which the mere conjoining of interests and power do not translate into effective mediation, as the issues at the heart of the conflict remain alive and well over a decade after the cease-fire.

Medium-sized or smaller powers mediate conflicts more out of necessity than interest; they may fear that a proximate conflict might spill over into their territory, draw outside intervention from a major power, foment instability on the domestic front, or undermine international norms and laws that benefit smaller powers. That said, like major powers, medium and small powers are also propelled to mediation out of a desire to enhance their prestige and interests. Libya's recent efforts to mediate ongoing conflicts in the Democratic Republic of the Congo (in 1998–1999), the Eritrea–Ethiopia war (1998–2000), and in the Darfur conflict (since 2003) are undoubtedly prompted by a mix of these motives.

With respect to mediation by states, common threads do exist regardless of a state's absolute or relative power. Nearly all states contemplating or carrying out mediation are prompted by the desire to increase regional (and possibly global) stability, and the direct material benefits that this conveys on the mediating state itself. States also rely on mediation to increase their own (and deny their rivals) influence over a particular conflict and its settlement, as well as to enhance their prestige on the world stage. In this sense it is important to remember that the vast majority of mediating states are status quo-supporting actors. Politically, legally, and theoretically, states are the central actors in the contemporary international system, and most states capable of, and interested in, serving as mediators are more likely to favor sustaining the status quo (and the distribution of power underlying it) to some radical transformation of it.

IGOs and RGOs

By virtue of their mandate and constitution, mediation by IGOs and RGOs typically resembles mediation by states. This is not altogether surprising, since they are organizations whose members are states, and as such they are beholden to represent (and attempt to reconcile) the various policies and interests of their member governments. As a result, the motives for mediation efforts led by the UN, the EU, or OAS (on a regional basis) have sometimes been called into question, with accusations that these organizations are captive to the foreign policy agendas or domestic political concerns of their most powerful and influential members.

One distinctive motive underlying both IGO and RGO mediation is the desire of these types of organizations to provide a counterweight to the great powers, and to establish and assert an independent role on global security matters (Zartman and Touval, 2007). EU mediation in the Balkans, the OSCE mission to Moldova, ASEAN mediation in Cambodia, and Intergovernmental Agency on Development (IGAD) efforts in the Sudanese civil war and the conflict in Darfur are all compelling examples in this regard.

Individuals

Most (if not all) mediation efforts feature a mix of self and other-regarding interests. Yet mediation by individuals, particularly those disconnected from and not representing any particular state or governing entity, may be the most other-regarding and humanitarian of all. Those who exhibit a willingness to devote their time, effort, resources, and in some cases lives to mediating difficult and dangerous intra-state conflicts clearly fit the bill as 'peacemakers,' and should be celebrated as such. Yet the extent to which playing the role of mediator may serve to gratify an individual's ego, to promote his or her historical legacy, to enhance the profile of (and increase contributions to) a thinktank or peace center, and so forth, are not inconsequential considerations.

NGOs

As was the case with individual mediators, efforts by NGOs may be more directly linked to the objectives of conflict resolution and peacebuilding, particularly those that are founded with the sole purpose of providing mediation and/or promoting non-violence. Yet while the motives of organizations founded out of religious or secular commitment to peace and humanitarianism are perhaps less self-regarding than other actors, these kinds of organizations are also not without pragmatic concerns and considerations. These concerns vary, but can include extending their own influence (particularly for religious organizations), maintaining or expanding organizational presence or solidarity, maintaining their reputation as effective peacemakers, and so forth. Still, in most cases the motives of such organizations are correspondingly more distant from the machinations of power politics. As a result of the neutrality and impartiality of most NGOs, they tend to possess additional legitimacy as mediators (see Box 6.7).

Box 6.7 Quaker mediation in Sri Lanka

Quaker mediator Joseph Elder's many interviews regarding his mediation activities in the Sri Lankan civil war reveal some of the unique features of the Quaker approach to international mediation. As a relatively small Protestant sect, whose values include pacifism and a tradition of peacemaking, the Quakers (officially, the Society of Friends) are noted for their efforts at non-violent conflict resolution. Due to their religious convictions and chosen strategy of 'practical powerlessness,' Quaker mediators are renowned for maintaining both a strict neutrality and a low profile.

Elder was sent by the London office of the Society of Friends, along with a colleague, to Sri Lanka in 1984, ostensibly to find out whether mediation might be a possibility. Around this time, the (Buddhist) Sinhalese majority controlling the government in Colombo had increased its repression of the (Hindu) Tamil minority concentrated in the north, roughly contemporaneously with calls for a separate Tamil state and the formation of various Tamil militia (including the infamous Liberation Tigers of Tamil Eelam (LTTE, or 'Tamil Tigers').

Elder determined that the Quakers could serve an essential function as a conduit for dialogue between the Sinhalese and Tamil factions. While Colombo steadfastly refused in public to negotiate with the Tamils (instead labeling them 'terrorists'), officials privately expressed to Elder that dialogue was imperative given the low likelihood that a military campaign could succeed in the rural hinterlands controlled by the Tamils. The Quaker offer to mediate came with two conditions: first, that neither party would reveal the involvement of the Quakers; and second, that if at any point either side felt Quaker involvement was no longer helpful, they inform the mediators, who would withdraw.

These conditions apparently surprised the parties, and were keys to the mediation effort's success. By rejecting any public recognition of their work, Quaker mediators reinforced the message that they had no agenda beyond ending violence and promoting reconciliation. At the same time, giving the disputants a 'veto' power over Quaker mediation reinforced the perception of the parties to the dispute that they were in control of the mediation process, while reinforcing what Elder refers to as the 'power of powerlessness.' In his view, Quaker intervention was acceptable in this case precisely because the mediators elected to forego the power to leverage disputants or pursue their own agenda, instead focusing on setting enforceable standards and influencing the tone of the dialogue.

(Excerpted and adapted from Thomas Princen. 1994. 'Joseph Elder: Quiet Peacemaking in a Civil War,' in Deborah Kolb (ed.). *When Talk Works*. San Francisco, CA: Jossey-Bass, pp. 428–445)

The essence of ripeness

A crucial consideration in the assessment of how mediation works, as well as a determinant of its effectiveness, is whether or not a conflict is 'ripe' for mediation to occur. Among scholars of mediation, I. William Zartman has made the most significant contribution in establishing the link between the conditions of a conflict, the timing of mediation, and the prospects for that mediation to succeed through the concept of 'ripeness.' The basis of that concept, and its relationship to the effective third-party mediation of contemporary conflict, lies in understanding that the success of a mediated settlement depends on the readiness of the parties themselves for said mediation to occur. A ripe conflict is one in which satisfactory results for both parties are unattainable, or more accurately, when attaining them cannot be done without incurring unacceptable risks and costs. At that moment of ripeness, the parties seek a way out – a precursor to effective mediation, which successful mediators can and must exploit.

There are three main elements of ripeness: a mutually hurting stalemate; an impending, recently experienced, or recently avoided catastrophe; and an alternative way out (Zartman, 2000). Mediation is most likely to occur when a conflict has gone on for some time, the efforts of the individuals or actors involved have reached an impasse, neither actor is prepared to countenance further costs or escalation of the dispute, and both parties welcome some form of mediation and are ready to engage in direct or indirect dialogue.

Mutually hurting stalemate

The notion of the mutually hurting stalemate is the single greatest factor in determining the ripeness of a conflict for mediation. This concept is well-established among diplomats; Kissinger once mused that 'stalemate is the most propitious condition for settlement.' The metaphor of a plateau is an instructive one for understanding the dynamics of a mutually hurting stalemate, and how it can foster effective conflict mediation. Reaching a mutually hurting stalemate requires reaching a point in which neither side perceives it can win; the conflict appears to both sides as if it will stretch out indefinitely into the future, with no possibility for escape and no hope of victory (the aforementioned plateau). Accordingly, the parties come to believe that continuation of the conflict is, at a minimum, harmful to its interests, if not catastrophic.

The perception of the parties to the conflict is a key factor here, and these perceptions can be skillfully manipulated by a mediator to further the negotiation process or heighten recognition of the negative implications and ramifications associated with the plateau that stretches before them. It is important to recognize that mutually hurting stalemates cannot be solely manufactured by mediators or any other outside parties; if the parties do not recognize that they are at an impasse, a mutually hurting stalemate has not occurred (though it still may).

Ripeness as a necessary condition

Ripeness is the key to many successful cases of negotiated settlements in post-Cold War conflicts; for instance, ripeness was a key determinant in the success of the Oslo Accords (Pruitt, 1997). At the same time, empirical studies of other attempts at mediating post-Cold War conflicts such as the civil wars in Liberia and Sierra Leone saw little relationship between the success or failure of mediation and various proxy measures of ripeness (Schrodt *et al.*, 2003). A third possibility are cases where ripeness was seemingly at hand, but not effectively seized in order to bring about a successful mediated agreement; examples here include Nagorny-Karabakh in 1994 and Cyprus in 2002 (Zartman, 2003).

One area of particular emphasis in terms of gaining a better understanding of ripeness is the location of cues indicative of its emergence. Subjective expressions of suffering, stalemate, and the inability or unwillingness to bear the costs and risks of continuing or escalating the conflict by authoritative spokespersons for one or both parties to the conflict provide strong signs of ripeness. Whether objective standards can be derived from empirical study of casualties, material costs, and other potential markers of ripeness is also a subject for further consideration.

Approaches to international mediation

Shuttle mediation

The idea of shuttle diplomacy is most closely associated with the efforts of Henry Kissinger to broker a Middle East peace accord after the 1973 Yom Kippur War. Kissinger employed a decidedly problem-solving, interest-based approach to mediation, advocating a blueprint to stabilization dubbed the 'American plan' that emphasized a cease-fire, tabled larger and potentially intractable issues, and was chiefly motivated by the objective of freezing the Soviets out of the process. Kissinger promoted, re-tooled, and promoted again this plan for months, shuttling from the various capitals of the Middle East via airplane and keeping in constant communication with the White House using all available means.

Shuttle diplomacy involving high-ranking, high-powered diplomatic emissaries functioning as mediators continues in much the same vein today. While significant improvements in information and communication technologies, as well as air transportation, make at least some aspects of shuttle mediation easier than in Kissinger's day, the act of mediation itself remains as challenging as ever. A particularly challenging aspect of mediating a conflict through such means is discerning whether the conflict is at a stage where the commitment of the significant material resources attendant in shuttle diplomacy is worthwhile. The most useful application of mediation through shuttle diplomacy comes in the early stages of a conflict, when direct communication between the parties is likely to be non-existent, or even counterproductive given the tenuousness of the situation.

Generating attention

Finding a third party to carry information between the main parties at an early juncture of a conflict can help defuse or de-escalate the situation by providing a reliable means of communication that would otherwise not exist. That intermediary can relay questions and answers between the parties, or even suggest ideas for de-escalating the conflict that the parties themselves could not (at least publicly) without compromising their position. The necessary balance to strike in such mediation efforts lies in cultivating enough publicity and outside attention to compel the parties to communicate with one another (indirectly, through the mediator) without jeopardizing the dynamic of the mediated relationship (by encouraging one or both parties to seek out favorable media exposure, employ brinkmanship, publicly grandstand, or engage in some other form of counterproductive behavior). Such a balance is especially difficult to strike since shuttle mediation is often employed by high-profile individuals such as Kissinger, Carter, Clinton, Rice, Blair, and the like. Though these individuals bring with them a degree of clout associated with officialdom, they are also typically subject to extensive media coverage and intensive political scrutiny.

Examples of shuttle mediation

Examples of shuttle mediation, especially those involving high-ranking and prominent officials representing governments, are numerous and varied. President Carter's mediation at Camp David traced its origin to his earlier shuttling between Tel Aviv and Cairo. His effort at Camp David itself amounted to shuttling of a sort, albeit between Begin and Sadat's cabins rather than capitals. The sudden outbreak of hostilities between Margaret Thatcher's Britain and Argentina during the Falklands/Malvinas conflict in the spring of 1982 provide yet another example, as then-US Secretary of State Alexander Haig attempted shuttle mediation (ultimately unsuccessfully) on behalf of the Reagan Administration between London and Buenos Aires.

Such efforts have continued apace since the end of the Cold War, with mixed results. The efforts of Richard Holbrooke (the Clinton Administration's special envoy to the Balkans during the 1990s) in shuttling between and among the various factions emerging from the former Yugoslavia were pivotal in generating the Dayton Accord, as well as the eventual cessation of the NATO campaign over Kosovo. Numerous attempts at shuttle mediation of the Israeli–Palestinian conflict since Oslo have been carried out by special envoys (Dennis Ross, Saudi Prince Bandar bin Sultan), US Secretaries of State (Colin Powell, Condoleezza Rice), and going forward by the special representative to the 'Quartet' (the United States, the UN, Russia, and the EU), former British Prime Minister Tony Blair. The persistent tension between India and Pakistan has elicited shuttle mediation from Blair, former US Deputy Secretary of State Richard Armitage and former US Defense Secretary Donald Rumsfeld, among others.

Shuttle mediation can be carried out by lower-profile representatives from humanitarian NGOs, religious leaders, scholars, or even business leaders. One prominent example was the effort by a sizeable number of Quakers in carrying messages between the LTTE and hard-line politicians among the Sinhalese majority in the Sri Lankan civil war. Whatever the Quaker missionaries lacked in political power or official authority, they made up for with a reputation for fairness; gaining the trust of each party led to the opening of indirect channels of communication which official mediation (from India, and later Norway) failed to do.

This outcome stands in contrast to the efforts by Norwegian envoys Vidar Helgesen and Erik Solheim. Though, like the Quakers, the Norwegian mediators were adept at controlling press intrusion, and steadfastly avoided directive strategies (preferring instead a facilitative role), they experienced little more than frustration in their meetings with Tamil groups as well as the Sri Lankan government (Martin, 2006: 112). The main difference was the reserve of trust that the Quakers possessed, and the Norwegians, despite their best efforts, did not.

Muscular mediation

The aforementioned structural constraints imposed by anarchy make power as important to effective mediation as to any other form of international behavior. If impartiality is the single most important prerequisite for effective conflict mediation, a mediator's influence – measured in part by the power the mediator can bring to bear on the proceedings – is a close second. While power, and the ability convert that power into influence, may be less important for communicative-facilitative strategies, when mediation may still be in the good offices stage, it is vital to procedural and directive strategies. These types of mediation, when done effectively, have been referred to as 'muscular mediation' (McIntosh, 1998).

Power as a backdrop

The exercise of power by mediators is increasingly seen in a positive light as the dynamics of many post-Cold War conflicts are better understood. Given the complex nature of many of these conflicts, the need to cajole actors into agreements, to 'deliver' recalcitrant parties, and in some cases to engineer ripeness in order to effectively manage said conflicts through the effective marshalling and application of power has become evident. The sources of power that underwrite muscular mediation are many and varied. Unlike the practice of coercive diplomacy, muscular mediation does not rely explicitly or primarily on threats of offensive military action backed by tangible power assets. Instead, the sources of a mediator's power are more nuanced. They may derive from a mediator's successful track record, from the lack of any other acceptable or willing mediator (each of which played a part in Algeria's successful mediation of the Iran hostage crisis), from the level of the mediator's commitment, the timing and context of the mediation, the merits and appeal of the mediator's proposals, and a myriad of other factors.

Another critical factor in the ability of a mediator to exercise power is the synergy between the mediator's efforts and those of other interested observers or third parties (in cases of multiparty mediation). When the positions and objectives of the mediators are in line with those of other important external parties, mediators are well-positioned to use muscular approaches. The successful use of muscular tactics by the United States in the Angola/Namibia negotiations in 1988 provide a good example; support for the US position from the USSR, the United Kingdom, Portugal, and the Front Line States helped the United States increase pressure on the warring factions.

One can think of numerous scenarios where the involvement of a powerful actor as a mediator lends something to the mediation effort that would otherwise be lacking. Such a dynamic was certainly on display in the Camp David example presented at the outset of this chapter. The direct involvement of one of the world's two military and economic superpowers certainly impressed upon both the Israeli and Egyptian delegations the momentousness of the occasion, and the importance the United States attached to striking an agreement. Furthermore, there were occasions during the talks – such as when Sadat's frustration with Begin's perceived intransigence led him to declare the talks finished – that the power assets of the mediator was brought to bear directly on the principals. In that specific instance, President Carter bluntly informed Sadat that: 'Our friendship is over. You promised me that you would stay at Camp David as long as I was willing to negotiate. ... I consider this a serious blow ... to the relationship between Egypt and the United States' (PBS.com).

At the same time, no direct or indirect threat was ever levied by the United States against Egypt (or Israel, for that matter), no matter the state of the talks, and both principals perceived US power as compelling rather than threatening. What this example and other cases of muscular mediation demonstrate is that while power in general, and a mediator's power in particular, can (and often does) provide an important backdrop to the mediation process, it cannot be its sole driving engine.

Multiparty mediation

The promise of third-party mediation, as well as the criteria that define a third party, have remained constant in the face of increasingly widespread changes in the sources and types of conflict mediation and the activities of mediators. One of the most significant of these changes has been the emergence and flourishing of multi-party mediation.

Sequential multiparty mediation

Multiparty mediation may occur sequentially over the duration of a conflict, as was more or less the case in the efforts by a wide range of mediators in the war in Bosnia-Herzegovina. The successive efforts of the UN, the EC (later the EU), the United States, and (in a private capacity) former President Carter to mediate the conflict in Bosnia-Herzegovina during the period 1992–1995 provide an excellent illustration of these kinds of multi-layered mediation efforts. These efforts were ultimately coordinated to some degree through the creation of the multi-state Contact Group in April 1994.

Simultaneous multiparty mediation

Multiparty mediation may also involve simultaneous mediation efforts by a variety of uncoordinated actors, as happened with the outbreak of the civil war in the former Zaire (now the Democratic Republic of the Congo) in 1996–1997. Overlapping diplomatic interventions and mediation overtures from the governments of Kenya, South Africa, and Canada, as well as the UN and the then-Organization for African Unity (OAU) (now the AU) further complicated an already complex mosaic, by simultaneously introducing into a fractured society a variety of inchoate objectives, interests, and priorities associated with the various third parties.

Advantages and drawbacks

Whether sequential or simultaneous, multiparty mediation offers both peril and promise. On the positive side of the ledger, the presence of multiple and alternative channels for mediation may provide the impetus for the resumption of stalled talks or the cultivation of further support for previously negotiated settlements. On the other hand, the cluttered mediation landscape may make the efforts of each mediator more difficult, by adding layers of complexity to the process and by offering 'opt-out' possibilities to parties that may solicit the most sympathetic mediator or pit mediators (or their proposals) against one another.

When multiparty mediation occurs, the life cycle of the conflict often dictates both the type and source of mediation. Non-official parties (such as individual mediators or NGOs) have typically been the main, if not only, third parties offering mediation in the early stages of many post-Cold War conflicts. Only later, when said conflicts have escalated and intensified, have IGOs, RGOs, and concerned and influential states committed themselves to mediation (and/or other forms of conflict management). The waning, or even cessation, of the conflict typically sees state-based mediators bow out, though international and regional organizations and especially NGOs have served important mediatory roles in implementing agreements and overseeing reconstruction and civil society building efforts.

Contemporary issues and debates

Impartiality

The assumption advanced at the outset of this chapter that all mediators are (or should be) impartial if they are to effectively manage contemporary conflicts requires revision and qualification. Mediators can and do bring their own interests to the table when mediating a dispute. An intense interest in securing those interests through a mediated settlement might even be said to be a prerequisite to successful mediation. The 'meddling' of third parties (up to and including their pursuit of their own interest in the process) is accepted by the adversaries *to the extent that they are seen as bringing about outcomes acceptable to the parties* (Touval and Zartman, 2001: 443 – emphasis added). To this end, good relations between the mediator and the parties, as well as a demonstrated skill and ability in performing the various tasks of the mediator (facilitator, communicator, catalyst, agenda-setter, etc.), are more important than any perceived 'bias.'

That qualification notwithstanding, effective mediation cannot occur if a mediator's own interests deviate from or transcend that of securing a durable and mutually acceptable ending to the conflict. This must be done so as to avoid leaving one party to the conflict more satisfied with the outcome than the other. The failure to avoid such scenarios compromises the credibility and effectiveness of the mediator, and may sow the seeds for a future renewal of hostilities. The key to avoiding this scenario lies in the mediator's ability to strike and maintain a tenuous balance between pursuing the interest(s) that prompted it to mediate in the first place without losing sight of the need and desire of all parties to reach an acceptable settlement.

Locating ripeness

The fact that most mediators are motivated by at least some degree of self-interest has the end result of making the timing of mediation a highly salient consideration for when mediation will occur. It is usually the case that mediation only becomes a valid possibility when a conflict has escalated to the point that its implications are perceived by possible mediators, which in turn generates calculations of interest, and if those interests 'register' with the mediator, action. The flip side to this scenario is that conflicts that have escalated to that point are likely to feature 'hardened' and confrontational positions between the parties, reducing any potential common ground for mediators to work from.

It is certainly one of the great conundrums of third-party mediation that the conditions that capture the attention of possible mediators are the very same conditions that work against effective mediation, and must be overcome if mediation is to succeed. The probability that mediation will succeed is dramatically increased if it occurs at the particular ripe moment when the adversaries' capacity for and commitment to continued conflict is exhausted, and their positions are therefore amenable to change. The oft-overlooked implication associated with ripeness, of course, is that some conflicts are by definition not ready for mediation. The issues at the heart of the dispute may be too intense, the level of violence too high, the positions too entrenched (all characteristics of what scholars call 'intractable' conflicts). The difficult conclusion that one is forced to confront here is that successful mediation may be impossible in such circumstances (though other conflict management operations could prove effective). Parties interested in mediating the conflict are best advised to wait for, or somehow bring about, that ripe moment.

Mediation by NSAs

NSAs play an increasingly significant role as mediators in contemporary conflicts. Irrespective of their particular emphasis, NSAs possess some advantages that individual mediators, and especially states, do not. Like unofficial individual mediators, mediation involving NSAs is a form of 'track two' diplomacy. Those engaged in mediation operate with less formality and secrecy than do states or high-profile official individuals, meaning that the mediation can take place without a concern for 'face-saving' by either the parties or the mediator. NSAs also generally find it easier to earn the trust of the parties, given that they usually possess at least the veneer (if not more) of impartiality in the first place. Unlike formal representatives of states, non-state mediators are not as obviously associated with national interests or strategic calculations by the parties they seek to work with. This may translate into greater access to the key actors in the conflict, lowered inhibitions and hostilities among parties to the conflict, and greater flexibility in mediation tactics and services than is possible in mediation efforts undertaken by mediators representing states.

Typically, at least one significant faction in the affected society, and perhaps even one of the parties to the agreement, is opposed to some facet of the settlement's proposed implementation, or is unclear or doubtful about it. As external mediators who have more or less commandeered the process are exiting, a void of 'local' ownership over the peace process emerges. As former UN Under-Secretary for Peacekeeping Marrack Goulding (2003) points out, this stage of conflict management presents a rather troubling scenario, given that the conflict that has just been settled has most likely undermined the credibility and effectiveness of local political, economic, and social institutions.

The civil society building orientations of NGOs in particular, along with their commitment to the encouragement of public participation in political and social life, make them valuable parties that can effectively fill that void. As a conduit for information between political officials and the public, NGOs provide opportunities for increased (and broadened) discourse about the proposed settlement and how it can be both faithfully and effectively implemented. At the same time, NGOs can and do participate in the actual process of implementation as well as oversight (as is on display in the activities of the hundreds of NGOs that have proliferated in Bosnia-Herzegovina in the wake of the Dayton agreement). Finally, NGOs can and do play a unique and important role in helping members of the fragile post-conflict society to build and strengthen their own civil society institutions.

Mediation by NSAs (NGOs or otherwise) is especially useful during the later phases of conflict management, when mediators may be called upon to assist the parties in working through the specifics of implementing an agreement that has been previously crafted. This is historically a phase of conflict management operations when the attention of more traditional mediators such as states or the UN has waned. Mediation efforts over a three-year period (from October 2001 to January 2005) by retired Kenyan General Lazaro Sumbeiywo to bring an end to Sudan's 21-year civil war illustrate the degree to which even the most effective individual mediator, acting on behalf of an RGO (the IGAD), provides only a small piece of the larger conflict management puzzle (McLaughlin, 2005; Martin, 2006).

Study questions

1   What lessons can be drawn from the success of the Camp David Accord? Are these lessons applicable in considering the mediation of contemporary conflicts?
2   What are the key defining features of mediation?
3   Is the mediation of contemporary international conflicts by actors other than states effective? Why or why not? What kind of non-state mediation do you feel offers the most potential?
4   What role do mediator motives and strategy play in the mediation of international conflicts? How and why do these factors vary?
5   What are the pros and cons of shuttle mediation, muscular mediation, and multiparty mediation?
6   How important is impartiality to the successful mediation of contemporary conflicts? How about ripeness? What other factors in your view help increase the prospects of successful mediation?

Suggested reading

Bercovitch, Jacob. 2005. 'Mediation in the Most Resistant Cases,' in C.A. Crocker, F.O. Hampson, and P. Aall (eds.), *Grasping the Nettle: Analyzing Cases of Intractable Conflict.* Washington, DC: USIP, pp. 99–122.

Bercovitch, Jacob and Jeffrey Z. Rubin. 1992. *Mediation in International Relations: Multiple Approaches to Conflict Management.* New York, NY: Macmillan/St. Martin's Press.

Carnevale, Peter J. and Dean G. Pruitt. 1992. 'Negotiation and Mediation,' *Annual Review of Psychology*, 43: 531–582.

Crocker, C.A., F.O. Hampson, and P. Aall (eds.). 1999. *Herding Cats: Multiparty Mediation in a Complex World.* Washington, DC: USIP.

Druckman, Daniel and Christopher Mitchell (eds.). 1995. *Flexibility in International Negotiation and Mediation*, The Annals of the American Academy of Political and Social Science, vol. 542. Thousand Oaks, CA: Sage.

Greig, Michael J. 2005. 'Stepping into the Fray: When Do Mediators Mediate?' *American Journal of Political Science*, 49 (2): 249–266.

Kydd, Andrew H. 2006. 'When Can Mediators Build Trust?' *American Political Science Review*, 100 (3): 449–462.

Princen, Thomas. 1992. *Intermediaries in International Conflict.* Princeton, NJ: Princeton University Press.

Regan, Patrick M. and Allan C. Stam III. 2000. 'In the Nick of Time: Conflict Management, Mediation Timing, and the Duration of Interstate Disputes,' *International Studies Quarterly*, 44 (2): 239–260.

Touval, Saadia. 1992. 'The Superpowers as Mediators,' in Jacob Bercovitch and Jeffrey Z. Rubin (eds.), *Mediation in International Relations: Multiple Approaches to Conflict Management.* New York, NY: Macmillan/St. Martin's Press.

Wall, James A. Jr., John B. Stark, and Rhetta L. Standifer. 2001. 'Mediation: A Current Review and Theory Development,' *Journal of Conflict Resolution*, 45 (3): 370–391.

Wilkenfeld, Jonathan, Kathleen J. Young, David M. Quinn, and Victor Asal. 2005. *Mediating International Crises.* London: Routledge.

Young, Oran R. 1967. *The Intermediaries: Third Parties in International Crises.* Princeton, NJ: Princeton University Press.

Zartman, I. William and Saadia Touval. 2007. 'International Mediation,' in C.A. Crocker, F.O. Hampson, and P. Aall (eds.), *Leashing the Dogs of War: Conflict Management in a Divided World.* Washington, DC: USIP, pp. 437–454.

7 A study in mediation
IGAD in Sudan

This chapter presents a case study of the mediation efforts of the IGAD in the Sudanese Civil War. This case illustrates the crucial impact of ripeness, the importance of commitment and flexibility on the part of the mediators, and the growing role of NSAs (in this case, an RGO) as mediators in contemporary intra-state conflicts.

Background and context

The signing of the Comprehensive Peace Agreement (CPA) in Nairobi, Kenya on 9 January 2005, after over three years of intensive mediation was hailed as marking the birth of a new era for Sudan after 21 years of civil war. Uganda's President Yoweri Museveni, in attendance as a witness to the accord, along with US Secretary of State Colin Powell and a raft of other dignitaries, attempted to put the agreement into appropriate context. Reflecting on the scene, and the years of laborious negotiations that preceded it, he observed:

> What we saw here was the reality of the Sudan when they were dancing, the people of the turbans and the people of the ostrich feathers. How do they continue to live together respecting each other's culture? This has been the problem of the Sudan.
>
> (Simmons and Dixon, 2006)

Political and social cleavages

The last 50 years of Sudan's history have been plagued by two civil wars (1955–1972 and 1983–2005), with the protracted conflict associated with these two wars and other related conflicts killing, wounding, and displacing millions while disrupting and destroying much of the country's economy and infrastructure. The leading – but hardly the only – dimension of the violence and instability in Sudan has been the armed conflict between the Sudanese government based in Khartoum (dominated by northern Sudanese, largely of Arab descent) and various factions in southern Sudan (largely of black African descent) who have long sought political autonomy. An additional fault line running through the civil wars is religion. Islam is dominant in the north, with a mix of animism and Christianity prevalent in the south; this fault line did, at various points during the civil war, lend a regional and international dimension to the crisis. Aside from a desire for political autonomy and religious differences, the two sides have been locked in a struggle to gain control over extensive oil reserves in the south.

The role of the state

While the second civil war between Khartoum and the southern Sudanese commanded a great deal of international attention during its 21-year tenure, organized violence between forces loyal to Khartoum and other factions has long prevailed in Sudan. Elements of various ethnic groups such as the Beja in the east, the Nuba in Kordofan, and especially the Fur in Darfur have been engaged in armed conflict by the Sudanese government or government-backed militias (such as the infamous janjaweed in Darfur) for years. At the heart of the armed violence in Sudan is the state itself; in much of the country, the state is viewed variously as oppressive, illegitimate, or simply a means for economic exploitation and personal enrichment (or some combination of the three). As el-Battahani (2006) points out:

> Successive regimes have manipulated administrative structures to undermine the control of local people and authorities over resources. Identity and ideology, particularly Arab nationalism and political Islamism, have been used to mobilize support and compensate for the governance and development failings of state policies. Elites have mastered the divide-and-rule tactics inherited from the colonial era through their territorial organization of the modern Sudanese state. The result has been underdevelopment, exclusion and violent conflict.

Indeed, as attention has shifted to the conflict in Darfur in recent years, the situation in Sudan has come to be seen for what it is: a series of interlocking civil wars, with interwoven causes such as resource scarcity, ethnic divisions, cultural and religious practices, and foreign intervention.

The Sudanese civil war

Issues and factions

Disaffection in the south mounted throughout the 1970s in response to the dominance of the northern Arabs in the government, symbolized by the introduction of shari'a law in various jurisdictions throughout the country. This disaffection came to a head around the same time that former army colonel John Garang (de Mabior), operating within Ethiopia, organized disparate elements among the southern Sudanese (including the previously adversarial Nuer and Dinka groups) into the Sudan People's Liberation Movement (SPLM) and Army (SPLA). The SPLM/A's aim was a unified and secular 'New Sudan' in the south; the movement's accompanying manifesto rejected the interference of Khartoum in the region, typified by the unconstitutional dissolution of regional political assemblies among other actions (Simmons and Dixon, 2006).

Rise of the National Islamic Front

Mounting pressure from the South led to a period of intense political turmoil and factionalization in conjunction with the civil war. Successive governments imploded, leaving an opening both for the rise of Islamist political parties (most prominently Hassan al-Turabi's National Islamic Front, or NIF) as well the proliferation of a

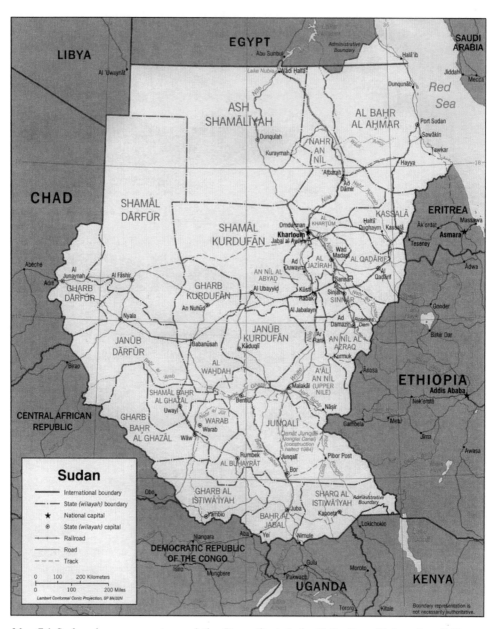

Map 7.1 Sudan (source: courtesy of the Perry-Castañeda Collection, University of Texas-Austin).

Timeline: Sudan's civil war

1955   Beginning of first civil war between northern and southern Sudanese factions.

1972   Addis Ababa Agreement ends 17-year civil war; grants limited autonomy to south Sudan.

1983	Second civil war between north and south begins, fueled by the struggle for control of rich oil reserves in southern regions of the country, as well as ethnic and religious differences and desire for greater autonomy among the south Sudanese. Northern/Arab-dominated government introduces some aspects of shari'a law.
1983–1984	John Garang organizes southern resistance into Sudan People's Liberation Army (SPLA).
1985	Fighting in southern Sudan escalates. Khartoum and central Sudan are flooded with refugees.
1989	Lt. Gen. Omar Hassan al-Bashir takes power in a bloodless coup.
1991	Osama bin Laden relocates the fledgling al-Qaeda organization to Sudan.
1992	Garang proposes referendum on southern self-determination. Government forces launch major offensive in response to failed SPLA invasion of southern city of Juba.
1996	Djibouti, Ethiopia, Kenya, Somalia, Sudan, Uganda, and Eritrea create the IGAD, a successor organization to the IGADD. The IGAD is given a broad mandate, with a priority on conflict management, prevention, and humanitarian affairs; Sudanese civil war becomes first major item on security agenda.
1996	Bin Laden is expelled from Sudan by the government in Khartoum; al-Qaeda relocates to Afghanistan.
1997	The Khartoum Peace Agreement is signed between government representatives and six splinter rebel groups; the SPLA remains outside the process.
2001	Kenyan General Lazaro Sumbeiywo is named chief mediator. Former US Senator John Danforth is designated US presidential envoy to Sudan.
2001–2004	Negotiations begin between the SPLA and Khartoum over the future of southern Sudan.
January 2005	SPLA chief Garang and government negotiator Ali Osman Taha sign a comprehensive peace accord ending the civil war. The US Secretary of State attends the ceremony and signs the accord as a witness. Most estimates of the death toll from 21-year civil war approach two million persons.
April 2005	An international donor conference held in Norway nets US$4.5 billion earmarked for recovery and rebuilding efforts in southern Sudan.
July 2005	A new interim constitution is drafted, with a six-year period of political autonomy for south Sudan to be followed by referendum on independence. President Omar Hassan al-Bashir signs the constitution and takes a new oath of office. John Garang takes oath of office as the first vice president.
August 2005	Garang dies in a helicopter crash in southern Sudan. The SPLA leadership pledges to fully implement the peace accord.
September 2005	A power-sharing government is formed in Khartoum.
October 2005	Autonomous government, dominated by former rebels, is formed in the south.

Sources: *Christian Science Monitor*; Sudanupdate.org; BBC.

number of brutal militia operating against the SPLA and the remainder of the civil-ian population in the south, chiefly at the behest of landowners and oil interests tied to Khartoum. The NIF was a particularly important actor at this juncture. When the National Salvation Alliance (acting on behalf of the government after the overthrow of the previous Nimeiri regime) and the SPLM/A reached an accord at the Koka Dam in Ethiopia, satisfying most if not all of the SPLM's demands in March 1986, NIF opposition was instrumental in the failure of the agreement and perpetuation of the violence (Institute for Security Studies, 2004). Likewise, a subsequent (and even more comprehensive) agreement between the SPLM/A and the majority party in government (the Democratic Unionist Party, or DUP) in November 1988 was also scotched by the NIF, which at that time was a key minority party in the governing coalition. When the National Assembly, prompted by widespread popular support, endorsed the agreement in April 1989, the NIF promptly left the coalition (ibid.).

Khartoum's divide and rule

This rising tide of instability and violence generated calls for stability in the northern region around Khartoum, paving the way for a bloodless coup led by General Omar al-Bashir in 1989. The al-Bashir regime embraced the NIF politically and ideologi-cally, quickly taking the offensive against the rebels while assuming the properties of a dictatorship with strong Islamist inclinations (de Waal and Abdelsalam, 2004). One of the first acts of the al-Bashir government, aside from banning political parties and disbanding parliament, was the creation of a new paramilitary force (dubbed the Popular Defense Force, or PDF).

The PDF was chiefly employed against civilians, with the goal of severing the link between the SPLA and the populace. A major government-led military advance on the south was also planned, with the goal of reversing territorial gains made by the SPLA in 1989–1990. This campaign culminated in the government's capture of Torit (the SPLM's administrative center) in the summer of 1992, in the process ratcheting up the intensity and violence of the conflict. The government's intensification of the military dimensions of the civil war was also linked to a political strategy of elimin-ating indigenous political leaders and replacing them with pro-regime elements. This occurred not only in the south, but in other rebellious areas such as Darfur and Kordofan. Most often the process included exploiting ethnic and tribal identity and playing on long-dormant grievances between ethnic and tribal groups; those groups who had lost political and economic power and social standing in the various regions were cultivated by Khartoum, and given the chance to reclaim these through collab-oration against prominent local leaders and families. Where religious differences existed, these were also utilized: not long after seizing power, the government began utilizing pan-Islamist rhetoric in an attempt to unite the Muslim population in a jihad-style campaign against the animist and Christian south.

Though these divide-and-rule tactics allowed the government to exercise more local control in far-flung parts of the country (with the additional benefit of a splin-tering among the SPLM/A during the early 1990s), they also helped galvanize wider opposition to Khartoum from various quarters around the nation. By the mid-1990s, the civil war had reached its apex in terms of intensity and bloodshed, and the polit-ical landscape of Sudan was fractured. Much of the south, as well as Darfur and Kordofan, were plagued by extreme violence and widespread and egregious human rights violations, including systematic rape and torture perpetrated by government forces, paramilitaries, and militias, as well as various elements of the opposition. By 1998, when a major famine erupted in the south and west as a direct result of the civil war, one of every five southern Sudanese had been killed as a result of the war, and 80 percent of the population had been displaced from their homes (BBC, 1998).

The IGAD mediation in Sudan

Such was the horrific and seemingly intractable state of the conflict in Sudan when mediation efforts by the IGAD began. The IGAD was actually a successor organization to the IGADD, formed in 1986 with a narrow mandate to combat drought and desertification in east Africa. By the mid-1990s, its founding member-states (Eritrea, Ethiopia, Djibouti, Kenya, Uganda, Sudan, and Somalia) decided to transform the IGADD into a regional political, economic, development, trade, and security entity similar to the Southern African Development Community (SADC) and ECOWAS (US Department of State, 2003). At that time, the new IGAD became the primary vehicle for security and conflict management in the region. The situation in Sudan quickly rose to the top of the organization's agenda, leading to the creation of a special committee by the IGAD Council of Ministers (to be chaired by Kenya) to seek ways of managing the conflict.

Prior mediation attempts

The IGAD was not the first entity to attempt to mediate the Sudanese civil war since its re-ignition in 1983. The overthrow of the SPLM/A's chief benefactor, Mengistu Haile Mariam, in Ethiopia, in concert with the fracture of the SPLM/A along ethnic lines (culminating in the defection of the Nuers in 1991) was of sufficient concern to Nigerian interests so as to prompt an attempt at mediation by then-President Ibrahim Babangida. Though multiple rounds of talks were held at Abuja in 1992 and 1993 under Babangida's good offices, the fissures among the southern factions, in combination with the renewed military assault by Khartoum, saw the government on the offensive and unwilling to offer any concessions on the matter of self-determination for the south. Ripeness was clearly not at hand, and the attempt at mediation by an aspiring regional hegemon went for naught (Prendergast and Mozersky, 2004).

Mounting international pressure in the wake of the failed Nigerian effort led the Sudanese government to propose IGAD mediation. The organization quickly accepted the challenge, with a combination of factors influencing the decision. Having already established a standing committee on Sudan, the organization was eager to demonstrate its relevance so as to position itself as a major regional player on security issues. The member-states themselves had a clear strategic incentive to contain Sudan's civil war, and shared a related desire to contain the spread of political Islam in the region. Prompted by these interests, the IGAD officially launched peace negotiations in Nairobi in March 1994.

The Declaration of Principles

As in Abaja, IGAD-brokered talks quickly broke down over the issue of self-determination. Seeking to break this impasse, IGAD mediators developed a

Declaration of Principles (DoP), presented to the belligerents in July 1994. Within the extensively detailed prescriptions of the DoP, the document emphasized several main points: (a) the maintenance of Sudan's unity; (b) the need for an equitable distribution of resources within the country; (c) a secular and democratic political system; and (d) the right of the south to seek self-determination through a referendum if these objectives were not shared by all parties (Adar, 2000). Not surprisingly, Khartoum rejected the agreement's provisions and the activist style of mediation that fashioned it. Positions hardened and the prospects for progress seemed distant.

Stalemate and regression

The next two years were marked by further fragmentation within Sudanese society, a renewal of violence, and a marked increase in regional and international support for the SPLM/A in conjunction with added pressure on the Sudanese government. These factors combined to increase war-weariness on all sides. The growing diplomatic isolation of Khartoum, in concert with the military engagement of Ethiopia, Eritrea, and Uganda on behalf of the SPLA and subsequent SPLA victories in the field in 1995 and 1996, prompted the government to return to the bargaining table and accept the DoP as a precursor to further negotiations in 1997 (Deng, 1999). An additional contributing factor was the Khartoum Agreement between the government and a splinter group, the South Sudan Independence Movement (an umbrella organization of Nuer militias that broke from the SPLM/A in 1991). Though the SPLM/A remained the main source of opposition to the government in the south, the Khartoum Agreement represented an important symbolic precedent.

The Sudanese government's acceptance of the DoP in 1997 produced little of substance, and the negotiations waned along with the commitment of IGAD member-states, especially after the outbreak of the Ethiopian–Eritrean War in May 1998. When a new round of talks held at Lake Bogoria (Kenya) in October 2000 ended in stalemate, it became clear to IGAD mediators that a new approach, to include additional pressure from external parties as well as a new mediator, was needed in order to change the context surrounding the mediated negotiations.

Enter Sumbeiywo

Such was the atmosphere when Kenyan President Daniel Arap Moi asked General Lazaro Sumbeiywo to assume leadership of the IGAD delegation in October 2001. Considered equally fair and brusque, Sumbeiywo was Kenya's special envoy to the talks during the bleak years of 1997–1999. He was also relatively new to mediation and as a result openly solicited the opinions and ideas of the parties as well as experts on the conflict. Sumbeiywo quickly determined that housekeeping was in order, including a recalibration of the IGAD's relationship with all of the regional and international actors with a stake in Sudan. His first act was to arrange for personal, one-on-one visits with Garang and al-Bashir. Sumbeiywo then lobbied President Moi to pay all of the debts incurred by IGAD mediation over the proceeding seven years, a move designed to increase his credibility with the states that had underwritten much of the peace process, including the United States and the United Kingdom (Young, 2005). Sumbeiywo's plan was to utilize his reserve of political capital to convince these actors to apply pressure to the parties from without, with a goal of changing the tenor of the proceedings upon their resumption.

Internationalizing the mediation

When negotiations reopened, Sumbeiywo elected to hold them in Khartoum, an important symbolic gesture given that most of the preceding rounds of negotiations had occurred outside Sudan. The communiqué produced by the Khartoum Summit, issued in January 2002, called for rejuvenation of the process through solicitation of new initiatives and perspectives. This statement bore the marks of Sumbeiywo's earlier handiwork relative to the donor states; shortly after the summit concluded, he created the IGAD Partners Forum, a consultative body consisting of many of the major economic sponsors of the peace process (principally the United States, the United Kingdom, Norway, and Italy), which he would rely upon to great effect in subsequent sessions. Sumbeiywo parlayed his early success into a diplomatic visit with Egyptian President Hosni Mubarak; Sumbeiywo extracted a pledge of support for the IGAD mediation from Mubarak, interpreting this as a sign that the competing Egyptian–Libyan Initiative (ELI) on Sudan would be shelved, at least in the short run.

Reframing the discourse

Having remade the external context enveloping the IGAD mediation process, Sumbeiywo and his delegation (including by this time the noted South African mediator Nicolas 'Fink' Haysom) turned his attention to reframing the process of the discussion itself. In doing so Sumbeiywo revisited his earlier close adherence as special envoy (in the late 1990s) to a point-by-point discussion of each of the provisions of the DoP. The IGAD team determined that a more holistic approach in which continuous negotiation was held on each element of the DoP, with points of concurrence added to a new document, would be more effective in generating a single negotiation text and distancing the parties from their previous and contradictory positions (Haysom, 2006). Divorcing the process from the DoP document itself increased the investment of the parties (especially the Sudanese government), putting distance between the current discussions and a notable and controversial talisman of the past. This move also allowed the parties to focus on the progress they were making, and granted them a view of the course ahead.

The outcome

The Machakos Protocol

Sumbeiywo's sagacity in transforming the external context as well as the internal tenor of the negotiations set the stage for the adoption of the Machakos Protocol in July 2002, viewed by many as the single most important breakthrough in the entire peace process. Unlike preceding rounds of negotiations surrounding the DoP, the talks at Machakos recast the two recurring sticking points between the government and the SPLM/A (self-determination and the relationship between the state and religion) as quid pro quo, rather than two disparate points to reconcile.

The government agreed to a major concession to the SPLM/A's demands for self-determination, agreeing to a six-year transitional period in which a federal system of government would be in effect, with local, provincial, and national government coinciding with two national chambers. Following this period of increased autonomy, a referendum in the south on secession would be held. In return, Khartoum rejected immediate unilateral secession, and proposed the maintenance of shari'a law as the source of law in the northern jurisdictions, though providing an opt-out clause for the south. Moving away from its earlier demands for a universally liberal and secular Sudan (as reflected in the DoP), which would have required the dismantling of the NIF, the SPLM/A agreed to these terms.

The IGAD as broker

IGAD mediators played a major part in facilitating this breakthrough, in large part by clarifying options for the way forward. The full engagement of the IGAD team was critical at this juncture. Accordingly, the mediators made a concerted effort to adopt a full-fledged problem-solving approach:

> In order to break the pattern of simply restating previously held positions, the General [Sumbeiywo] suggested that I present a workshop to the parties dealing with constitutional negotiations and problem solving. The workshop format was itself useful in that it placed both parties on the same side of the table, as workshop participants, rather than in an adversarial setting. As the subject of the problem-solving exercise it was decided that we should take the state and religion problem, canvass alternative solutions from the parties and have the parties rank them against shared criteria. Using this exercise as a basis, we prepared a single negotiating text reflecting these discussions, and from the alternatives generated in the exercise we were able to suggest the compromises that would form the basis of a protocol containing a model of asymmetrical federalism.
>
> (Haysom, 2006)

At the same time, as an agreement came into full view, the chief obstacle was no longer obtaining commitment from the parties, but assuring them that they had not overreached their mandate, and not allowing them to utilize such a claim as an excuse for failing to reach an agreement.

In responding to this concern, the IGAD delegation increased pressure on the parties; the culmination of this more directive strategy was the imposition of a one-hour deadline to finalize the agreement imposed by Sumbeiywo. The delegates at the table took the opportunity to inform the principals (including, by this time, Sudanese First Vice President Ali Osman-al-Taha, as well as John Garang) of the details, which they agreed to, and signed on 22 July 2002.

The road to Naivasha

Realization of the Machakos Protocol set the stage for a confluence of events that would produce the CPA signed amidst much fanfare in January 2005. Some of these events seemed more problem than opportunity, and the talks appeared doomed at several junctures. One critical challenge was the initiation of a new SPLM/A offensive to retake Torit in September 2002. The offensive caused the government to pull out of the talks, vowing to refrain from further negotiations until a cease-fire was established.

Cultivating ripeness

Sumbeiywo saw in this ultimatum an opportunity to cultivate ripeness. Aware that the SPLM/A offensive was prompted in large part by frustration at the pace of the talks after Machakos, he returned to the role of facilitator-communicator, meeting with Garang and the SPLM leadership to inform them that while Khartoum was seriously committed to turning Machakos into a comprehensive peace agreement, the government was equally as committed to a cease-fire as a precondition to any such agreement. Remarkably, within a month Sumbeiywo had extracted a signed pledge for the cessation of hostilities from the SPLM/A, which he presented as a fait accompli to Khartoum, sealing the final transformation of the process and paving the way for a successfully mediated agreement.

Interpersonal rapport

Another major development on the road to peace was the emergence of a genuine personal commitment on the part of the lead negotiators representing each of the parties in bringing the Machakos Protocol to fruition. This in turn facilitated the growth of a genuine rapport and trust between the principal representatives, most notably in the case of Garang and Taha. Beginning with a series of talks held at Naivasha (Kenya) between September 2003 and May 2004, the two leaders became progressively more engaged, intervening directly to finalize the cease-fire in Nairobi in October 2004. From the Naivasha negotiations forward, Garang and Taha (and their delegations) started meeting directly, without the presence of IGAD mediators, hammering out the details of what would become the CPA.

Mediator flexibility

With this welcome development over the six months of talks at Naivasha, Sumbeiywo was content to retrench once the parties themselves demonstrated sincere commitment. Having been directive on matters of process, he became equally as laissez faire as the parties concluded agreements on various matters of substance (including joint security arrangements, wealth distribution, the status of contested territorial areas, and so forth) – an approach that was roundly criticized in some quarters. Importantly, both Garang and Taha were positioned strongly enough politically so as to sustain progress over the two-year period of negotiations following Machakos while also consolidating their constituencies and heading off any potential 'spoilers.' Garang's profile aided him in bringing back some of the factions that had earlier deserted the SPLM, while Taha's popularity allowed him to seriously broach the southerners without losing face with his core supporters among the Arabs in the north.

Cultivating external commitments

Still a further change in the climate surrounding the IGAD mediation was the increased external pressure on the parties, a culmination of earlier efforts on the part of Sumbeiywo (such as the creation of the Partners Forum). The increased involvement of the United States in the process, particularly after the September 11 attacks, was especially noteworthy. An intensified commitment to combating pan-Islamism driven both by the Bush Administration's new national security strategy and by the lobbying of the Administration by conservative Christian groups each played a major part in rendering Sudan an object of concern, especially given previous ties between the al-Bashir regime and al-Qaeda.

Osama bin Laden had been a warmly received guest of the government in the early and mid-1990s, and these and other factors were key to the intensified interest of the United States in seeing a lasting end to the civil war. The Bush Administration's new approach toward Khartoum included a mix of carrots and sticks directly linked to a successful peace accord, as well as the commission of a new special envoy, former US Senator John Danforth, in 2001. The IGAD mediators were again shrewd in seizing upon this development. Sumbeiywo himself placed several calls to US Secretary of State Colin Powell when stalemate loomed, and Powell was an observer both at Naivasha and at the signing of the CPA in Nairobi in January 2005 (Sumbeiywo, 2006).

The Comprehensive Peace Agreement

As with most mediated settlements, the CPA was equal parts formalization of previous negotiations and high-profile photo-op. That disclaimer aside, the CPA stands as a by-product of years of tense and difficult negotiations, and a testimonial to the efforts of dedicated and effective mediators operating in a dangerous and seemingly intractable conflict. It finalized the details pertaining to the six-year interim period of increased autonomy for the south. Such details included the process of withdrawing armed forces from contested areas; the creation of new, integrated forces; an equitable split of oil wealth and resources; the creation of a dual banking system and introduction of a new currency (the Dinar) for the south; the specific terms of a consociational power-sharing arrangement at the national, provincial, and local levels of government; and the formalization of the status of shari'a law.

The CPA shares with most mediated settlements the bittersweet properties of a peace agreement that goes a long way toward peace, but perhaps not far enough. As critics and supporters alike have pointed out, the CPA is a bilateral agreement between the government of Sudan and the SPLM/A. Thus the grievances of other factions and the status of other ongoing conflicts throughout the country – which are both directly and indirectly linked to the civil war – were steadfastly left outside the bounds of the agreement. The affect of this limited scope has hardly been benign. Observers of the conflict in Darfur, for instance, have linked the intensification of the conflict there to the reality that the attention and resources of Khartoum have been redirected from the conflict in the south. Likewise, the various anti-government forces in the region have concluded from the exclusion of their voices from the peace process that violence is the only available option.

Even with the limited scope of the dispute contained with the CPA, progress to fully implement the terms of the agreement has been slow. Application of the interim tag to the constitution, national assemblies, integrated military forces, and the government in the south has hardly helped facilitate matters, nor did the sudden death of Garang in a plane crash on 30 July 2005, mere weeks after being sworn into office as First Vice President. Furthermore, 'spoiler' factions (of both a pro- and anti-government bent) have viewed the CPA as a betrayal by their leaders, and have thus sought to seek redress in Darfur and elsewhere. At the same time, the IGAD and the international sponsors of the process that led to the CPA began to suffer from a period of 'Sudan fatigue.'

Lessons learned

In seeking to grasp the changes that have affected third-party conflict management techniques in contemporary usage and settings, it is important to highlight the major differences (and any similarities) between the IGAD mediation in the Sudanese civil war and Jimmy Carter's mediation of the Middle East conflict at Camp David in 1978 (discussed in the opening of the previous chapter). Clearly some similarities in the two examples of mediation did entail; by the time mediation proved an effective form of conflict management, ripeness was certainly evident – and the conditions of ripeness were at least in part cultivated by the mediators. Furthermore, the mediators in each case showed remarkable flexibility in employing multiple mediation strategies (sometimes concurrently!). Yet at the same time, it is the differences between the two cases that are most striking, and enlightening.

The first, and most obvious, difference between the two situations stems from the fact that Carter's efforts were devoted to resolving (part of) an inter-state regional war, whereas the IGAD mediation attempted to bring together disparate factions in a long-running intra-state civil conflict. It is, of course, the operating premise of this book that the latter form of conflict has grown far more common than the former, so whatever differences might be discerned from the Sudanese case with regard to third-party mediation should be taken to heart. Among these is the iterative nature of the peace process; as this case study of the Sudanese civil war illustrates, the success of IGAD mediation was very much a product of the incremental fits and starts, as well as significant setbacks, over the years preceding it. This stands as a study in contrasts with the Camp David Accords, which came together in a relatively short time and were treated, by all parties concerned, as something of an 'all-or-nothing' proposition.

Another difference is the larger environment surrounding the mediation process. Whereas, as we have seen, in the IGAD case mediation was in part successful as a result of external sponsorship and pressure (cultivated by Sumbeiywo), the Camp David talks took place in isolation. Of course, one could argue that one of the world's two superpowers at the time was serving as the mediator, making the cultivation of external pressure on the parties a moot point. While this is true, it also raises the larger point of whether major powers, and especially superpowers (if not states in general) make effective mediators. If his efforts had fallen short, Sumbeiywo could have appealed to the Partners Forum to ratchet up the pressure, whereas Carter would have simply had to abandon talks. Whether these all-or-nothing views and self-imposed 'high stakes' environments are a function of mediation efforts led by, and confined to, states and their leaders is surely something to consider as the options for mediation by NSAs become more numerous and more viable.

An additional and striking contrast between the Sudan case study and the Camp David vignette is that Carter's efforts were delivered, and received, in an individual-istic and exceedingly personal way, whereas the IGAD mediation was spearheaded by an RGO (after the failure of shuttle-style mediation by Babangida and, later, Mubarak and Quaddafi). This is an important point, in that the Sudanese case reflects the growing institutionalization of world politics, an institutionalization which has also seeped into the realm of intra-state conflict management. As the Sudanese case shows us, the days in which shuttle diplomacy between heads-of-state was the 'only game in town' with respect to mediation are well in the past, and whether such high-profile and highly personal ventures between top-level political officials even remain viable in the face of intra-state conflicts is certainly a subject of some debate, as we have seen.

Accordingly, the fact that effective mediation of the Sudanese civil war came from an RGO, as opposed to the UN, is telling. The increasing involvement of RGOs is a wider phenomenon, as earlier chapters on peacekeeping and peace enforcement convey. Clearly, the desire of the combatants for third-party involve-ment from culturally and politically, as well as geographically, proximate actors combined with the appeal of that involvement taking place through an institutional structure (rather than through the individualism and informality of shuttle diplo-macy or the more coercive and self-interested means of a single regional hegemonic power) is strong.

However, the IGAD-led mediation in Sudan also shows us that intra-state con-flict management by third parties is very much at a crossroads. Whereas the level of institutional activity and 'track two' activity in the Sudanese civil war was great and indicative of larger shifts in the landscape of intra-state conflict management, it is also the case that individual actors and the 'personal touch' – first in the form of Sumbeiywo's enormous contributions to bringing the parties together, and later in the rapport that emerged between Garang and Taha leading up to the CPA – remains vital. Of course, this vitality is likely to vary by conflict, as the effectiveness of personal appeals varies with historical, cultural, and other factors (Woodward, 2004). Yet the larger point is that while the days of mediating intra-state conflicts in a high-profile way by (often self-styled and self-serving) 'great men' seem to be over, the role of individuals working in conjunction with organs of global gover-nance in managing intra-state conflicts is not.

In sum, as this case study undoubtedly demonstrates, the mediation of the 21-year civil war in Sudan was every bit as complex as the conflict itself. The fact that Sudan remains torn by internecine conflict even after the parties reached a success-fully mediated agreement only illustrates the complexity and obscures the legacy of the IGAD mediation of that war. The escalation and intractability of the genocidal conflict in the Darfur region – a conflict with distinct ties to the recently 'concluded' civil war – is particularly telling in this regard.

Study questions

1   Consider the IGAD as a mediator of the Sudanese civil war.

    a   What were the IGAD's primary motives?
    b   What made the IGAD viable and legitimate?

2   What were the primary mediation strategies employed by Sumbeiywo and the IGAD delegation?
3   How did ripeness factor into the IGAD's mediation efforts? At what point (if any) did the parties reach a mutually hurting stalemate?
4   What was the role of external actors and the 'international community' in the mediation of the Sudanese civil war? Could other actors (pivotal states, major powers, the UN, NGOs) be as or more successful? If so, under what conditions? If not, why not?
5   On balance, was the IGAD mediation of the Sudanese civil war a success? Why or why not?

Suggested reading

Adar, Korwa G. 2000. 'Conflict Resolution in a Turbulent Region: The Case of the Intergovernmental Authority on Development (IGAD) in Sudan,' *African Journal of Conflict Resolution*, 1 (2): 39–66.

de Waal, Alex. 2007. 'Sudan: International Dimensions to the State and its Crisis,' Social Science Research Council Occasional Paper no. 3, Crisis States Research Centre, London School of Economics.

el-Affendi, Abdelwahab. 2001. 'The Impasse in the IGAD Peace Process for Sudan: The Limits of Regional Peacemaking?' *African Affairs*, 100: 581–599.

Haysom, Nicholas. 2006. 'Reflecting on the IGAD Peace Process,' in *Peace by Piece: Addressing Sudan's Conflicts*, Accord: An International Review of Peace Initiatives, no. 18. London: Conciliation Resources.

Institute for Security Studies. 2004. *The Sudan–IGAD Peace Process: Signposts for the Way Forward*, African Security Analysis Program, Occasional Paper no. 86.

Prendergast, John and David Mozersky. 2004. 'Love Thy Neighbor: Regional Intervention in Sudan's Civil War,' *Harvard International Review*, 26 (1): 70–74.

West, Deborah L. 2006. *The Sudan: Saving Lives, Sustaining Peace*, Belfer–WPF Report 42, Program on Intrastate Conflict.

8   Peace enforcement

The first application of peace enforcement – ONUC – serves as a prelude to examination of the emergence, application, revision, and challenges of this expansive form of conflict management. Major themes include the transformed ROE, legal status, and resource requirements associated with peace enforcement operations, factors impacting the timing, provision, and sources of peace enforcement, and the continuing debates surrounding it.

Peace enforcement in brief: insights from ONUC

The first definitive example of a peace enforcement operation in an internecine conflict was ONUC. Rooted in Security Council deliberations dating to 13 July 1960, ONUC was transformed into a peace enforcement operation with UNSC Resolution 161 (21 February 1961), continuing until the withdrawal of forces on 30 December 1963 and the termination of the operation in June 1964. Prior to the end of the Cold War, ONUC was the largest UN operation on record; it peaked at approximately 20,000 uniformed personnel, along with an extensive civilian contingent (DPKO, 2007b).

Crisis in the Congo

The primary catalyst for UN involvement in the Congo was the declaration of independence from the new Congolese republic by Moise Tshombe, head of the provincial government in Katanga. Tshombe enjoyed significant support from the Belgian business community, which had exclusive mining rights in Katanga. Complicating this situation was the fact that two military bases in the Congo remained in Belgian hands, and absorbed the arrival of Belgian military reinforcements (ostensibly to protect Belgian nationals and property) on 9 July, in violation of the new republic's sovereignty. This led President Joseph Kasavubu and Prime Minister Patrice Lumumba to issue a joint appeal for assistance to UN Secretary-General Dag Hammarskjöld on 12 July 1960, calling for UN action.

The situation in the Congo represented a litmus test for the UN's commitment to decolonization, as well as its ability to provide security to a newly independent member-state. Additionally, Hammarskjöld was concerned about the possibility that the void of security and authority could be filled by superpower intervention or by Lumumba delivering on his threat to invite forces from the Non-Aligned Movement (NAM). Hammarskjöld's response to the crisis was precedent-setting. Utilizing Article 99, he referred the matter for action to the Security Council. Convening in emergency session on 13 July 1960, the UNSC drafted a resolution (Resolution 143) calling for withdrawal of all Belgian troops and authorizing the Secretary-General to 'take the necessary steps, in consultation with the Government of the Republic of the Congo, to provide the Government with military assistance as may be necessary for security forces of the Congo to reassert themselves.'

The resolution, introduced by an aspiring middle power (Tunisia), was supported by each of the two superpowers and passed easily. The next day, Tunisian forces operating under UN auspices entered the Congo, followed by contributions from 17 member-states commanded by Swedish General Carl von Horn.

Tentative beginnings

The ONUC mission evolved in conjunction with both the deteriorating situation on the ground in the Congo and the debate over the mission in the Security Council. This evolution was reflected in several subsequent resolutions attempting to refine and cement the purpose, authority, and scope of the operation. Resolution 145 (22 July 1960) called for the 'complete restoration of law and order' in the Congo, linking it for the first time to the instrumental clause 'the maintenance of international peace and security' in Chapter VII of the UN Charter. Resolution 146 (9 August 1960) further emphasized the need for *immediate* Belgian withdrawal, specifically mentioning Katanga. This resolution also included the first direct reference to the legal basis of ONUC in the UN Charter, citing both Chapter V (Article 25) and Chapter VII (Article 49) in making the case for UN forces to enter Katanga to implement the resolution.

While stressing the necessity of the presence of UN forces for full implementation, none of these resolutions named Belgium as an aggressor nor imposed any specific timetables. Each also stressed the impartiality of the mission, and accordingly, none received any dissenting votes. However, the escalating violence and disorder in Katanga, along with the presence on the ground in the Congo of Hammarskjöld and special envoy Ralph Bunche, significantly altered the debate around the scope and authority of ONUC. Lumumba, motivated by a desire to secure his position by ending the Tshombe-led insurrection, lobbied Hammarskjöld for ONUC to use force in Katanaga. The reluctance of Hammarskjöld and the Security Council to do so prompted Lumumba's decision to dispatch loyal militants to Katanga on 26 August 1960.

State collapse

Lumumba's action intensified the conflict and triggered a constitutional crisis. On 5 September Kasavubu dismissed Lumumba, who responded in kind, hastening the collapse of the state. The resulting power vacuum left ONUC forces deployed at the behest of a government that no longer existed. Furthermore, elements of the Congolese armed forces were openly hostile to the UN presence. The prospects for impartiality, along with the non-interference associated with consent, disappeared along with the central government. With the situation in the Congo radically transformed, debate was referred to an emergency session of the UNGA (17–20 September 1960). This session yielded Resolution 1474, reaffirming prior UNSC resolutions and calling on the Secretary-General to take 'vigorous action' (UN, 1960c). The first such action came on 5 September, when ONUC closed the airports and seized the radio station in Leopoldville (Kinshasa) on the orders of the Secretary-General's special representative.

Escalation

These moves by ONUC were deemed hostile by Lumumba and his supporters; accordingly, they fled Leopoldville to establish a new government in Stanleyville. Lumumba was arrested there by forces loyal to Kasavubu on 1 December. ONUC troops refused involvement in the matter, a legacy of the persistent emphasis on impartiality and non-interference attached to the mission. The transfer of Lumumba to a prison in Katanga on 17 January 1961, along with his death under clouded circumstances days later, underscored the perils of clinging to such strict parameters of peacekeeping in the absence of any peace to keep. Further complicating matters, the USSR and France had become openly critical of ONUC in the Security Council, claiming that it had outstripped its original mandate and become exceedingly costly.

Lumumba's death generated renewed support for an intensified operation, given the prospects for the total collapse of order in the Congo. This support materialized in the form of Resolution 161 on 21 February 1961. This comprehensive resolution stands as a landmark in the annals of UN peace enforcement due to its precise wording in paragraph 1 (UN, 1961a):

> The Security Council urges that the United Nations take immediately all appropriate measures to prevent the occurrence of civil war in the Congo, including arrangements for cease-fires, the halting of all military operations, the prevention of clashes, and the use of force, if necessary, in the last resort.

While linked to the promotion of a cease-fire, the resolution's wording reflected a clear change in the Security Council's approach to ONUC's mandate. This change spawned numerous episodes of direct clashes between ONUC forces and security forces loyal to Tshombe, as well as mercenary and foreign elements and even rogue elements of the Congolese army.

Metamorphosis

Though precluded from involvement in the internal affairs of the Congo, UN forces were authorized by Resolution 161 to use necessary force to: (a) prevent civil war; (b) enforce the conditions of peace; and (c) protect themselves from hostile acts. These ROE would later be further expanded to authorize ONUC to use force to pursue and disarm combatants; pursue and detain mercenaries; protect civilians from violence; and arrest and detain civil and political leaders. With Resolution 161, the metamorphosis of ONUC into a peace enforcement operation was complete.

It is instructive to note that ONUC's fundamental goals remained the same throughout the operation. From its earliest days, the Security Council and the Secretary-General sought to use ONUC forces to obtain the full withdrawal of Belgian forces, and to provide military assistance to Congolese forces for the realization of internal security. Even the final UNSC resolution dealing with the Congo crisis (169 on 24 November 1961), expanding ONUC authority to include the use of force in apprehending and detaining foreign mercenaries, hewed to the same underlying objectives. Yet as this brief vignette illustrates, ONUC's ROE changed drastically over the life of the operation. While the pivotal article (42) of Chapter VII was never specifically invoked, ONUC bore all the hallmarks of a peace enforcement operation. As such, it provides a useful baseline for consideration of the problems and possibilities facing peace enforcement.

What is peace enforcement?

As a concerted initiative organized under international auspices to impose the conditions for peace, including the prevention of a resurgence of violent conflict, peace enforcement is a unique form of peace operation (Johnston, 2001). Peace enforcement was born of recognition that the limitations associated with peacekeeping rendered that particular form of peace operation insufficient for the management of certain types and forms of conflict. Peace operations in general have traditionally been defined by the UN to exclude the use of coercive force, with the exception of the rare occasion in which the Security Council deemed it necessary to facilitate the peace process. As Article 33 (Section 1) of the UN Charter states:

> The parties to any dispute, the continuance of which is likely to endanger the maintenance of international peace and security, shall first of all seek a solution by negotiation, enquiry, mediation, conciliation, arbitration, judicial settlement, resort to regional agencies or arrangements, or other peaceful means.

Outside the UN context, peace operations have long possessed a wider and less legalistic connotation. This broader conception created space for military intervention, under the guise of peace enforcement, to enter the conflict management realm during, and especially after, the Cold War.

Defining features of peace enforcement

The term 'peace enforcement' as conventionally understood was popularized by former UN Secretary-General Boutros Boutros-Ghali's 1992 policy proposal, *An Agenda for Peace*. That document called for the creation of 'peace enforcement' units consisting of military forces to be put at the disposal of the UN, chiefly to monitor and enforce cease-fire agreements. Boutros-Ghali's use of the term 'peace enforcement' was designed to distinguish it from peacekeeping. In the complex, dynamic, and intensely violent environments characterizing most contemporary intra-state conflicts, the interposition of impartial and lightly armed forces as a buffer between the warring parties is unlikely to provide a sufficient deterrent to the continuation, and in some cases intensification, of armed conflict. The limited mandate and ROE, as well as the requisite of consent from the parties to the conflict, associated with peacekeeping operations further undermine their ability to contain such conflicts.

Peace enforcement falls on the other end of the spectrum of peace operations. As a form of third-party intervention in a violent conflict undertaken to bring about a cessation of that conflict, peace enforcement can be understood as a subsidiary of peacemaking and peacebuilding – albeit an unusual one given its central emphasis employing military coercion to that end. Peace enforcement operations seek to create or impose, by force, a cessation in hostilities so as to provide the conditions amenable to the negotiation of a cease-fire or peace agreement (or to help maintain that cessation). This difference is not merely one of degree but of kind, as the defining features of peace enforcement outlined below suggest.

Rules of engagement

The single most distinguishing feature of peace enforcement stems from the ROE regarding conduct on the battlefield. Unlike peacekeeping operations, personnel engaged in peace enforcement operations generally possess the authority to use armed force not only in self-defense, but in other circumstances as well. Chief among these circumstances are the imperatives of defending non-combatants who are under attack or threat of attack, or to engage on a military basis with armed combatants who are violating the terms of the cease-fire or other peace arrangement being enforced or introduced. In this sense, in conjunction with a peace enforcement operation, coercive force may be used in a traditional (strategic) fashion.

Resource requirements

The provision and maintenance of public security, safety, and order is paramount to peace enforcement operations. This goal is what ostensibly animates such extensive ROE, and may require coercive action against any parties opposed to the provision and maintenance of those conditions. Accordingly, peace enforcement operations require extensive and sophisticated training and weaponry, far beyond that of traditional peacekeeping operations. The condition of non-compliance eliciting peace enforcement in the first place also requires personnel engaged in such operations to possess advanced and customized military training, as well as a level of sophisticated armaments, support equipment, and infrastructure befitting a military operation in which significant opposition is likely to be encountered.

Legal authority

The militarily robust nature of peace enforcement suggests an important qualitative difference between peace enforcement and most other forms of conflict management. A related difference is that peace enforcement operations require (and receive) a different form of legal authorization than do peacekeeping missions or other conflict management initiatives. This difference in the sanctioning of peace enforcement operations is perhaps best explained with reference to the UN Charter. Although peace enforcement can be (and is) provided by non-UN sources, the distinction made in terms of legal sanction and within the UN Charter applies conceptually to non-UN operations as well.

As we have seen, peacekeeping operations fall under the heading of Chapter VI of the UN Charter. Historically, Chapter VI has also provided authority for mediation, negotiation, and a range of other diplomatic ventures emanating from the UN organization. Peace enforcement operations, on the other hand, fall under the heading of Chapter VII of the Charter. Chapter VII authorizes the UN and/or its member-states to undertake remedial action, up to and including the use of coercion and military force, in responding to threats and breaches to peace and security and acts of aggression. Specifically, as Article 42 of the Charter elaborates:

> [the Security Council] may take such action by air, sea, or land forces as may be necessary to maintain or restore international peace and security. Such action may include demonstrations, blockade, and other operations by air, sea, or land forces of Members of the United Nations.

Imperfect consent

Peace enforcement operations are conducted when it has been determined that the conditions for peace need to be imposed by an outside party. Peace enforcement necessarily occurs when peace itself does not entail; in some cases, a desire for peace on behalf of the parties may not even exist. Peace operations undertaken in this sort of conflict environment almost always require the interposition of armed forces into the conflict, along with the introduction of the quasi-offensive ROE discussed above. Taken together, these factors contribute another key distinguishing feature of peace enforcement operations; namely, that they typically do not feature the full consent of the parties to the conflict, and may proceed without securing consent at all.

Impartiality

The operational requirement of impartiality is an additional dimension of peace enforcement. The main 'enemy' of any peace enforcement operation is the persistence of organized aggression. A central tenet of peace enforcement operations is that the persistence of violence is the chief destabilizing force that peace enforcement must surmount, in order for the order and stability necessary for furtherance of the peace process to entail. In this sense, peace enforcement is not appreciably different from other conflict management techniques.

By design peace enforcement operations usually strive to maintain neutrality, and implement their mandate in an even-handed fashion that maintains and enhances the conditions for peace, but does not target or assist any party to the conflict. Military force is applied with regard to the compliance (or non-compliance) of the parties with the mandate which the operation has been tasked to enforce, rather than any other extraneous factors, though this ideal is not always easy to maintain after implementation.

Peace enforcement: a narrative history

The birth of peace enforcement

Conceived of as a successor to the League of Nations, the UN was introduced in a context remarkably similar to its predecessor. The utter devastation of a world war brought with it recognition that averting such a fate in the future required a robust and effective means of providing for collective security. At the same time, a much-enhanced mandate for peace operations made the fledgling UN a more viable collective security actor from its inception.

Indeed, it was this changed security landscape that put said mandate to its initial test, in the Cold War struggle over the Korean peninsula in 1950 (see Box 8.1).

Box 8.1 UN enforcement actions: the Korea precedent

Under the guise of a counter-attack, the military forces of the Democratic People's Republic of Korea (DPRK) (North Korea) crossed the 38th parallel separating it from the Republic of Korea (South Korea) on 25 June 1950, initiating what is commonly referred to as the Korean War. Equipped with over 200 Soviet-made tanks, a substantial air force, and ground forces numbering approximately 130,000, North Korea surprised its adversary, as well as much of the rest of the world. In the immediate wake of the attack, on 25 June, the UN drafted UNSC Resolution 82, calling for: (a) the immediate cessation of hostilities and the withdrawal of the DPRK to the 38th parallel; (b) creation of a UN Commission on Korea to monitor the situation on behalf of the Security Council; (c) the unanimous support and assistance of member-states in achieving these goals; and (d) a ban on any assistance by UN member-states to the DPRK.

The unanimous passage of Resolution 82 (the Soviet delegation was absent due to a decision to boycott the Security Council over the decision to grant the 'China' seat to the nationalist government in Formosa/Taiwan) set the stage for the first ever UN enforcement action, elaborated in UNSC Resolution 83 on 27 June. This resolution called upon members to 'render such assistance to the Republic of Korea as may be necessary to repel the armed attack and restore international peace and security' (Billings-Yun, 1983). UNSC Resolution 83 precipitated a direct military act under UN auspices, commanded by the United States and including combat and support forces from Canada, Australia, New Zealand, the United Kingdom, France, South Africa, Turkey, Thailand, Greece, the Netherlands, Ethiopia, Colombia, the Philippines, Belgium, and Luxembourg. This multilateral enforcement action was sustained through multiple reversals of fortune and intense fighting with high casualties on both sides and until the signing of an armistice on 27 July 1953, effectively returning the Korean peninsula to its pre-war borders along the 38th parallel.

The US-led military intervention, conducted under UN auspices and involving troops, materiel, and other resources from 21 nations, provided the first test of the UN's capacity in the collective security realm. The UN response – in the form of a major enforcement action – distinguished the organization as a more viable actor than its predecessor. UNOK also cast in broad relief the difficulties of such operations, even when the legal authority for doing so was clear (North Korea had invaded South Korea in a flagrant violation of the UN Charter). As the consideration of ONUC in the opening vignette also highlighted, the combination of changing circumstances on the ground and intense political debate surrounding the operation's mandate posed significant obstacles in maintaining operational effectiveness.

Peace enforcement during the Cold War

As the UNOK and ONUC operations reflect, neither peace enforcement under UN auspices, nor the perceived need for peace enforcement operations, is a new phenomenon. Between 1946 and 1989, Chapter VII of the UN Charter was invoked in Security Council discussions a total of 24 times (Chesterman, 2004). However, the sizeable costs entailed in mounting peace enforcement operations (financial, human, and materiel) as well as the problems of legitimacy and legal authority associated with them often worked against such action. These costs and problems were magnified by the institutional paralysis imposed by Cold War bipolarity. As a result, UN peace operations during the Cold War tended toward the more limited forms of preventative diplomacy and peacekeeping, even when conditions seemed to warrant more extensive action.

The Gulf War and the 'new world order'

While peace enforcement was not a creation of the post-Cold War security landscape, the end of the Cold War did bring a major transformation in prevailing views of the prospects of attaining collective security. For a brief period in the early 1990s, the headiness of post-Cold War realignment made collective security provision through the vehicle of the UN fashionable. The success of Operation Desert Shield/Desert Storm (1990–1991), itself an enforcement operation backed by an extensive multinational military force, furthered this sentiment. In removing Iraqi occupation forces from Kuwait and restoring Kuwaiti sovereignty, Desert Shield/Desert Storm symbolized the promise of a unified international community acting decisively with the full support of the UN to stop, and reverse, acts of aggression.

As subsequent UN peace operations revealed, Desert Shield/Desert Storm proved to be the exception rather than the rule. As was the case with UNOK, UN involvement came chiefly in providing the legal and political sanction for the operations of member-state militaries operating under their own unified coalition command. That command did remain more or less faithful to the Security Council Resolutions (660 and 661) that had authorized the mission, and the political leadership of the coalition (including the George H.W. Bush Administration in the United States) continued to tout the benefits of 'assertive multilateralism' and the major part of the UN in creating, maintaining, and enforcing a 'new world order.' Yet for all the optimism associated with the operation, the military aspect of the mission was a product of a full-fledged multinational coalition only tangentially associated with the UN.

An Agenda for Peace

The much-celebrated triumph of the international community against aggression in the Gulf War magnified the newfound belief in the management of international conflict by an activist and effective UN. At the same time, the proliferation of intense, complex, and dynamic intra-state conflicts demanded a more assertive and expanded form of peace operation, and the increased capacity necessary to mount such an operation. At the juncture of these two cross-currents came the release of *An Agenda for Peace* by then-UN Secretary-General Boutros Boutros-Ghali in June 1992.

The *Agenda for Peace* report was a landmark document for a variety of reasons, not least of which being that it represented an attempt by Boutros-Ghali to seize upon the prevailing optimism to redefine UN peace operations (Boutros-Ghali, 1992a). Boutros-Ghali was hardly alone in his recognition of the need to overhaul the UN's peace operations architecture so that it might better respond to the changing security environment (Urquhart, 1990; Mackinlay and Chopra, 1992). In calling for the UN to do a better job of upholding its obligations under Chapter VII, Boutros-Ghali outlined the case for peace enforcement in paragraph 44:

> The mission of forces under Article 43 [Chapter VII] would be to respond to outright aggression, imminent or actual.... Cease-fires have often been agreed to but not complied with, and the UN has sometimes been called upon to send forces to restore and maintain the cease-fire. This task can on occasion exceed the mission of peace-keeping forces and the expectations of peace-keeping force contributors. I recommend that the Council consider the utilization of peace-enforcement units in clearly defined circumstances and with their terms of reference specified in advance.
>
> Such units from Member States would be available on call and would consist of troops that have volunteered for such service. They would have to be more heavily armed than peace-keeping forces and would need to undergo extensive preparatory training within their national forces. Deployment and operation of such forces would be under the authorization of the Security Council and would, as in the case of peace-keeping forces, be under the command of the Secretary-General. I consider such peace-enforcement units to be warranted as a provisional measure under Article 40 of the Charter. Such peace-enforcement units should not be confused with the forces that may eventually be constituted under Article 43 to deal with acts of aggression or with the military personnel which Governments may agree to keep on stand-by for possible contribution to peace-keeping operations.

At the most basic level, *An Agenda for Peace* represented a resurrection of the long-dormant idea (elaborated in Article 45 of Chapter VII) of creating a standing UN force under the command of the UN Military Staff Committee. Such units would be purposed to rely on the use of force beyond self-defense. Boutros-Ghali viewed such an arrangement as crucial for deterring potential aggressors; as he saw it, a 'UN with teeth' would have a generally pacifying effect, allowing the organization to create the conditions of peace where they did not entail.

Peace enforcement exposed

With the promotion of the Secretary-General and the support of the major Western powers, 'peace enforcement' became a popular catch-all used in reference to operations using military force in support of Security Council mandates or tentative peace accords. Beyond any imprecision in the lexicon, the most troubling problem facing UN peace operations was the prevailing and persistent capacity problems identified but not solved by the *Agenda for Peace* report. This problem was a product of two highly correlated factors: constraints on available and appropriate resources and a lack of political will. These problems were exposed by a series of high-profile UN operations occurring between 1992 and 1995. Three operations in particular required a peace enforcement component that the UN was unable (in Somalia and Bosnia) and/or unwilling (in Rwanda) to effectively deliver; remaining in the 'gray area' between traditional peacekeeping and peace enforcement, they proved colossal failures for all parties concerned.

UNOSOM

The UN Operation in Somalia (UNOSOM) was commissioned in 1991 with a specific charge to address the chaos that prevailed in the wake of the collapse of the Mohammed Said Barre regime and, with it, the Somali state. With the passing of Resolution 751 in April 1992, UNOSOM-I was born. UNOSOM was initially enacted with the consent of the warring parties (though none were representatives of the Somali state, since no such state existed) and was impartial, tasked with monitoring a cease-fire and securing and distributing emergency relief aid. The scope of the ROE was correspondingly limited. Despite the cease-fire agreement and their pledges to welcome a UN presence, militias loyal to the various clan leaders continued to engage in armed clashes. Such clashes, and the repeated looting of food aid and other emergency supplies (and their re-sale on the informal market), led the Security Council to authorize an additional 3,000 troops for UNOSOM in August 1992.

With no substantial change in the operational mandate, conditions worsened: looting of humanitarian aid continued; aid workers came under attack by militias; and the famine expanded to threaten 1.5 million Somalis (UN, 2003). It was evident to all that the narrow mandate and circumscribed ROE of UNOSOM was insufficient to alter the situation in Somalia. In November 1992, the United States proposed the deployment of an expanded operation to ensure the delivery of humanitarian assistance. This operation, dubbed UNITAF (Unified Task Force), was intended to serve as both a supplement and complement to UNOSOM. In December 1992, the Security Council passed Resolution 794, granting UNITAF forces the authority to employ 'all necessary means' to establish a secure environment in Somalia.

The creation of UNITAF marked the dawn of peace enforcement in Somalia. Fortified by military contingents from 24 countries, all major distribution points for food and emergency aid were secured, while UNOSOM remained committed to the delivery of that aid to the populace as well as to continuing its diplomatic overtures to the combatants. In conjunction with a series of UN-brokered agreements, in March 1993 the Security Council decided to replace the limited UNOSOM-I and absorb the largely autonomous US-led UNITAF with a new UN-led operation.

UNOSOM-II (established by Resolution 814) took on UNITAF's expanded mandate and ROE, each representative of peace enforcement. Violence and lawlessness persisted, punctuated by an attack on UN forces by militia loyal to the warlord Mohammed Farah Aideed on 5 June 1993, killing 23 (Pakistani) UNOSOM personnel. UN operations in Somalia unraveled throughout the summer, as the well-armed and equipped US forces became preoccupied with the manhunt for Aideed, while UNOSOM forces struggled to secure civilians and relief depots. The death of 18 US Army Rangers (and over 500 Somalis) in a firefight on 3–4 October 1993 in Mogadishu sounded the death knell for UNOSOM-II. Within days the Clinton Administration announced a timetable for withdrawal. Now, 15 years later, Somalia remains a disordered and stateless society defined by violence.

UNPROFOR

After months of internecine warfare among Serbs (with support from the Federal Republic of Yugoslavia) and Croats in the breakaway republic of Croatia, the UN initiated UNPROFOR via Security Council Resolution 743 on 21 February 1992. The initial UNPROFOR deployment was to three UN Protected Areas (UNPAs) in Croatia, a deployment consistent with the operation's initial mandate to create 'safe areas' to provide for the immunity of non-combatants (UN, 1999a). In a recurring theme of this chapter, the complexities of the conflict required a significant, if unanticipated, expansion of the mission. By the end of 1992, UN personnel had taken on a range of tasks such as administering the movement of persons and goods into and out of the UNPAs and supervising the Croat–Serb cease-fire. The latter task included supervision of demilitarization, protection of critical infrastructure, and other related tasks.

As the conflict spread to and intensified in Bosnia, UNPROFOR's mandate was expanded to include the use of force in self-defense. However, the operation's primary concern remained the creation of safe areas. The insufficiency of this approach was quickly exposed by the problems Boutros-Ghali outlined in *An Agenda for Peace.* As hundreds of thousands of civilians became trapped in the escalating warfare among an array of paramilitaries and militias, the Security Council was unwilling to provide UN forces with Chapter VII authorization to use force to defend the UNPAs. With UNPROFOR personnel lacking in supplies and adequate reinforcements, pursuit and disarmament of the combatants was impossible, rendering the entire safe-areas policy a disaster. While the UNPAs served as a magnet to civilians, the inability of the UN to protect those centralized concentrations of civilians had the perverse effect of facilitating the 'ethnic cleansing' activities of ethno-nationalist paramilitaries.

The catastrophic failure of the safe-areas approach culminated in the horror of Srebrenica. Over a ten-day period in July 1995, 23,000 Muslim girls and women were expelled, and over 7,600 Muslim boys and men apprehended and executed while Dutch forces attached to UNPROFOR stood by without the authority, will, or weaponry necessary to act. The shocking nature of what happened at Srebrenica provided the final measure of the insufficiency of UNPROFOR's mandate and operational strategy. In response the Western powers authorized a full-blown enforcement action utilizing NATO air power and rapid-reaction forces, which succeeded in bringing about a cessation of the conflict.

UNAMIR

The UN Assistance Mission in Rwanda (UNAMIR) was established by Security Council Resolution 874 in October 1993. The operation was intended to assist in implementation of the Arusha Accord, a peace agreement brokered in August 1993 by the OAU between the armed forces of the Hutu-led government of Rwanda and the Tutsi-led Rwandan Patriotic Front (RPF). UNAMIR was requested by representatives of both the Rwandan government and the RPF, and its objectives (including establishment of a demilitarized zone in Kigali) and size (initially 400 Belgian and 400 Bangladeshi forces) bore all the hallmarks of a limited observer mission.

The deep social cleavages underlying the Rwandan conflict were soon underscored by the death of President Juvénal Habyarimana along with Burundi's President Cyprien Ntaryamira in a plane crash on 6 April 1994. The death of the two leaders under clouded circumstances served as the catalyst for both genocide and civil war. That event prompted a campaign of premeditated killings of Tutsi and moderate Hutu political leaders by the Rwandan armed forces, the special presidential guard, and roving bands of Hutu militia (*interhamwe*). In response, the RPF initiated a military advance from the northeast of Rwanda toward Kigali.

The UN response centered mostly on efforts to restore the cease-fire. With one of the parties using the levers of the state to carry out a policy of genocide, and the other reliant on military force to stop that program by seizing control of the very same state, such diplomatic overtures bordered on the absurd. The UNAMIR deployment (now totaling approximately 2,500) was bound by a limited mandate that did not include pursuit, disarmament, or direct armed engagement. With UNAMIR's commanders receiving little guidance from UN headquarters, they adopted a variation on a 'safe areas' strategy in Bosnia, and the centralization of large numbers of civilians in 'shelters' again rendered them easy prey for the depredations of the Hutu extremists.

The murder of ten Belgian peacekeepers attached to UNAMIR at the hands of the *interhamwe* on 7 April 2004 further emasculated the operation. The Belgian government immediately withdrew all of its personnel from UNAMIR, with Bangladesh soon following. Other military deployments to Rwanda (from France and the United States) were carried out with the sole purpose of securing the withdrawal of national citizens and property. Disregarding the calls of UNAMIR's commander (Canadian Major-General Romeo Dallaire) for reinforcements, the Security Council passed Resolution 912 (21 April 1994), reducing the operation to a rump force of 270. This decision occurred precisely as the premeditated mass killing in Rwanda was reaching its apex.

The scaling back of UNAMIR in concert with political paralysis in the Security Council removed any possible impediments to genocide. Hutu extremists took full advantage, relying on rudimentary implements and exhorting their compatriots to join in the mayhem through the national radio station. The daily death tolls were staggering. In a period of 100 days in April–June 1994, over 800,000 Tutsi and Hutu moderates were killed in the genocide, which created two million refugees (mostly in Zaire) and another two million IDPs. Though subsequent Security Council Resolutions 918 (17 May 1994) and 929 (22 June 1994) did authorize more direct action, and even in the latter case granted Chapter VII authorization for a multinational humanitarian operation (Operation Turquoise) led by France, it was too little (forces were deployed only to southwestern Rwanda) and certainly too late. The genocide persisted until the successful conclusion of the RPF offensive in July, at which point a transitional government similar to that called for in the Arusha agreement was established.

Supplement to an Agenda for Peace

UNOSOM, UNPROFOR, and UNAMIR all revealed different facets of the problematic nature of peace enforcement. Collectively, the three operations reflected a continuum of retrenchment with respect to the concept and application of peace enforcement. Having been fully authorized in Somalia, UNOSOM-II failed to significantly alter the lawlessness and chaos of a stateless society. Subsequently, when authorization for peace enforcement was needed in Bosnia, it was never fully granted, resulting in the disastrous safe-areas policy. Twice bitten, the UN refused to commit a meaningful military presence to Rwanda, thereby facilitating genocide.

Forced to confront the legacy of these failed operations, Secretary-General Boutros-Ghali cemented this retrenchment with publication of the 'Supplement to an Agenda for Peace' in January 1995. The Supplement took great pains to down-play peace enforcement, implicitly acknowledging the hazards of undertaking such expansive and assertive operations given the UN's insufficient capacity for doing so. The term 'peace enforcement' is almost completely absent, appearing only once in reference to the 'many instruments for controlling and resolving conflicts between and within states' (Boutros-Ghali, 1995).

Perhaps more telling is the treatment that peace enforcement receives in the section of the report devoted to 'enforcement action.' In that section, the third option that peace enforcement was supposed to offer (somewhere between coercion and non-coercion, full and no consent, and impartiality and partiality) was replaced with a reversion to the stark, pre-*Agenda* practice of associating 'enforcement' only with major military actions such as UNOK or Operation Desert Shield/Desert Storm, while retaining the term and strictures of 'peacekeeping' for all UN-led and staffed operations. The Supplement's admonition against 'blurring the distinction between peace-keeping and enforcement' is telling. Accompanying that distinction was a newfound distance imposed between the UN and enforcement action, as the document placed repeated emphasis on the notion that such actions were most effective when authorized by the Security Council, but carried out by coalitions of member-states or regional security institutions.

The peace operations launched either directly by the UN or with UN consent in the mid-to-late 1990s reflected the revisionism of the Supplement. The shift in post-*Supplement* UN operations was both quantitative and qualitative; whereas in 1993 over 70,000 military personnel were deployed under UN auspices in peace operations, by 1996 this figure had been reduced to less than 20,000 (Bellamy *et al.*, 2004). Furthermore, between 1995 and 1999 only four new UN operations were commissioned by the Security Council: UNSMIH and UNTMIH (both in Haiti); UNOMSIL (Sierra Leone), and MINUGUA (Guatemala). Each of these operations was granted a very limited mandate and an accordingly limited number of personnel.

The Brahimi Report

If the 'Supplement to an Agenda for Peace' sought to prevent further discussion and application of peace enforcement, it failed. In reality, many of the humanitarian crises considered appropriate for more limited UN action were linked to, if not directly triggered by, the upheaval associated with 'new wars' – the type of upheaval necessitating the larger commitments originally envisioned by Boutros-Ghali. This connection was more clearly revealed with the authorization of four new operations by the UNSC in 1999 (UNTAET, in East Timor; MONUC, in the Democratic Republic of the Congo; UNAMSIL, in Sierra Leone; and UNMIK, in Kosovo). The individual and collective size of the force authorizations (which more than doubled the total number of active UN peacekeepers), as well as the fact that they were all commissioned within the span of a year to respond to intra-state conflicts in societies with deep and profound social, economic, cultural, and/or ethnic divides, served notice that another reversal of course for UN peace operations was at hand. It was clear that at the dawn of the twenty-first century, the term and concept of peace enforcement was undergoing a further redefinition.

This redefinition was fully codified in the report of an independent review of peacekeeping operations (in conjunction with the UN's 'Millenium Summit') chaired by the prominent diplomat and UN functionary Lakhdar Brahimi in 2000. The report stressed that peace operations were the 'yardstick with which the Organization is judged,' while subsequently acknowledging that 'over the last decade, the UN has repeatedly failed to meet the challenge, and [it] can do no better today' (Brahimi, 2000: paragraph 1). The panel's answer for this problem was a return to the arguments that had originally prompted the shift toward peace enforcement. While the report emphasized that the UN exercise discrimination in the missions it chose to undertake, it also argued that even discretion would not address the fundamental problem of insufficient capacity.

Accordingly, the Brahimi Report sought to galvanize member-states to act more quickly and decisively in responding with appropriate force, detailing a number of recommendations for revised and robust peace enforcement. It staked out new territory with respect to how to transcend the limiting conditions of traditional UN peace operations. In the direct language of the report itself, 'no failure did more to damage the standing and credibility of UN peacekeeping in the 1990s than its reluctance to distinguish victim from aggressor' (Brahimi, 2000). Following on from this, the report underscored that an insistence on the equal treatment of all parties to a conflict was not only likely to inhibit effectiveness but was tantamount to 'complicity with evil' (ibid.).

The Brahimi Report reintroduced (and sought to alter perceptions of) peace enforcement as a tool of conflict management. The ultimate implication of the report was its insistence that traditional considerations of consent, impartiality, and self-defense should not inhibit an appropriate response to ongoing conflicts. Whether in terms of the necessary criteria for authorization or the extent of the tasks required by such operations, the Report stressed that a strict adherence to impartiality would be counter-productive, and that consent could be manufactured when necessary. As such, it raised questions that remain very much at the forefront of the debates surrounding enforcement today.

The current landscape

A sustained demand for peace enforcement has triggered a sustained increase in the number of military operations commissioned under the guise of maintaining international peace and security since the end of the Cold War. While the bulk of peace enforcement operations have been expressly commissioned by the UN, those that have not have typically been subordinated to UNSC command and oversight. As of the time of this writing, there are six active UN peace operations authorized under a Chapter VII mandate, involving a total of nearly 62,000 UN personnel, including military, policing, and civilian staff (see Table 8.1). These six deployments account for 74 percent of the total of 83,445 DPKO personnel deployed throughout the world.

The most recently authorized peace enforcement operation at the time of this writing is the UN Mission in the Central African Republic and Chad (MINUR-CAT), an EU-led force authorized for deployment to the Central African Republic and Chad under UNSC Resolution 1778 (25 September 2007). Like the other six currently active UN peace enforcement operations, MINURCAT's chief mission is

Table 8.1 Current UN-authorized peace enforcement operations (*ca.* November 2007)

Mission	Date commissioned	Initial authorization/ current deployment	Current budget allocation (million $)	Largest contributor (personnel)
United Nations Organization Mission in the Democratic Republic of the Congo (MONUC)	30 November 1999	16,700/18,352	1,166.72	India
United Nations Mission in Liberia (UNMIL)	19 September 2003	15,000/15,318	721.72	Pakistan
United Nations Operation in Côte d'Ivoire (UNOCI)	27 February 2004	6,240/9,196	493.70	Bangladesh
United Nations Mission in the Sudan (UNMIS)	24 March 2005	10,000/10,066	887.33	India
United Nations Stabilization Mission in Haiti (MINUSTAH)	1 June 2004	6,700/8,836	561.34	Brazil/Nepal
African Union/United Nations Hybrid Operation in Darfur (UNAMID)	31 July 2007	19,555/230	Not yet available	Not yet available

Source: DPKO, 'Monthly Summary of Contributors to UN Peacekeeping Operations,' September 2007 (www.un.org/Depts/dpko/dpko/contributors/).

the provision of humanitarian relief and refugee protection and repatriation, and the provision of security and protection to both affected populations and UN personnel attempting to fulfill that mission. In this, MINURCAT possesses Chapter VII authorization to, as its mandate indicates, take 'all necessary measures' to fulfill its responsibilities.

In recent years, operations of a peace enforcement nature have also been undertaken by regional arrangements. Examples include AU missions in Burundi (2003–2004) and Sudan (since 2004), and NATO's operations in Kosovo since 1999 and in Afghanistan (in commanding the International Security Assistance Force) since 2003. Peace enforcement operations have also been prosecuted by so-called 'coalitions of the willing,' including the French-led Operation Artemis in the Democratic Republic of Congo (2003) and the Multinational Interim Force in Haiti (2004). Finally, in some cases, individual states such as France (Operation Licorne in Côte d'Ivoire in 2003), South Africa (Protection Support Detachment in Burundi 2001–2003), and the United Kingdom (Operation Palliser in Sierra Leone since 2000) have carried out peace operations with an enforcement dimension.

How peace enforcement works

Why peace enforcement?

Whereas peacekeeping operations are contingent on the consent of the parties, in settings featuring peace enforcement as a tool of conflict management, it is usually the case that one or more of the parties to the conflict do not desire the cessation of hostilities. The continuation of conflict is neither considered pointless nor an untenable burden by all engaged in that conflict; by definition, a 'mutually hurting stalemate' and the ripeness it engenders are not fully evident prior to the commitment to undertake peace enforcement, making the consent to the introduction of peace enforcers incomplete at best. What is evident is a determination by external parties, perhaps in collaboration with internal stakeholders within the state or society in question, that introducing an armed presence can help manufacture that commitment to peace.

Most contemporary applications of peace enforcement are predicated on the notion of utilizing the presence of military personnel operating with greater authority and resources as a catalyst for the process of restoring services and rebuilding infrastructure. To that end, peace enforcement would seem complementary rather than contradictory to the goal of state-building and the associated end of peacemaking. It is at least possible to view peace enforcement operations, despite their reliance on coercive force, as facilitating peacemaking rather than running at cross-purposes to it.

When peace enforcement?

Any combination of factors associated with peace enforcement operations (the inherently dangerous operational environment; problems in coordinating joint command-and-control; the often shifting tides of political support within the wider international community; the evolving nature of the operational mandate; persistent problems of resource capacity and shortfalls) combine to make peace enforcement a risky, if not unattractive, venture. These factors become even more daunting when one considers that clear-cut justifications for peace enforcement operations are usually not evident. Unlike the two enforcement actions referenced above (UNOK, 1950–1953; Operation Desert Shield/Desert Storm, 1990–1991), peace enforcement is rarely prompted by a blatant violation of a state's territorial and legal sovereignty or a massive and documented campaign of human rights violations. What then prompts peace enforcement to occur when it does? In other words, given the level of risk and danger associated with such operations, why are they ever attempted at all?

Domestic support

The first essential condition for a peace enforcement operation is the presence of some degree of domestic support for the operation among those actors (states or otherwise) that are in a position to contribute to (or prevent) such an operation. This support may emerge organically from heightened public awareness of some apparently egregious violation of law, ethics, political sensibilities, and so forth. Conversely, domestic support may be cultivated via the activist efforts of lobbies and interest groups, or a government itself. In this 'top-down' scenario, a concerted effort is made to frame a particular situation so as to elicit popular support for a potentially costly and risky third-party military intervention. Regardless of the manner in which domestic support is achieved, it is clearly crucial to a third party's decision to support a peace enforcement operation, especially with the end of the Cold War and the dissolution of the ever-present justifications provided by that ideological and political struggle.

Media coverage

Closely linked to the presence of domestic support is the role played by media coverage of the conflict. A key development in this area is the emergence and development of the so-called '24-hour news cycle' and the global proliferation of the mass media. This change in the extensity and intensity of mass media (including its highly visual and 'real-time' character) has greatly enhanced the ability of journalists, pundits, and other opinion leaders to shape public perception of issues and events in ways that also shape the debate surrounding the appropriate policy response to them, a phenomenon dubbed the 'CNN Effect' (Livingston, 1997). Whether through the simple determination to train (or not to train) the spotlight on a particular situation, or to 'frame' those issues and events they have elected to cover (by virtue of the tenor and scope of their coverage), the media may either accelerate or impede the likelihood of peace enforcement.

(Perceived) national interest

A third factor influencing the decision of states to contribute to peace enforcement operations is consideration of the national interest. The notion of the national interest as a crucial influence on such a decision is undoubtedly a product of realist theory that retains validity here. The ability of states and their leaders to effectively identify and agree upon what the 'national interest' is, as well as whether or not it might be served by a peace enforcement operation (if it can even be said to exist in unitary form) presupposes a degree of rationality and perfect information that rarely, if ever, entails. Further it is possible, if not likely, for states to act for reasons other than the advancement of their own interests at the expense of others. These (and other) sensible critiques of the concept of the national interest notwithstanding, it is hard to imagine a state contemplating a potentially risky enterprise such as peace enforcement proceedings without that action being interpreted as in some way serving the state's own interests – whether material, strategic, ideological, or ethical.

Feasibility and efficiency

Such pragmatism is also reflected in yet another factor affecting the provision of peace enforcement, especially (but not exclusively) by states and their leaders – namely, considerations of feasibility and cost-to-benefit ratios. It is safe to say that whether an operation can be carried off, whether or not it has a reasonable chance of success, and whether or not the benefits of undertaking the operation outweigh the potential costs and risks are factors that weigh on the minds of political leaders mulling over the decision. To begin with, it is important to distinguish military from political success. Success in either area is both difficult to achieve and difficult to assess, while at the same time different strategies, tactics, and commitments are needed to succeed in each of these distinct realms. In terms of cost, probably the greatest inhibition is the specter of casualties. Concerns with both feasibility and cost-to-benefit ratios are crucial to the initial determination to support an operation.

Who are the peace enforcers?

Political and legal authority for peace enforcement missions may be secured through a variety of multilateral conventions and procedures (such as Chapter VII of the UN Charter; Article 5 of the NATO Charter; ECOWAS's Protocol on Conflict Prevention, Management, Resolution, Peace-keeping, and Security, and so forth). However, any and all of these organizations must turn to their constituent member-states in order to secure the necessary financial, materiel, and human resources to mount such operations. A division of labor defines peace enforcement; typically, legal authority and political cover for an operation is conveyed by an international organization, while the military and financial contributions come from sufficiently concerned states.

Two defining features of the international system cement this division of labor: the prominence of military force and coercion to peace enforcement operations on the one hand, and the reality that no international or regional governing authority possesses a standing military capacity on the other. This structurally-imposed division of labor sometimes fails to materialize; in such cases, an operation may proceed without sanction (e.g., NATO's KFOR in Kosovo, or ECOWAS missions in Liberia in 1990 and 2003) or, conversely, be approved by one or more international organizations but fail to go forward due to a lack of commitment on the part of states (numerous examples abound).

The UN

In paraphrasing former UN Secretary-General Boutros-Ghali, peace enforcement is in many ways a 'UN invention.' As one recent study of peace enforcement (Coleman, 2007) illustrates, all peace enforcement operations commissioned and terminated since ONUC (a total of 18 to date) have been granted a mandate from at least one formal international organization. In the majority of cases (ten of the 18), the mandate has been provided solely by the UN (see Table 8.2).

Organizational capacity

Given that the UN is so often prevailed upon, it is not at all surprising that the organization has reformed itself over the past two decades with an eye toward precisely the types of complex security and humanitarian crises that dot the contemporary international landscape. The reforms were prompted by the inability of the organization to adequately address a number of such crises in the waning days of the

Table 8.2 Peace enforcement operations, 1945–2006

Target country	Lead state	Dates	Force status	Source of mandate
Congo	n/a	1961–1964	UN	UN
Liberia	Nigeria	1990–1997	ECOWAS	ECOWAS
Somalia	US	1992–1993	Multi-national	UN
Bosnia-Herzegovina	NATO/US	1993–1995	NATO	UN
Somalia	US	1993–1995	UN	UN
Tajikistan	Russia	1993–2000	CIS	CIS
Rwanda	France	1994	Multi-national	UN
Haiti	US	1994	Multi-national	UN
Albania	Italy	1997	Multi-national	UN
Central African Republic	France	1997–1998	Multi-national	IMC
Sierra Leone	Nigeria	1997–1999	ECOWAS	ECOWAS
Guinea-Bissau	Senegal/Guinea	1998–1999	ECOWAS	ECOWAS
Lesotho	South Africa	1998–1999	SADC	SADC
Democratic Republic of the Congo	Zimbabwe	1998–2002	SADC	SADC
Kosovo	US	1999	NATO	NATO
East Timor	Australia	1999–2000; 2006–present	Multi-national	UN
Sierra Leone	n/a	2000–2005	UN	UN
Democratic Republic of the Congo	France	2003	EU/ Multi-national	UN

Source: Coleman, 2007: 8; UN DPKO.

Cold War. In response to the exposure of the UN's limitations, many key member-states (including the P-5) pushed for extensive reform, with an emphasis on bolstering the UN's capacity. Of particular concern was redesigning the UN as an institution in ways that would augment its capabilities in the field, and provide better coordination between and among UN headquarters, member-states, and NGOs.

Among other changes, this prompted a reorganization of existing resources and units under three departments: the DPKO, the Department of Political Affairs (DPA), and the DHA. Other specific operational reforms included the introduction and expansion of institutionalized vehicles for inter-agency cooperation, mission planning, financial appeals, and the emergence of features such as a 24-hour situation room and communication center, as well as standardized arrangements for force training and deployment, and intelligence gathering and dissemination.

Legal and political authority

The UN exercises supreme legal authority over peace enforcement in concert with the powers granted to it by the UN Charter. In practical terms, however, the UN is a reactive body and responds to requests for peace enforcement from a representative government or, in some instances, an NGO or other civil society organization. The chief exceptions to this reactive scenario are when extremely urgent and dire circumstances prevail, or when no legitimate and functioning government is in place to render such a request, in which case the Security Council is permitted to act pre-emptively in lieu of any request.

The first concrete step in any UN peace enforcement operation is the invoking of the assessment powers granted by Chapter VII, Article 39. The Security Council then undertakes consideration of the request and engages in a Strategic Assessment (SA) of the alleged 'breach of international peace and security' to determine the appropriate course of action (if any). In the event that peace enforcement is determined to be necessary, the lead implementing agency is the DPKO, with the DPA and DHA providing support functions.

The Secretary-General assumes a directorate capacity and reports to the Security Council on the progress of the operation in accordance with a pre-established timetable. These progress reports are derived from the larger UN missions created and assigned to the conflict in question. These missions, staffed by UN civilian personnel and overseen by special representatives reporting directly to the Secretary-General, typically serve as the superstructure for most peace enforcement operations, providing the overarching political mechanism and as well as coordination for the mission.

Operational characteristics

UN peace enforcement operations typically differ in their constitution. The activities and personnel attached to a particular operation are determined by decision-makers and analysts in their assessment of what is necessary to successfully implement the mandate given to the operation. That said, the vast majority of UN peace enforcement operations have included a sizeable contingent of armed military personnel, an international civilian police force, and a varying number of civilian personnel with a wide array of duties.

Member-states are responsible for committing military, police, and civilian support personnel to the levels determined as necessary by the Security Council in consultation with the Secretary-General on a voluntary basis. Senior military personnel are typically employed by the UN, on loan from their national armed forces; senior police officers enjoy a similar arrangement. Military personnel committed to a UN peace enforcement operation are paid by their own governments according to their rank (and attendant salary) in their home military, while the UN reimburses contributing governments at a rate of roughly $1,000 per soldier per month. Rank-and-file police and civilian support staff are paid directly from the budget established for the operation, although these funds are also derived from the member-states via payment of annual UN dues.

RGOs

The involvement of regional organizations (whether singly or in conjunction with the UN) is also a major factor in determining whether or when peace enforcement will proceed, and if it does, whether or not it will succeed. In the 18 total cases of peace operations since the inception of ONUC in 1960, only one (the 1997–1998 intervention in the Central African Republic, initiated and underwritten by France, and prosecuted by Burkina Faso, Chad, Gabon, Mali, Senegal, and Togo) was not commissioned by either a standing IGO or RGO, or both.

Organizational capacities

Given the UN's traditional domination of the international peace and security agenda, it should come as no surprise that Cold War bipolarity rendered peace operations (of any type) by RGOs both rare and controversial. The scarcity of such RGO involvement during the Cold War stems from a variety of factors, including organizational imperatives within the UN to 'own' peace operations (and to control any associated resources). At the same time, the capacity of regional organizations during much of the Cold War period was rather underwhelming. Even on those rare occasions where regional organizations did wade into conflict management waters, the larger structural constraints that bipolarity imposed upon the UN (particularly on security matters) had a similar effect on RGOs, rendering them ineffective and prone to capture by one or the other superpower.

The circumscribed role for RGOs changed significantly with the end of the Cold War. The heightened emphasis on the possibilities for peace enforcement had much to do with this shift, as did a change in the views of the UN toward the provision of peace operations by RGOs. As the agency of the UN was enhanced by the removal of the strictures imposed by Cold War bipolarity, so too did the need for peace operations in general, and for peace enforcement in particular, increase. RGOs have accordingly been portrayed (especially within UN circles) as an increasingly appropriate vehicle for the delivery of peace enforcement. Beginning with the *An Agenda for Peace* report, regional organizations have taken on a steadily expanded role in peace enforcement, as borne out by Boutros-Ghali's assertion that regional institutions could 'not only lighten the burden, but contribute to a deeper sense of participation, consensus, and democratization in the process' (Boutros-Ghali, 1992a: 4–6).

Legal and political basis

The relationship between the UN and RGOs on matters of security and conflict management is clearly defined legally, less so in operational terms. Chapter VIII of the UN Charter provides for the delegation of authority for the provision of peace and security to regional organizations. This reserved right of delegation lends de jure supremacy to the UN within any prospective security partnership involving an RGO. The Security Council retains ultimate jurisdiction and coordinating authority over any operation commissioned under regional auspices. At the same time, matters of jurisdiction and operational command and control have varied widely from case to case. In some instances, obstacles have proven great enough that regional institutions have proceeded without Security Council authorization. Recent examples along these lines include NATO's 1999 intervention in Kosovo and the ECOWAS interventions in Liberia in 1990 and again in 2003.

RGO authorization confers a significant legal and political 'cover' for peace enforcement operations. This is due not only to the perceived legitimacy this authorization lends to the operation, but also because it helps decision-makers contemplating peace enforcement to 'sell' participation (and its attendant costs) to domestic constituents. Receiving sanction for an operation from a regional governing entity may be even more important than receiving it from the more distant (geographically and symbolically) UN, due to perceptions of greater legitimacy and credibility associated with regional organizations, as well as perceptions of greater efficacy associated with regional peace operations.

Operational characteristics

While peace enforcement remains a necessary tool of conflict management in certain circumstances, obvious impediments to the adequate supply of peace enforcement by the UN have propelled that body to focus on a regional approach as a feasible solution. The feasibility of the 'new regionalism' introduced in the early 1990s was buttressed by the fact that a significant number of RGOs were concurrently engaged in identifying collective security and conflict management as priorities. Examples of this expanded interest in, and capacity for, regional security provision abound, including ECOWAS's Protocol on Mutual Assistance and Defence (1981), the CSCE's Helsinki-II agreement (1992), the OAU's Mechanism for Conflict Prevention, Management, and Resolution (1993), the SADC's Organ for Politics, Defence, and Security (1996), and so forth.

While the regional approaches presaged in Chapter VIII have become more frequent since the early 1990s, they have proceeded in a rather ad hoc and incremental way. The bulk of regional peace enforcement operations have been undertaken by those institutions with the longest standing and most robust security capacities, namely NATO and the OSCE. Generally speaking, those peace enforcement operations that have involved regional organizations have tended to fall under one of two headings. The first is a 'joint' or 'cooperative' arrangement where UN and regional forces carry out an operation cooperatively and concurrently. Examples of this arrangement include the CIS involvement in Tajikistan in conjunction with the UN Mission of Observers in Tajikistan (UNMOT) (1993–2000) and the ECOMOG/ UNOMIL mission to Liberia (1993–1997). The second type of regional operation is consistent with a 'sub-contracting' arrangement in which the Security Council delegates authority to the appropriate regional organization and then assumes a supervisory/consultative status. Examples of this approach include the NATO MNF mission to Bosnia-Herzegovina (1993–1995) as well as the US/OAS-led MNF commissioned and deployed to Haiti (1994).

Pivotal states and coalitions

Peace enforcement operations organized and led by individual states are relatively rare, and when they do materialize are usually linked to international or regional organizations. Nonetheless, peace enforcement operations led by states are clearly distinguishable, most notably with respect to the extent of the contribution by the lead state(s) and the degree that operational command and control lies with the state or states heading up the operation.

Pivotal states

Typically, states assuming a leadership role in the provision of peace enforcement possess the requisite material capabilities to mount and oversee such an operation, including, at a minimum, a relative advantage in military (and most likely economic) power in comparison to the actors involved in the conflict, as well as most other states in a position to potentially intervene. Material capabilities, while crucial to the provision of peace enforcement, represent a necessary but not a sufficient condition. Equally imperative is the perception that the imposition of the conditions of peace in a particular conflict setting is in the interests (material or ideological) of the state considering the undertaking.

Given their material capabilities and overriding interests, leading states engaged in peace enforcement operations are often referred to as 'pivotal states.' The underlying motives for peace enforcement by pivotal states vary. Often, the decision-making calculus of the potential peace enforcer(s) is strongly influenced by geographic proximity. In such cases, a third-party state considering peace enforcement may be prompted to act out of a desire to expand its regional influence and/or prestige, to alter the direction of the post-conflict trajectory, or to prevent a spillover of the conflict.

REGIONAL HEGEMONS

In any or all of these instances, a pivotal state may act as a function of its status as a regional hegemon, or out of desire to attain that status. The overriding imperative of the pivotal state in such instances is the maintenance of the regional status quo, which by design benefits the (regional) hegemon but is potentially undermined by the persistence of conflict and instability within the region. In these cases, peace enforcement may be undertaken directly by a regional power, such as Australia's leadership of INTERFET (International Force for East Timor) in East Timor in 1999–2000, or through institutional arrangements dominated by the regional power, such as South Africa's Operation Boleas in Lesotho (under the auspices of the SADC) in 1998.

CONCERNED NEIGHBORS

Regional hegemonic aspirations or imperatives need not come into play with respect to peace enforcement operations led by pivotal states. When previously internalized conflicts threaten to expand beyond borders and involve others in the region, 'concerned neighbors' may act decisively to arrest or subdue those conflicts. Amid the near collapse of the Albanian state as a result of extensive economic instability and social unrest in 1996–1997, Italy mounted Operation Alba as a means of stabilizing Albania itself, as well as averting any regionalization of the crisis through refugee flows, externalization of violence and organized crime activity, and so forth.

HISTORICAL LEGACIES

Yet another incentive for the provision of peace enforcement by pivotal states stems not from regional ties but historical ones, particularly in the form of residual links held over from previous colonial arrangements. In such cases, pivotal states that are decidedly not proximate to the conflict in question may nevertheless have a significant interest in providing peace enforcement. Such interests are a particularly salient factor when the conflict threatens to disrupt or unseat economic and diplomatic arrangements beneficial to the former colonial power. Examples of pivotal state peace enforcement operations in such instances are numerous, particularly in sub-Saharan Africa: the engagements of France in the Central African Republic (1997–1998) and Côte d'Ivoire (since 2004), or the United Kingdom in Sierra Leone (Operation Palliser, 2000–2001) are illustrative in this regard.

Ad hoc coalitions

As the choice of terminology implies, pivotal states possess the requisite interest and ability to impose the conditions of peace. They may also possess the interest and ability to act in concert with others to do so; that is, to serve as the pivot point for the assembly and coordination of an ad hoc coalition to carry out a collective peace enforcement operation. This is an important dimension of peace enforcement provision by pivotal states, since unilateral actions (such as the British and French actions cited previously) are increasingly rare. Any operational efficiencies gained by singular command and control of the deployment are undermined by perceptions that the peace enforcer is acting for selfish motives; these perceptions have a very real impact on the success of the operations, oftentimes generating a backlash from the original combatants.

Peace enforcement by pivotal states in the post-Cold War environment is most often pursued through the assembly by said states of so-called 'coalitions of the willing' – ad hoc assemblages of states of varying capabilities and interests who share a commitment to the provision of peace enforcement in the conflict in question. Typically the military, logistical, and economic burdens for the operation are dramatically skewed toward the pivotal state(s) assembling it. Still, the political legitimacy of an assertive peace operation is greatly enhanced when that operation is carried out by a broad-based multilateral coalition of disparate states rather than a powerful unilateral actor.

Recent examples of peace enforcement carried out by such coalitions include the Australian-led INTERFET (1999–2000), as well as the International Stabilisation

Force (2006–present) in East Timor; the French-led Interim Emergency Multinational Force (IEMF) in the Democratic Republic of the Congo in 2003; and the US/-NATO-led ISAF in Afghanistan (2002–present). UNSC authorization is not automatic for peace operations undertaken by 'coalitions of the willing'; while in the previous examples it was, it was not granted to NATO's Operation Allied Force in Kosovo (1999) or Australia's Regional Assistance Mission to the Solomon Islands (RAMSI) in 2003.

Contemporary issues and debates

Legality

Peace enforcement poses a problem for an international system predicated on the normative and legal construct of state sovereignty. As peace enforcement operations hold out the prospect that the blunt instrument of military force can be employed by actors other than states (such as the UN and various RGOs), and that these actors can legitimately exercise the authority to determine why, when, and how military force may be employed by an outside (third) party, it becomes harder to maintain the central tenet that the state reserves the sole right to (legitimately) employ organized violence. In this way, peace enforcement offends the sensibilities and challenges the logic of those who would point to the state as the central and most legitimate actor in the international system.

At the very center of the debates over the legality of peace enforcement is the potential incompatibility of peace enforcement with the norm of non-interference, itself derived from and sustained by the concept of state sovereignty. As a form of third-party military intervention, peace enforcement faces the same legal and normative challenges that more conventional (read: strategic and interest-driven) examples of military intervention do. In many ways peace enforcement occupies an even more tenuous legal position than those 'traditional' forms of military intervention, in that it is not even linked to *raison d'etat*. The legality of peace enforcement is challenged both by staunch defenders and fierce critics of a state-based international order – the former on the basis that peace enforcement represents a dangerous appropriation of military power from the state, the latter on the grounds that it represents an example of military might trumping the institutional and legal basis of global governance.

Authorization

The source and extension of sanctioning authority for peace enforcement is a question with both legal and political dimensions. Whereas the resources necessary to act are derived from member-states themselves, the authority to determine the need for acting flows first and foremost from the UN. Undoubtedly, the importance of support, sanction, and/or an explicit mandate from the UN for peace enforcement stems from the fact that the chief legal basis for these kinds of peace operations lies in Chapter VII of the UN Charter, which grants the Security Council power to authorize 'action with respect to threats to the peace, breaches of the peace, and acts of aggression.'

While the UN's custodial role confers a formal authority to sanction the use of military force via a peace enforcement operation, that power has not always translated effectively – meaning that peace enforcement has proceeded without UN authorization, while UN calls for peace enforcement have been late in coming, or have gone unheeded. This disconnect is a direct result of the capacity problems associated with UN peace operations, and is brought into broad relief with the introduction of peace enforcement as a distinct form of conflict management in *An Agenda for Peace*. Whereas the prevailing norm of non-interference can serve as an impediment to an effective UN response to contemporary conflicts (via a strict adherence to consent), so too can the UN's resource shortfalls undermine the organization's collective security role and authority.

Managed consent

To the same degree that the necessity of procuring consent from the combatants themselves is a defining feature of traditional peacekeeping, peace enforcement is defined by the low likelihood of obtaining consent from the warring factions. This is a derivative of the reality that peace enforcement operations are explicitly designed to impose the conditions of peace, rather than an attempt at lending security and stability to an emergent (if fragile) peace evinced by a cessation in hostilities. In the absence of either, gestures by the combatants toward one another (such as a cease-fire), or overtures to a third party by the combatants (such as a request for the interposition of a neutral force), the conditions for continuation of the conflict remain in place.

The primary way in which this situation has been dealt with by proponents of peace enforcement is through advancing the case for the management of consent when political, legal, and even ethical obligations necessitate the introduction of peace enforcement. In particular, it was the Brahimi Report's emphasis on the need for more expansive peace operations that demanded the challenge of consent be met head on. In fact, it was by the Report's prioritization of the UN's responsibility to provide peace and security over its responsibility to uphold the norm of non-interference. In presenting the former responsibility as a moral obligation, the Brahimi Report downplayed the longstanding debate over consent, implying that while consent was not inconsequential, it would be better to procure it ex post facto from a society enmeshed in conflict rather than to delay in providing peace enforcement at a critical juncture.

Timing and exit strategies

Comprehensive studies of peace operations have found that the presence of third parties as peace enforcers has a significantly positive impact on the durability of the peace that they seek to provide or sustain (Doyle and Sambanis, 2006; Fortna, 2004). However, this positive effect is qualified by the parallel finding that any cessation in hostilities that is forcibly imposed solely through pressure by a third party is also significantly likely to unravel (Werner and Yuen, 2005). Furthermore, most studies of the question seem to conclude that peace enforcement operations require extensive long-term commitments and can outlive their usefulness (Benson and Thrash, 1996; Rose, 1998; Chesterman, 2004).

These conflicting findings introduce and frame one of the larger dilemmas concerning peace enforcement: namely, at what juncture should it be provided, and how long should it last? In other words, is there a point when peace enforcers outlast their welcome, and are not only no longer necessary but perhaps counter-productive? These questions defy easy answers, given the sensitivity involved in getting the timing 'right,' and the high degree of variability from conflict to conflict. As the recurring theme of ripeness suggests, while a well-timed peace enforcement operation can prevent the intensification of a conflict, a premature one can trigger intractability. Perhaps just as importantly, peace enforcement operations have a shelf-life. Though difficult to forecast, peace enforcement missions can and do reach a point beyond which they may actually inhibit the ability of the peace they have enforced to take root. This can occur either by their 'freezing' the conditions of the conflict, or by impeding local stakeholders from expanding their own role in, and responsibility for, a sustainable peace.

Study questions

1   Did ONUC shape the civil war in the Congo, or vice versa? Are there lessons evident from the first true peace enforcement operation with wider applicability to peace enforcement in contemporary (especially) intra-state conflicts?
2   What are the defining conditions of peace enforcement? How do they differentiate it from other approaches to conflict management, and what prospects and problems do they raise?
3   What was the trajectory of the debate surrounding peace enforcement in the 1990s? What explains the major reversals in prevailing views, especially at the UN, toward peace enforcement?
4   What was the significance of the Brahimi Report, and why does it remain significant nearly a decade after its introduction?
5   What are the necessary conditions for the provision of peace enforcement operations?
6   How do peace enforcement operations vary by their source? Are there major differences in such operations when provided by the UN, RGOs, or pivotal states and ad hoc coalitions?

Suggested reading

Abi Saab, G. 1978. *The United Nations Operation in the Congo, 1960–1964.* Oxford: Oxford University Press.
Boulden, Jane. 2001. *Peace Enforcement: The United Nations Experience in Congo, Somalia, and Bosnia.* Westport, CT: Praeger.
Boutros-Ghali, Boutros. 1992. *An Agenda for Peace.* New York, NY: United Nations. Available at: www.un.org/Docs/SG/agpeace.html.
Boutros-Ghali, Boutros. 1995. 'Supplement to an Agenda for Peace.' Position paper of the Secretary-General on the occasion of the Fiftieth Anniversary of the UN. In Boutros Boutros-Ghali, *Agenda for Peace*, 2nd edn. New York, NY: United Nations, pp. 5–38.
Brahimi, Lakdar. 2000. 'Report of the Panel on United Nations Peace Operations,' A/55/305-S/2000/809, 21 August. Available at: www.un.org/peace/reports/peace_operations/docs/a_55_305.pdf.
Coleman, Katharina P. 2007. *International Organizations and Peace Enforcement: The Politics of International Legitimacy.* Cambridge: Cambridge University Press.
Crigler, T. Frank. 1993. 'The Peace Enforcement Dilemma,' *Joint Forces Quarterly*, Autumn: 64–70.

Jakobsen, Peter Viggo. 1996. 'National Interest, Humanitarianism, or CNN: What Triggers UN Peace Enforcement after the Cold War?' *Journal of Peace Research*, 33 (2): 205–215.

Roberts, Adam. 1995. 'From San Francisco to Sarajevo: The UN and the Use of Force,' *Survival*, 37 (4): 7–28.

Thakur, Ramesh C. 2006. *The United Nations, Peace and Security: From Collective Security to the Responsibility to Protect*. Cambridge: Cambridge University Press.

9 A study in peace enforcement
INTERFET in East Timor

This chapter features a case study of INTERFET, an Australian-led peace enforcement operation deployed to quell the outbreak of communal violence in East Timor in the aftermath of an UN-administered referendum on self-determination in 1999. This case illustrates the unique possibilities and problems of peace enforcement operations led by pivotal states, while also elaborating on the general dilemmas surrounding authorization, consent, impartiality, and exit strategies.

Background and context

Between May 1999 and August 2006, six overlapping and interrelated peace operations were sanctioned by the UN in the turbulent eastern half of the Southeast Asian island of Timor (see Table 9.1) (while East Timor is officially referred to in Portuguese (Timor-Leste) it will be referred to throughout in the English form). This chapter focuses on one of these operations – INTERFET, a major peace enforcement operation commissioned by the UN under Australian command in September 1999. From well-documented dilemmas concerning consent, impartiality, and resource constraints to specific concerns posed by the transition between operations and establishing a workable division of labor between and among the UN and pivotal states, this profile of INTERFET provides an instructive baseline for the evaluation of future peace enforcement actions.

Colonial administration

The social upheaval and violence that marked East Timor's push for self-determination in 1999 were deeply rooted in the nation's colonial experience. Most of this foreign presence came from the Netherlands (who administered the western half of the island via the Treaty of Lisbon in the eighteenth century) and Portugal (who assumed the eastern portion). Like other European states, the Netherlands came under significant pressure to decolonize after World War II. This pressure was particularly intense in Southeast Asia, as the Dutch government sought to wage a difficult counter-insurgency operation in response to violent challenges in Indonesia, Papua New Guinea, and elsewhere. With such operations costly and difficult to mount, and facing international condemnation for its heavy-handed responses to these national liberation movements, the Dutch ceded control over West Timor to the newly established Republic of Indonesia in 1949.

Table 9.1 UN operations in East Timor, 1999–2008

Operation	Authorization	Chief mandate responsibilities	Date initiated	Date terminated
United Nations Mission in East Timor (UNAMET)	UNSC Resolution 1246	Oversee and coordinate 'popular consultation'	11 June 1999	25 October 1999
International Force for East Timor (INTERFET)	UNSC Resolution 1264	Restoration of peace and security; support UNAMET in delivery of humanitarian assistance	15 September 1999	28 February 2000
United Nations Transitional Administration in East Timor (UNTAET)	UNSC Resolution 1272	Provision of security; maintenance of law and order; territorial administration and governance; assistance in development and delivery of civil and social services; coordination and delivery of humanitarian and development aid; capacity building for self government; establishment of conditions for sustainable development	25 October 1999	20 May 2002
United Nations Mission of Support in East Timor (UNMISET)	UNSC Resolution 1410	Provision of assistance and support in post-transition independence	20 May 2002	20 May 2005
United Nations Office in Timor-Leste (UNOTIL)	UN Security Council Resolution 1599	Dispatch advisers to support development of critical state institutions, policing, border security, and observance of human rights and democratic governance	20 May 2005	20 May 2006
United Nations Integrated Mission in Timor-Leste (UNMIT)	UN Security Council Resolution 1704	Support and stabilize East Timorese government and institutions; support parliamentary and presidential elections; restore and maintain public security and assist in security sector reform; aid in ongoing relief and recovery efforts; aid in investigation and prosecution of major human rights crimes	25 August 2006	26 February 2009 (projected)

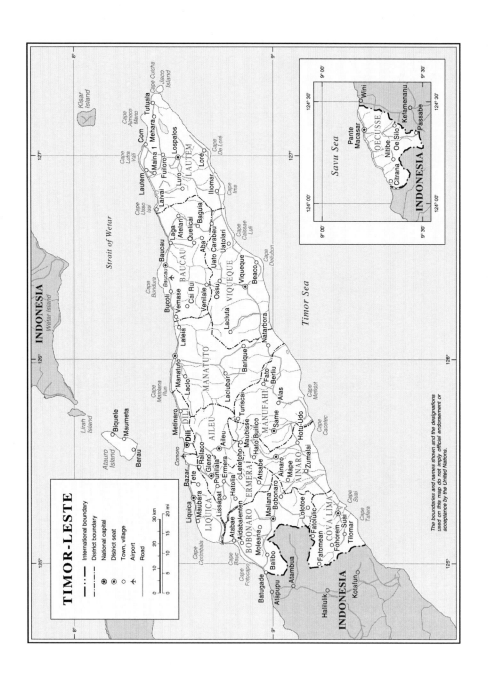

Map 9.1 The island of Timor (source: courtesy of UN).

The situation in the remainder of Timor, however, remained very much status quo. The autocratic Salazar regime in Portugal (dubbed 'Estado Novo,' or 'New State') resisted both international overtures and local calls to decolonize. If anything, Lisbon consolidated its hold over Timor in the post-war period, relying on a mix of direct repression, selective cultivation of local elites into administrative capacities, and various means of acculturation – including, but not limited to, the institutionalization of the Catholic Church.

The 'Carnation Revolution' of 1974, prompted in part by the tangible costs of maintaining a widely dispersed system of colonial administration as well as the symbolic costs of isolation associated with colonialism, moved Portugal definitively toward decolonization. Tentative steps toward decolonization undertaken by the provisional government in Lisbon were accelerated by a campaign of organized violence in East Timor. Violence was employed by factions intent not only on advancing the cause of self-determination, but cementing their own post-independence positions. Chief among these were two nascent parties formed in 1974 the conservative União Democrática Timorense (Timorese Democratic Union, UDT), and the leftist Associação Social Democrática Timor (Timorese Social Democratic Association, ASDT). While the UDT advocated for an extended period of 'association' with Portugal during the transition to independence, the ASDT strongly favored immediate independence.

Post-colonial Timor

Facing the immediate challenges of consolidating democracy at home while divesting itself of other colonial holdings, the newly elected Portuguese government of socialist Mário Soares unexpectedly issued a declaration of the right of the East Timorese to self-determination in the summer of 1975. This declaration was issued at roughly the same time as the removal of the entirety of the colonial administration to the nearby island of Atauro, in advance of a return to Portugal. With the sudden removal of the political administration (and most of the portable assets), conflict engulfed the eastern half of the island.

Clashes were most intense between the UDT and FALINTIL (Forças Armadas de Libertação Nacional de Timor Leste, the Armed Forces for the National Liberation of East Timor), the armed wing of FRETILIN (the Frente Revolucionária do Timor Leste Independente, or Revolutionary Front for an Independent East Timor, the chief successor to the ASDT). The abrupt departure of the Portuguese administration also prompted expanded interference in East Timorese affairs by the authoritarian Suharto regime in Indonesia, mostly through infiltration of the UDT.

Indonesia invades

FRETILIN unilaterally declared independence and the establishment of the Democratic Republic of East Timor on 28 November 1975. Two days later, the UDT declared East Timor's integration into Indonesia. The internal divide and mounting violence in East Timor triggered concern over the rising tide of instability in neighboring Indonesia. Acting on the basis of the alleged ties between FRETILIN/FALINTIL and the Soviet bloc, and with the assent of both the US and Australian governments, the Western-backed and staunchly anti-Communist

Suharto government invaded and occupied East Timor on 7 December 1975. Indonesia's designs on East Timor were laid bare with its formal incorporation as Indonesia's twenty-seventh province in 1976.

Whereas Portuguese withdrawal from East Timor was prompted by overwhelming international condemnation of its persistent colonialism, the Indonesian invasion and occupation drew a much more tepid response. The invasion was roundly denounced in both the UNSC and the UNGA, and Indonesian sovereignty over East Timor was never formally recognized by either body. At the same time, acting chiefly out of a *realpolitik* concern with maintaining regional stability and Cold War equilibrium, the United States afforded de facto recognition to Indonesia's control over East Timor until the early 1990s, while Australia extended a more formal and complete recognition of Indonesian sovereignty over East Timor in 1979.

Indonesia's about-face

Given this prevailing context, it is not surprising that Indonesia's annexation of East Timor was accepted as a fait accompli by the bulk of the international community. By the early 1980s, resolutions condemning the Indonesian occupation attracted little support even in the UNGA. Notwithstanding the persistence of the FRETILIN-led opposition, the situation stagnated until the sudden collapse of the Suharto regime in the face of domestic political and international financial pressures in the spring of 1998. Shortly after assuming office in June 1998, Suharto's successor (and former vice-president) B.J. Habibie conceded his willingness to grant East Timor 'special autonomy.' Few specifics were revealed, other than that East Timor would remain a part of the Indonesian republic.

What was clear was that the mounting pressure on the Habibie government for financial and political reform opened a 'window of opportunity' for East Timorese independence – a window that Australia, for one, recognized. Seeking to maintain a continued alliance with post-Suharto Indonesia as well as to confirm its status as the major regional power, the Howard government declared unequivocal support for East Timorese self-determination in August 1998. This position was reiterated in more explicit detail in a subsequent letter from Howard to Habibie in December 1998, a letter drafted at least in part to placate critics of Australia's two decades of calculating pragmatism on the East Timor question.

Chastened by a perceived deception from a previously silent partner, Habibie undertook another gambit. In January 1999, he announced Indonesia's support for a 'popular consultation' in East Timor, with the choice of special autonomy or independence. This ultimatum presented the East Timorese (and, by extension, Australia, Portugal, and the UN) with a compressed and accelerated timeline for action in order to realize the opportunity. The resulting 5 May Agreement provided for submission of the choice to the East Timorese population through administration of a direct popular referendum. While the UN would contribute election observers (including civilian police) via the establishment of UNAMET (the UN Assistance Mission to East Timor), Indonesia insisted on maintaining sole responsibility for the provision of peace and security in East Timor in advance of, and during, the referendum.

Timeline: the conflict in East Timor

April 1974	Transitional administration in Portugal commences the process of decolonization, to include abandoning its presence in East Timor after more than 400 years.
Summer 1974	East Timor is gripped by sectarian violence and power struggles between rival political groups, some backed by Indonesia. FRETILIN constitutes the largest and most effective pro-independence faction.
7 December 1975	Indonesia launches a full-scale invasion of East Timor to 'prevent communist infiltration and takeover.' According to a 2006 UN report, the Indonesian occupation results in the death of over 100,000 Timorese and approximately 20,000 members of the Indonesian armed forces, either through armed conflict or famine.
July 1976	The Indonesian President, Suharto, formally annexes East Timor, declaring it the country's twenty-seventh province.
12 November 1991	The massacre of over 100 pro-democracy and pro-independence supporters at Dili's Santa Cruz cemetery triggers a wave of international attention to East Timor's plight.
November 1992	Former FRETILIN commander and resistance leader, Xanana Gusmão, is taken into custody in Dili by Indonesian armed forces. Dili is convicted of subversive activities under Article 108 of the Indonesian Penal Code, and given a life sentence (later commuted to 20 years).
21 May 1998	The Asian financial crisis spawns widespread protests, prompting resignation of Suharto after 31 years.
9 June 1998	In a significant policy shift, Indonesia's new president B.J. Habibie indicates willingness to give East Timor 'special status' within Indonesia; he stops short of offering independence.
5–6 April 1999	Pro-Indonesia militiamen, with alleged support of the TNI, kill dozens of refugees seeking asylum in a churchyard in Liquisa. A series of militia attacks in Dili follow; at least 21 people are killed.
May 1999	Following a series of UN-brokered 'Tripartite Process' talks, Indonesia and Portugal agree to allow the East Timorese to determine their political future via a referendum, to be administered by the UN in August 1999.
23 June 1999	Indonesia announces the plan for East Timorese autonomy, to be subject to ballot initiative.
30 August 1999	A UN-supervised referendum is held; the East Timorese are given a choice between the Indonesian offer of autonomy and full independence. Over 98 percent of registered voters participate.
31 August–4 September 1999	Violence initiated by pro-Indonesian militias and elements of the Indonesian armed forces erupts in anticipation of a pro-independence vote. Scores of East Timorese and five UN staff are killed, triggering wide-

	spread condemnation of Indonesian involvement, as well as the withdrawal of UN personnel. More than 200,000 East Timorese flee to Indonesian West Timor. Indonesia's President Habibie concedes to an Australian-led international stabilization force (INTERFET) to stem the violence.
4 September 1999	Results of the referendum are determined and announced; 78.5 percent of East Timorese choose full independence over Jakarta's offer of autonomy within Indonesia.
20 September 1999	INTERFET forces begin to arrive in Dili. Pro-Indonesian demonstrators congregate outside the Australian embassy in opposition to the intervention.
18 October 1999	The Indonesian parliament endorses the referendum and declares the 1976 annexation of East Timor void.
25 October 1999	The UN Transitional Administration in East Timor (UNTAET) is established to aid the East Timorese in the transition to independence.
1 November 1999	Indonesian forces complete a full withdrawal from East Timor; the UN and various relief agencies begin the process of repatriating over 200,000 refugees from the violence.
28 February 2000	Command over INTERFET forces is transferred to UNTAET.
30 August 2001	East Timor holds its first parliamentary elections, electing the 88-member Constituent Assembly. The first task of the national assembly will be drafting a constitution for an independent East Timor.
14 April 2002	East Timor holds its first ever presidential election. The former rebel leader Gusmão wins in a landslide.
20 May 2002	East Timor becomes fully independent. The massive celebrations include UN Secretary-General Kofi Annan, former US President Bill Clinton and Australian Prime Minister John Howard among attendees.
20 May 2005	The UNTAET mission is terminated; the UN is to withdraw forces from East Timor by late June.
March/April 2006	Mass desertions from the East Timorese security force over accusations of discrimination triggers a political upheaval. Of 6,000 members of the military, 1,400 are dismissed. A rally in support of the dismissed soldiers on 28 April turns into riot as government forces fire on crowd. Up to 25 people are killed and 100,000 displaced from homes by June.
9–11 May 2006	Australia puts two warships on alert after East Timorese Prime Minister Mari Alkatiri characterizes unrest as an 'attempted coup.' The UN Office in Timor-Leste (UNOTIL), a small mission consisting of administrators, police, and military advisers, is extended.
23–24 May 2006	Ongoing clashes between rebels and government forces leave two people dead and five wounded. The government requests assistance from Australia, New Zealand, Malaysia, and Portugal to quell the unrest;

	Australia agrees to send up to 1,300 troops as part of the International Stabilisation Force (ISF).
25 June 2006	Foreign minister José Ramos Horta resigns from the Alkatiri government in protest.
26 June 2006	Prime Minister Alkatiri resigns; he is summoned to court by prosecutors a day later over allegations that he organized a hit squad for use against opponents.
8 July 2006	José Ramos Horta is named as the new prime minister.
August 2006	UNMIT (UN Integrated Mission in East Timor) is established.
April/May 2007	Presidential elections are held; José Ramos Horta is elected second president of East Timor.
June 2007	Parliamentary elections are held; FRETILIN, led by Alkatiri, wins the largest number of votes but falls short of a majority; CNRT forms a governing coalition with a number of smaller parties.
August 2007	Xanana Gusmão is named prime minister by the CNRT-led (the Conselho Nacional Da Resitência Timorense) coalition, prompting violent protests.
February 2008	An assassination attempt is made on President Ramos Horta and Prime Minister Gusmão, allegedly by forces loyal to the rebel leader, Alfredo Reinado; UNMIT and ISF operations are extended.

Sources: BBC, CNN, ABC News; Smith (2003).

The conflict in East Timor

UNAMET and the 'popular consultation'

Despite an attachment of 271 civilian police, and an additional 50 military liaison officers, from its very inception UNAMET (established by UNSC Resolution 1246 on 11 June 1999) was defined as an observer mission, albeit with a twist. Whereas similar missions in the past had been limited to the role of monitoring election behavior and documenting and reporting irregularities, UNAMET's mandate was unique. The nearly 250 international staff (supplemented by over 400 volunteers, and over 600 local staff hired by the UN) were tasked with actually organizing and conducting the election. UNAMET activities included ensuring the secrecy of the ballot, guaranteeing universal participation, conducting registration drives, and providing necessary information to voters regarding the procedural details of the election, as well as the two choices listed on the ballot.

The open-ended nature of UNAMET's mandate came into conflict with a sobering practical reality. Upon commissioning UNAMET, the UN had conceded responsibility for maintaining peace and security within East Timor to Indonesian military authorities. In fact, the UN had little legal room for maneuver on the question, since prior to the referendum East Timor was considered by most of the international community to be an integral part of Indonesia. While Indonesia's de facto sovereignty over East Timor did not prevent the UN from inserting itself into the situation, it did severely constrain the UN from exercising any direct responsibility for providing said peace and security (Martin, 2001).

Voting and violence

Even the most optimistic observers at the outset of UNAMET could have foreseen the potential for problems as a result of this arrangement. The documented involvement of the Indonesian military (Tentara Nasional Indonesia, or TNI) and its Kopassus special forces units in organizing pro-Indonesian militias, beginning in 1997–1998 (and in covertly training and equipping the so-called 'ninja' gangs), provided the pretext for what was to come. Several violent episodes in the spring of 1999 foretold significant trouble, with the single most egregious event on the 6 April 1999 killing of 62 civilians at a church in Liquiça (eyewitnesses alleged on presence of uniformed Indonesian military personnel; see Dickens, 2001). Also unsettling were a series of open letters from militia leaders promising the targeting and killing of anyone involved in the ballot.

UNAMET personnel had little ability to stem the growing campaign of violence and intimidation. At the same time, UNAMET's presence served as a reminder that the referendum was an impending reality, which intensified the efforts of pro-Indonesian militias to terrorize the populace and derail the referendum. The planned and systematic nature of these efforts against civilians (including the displacement of hundreds of thousands from their homes) was linked to periodic attacks on FALINTIL and the pro-independence umbrella party CNRT as well as extensive pro-Indonesia propagandizing among the public.

For a variety of reasons, including FALINTIL's restraint, Australia's coercive diplomacy (including a March 1999 decision to place two brigades on 'high readiness'), and increasing internal fragmentation of the Indonesian position, the referendum did proceed (after two delays) on 30 August 1999. Four days later, in New York, Secretary-General Kofi Annan announced the result: 98 percent of eligible voters participated, with 78.5 percent voting in favor of independence from Indonesia. On the eve of that announcement, violence erupted in East Timor, with pro-autonomy paramilitaries rampaging through the streets of Dili and other major population centers with impunity.

INTERFET and peace enforcement in East Timor

A case for action

International press coverage of the violence, looting, arson, and wanton destruction of public infrastructure was extensive given the presence of the media covering the referendum. This press coverage not only exposed the graphic and extensive nature of the carnage, but also the obvious complicity of the TNI and the equally obvious impotence of UNAMET personnel. Within days, over 500,000 East Timorese had been expelled from their homes, with an untold number killed, while the Secretary-General ordered the evacuation of most UNAMET personnel to Australia (Smith, 2003).

On 8 September 1999, an emergency observer mission consisting of five UN emissaries was hastily raised and dispatched by the Security Council to visit both Dili and Jakarta. The mission concluded its observations with a report to the Security Council and Secretary-General on 12 September. Included in that report was a statement that the violence in East Timor 'could not have occurred without the involvement of large elements of the Indonesian military and police,' and further, that 'the Indonesian authorities were either unwilling or unable to provide the proper environment for the peace implementation of the 5 May agreement' (UN, 1999b). This determination, in conjunction with UNAMET's delivery of its primary task (the referendum), profoundly transformed the debate over what the international community should do in East Timor.

Emergence of a pivotal state

In the aftermath of the observer mission's report, international support for a multi-lateral stabilization force for East Timor was extensive. Since popular participation in the referendum had been hedged on the promise to the East Timorese to maintain and restore stability and order, the UN itself was perhaps the chief beneficiary when a commitment to deliver on such a promise emerged. In the run-up to the vote, Australia had expressed strong support for East Timorese independence as well as a willingness to contribute forces to stabilize the post-ballot situation if needed. This offer, which coincided with widely publicized military readiness exercises carried out over a period of several months, positioned Australia as a viable lead state. The United States, Britain, Canada, New Zealand, Japan, and South Korea all voiced support for mounting such an operation under Australian leadership, as did ASEAN (Dupont, 2000).

The consent question

Given the emerging consensus for action, the Habibie government had little choice but to formally request on 12 September that 'allied nations and the United Nations provide peacekeeping troops for East Timor' (quoted in Dickens, 2001: 216). On 15 September 1999, the UNSC invoked Chapter VII of the UN Charter in Resolution 1264, unanimously authorizing establishment of a 'multinational force to restore peace and security in East Timor,' to 'protect and support UNAMET in carrying out its tasks,' and most importantly, to 'undertake all necessary measures to fulfill this mandate' (UN, 1999c). So it was that the most strongly worded UN mandate since the Gulf War was granted to INTERFET, with lead responsibility granted to the Australian command of what was dubbed Operation Stabilise, led by Major General Peter Cosgrove.

The consent question was solved procedurally by Habibie's concession to the inevitable, and substantively by the extensive documentation of Indonesia's interference in Timorese affairs. Yet despite obtaining this 'managed' consent, most UN member-states (with the primary exception of Australia) remained reluctant to contribute to such a high-stakes and high-cost deployment. This reluctance in turn posed a serious problem for the operational design, planning, and deployment of INTERFET. The persistent capacity problem facing peace enforcement operations led to the assumption of a heavily disproportionate degree of the burden by Australia (and, to a lesser extent, New Zealand). While INTERFET eventually included contributions of forces from 22 states, in the first two weeks of the operation (when

Table 9.2 Contributions to INTERFET (total force strength at peak deployment: approx. 10,000)

Country	Contribution(s)	% of total contribution at peak deployment
Australia	*Maritime:* 3 × Frigates, 1 × Landing Ship, 3 × Landing Craft, 1 × Tanker, 1 × Jet Cat, 1 × Clearance Diving Team. *Land:* HQINTERFET, 1 × Joint Support Unit, Brigade Headquarters, 10 Signals Squadron, 2 × Infantry battalion groups, 1 × Mechanized battalion group, Special Forces, 1 × Armoured Reconnaissance Squadron, 1 × Armoured Personnel Carrier Squadron, 2 × Construction Squadron, 1 × Aviation Regiment, 1 × Reconnaissance Squadron, 1 × Brigade Administrative Support Battalion, 1 × Forward Logistic Support Group, 1 × Forward Support Base, Combat Engineer Regiment. *Air:* 12 × C130, 2 × 707, 4 × Caribou aircraft.	41.0
Brazil	*Land:* Reinforced MP Platoon (50 members).	0.4
Canada	*Maritime:* 1 × Tanker, 2 × Helicopters. *Land:* Infantry company group, 1 × Construction Troop. *Air:* 2 × C130, Air Support Team.	4.7
Denmark	*Land:* Staff Officers.	Unknown
Egypt	*Land:* Contribution to medical facility, 70 hospital staff.	0.5
Fiji	*Land:* Infantry company group.	Unknown
France	*Maritime:* 1 × Frigate, 1 × Landing Ship. *Land:* Surgical Team Protection Element. *Air:* 3 × C130, 3 × Puma Helicopters.	4.7
Germany	*Land:* Casualty Evacuation Support. *Air:* 2 × C160.	0.6
Ireland	*Land:* HQ Element, Ranger Platoon.	Unknown
Italy	*Maritime:* 1 × Landing Ship. *Land:* 1 × Company Group. *Air:* 2 × G222, 4 × Helicopters.	4.0
Jordan	*Land:* Infantry Battalion Group.	Unknown
Kenya	*Land:* Infantry Company, Engineer Troop.	Unknown
Malaysia	*Land:* Staff Officers.	0.2
New Zealand	*Maritime:* 1 × Frigate, 1 × Tanker. *Land:* Infantry Battalion Group. *Air:* 2 × C130, 6 × Helicopters.	8.4
Norway	*Land:* Staff Officers.	Unknown
Philippines	*Land:* Humanitarian Task Force. *Air:* 2 × C130.	4.2
Portugal	*Maritime:* 1 × Frigate.	Unknown
South Korea	*Land:* Infantry Battalion G roup.	3.0
Singapore	*Maritime:* 2 × Landing Ships. *Land:* 1 × Medical Team.	1.9
Thailand	*Maritime:* 3 × Vessels. *Land:* 1 × Task Group (Battalion size). *Air:* 2 × C130.	13.0
United Kingdom	*Land:* Infantry company group. *Air:* 2 × C130.	2.4
United States	*Maritime:* 1 × Cruiser, 1 × Helo Support Ship, 2 × Support Ships. *Land:* Logistic Group, J2 and J6 Staff, CMOC Signals Company. *Air:* 4 × C130, 1 × C12, 1 × EP3.	11.5

Sources: Coleman, 2007; Ryan, 2000.

costs and risks were at their highest), Australia supplied over two-thirds of the troops. Even at the deployment's peak strength at the end of October (more than a month into the operation) Australia still accounted for over 40 percent of INTER-FET forces (see Table 9.2).

Cultivating 'impartiality'

INTERFET commanders demonstrated a strong command of the overtly political nature of the mission they were poised to undertake. As such, Cosgrove and his fellow officers considered diplomatic overtures to their counterparts within the TNI, an essential precursor to force deployment. The INTERFET tactical command specifically sought to cultivate a working relationship with Indonesian Major General Kiki Syahnakri and the senior commanders in the TNI. With the goal of keeping the TNI informed of INTERFET plans from the outset, Cosgrove and other INTERFET commanders participated in daily briefings with Syahnakri and his subordinates, and carefully selected liaison officers for attachment to the TNI.

The establishment of this multifaceted structure for consultation was driven by an estimation that both the effectiveness of the mission (and the security of the personnel attached to it) would be contingent on securing as much 'buy-in' from the TNI as possible. This estimation was based in large part on the obvious links of the Indonesian armed forces and police to the militias, as well as of the belief of INTERFET commanders that the militias, not the TNI, would likely provide the main opposition to restoring stability. In the end, this structured interaction served as a means of defusing potential tensions and convincing the TNI that INTERFET was for all intents and purposes an impartial force solely interested in the restoration of order to East Timor.

This working relationship at the command level was put to the test on several occasions during the operation, particularly as INTERFET forces faced hostility and interference from TNI units on the ground, and as they encountered the levels of devastation wrought by the TNI in Dili and elsewhere. Nonetheless, it held to a sufficient degree to yield operational benefits. Among those benefits was the development of a timetable (the 19 September Agreement) for coordinating the insertion of INTERFET forces with the full withdrawal of TNI and Indonesian police (POLRI). This timetable called for a phased withdrawal of remaining Indonesian forces, so as to allow Jakarta to save face and to stave off direct confrontations with TNI forces once INTERFET commenced in full.

The outcome

On the immediate heels of the 19 September Agreement, INTERFET forces deployed to East Timor. Force projection, under the coercive ROE associated with peace enforcement, was directed at what INTERFET commanders determined to be the primary threat to achieving their mandate – the pro-Indonesian militias. From an operational standpoint, however, INTERFET was forced to grapple with the reality that TNI commanders were unable (or in some cases unwilling) to compel junior officers and enlisted personnel to cease and desist in supporting and equipping the militias. Whereas the presence and activities of even the least disciplined and organized militia posed a significant threat to the security of the civilian population, the operations of those militia closest to the TNI and those consisting of TNI special forces dressed as militia constituted particular challenges (Robinson, 2001).

'Ubiquity' and 'ink spots'

The INTERFET deployment was led by a vanguard of nine warships, including HMS *Glasgow* and the USS *Mobile Bay*, which delivered approximately 1,000 ground forces to Dili on 20 September. This detachment was followed in a matter of days by an additional 4,000 troops. The force structure in the first week was constituted chiefly of Australian light infantry and special forces, with smaller contingents of light infantry and special forces from New Zealand and the United Kingdom; the United States provided logistics and intelligence personnel, as well as naval support.

The speed with which INTERFET's well-equipped and highly trained force was deployed immediately spawned a massive outflow of militia forces across the border into Indonesian-controlled West Timor. This exodus occurred despite the fact that TNI/militia forces outnumbered INTERFET by a ratio of approximately 3-to-1 (Dickens, 2001). The swift and decisive nature of the initial deployment had the secondary effect of discouraging the TNI from openly reneging on the 19 September Agreement. Although provocations involving Indonesian naval and aircraft occurred periodically throughout the operation, they diminished in frequency and significance after the first two weeks.

The strategic plan of Operation Stabilise was likened by Cosgrove to an ink spot. Ground forces were first concentrated in Dili; once security was established, they were dispersed to neighboring areas, with an eventual goal of incrementally linking all the 'ink spots' and consolidating INTERFET's hold on the whole of the territory. Naval and air power (incorporating contributions from the United States, the United Kingdom, France, and New Zealand) played a key supporting role, allowing ground forces to carry out the robust ROE without significant concern for external interference. The effective combination of maritime and air power with the light infantry and special forces dislocated the militias, in part by undermining their resolve through a demonstration of political will, according to the characterization of one senior INTERFET commander (Robertson, 2000). In a retrospective lecture, Cosgrove himself echoed this sentiment, pointing in particular to the extensive naval deployment as an 'important indicator of national will and international resolve' and further adding that the 'high end capabilities' of INTERFET made the force seem 'ubiquitous' and, as a result, discouraged 'more adventurist behavior by our adversaries' (Cosgrove, 2000).

Mission accomplished

With respect to its immediate mandate, INTERFET was an unqualified success. Within five days of the arrival of the initial contingent of INTERFET forces in Dili, the TNI began a rapid withdrawal. This withdrawal reduced the Indonesian presence in East Timor from 15,000 to 1,200 by 28 September, to a few hundred by the end of September, and culminated in complete withdrawal by 1 November. Indonesian submarine and aircraft activity similarly diminished significantly within two weeks of INTERFET's deployment. There were no major incidents between

INTERFET and the TNI, and overall there were few exchanges of gunfire and only minimal casualties (Dickens, 2001).

As INTERFET planners had anticipated, the effectiveness of the militia was significantly curtailed by the uprooting of their patrons, and the vast majority of the militias rapidly dispersed or disbanded, with most of the combatants fleeing for sanctuary in Indonesian West Timor. With stability restored and the mandate established in UNSC Resolution 1264 satisfied, INTERFET began the process of transferring responsibility for security operations to UNTAET (the UN Transitional Administration in East Timor), as stipulated in the resolution establishing that successor operation; that process was completed, and the INTERFET operation officially terminated, on 28 February 2000.

Lessons learned

The instructiveness of this profile of INTERFET stems in part from the fact that the operation was undertaken at a crucial juncture in the history of UN peace operations. To the extent that INTERFET represented a litmus test of sorts of the UN's ability to deliver peace enforcement to societies torn by internal conflict, its outcome was mixed. On the positive side of the ledger, decisive Security Council action afforded the Secretary-General's office and the DPKO the opportunity to demonstrate a newfound political resolve. Even more importantly, Australian leadership facilitated the UN's assembly of the needed resources to tangibly underwrite that resolve. At the same time, the longstanding misalignment between ambition and capacity created a division of labor problem for INTERFET, as Australia was forced to bear a disproportionate share of the burden for the operation at its most crucial juncture. In the end, this summary of INTERFET reveals several crucial lessons when thinking about the feasibility and effectiveness of contemporary peace enforcement.

Contemporary context

INTERFET bears some resemblance to the UN's first full-fledged peace enforcement operation, ONUC (discussed at the outset of the preceding chapter). For one, each operation began from a point of origin as a limited mission deployed with the full (if managed) consent of appropriate parties. Each operation was tasked to carry out a very narrowly defined task amidst a turbulent internal conflict. Further, both operations were quickly and unexpectedly (from the UN vantage point at least) transformed into broad-based exercises in peace enforcement.

Yet at the same time, INTERFET differed greatly from ONUC or any previous UN operation, due to the profound differences in the political context surrounding the operation. The main point of departure was the extent to which INTERFET served as an intermediary between the rump detachment of UN election officials that preceded it (UNAMET), and the extensive state- and civil society-building effort that followed it (UNTAET). In this way, INTERFET can be thought of as one installment in the larger saga that was the creation, defense, administration, and crafting of a nation-state under UN auspices.

This difference had significant implications on how these two 'historical bookends' (ONUC and INTERFET) were carried forth at the operational level. Upon its deployment, ONUC was forced to evolve toward the embrace of a peace enforcement role as a reaction to the changing dynamics of the conflict and the changing political environment sustaining that conflict. As a result, ONUC's assumption of tasks normally carried out by the state, particularly with respect to maintaining law and order, occurred more or less by default as the social order disintegrated along with the Congolese state. In the case of INTERFET, no East Timorese state had ever existed. Indeed, it was with the intent of creating such a state (or, perhaps more charitably, affording the East Timorese the opportunity) that peace enforcement was introduced. In picking up the pieces of UNAMET, INTERFET inherited the responsibility for expelling unwanted and unwarranted interference in the political self-expression of a nation by another state.

Getting the mandate right

In the specific case of INTERFET, one of the best illustrations of what went 'right' was that the demands of the mission shaped the terms of the mandate, rather than the inverse (and more frequent) scenario. With the situation on the ground devolving into chaos, the Security Council and the Secretary-General's office correctly adduced what was required to restore order. Much of INTERFET's success stems from the fact that a circumscribed mandate lent cohesiveness of purpose to the operation. At the same time, a broad degree of authority for action attached to that mandate lent the mission the ability to pursue that objective on the ground without significant operational constraints.

Managing consent

Along with the legal and ethical diminution of Indonesian claims to dominion over East Timor, Indonesia's forced call for an outside stabilization force helped confer legitimacy on INTERFET by encouraging the perception of consent for the operation, even among previously skeptical parties such as China. This was especially crucial to securing Australian leadership of INTERFET. Though Australia had envisioned and expressed the need for a limited force for post-ballot stabilization well before the vote, its rather minimalist projection of what that force would actually do was certainly a reflection of an overriding interest in placating Indonesia. The removal of customary international legal obstacles to a more extensive involvement was facilitated by Indonesia's political capitulation. In this way, Habibie's extension of a highly managed consent made it palatable for Australia to lead a stabilization force and for other member-states to contribute to that force.

The limits of peace enforcement

Most retrospectives of INTERFET have roundly celebrated the operation as an overwhelming success. Clearly INTERFET did successfully deliver on its mandated responsibility for conferring stability and security in East Timor, by quelling (if not ending) the rampant violence wrought by the militias. INTERFET did less to reintroduce law and order or aid UNAMET in the delivery of humanitarian assistance, though it seems plausible that gains were made on these fronts as a result of the stability INTERFET restored. To the extent that INTERFET did succeed, however, it should be pointed out that this success was a derivative of the clearly defined and circumscribed nature of that mandate. While this should not be taken as a diminution of INTERFET's accomplishments, it is critical to point out that INTERFET succeeded in large part because its goals were exceedingly limited in scope and few in number.

It is equally important to point out that celebrations of INTERFET as a success story tend to overlook that the operation itself only came to pass due to the drastic overreach and subsequent failure of UNAMET. In the same way that INTERFET's success was derivative of its limited goals, so too was it derivative of the UN's short-sightedness with respect to its initial commitment to East Timor. Though again this should not be construed as a critique of INTERFET per se, it does reveal a fundamental absence of contingency planning and a troubling resource shortfall at the heart of UN operations in East Timor.

In the end, assessing INTERFET, or any conflict management operation (including those that preceded and followed INTERFET in East Timor), requires consideration of the operation's effects from the oft-overlooked vantage point of the population targeted for assistance. East Timor was stabilized, and the violence and human rights abuses were quickly and effectively suspended by INTERFET's display of measured military force and the withdrawal of most of the pro-Indonesian militia. Yet INTERFET also encountered a mounting humanitarian disaster and a looming crisis of governance which – as a peace enforcement operation – it was intentionally and by design unable to forestall. These larger structural problems, insufficiently treated, paved the way for a return to violence and insecurity after INTERFET's termination.

Study questions

1   Consider the UN-authorized, Australian-led INTERFET operation.

   a   What were the UN's chief interests? What were Australia's primary motives?

   b   What (or who) were the primary obstacles to the successful implementation of INTERFET?

   c   What role did military force play in this operation? Political and diplomatic leverage? Legal and normative debates?

2   Could an operation like INTERFET be carried out directly by the UN? How might such an operation be similar to, or different from, INTERFET?

3   On balance, was INTERFET a successful effort at conflict management? Why or why not?

4   Is peace enforcement a reactive approach, dictated by events, or a proactive response, determined at the place and time of the peace enforcer's choosing?

5   What does this case study suggest about the prospects for, and problems of, peace enforcement in contemporary application? Is peace enforcement too ambitious, or insufficient?

Suggested reading

Beauvais, Joel C. 2001. 'Benevolent Despotism: A Critique of UN State-Building in East Timor,' *New York University Journal of International Law and Politics*, 33 (4): 1101–1178.

Chesterman, Simon. 2001. *East Timor in Transition: From Conflict Prevention to State-Building*. New York, NY: International Peace Academy, Project on Transitional Administrations.

Chopra, Jarat. 2000. 'The UN's Kingdom of East Timor,' *Survival*, 42 (3): 27–39.

Cotton, James. 1999. 'Peacekeeping in East Timor: An Australian Policy Departure,' *Australian Journal of International Affairs*, 53 (3): 237–246.

Dee, Moreen. 2001. 'Coalitions of the Willing and Humanitarian Intervention: Australia's Involvement with INTERFET,' *International Peacekeeping*, 8 (3): 1–20.

Dickens, David. 2001. 'The United Nations in East Timor: Intervention at the Military Operational Level,' *Contemporary Southeast Asia*, 23 (2): 213–232.

Krieger, Heike (ed.). 1997. *East Timor and the International Community*. Cambridge: Cambridge University Press.

Martin, Ian. 2001. *Self-Determination in East Timor: The United Nations, the Ballot, and the International Intervention*. Boulder, CO: Lynne Rienner.

Smith, Michael G. (with Moreen Dee). 2003. *Peacekeeping in East Timor: The Path to Independence*. Boulder, CO: Lynne Rienner.

Suhrke, Astri. 2001. 'Peacekeepers as Nation-Builders: Dilemmas of the UN in East Timor,' *International Peacekeeping*, 8 (4): 1–20.

Traub, James. 2000. 'Inventing East Timor,' *Foreign Affairs*, 79 (4): 74–89.

10 International adjudication

This chapter profiles the contours of international adjudication as a method for settling international conflicts. It begins with a brief synopsis of a resort to arbitration in one installment of the protracted conflict between India and Pakistan. The chapter then explores the defining criteria, legal, theoretical, and political debates, historical evolution, and inner workings of arbitration and judicial settlement in the context of international conflict management.

International adjudication in brief: insights from the Rann of Kutch case

The origins of the Rann of Kutch crisis of 1965 can be traced to arrangements associated with partition of the Indian subcontinent by Britain in 1947. The terms of partition ignored a longstanding territorial dispute between the Indo-British authority in the province of Sind and the rulers of the neighboring autonomous state of Kutch over the Rann (roughly translated as 'desolate place'), a salty desert-like area alternating as a body of water during the rainy season. While allusions were made to the potential for mineral and natural resource deposits in the Rann, its chief importance was its status as a boundary marker. By not addressing or even referencing the area in the redefinition of political authority and jurisdiction on the subcontinent, the British allowed the underlying sources of the dispute to fester.

Competing claims

With the accession of the princely state of Kutch to Indian control, and the reallocation of the province of Sind to the new state of Pakistan, the dispute over the Rann joined a long litany of grievances between the two adversaries. The positions of both India and Pakistan were consistent with those expressed prior to partition. India held that the boundary between Sind and Kutch was well-defined. Moreover, the Indian government cited the administrative records of the British authorities and various maps dating to British rule as evidence that the Rann was entirely within the state of Kutch. Pakistan countered that a new demarcation of the border was needed, citing the historical precedent of Sind jurisdiction in that area since its annexation by the British in 1843 as proof that it was entitled to control the Rann's northern half (Wetter, 1971).

An intractable dispute?

The ongoing dispute over the Rann resulted in numerous diplomatic rows between the two adversaries, even prompting a brief exchange between military forces in 1956. It was fueled by disagreement over the validity of the maps and other documents dating to the period of British rule. Pakistan repeatedly called for internationalization of the matter, first in the creation of a Joint Boundary Commission in 1949, and later (in 1953) for reference to an impartial tribunal. Some potential for progress was exhibited in a joint agreement in 1959 in advance of the Indo-Pakistani Border Conference of 1960. This agreement called for resolution of all border disputes by negotiation and for 'referral to an impartial tribunal for settlement and implementation of that settlement by demarcation on the ground and exchange of territorial jurisdiction, if any.' However, subsequent dismissals of the validity of any dispute over the Rann by the Indian government ushered in a period of increasing tension (Untawale, 1974).

Escalation and mediation

The situation worsened significantly in January 1965, when Pakistani police units commenced patrols in Indian-held territory. Tensions mounted throughout the spring, coming to a head on 8 April when each side engaged in reciprocal attacks on one another's police posts. A hurried cease-fire was quickly broken as hostilities renewed during the last week of April 1965. By summer the situation threatened to devolve into all-out war, as the deterioration of the situation coincided with a similar clash over territory in the disputed area of Jammu-Kashmir. Fearing the outbreak of major war in a volatile region, British Prime Minister Harold Wilson intervened, offering to broker a cease-fire based on the principle of restoring the territory to the status quo *ex ante* (Wetter, 1971).

Wilson's mediation helped facilitate the India–Pakistan Cease-Fire Agreement on 11 May, with the full terms of the agreement accepted by India and Pakistan on 30 June. The Agreement contained provisions for the mutual withdrawal of each side's forces to their positions of 1 January 1965 and continuation of direct negotiations toward a comprehensive peace settlement. In addition to these standard elements of a cease-fire, the Agreement of 30 June also provided for a precise and elaborately detailed procedure for revisiting the disputed boundary in the Rann of Kutch (Sharma, 1997).

Enter adjudication

Terms of arbitration

According to the terms of the compromis specified within the Agreement, after fully implementing the cease-fire the two sides agreed to seek mutual accord on the boundary. If unable to do so, the parties conceded to submission of the matter to an impartial tribunal with binding authority. As stipulated by the parties, this tribunal was to function in a manner consistent with an arbitration body, and had to be constituted within four months of the cease-fire. The tribunal would ultimately consist of three arbitrators – one nominated by each party, with the chair jointly selected. Indian and Pakistani nationals were ineligible, and failure to come to terms within three months would result in appointment by the UN Secretary-General. With the Jammu-Kashmir dispute as a backdrop, planned negotiations at the ministerial level over the Rann of Kutch matter were cancelled, triggering the creation of the Tribunal. On 15 February 1966 the Indo-Pakistan Western Boundary Case Tribunal was constituted in Geneva, Switzerland. When the two governments proved unable to concur, UN Secretary-General U Thant nominated Gunnar Lagergren (President of the Court of Appeal for Western Sweden) to preside as Chair.

Implementation difficulties

Adjudication was fraught with problems stemming from the poor state of Indo-Pakistani relations at the time. The two sides disagreed over the nature of the dispute, as India referred to it as a 'territorial' matter while Pakistan claimed it was a 'boundary dispute.' Within months of signing the agreement, each party expressed divergent views of the scope and intent of the tribunal. India pointed to the wording of the 1959 Indo-Pakistan Agreement (which first referenced introduction of a tribunal, providing the basis for the British delegation's advocacy) in support of its claim that the Western Boundary Case Tribunal was not to arbitrate, but merely to hear arguments and weigh evidence. India also contended that neither the consultation nor eventual decision of the Tribunal should constitute a legal precedent with reference to other disputes between the two sides. This was a position consistent with India's earlier expressed opposition to submitting the issue to the ICJ (Pavri, 1997).

Conversely, external arbitration was appealing to Pakistan, who had previously made overtures toward this end. Not surprisingly, Pakistan interpreted the creation of the Tribunal as precedent-setting, and appealed for application of the adjudicatory model for dispute resolution to other outstanding boundary disputes between India and Pakistan. While eventually (with prodding from the British mediators) India did accept the Tribunal's arbitration authority and Pakistan agreed to consider the Rann arbitration a stand-alone arrangement, the divergence between the two sides betrayed their wariness of the Tribunal, as well as lack of optimism regarding the prospects of a lasting political settlement.

Proceedings of the Tribunal

The first hearings convened by the Tribunal occurred in September 1966 at the UN Office in Geneva. Partly to accommodate Indian reticence on establishing precedent, the Tribunal was technically created as an independent institution with no official connection to the UN; its activities were financed by the parties themselves. The Tribunal continued to convene and assess evidence until 14 July 1967, holding 172 sessions and hearing the presentation of arguments for a total of 550 hours during that 11-month period. Over 350 maps of the Rann of Kutch were introduced, and approximately 1,000 other documents were filed as exhibits in the case (Untawale, 1974).

Issues and evidence

The arguments presented by the parties to the Tribunal were detailed and complex, turning chiefly on three key points: the geophysical properties of the Rann (Was it a body of water, and if so, what type?); the applicability of customary law regarding the introduction of a 'median line' (if found to be a land-locked sea or boundary lake, customary law generally provided for partition of such bodies of water in roughly equal proportion); and the historical precedents for administration of the territory established under British rule (as well as their admissibility). Competing depictions of the border as featured on various maps produced by both sides proved to be the key form of evidence in the case.

Both parties agreed that the Tribunal was free to declare a boundary distinct from either of the two options presented by the parties if it saw fit, though the Indian position held that the Tribunal was established to ascertain where the boundary had been, whereas Pakistan contended that the boundary should be fixed in consideration to where it should be based on principles of equality gleaned from international law. Being in possession of an older and more detailed set of maps, India enjoyed a distinct advantage with respect to cartographic evidence. Most of the maps introduced by India depicted boundary lines dating to the British period and roughly consistent with its claims; the Pakistani delegation introduced a set of maps produced specifically for the Tribunal.

The award

The decision of the Tribunal was rendered on 19 February 1968, at which time the opinions of the members of the Tribunal were distributed. Subsequent analyses of the content and tenor of the Award demonstrate a striking degree of political sensitivity and nuance. The term 'judicial inquiry' was used in place of 'arbitration,' while the evidentiary basis for a ruling was tempered with acknowledgment of the international legal principle of equity and with the wider interest of the international community in conflict management and the promotion of peace (Untawale, 1974). The balancing act struck by the Tribunal culminated in a ruling reflecting a compromise between the competing perspectives of India and Pakistan.

The decision of the Tribunal was by majority vote; Nasrollah Entezam of Iran (nominated by Pakistan) concurred with the Chair, while Ales Bebler of Yugoslavia (the Indian nominee) dissented. The decision determined a boundary which recognized roughly 90 percent (3,180 square miles) of the disputed territory as Indian, allocating the remainder (320 square miles) to Pakistan (Wetter, 1971). However, the Award modified India's claimed boundary in a number of instances, principally in allocating to Pakistan a large portion of the most usable land in the northern half of the Rann (a principal source of contention between the two sides).

The terms of the Award elicited serious misgivings in India; though Prime Minister Indira Gandhi denounced the ruling as political in nature, the specifics of the cease-fire agreement bound the parties to implement the Tribunal's findings. Accordingly, in February 1968 her government expressed its willingness to abide by the decision, braving a vote of no-confidence and a massive campaign of civil disobedience in the process (Untawale, 1974). Fashioned from an implementation agreement, a joint Indo-Pakistan team began the work of demarcating the boundary according to the terms of the ruling in March 1968, completing the task of erecting nearly 1,000 concrete pillars denoting the new boundary the following June. The new boundary came into effect at midnight on 5 July 1969, while the Tribunal itself was formally disbanded on 22 September 1969.

What is international adjudication?

The use of adjudication in response to international political disputes such as that over the Rann of Kutch is considered by some the epitome of the utopian idealism of the inter-war period of the 1920s and 1930s (Posner and Yoo, 2004). Yet despite the continued absence of a world court or arbitrator with compulsory jurisdiction sufficient to contain the scourge of war, the existence and use of international tribunals to adjudicate international disputes has grown dramatically over the course of the twentieth century. Whether through the use of arbitrators (a 'dependent' form of adjudicatory tribunal that is formed by and linked to the parties to a dispute) or more independent standing courts, international adjudication has taken on particular importance since the end of the Cold War. As one recent longitudinal study found, 63 percent of all international judicial activity (5,598 out of 8,895 cases) occurred after 1989 (Alter, 2003). The 1990s witnessed the creation of more international courts than any other decade (Romano, 1999: 729). There are now 20 different international legal bodies issuing binding decisions in trade disputes, enforcing rules pertaining to the law of the sea, and rendering judgments designed to promote and protect the rights of citizens, refugees, and civilians during wartime, among other things.

International adjudication as conflict management

Aside from its broader contribution to the resolution of disputes between and among states (and, increasingly, NSAs such as MNCs, NGOs, and individuals), international adjudication also serves as a form of conflict management. Adjudication involves referral of an ongoing dispute to an impartial third-party tribunal for the rendering of a binding decision, usually steeped in the treaties, customs, and/or cases providing the basis of international law (Lucy, 1999). Defined by the attempt of an impartial third party to utilize legal, extra-legal, and normative approaches and institutions to craft and reach legal settlements between parties to a conflict, adjudicatory approaches still reside squarely in the general space associated with third-party conflict management (Bercovitch and Regan, 2004).

Adjudication relies on legal processes and systems, in conjunction with standing or ad hoc legal institutions, to contain and manage the deleterious effects of international conflicts, ruling out the use of coercive force for such purposes. Yet in its reliance on a purportedly neutral third party to bridge the gap between two parties to a conflict, adjudication is functionally similar to other forms of international conflict management. This characterization is borne out in the correspondence between adjudication and other approaches to international conflict management (Bilder, 2007). In one recent empirical study of conflict management, the use of adjudication was shown to correlate closely with the use of 'communication' (e.g., negotiation) between the parties to a conflict, as well as with the involvement of mediators (Dixon, 1996).

Like other forms of third-party conflict management, adjudication is steeped in the normative and political climate of collective security provision, and as such is typically a reaction to some threat or challenge to international peace and security. However, the parallels between adjudication and other approaches to international conflict management are not limited to a point of common origin in the promotion of collective security. Adjudication shares with other forms of conflict management (such as peacekeeping and mediation) a traditionalist regard for the prevailing normative constructs of the international system, including the inadmissibility of coercive force as a means for resolving disputes (except in self-defense) and the central position of the organizing tenet of state sovereignty (as reflected in the jurisdictional authority of adjudicatory bodies). Similarly, adjudication is also generally only attempted after some exhibition of ripeness in the conflict, and with the consent of the parties themselves to submit the matter for adjudication (Bilder, 1989: 476). As one former ICJ justice noted, 'every recourse of states to international adjudication proceeds from their free will' (De Visscher, 1956: 467).

Defining features of international adjudication

International adjudication is not monolithic. Adjudication comes in two main forms (arbitration and judicial settlement), and significant differences in the structure and functioning of arbitration panels and international courts (considered in detail below) exist (Brownlie, 1999). At the same time, the empirical record of international adjudication suggests a sizeable degree of overlap in the two approaches. Indeed, the convergence in practice between courts and arbitration suggests that for the purpose of assessment as a form of conflict management, they can be treated as functionally similar (Simmons, 1999).

A strict interpretation of the workings of international courts suggests that they are to be guided solely by legal criteria and considerations, whereas arbitrators may have to consider claims in light of other, non-legal, factors. At the same time, the rulings of courts are sometimes shaped by quasi-legal considerations such as the 'equity principle,' while the frequent use of arbitration in matters of customary international law have lent it an unquestioned degree of legal status and authority. Whichever approach is used, the result is a legally binding ruling betraying similar obligations for compliance. In sum, whether an adjudication effort involves the use of arbitrators or international courts, the attempt to manage armed conflicts is defined by several common features.

Reliance on legal principles

International adjudication is typically distinguished from other forms of international conflict management by the essential condition that it involves a formally binding decision reached according to a legal rule, principle, or precedent (Gray and Kingsbury, 1993). The basis of the adjudicatory approach in this legalist paradigm is evident in the use of standing and ad hoc legal bodies, reliance on and search for legal precedent, and emphasis on assembling evidence and presenting arguments outlining conflicting positions. This is unlike other approaches to conflict management which reside in the decidedly 'grayer' political realm of compromise and ambiguity. A chief implication of the legalist basis of adjudication is the extent to which third-party adjudicatory bodies and processes feature an accompanying concern with the underlying causes of an ongoing conflict. To a degree far in excess of other forms of conflict management (such as peacekeeping, mediation, and peace enforcement), adjudication approaches are prompted not only by an interest in managing a particular conflict, but also by a motivation to settle and resolve the disputes that animate it.

One significant example of the rootedness of adjudication in the legal process is the fact that the process itself is dependent on the presence and involvement of one or more judges. Regardless of the nature of the claims, the arguments of the disputants, or the nature of the parties to the dispute, adjudication (whether through arbitration or the use of a standing court) cannot be said to apply in the absence of an impartial arbiter (Kelsen, 1943). Likewise, a related distinguishing characteristic of adjudication as a form of conflict management is the space it affords to affected parties to assemble legal arguments backed by reasoned proof and evidence. In this sense, adjudication is a mechanism for managing conflicts that grants formal and institutional expression to rationality and argument in the social realm (Fuller and Winston, 1978).

Ex ante *compliance*

Whether adjudication involves arbitration or judicial procedure, it is defined by an agreement of parties to the dispute *in advance* to comply with the ruling or award of the tribunal. Under international law, an international court or arbitration panel can render a binding decision only when the states or other parties in question have expressly or implicitly consented to the court or arbitrator exercising jurisdiction over the particular dispute, or to the area of the law in which that dispute resides (Bilder, 2007: 198). That consent may be granted to the court or arbitrator prior to consideration of the matter, or in advance through some standing treaty or other legal instrument. Regardless of the arrangement, extending such consent binds the state or other party to comply with the ruling or award in advance of its determination – what is called *ex ante* compliance.

Given the persistence of anarchy as the primary organizing principle of the international system, this extension of *ex ante* compliance may seem paradoxical. States are hardly compelled to submit disputes to adjudication, and no mechanism to enforce compliance with any ruling or award once it is rendered exists. The fact that the compliance in question is of a secondary nature – meaning that it consists of compliance with the rulings of a court rather than with some pre-established rule or accepted norm – only adds to the unlikely nature of *ex ante* compliance (Bulterman and Kuijer, 1996; Fisher, 1981). Indeed, compliance has become the central focus of analysis by scholars concerned with adjudication, and as such will be revisited later in this chapter.

Independence

The use of international adjudication as a tool of international conflict management typically proceeds without direct or undue interference from the parties to the conflict. The independence of adjudicatory bodies can be measured both formally and functionally. Strictly speaking, international tribunals are fully independent when they can be said to exercise compulsory jurisdiction over the parties to the conflict in advance of the dispute, and are staffed by appointed or elected judges who are protected from removal for any reason other than poor performance. From a practical standpoint, international tribunals exhibit independence when the rulings they produce, and the deliberations underlying those rulings, are based on applicable legal principles and precedents rather than political expediency (Helfer and Slaughter, 2005).

Table 10.1 Assessing independence of tribunals

Characteristic	Dependent	Independent
Term	Duration of dispute	Permanent
Jurisdiction	Dispute/treaty	Area of law
Initiation	Victim	Independent party
Number of states	Bilateral	Multilateral
State consent to jurisdiction	After dispute occurs	Before dispute occurs
Source of panel members	Chosen by disputants	Chosen by other parties

Source: Adapted from Posner and Yoo, 2004.

Independence further varies within and across the two major sub-categories of international adjudication, depending on the particular context surrounding a dispute or ruling (see Table 10.1). For instance, arbitration carried out by a single arbitrator is considered more dependent than that undertaken by a panel, as evinced in the concentration of authority in one individual selected jointly by the parties. Because they are typically constituted on an ad hoc basis by the disputants themselves, arbitration panels in general are dependent to varying degrees on the parties to the dispute (Merrills, 2005). The greater independence of courts relative to arbitration panels is reinforced by the fact that international courts have permanent jurists and legal staff who do not depend on the disputants for their appointment or salary; furthermore, they operate in accordance with established rules and procedures with a wide range of legal jurisdiction afforded to them. Yet while a permanent court possesses more structural independence as a function of its permanence and its compulsory jurisdiction, states may paradoxically find it easier to evade or delay compliance with the rulings of a court than an arbitration panel of their own creation (Posner and Yoo, 2004).

Legal and theoretical parameters

Like other approaches to the management of armed conflict, adjudication is a form of third-party intervention. However, the distinct nature of adjudication within the pantheon of conflict management approaches corresponds with an equally distinct set of theoretical and legal concerns stemming from its application. While this chapter is concerned with the practice of international adjudication as a method of third-party conflict management and not international law per se, the basis of the former in the latter requires at least some engagement with and understanding of the standards and practices of international law.

Adjudication and international law

The adjudication of armed conflicts and their underlying disputes by courts and arbitrators has both clear advantages and disadvantages (see Box 10.1). Adjudication is typically concerned only with the immediate dispute, and proceedings unfold according to a particular set of rules and processes associated with the immediate tribunal. As a result, while the rulings and awards produced can and do establish precedents, particularly with respect to the applicability of adjudication in other similar conflicts, the immediate and major impact of most rulings and awards generally extends only to the parties in the dispute (Sarat and Grossman, 1975). In the end, adjudication is an inherently adversarial process. Legal arguments are presented which can in some cases lead courts or arbitrators to render 'zero-sum' rulings – rulings which may be binding, but which may also lead to intense dissatisfaction in one or more parties to the conflict, potentially sowing the seeds for a renewal of hostilities.

Box 10.1 Advantages and disadvantages of international adjudication

As a conflict management process, international adjudication offers a number of distinct advantages over other approaches. Adjudication imposes a detailed, fixed, and final decision that the parties to the conflict – in the event they have expressed their willingness to consent to the tribunal's authority – are obligated to accept. Upon doing so, the parties to the conflict subject their grievance to due process. This shifts the contextual environment surrounding the dispute from the ambiguity, polarization, and volatility that typically surrounds inter- and intra-state conflicts to one that is defined and governed by established, consistent, and fair legal rules, principles, precedents, and procedures. Furthermore, adjudication through an international court is institutionalized – meaning that the court provides a standing avenue for redress that any party may use at any time, and which may render verdicts that said party may dislike, without fear of reprisal.

At the same time, adjudication has its disadvantages. Adjudication clearly shifts a great deal of control to the court or arbitrator(s); while pledged to principles of fairness and equity, this enhanced agency could be interpreted as threatening by the parties, while also quickly overwhelming the existing resources available to the court or arbitrator(s). Though not as great of a hazard in arbitration panels, adjudication by international courts may proceed in the absence of sufficient specific or relevant expertise to the matter at hand, as judges tend to be generalists. This problem is compounded by the fact that the jurisdiction of a relevant international court (such as the ICJ or ICC) may not be accepted by both or all of the parties. Even in the event that these problems are overcome, international courts tend to be slow-moving, with significant delays between petition of the court and the case appearing on the docket – delays which may prompt a return to violence in heated and protracted international conflicts. Finally, in the view of its critics (especially advocates of conflict resolution), adjudication is an adversarial process that typically produces zero-sum judgments, and may work at cross-purposes with the development of joint or collaborative solutions to the problems driving the conflict.

(Adapted from Spangler, 2003a, 2003b)

Westphalian orientation

Adjudication is an intriguingly complex form of international conflict management that is at once traditional and innovative, familiar and unique. Like other forms of conflict management, adjudication places a great deal of emphasis on upholding the conventional principles and practices of international politics. Adjudication's overlap with the more limited scope and intent of conflict management places it well within the trajectory of approaches outlined in this book. Indeed, adjudication is decidedly more 'traditional' or 'conventional' (at least to the extent that such terms apply to the relatively new phenomenon of conflict management) than, say, peace enforcement and its front-and-center challenges to state sovereignty, non-interference, and limited force.

In the case of international adjudication, such an orientation stems from adjudication's link to international law. As advanced and codified by the Dutch jurist Hugo Grotius, the modern tradition of international law emerged from support of the practice of conventional statecraft. Indeed, for much of its history the structure and conduct of international law has been rooted in the statist orientation of a Westphalian international system. As a result, adjudicatory approaches to international conflict management have been closely bound by concepts such as state sovereignty and non-interference.

As the experience of the Western Boundary Case Tribunal in the Rann of Kutch crisis demonstrates, the use of courts and tribunals to manage international conflicts has largely been limited to disputes submitted by, and occurring between, states. These disputes have typically concerned matters of interest to the state, such as disputes over territory, property, treaty obligations, and the like. Though often misrepresented as an encroachment on the practice of statecraft, until recently international law has largely been a reflection and extension of it, with little regard or role for NSAs or disputes not filtered through the unit of the state (Schreuer, 1993).

Post-Westphalian leanings

Despite its roots in the state-centric realm of international law, the concept of employing adjudicatory bodies to render binding decisions as a method of managing international conflict has always been at least mildly subversive of that paradigm. This subversion stems from the fact that international adjudication is steeped in a form of legal and political theorizing that seeks to draw an analogy between the legal systems and rules governing most domestic societies and polities and the nascent and much weaker body of international law.

Simply put, international adjudication is seen by proponents as a first step toward installing the rule of law that prevails in domestic society to the international stage. This is especially true of those seeking to increase the scope and jurisdiction of adjudication through the use of international courts. As one leading scholar of the phenomenon contends, 'it has generally been assumed that the hallmark and *sine qua non* of an effective domestic legal system is the compulsory settlement of disputes by permanent courts' (Bilder, 2007: 195–197). The use of court-based adjudication has been portrayed by some as reflective of a vital opportunity not just to manage the deleterious effects of any single conflict, but to advance the development of international law and global governance (Simmons and Martin, 2002).

Internationalizing the rule of law

Drawing an analogy between domestic and international society with respect to the position of laws and norms clearly opens the door for efforts to expand the power and reach of international law. Universal adherence to the 'rule of law' on the domestic plane has long been a goal sought by the international human rights movement and tacitly supported by the UN, as well as a predicate for membership in regional and international organizations such as the Council of Europe and the

OAS. With this condition front-and-center in contemporary international political discourse, it has taken on normative weight to such a degree that non-compliance incurs costs, especially of a reputational nature.

Defining the 'rule of law'

Though conditions vary, the minimum conditions for the rule of law include a representative form of government elected freely and fairly and fully subservient to the law; a separation between the state and political parties; accountability of military, security, and police forces to civilian authorities; transparency and effective means of redress in the administrative functions of the state; an independent judiciary; and commitment to equal access to and equal protection under the law (Kritz, 2007). Beyond the development of legal institutions or the application of legal technicalities, however, the rule of law is an evolutionary phenomenon that takes root in the political culture, germinating into a set of consensual norms that can produce and sustain a set of legal rules, principles, and procedures to hold all parties equally accountable for their actions.

Upholding the rule of law in any society requires universal or near-universal adherence to the principle of equality under the law for all members of that society. Strong advocates for constructing a parallel rule of law in global politics emphasize the existence of overlap and possibility for harmonization between and across legal traditions and their normative underpinnings, an argument with a strong basis in natural law. The chief implement for this process is the institution of effective international courts with compulsory jurisdiction to serve as strong adjudicators in a wide variety of disputes, including, especially, those involving the use of force and armed conflict. This in turn raises a crucial question related not only to international adjudication as a form of conflict management, but international law in general – what comes first, courts or rules?

Courts or rules?

Courts provide an agent and an arena for the peaceful settlement disputes, and as a result are universally considered essential to maintaining the rule of law. Whether courts can and should be crafted in advance of other facets of a legal order, and used to impose rules and rulings reflective of principles of fairness, equity, and so forth, is a subject that is far more controversial. Critics of such an approach oppose the extent of judicial activism it leads to, as well as the assumption that all matters can and should be subject to adjudication by courts – itself a decidedly Western proposition (Bilder, 2007). Proceeding from a positive law orientation, such critics argue that advocates of international juridical authority tend to overlook or dismiss the extent to which the normative basis of legal systems and codes differs between, among, and in some cases within, the nearly 200 nation-states currently in existence. In either case, it is clear that the effective functioning of an adjudicatory body (whether a standing court or ad hoc tribunal) ultimately hinges on fairness. Establishing such fairness in turn depends on some common understanding of rights and responsibilities derived from commonly-held normative principles, as well as the rules and laws derived from those principles. As Fuller and Winston (1978: 373) note:

you cannot be fair in a moral and legal vacuum ... adjudication cannot function without some standard of decision, either imposed by superior authority or willingly accepted by the disputants. Without some standard of decision the requirement that the judge be impartial becomes meaningless.

International adjudication: a narrative history

In moving beyond the sometimes paralyzing theoretical debates and thinking of adjudication in relation to the more pragmatic concern of international conflict management, adjudication offers promise. Given the inherent ambiguity embedded within so many inter- and intra-state conflicts, adjudication offers the prospect of clarifying the terms of the disputes underlying them, the positions of the parties engaged in them, and the basis for those positions. Rather than representing an embodiment of cosmopolitan utopianism, the practice of third-party adjudication offers the potential for 'attaining a realism that neither expects law to guarantee a peaceful world, nor concludes that law is irrelevant to international peace' (Falk, 1971: 192).

Whereas the practice of adjudication itself is one with a long, rich, and varied history beyond the scope of this book, the application of that practice to inter- and intra-state armed conflict is a fairly recent one that has been shaped in critically important ways by the activities of a small sample of international legal institutions commissioned with such authority. To a greater degree than the other approaches reviewed in this book, the evolution of international adjudication as a means for managing armed conflict is a process that is best understood in conjunction with the introduction and scope of a number of international institutions in the nineteenth and twentieth centuries.

Arbitration in history

Before the establishment of standing repositories of international judicial authority, those seeking adjudicatory remedy in ongoing disputes and conflicts turned to arbitrators. Arbitration dates at least to classical Greece, and was widely used by feudal lords during the Middle Ages (Collier and Lowe, 1999). The dawn of the modern era of international adjudication is frequently associated with the arbitration of the Jay Treaty of 1795 (also known as 'The Treaty of Amity, Commerce, and Negotiation'), establishing the terms of diplomatic relations between Britain and the newly independent United States, as well as the process leading up to the Treaty of Ghent (1814), ending hostilities between those two parties in the War of 1812 (Yoo, 1999). The apex of international arbitration was the first two decades of the twentieth century, coinciding with the creation of the Permanent Court of Arbitration (PCA) at The Hague (see Box 10.2).

Box 10.2 The Permanent Court of Arbitration

The process of arbitration was strongly endorsed in The Hague Conferences of 1899 and 1907, which established a Convention for the Pacific Settlement of International Disputes and, eventually, the Permanent Court of Arbitration based at The Hague at what was the historical peak of the frequency of international arbitration (Bilder, 2007).

While not technically a court at all, the PCA was the first permanent arbitral body, and featured a registry of international arbitrators as a means for promoting the use of adjudication in place of armed conflict. Of the 25 cases heard by the PCA, 21 were dealt with in its first 30 years of existence; though it technically still exists, it has not arbitrated an inter-state dispute since 1932, and has not been consulted at all since 1970 (Butler, 1992; Ginsburg and McAdams, 2004).

The past two centuries have born witness to hundreds of arbitrations, with the most comprehensive estimate to date pointing to the existence of over 450 cases of international arbitration between or among states (Stuyt, 1990). According to that data, the most common types of international conflicts subjected to arbitration stem from border disputes, maritime seizures, arbitrary acts, civil insurrections, and direct inter-state military actions. A significant number of arbitrations convened for the purpose of conflict management (especially of armed conflicts stemming from territorial disputes) have occurred since the end of World War II. These include the Rann of Kutch case in 1968, the 1977 Beagle Channel arbitration (in response to an international crisis between Argentina and Chile), the 1988 Taba arbitration between Egypt and Israel, and the numerous rulings of the Eritrea–Ethiopia Boundary and Claims Tribunals established by the December 2000 peace agreement and in conjunction with UNMEE. Two prominent and active examples of arbitration with respect to armed conflict are the UN Compensation Commission, established by the UN to address claims pertaining to Iraq's invasion of Kuwait in 1990, as well as the Iran–United States Claims Tribunal created in the aftermath of the 1979–1981 hostage crisis (see Box 10.3).

Box 10.3 The Iran–United States Claims Tribunal

Following the Islamic Revolution of 1979 and the subsequent seizure of the US embassy in Tehran by student militants, the United States froze all Iranian financial assets. Following the Iranian agreement to release the American hostages in 1981, the United States agreed to gradually release Iranian assets to the custody of a third-party bank. Through a complex set of negotiations involving the Algerian government as an intermediary, the United States and Iran agreed to create the Iran–United States Claims Tribunal as a means of releasing said assets as well as resolving any outstanding commercial or other disputes between the two parties (Aldrich, 1996). The nine-member panel was constructed in accordance with the classic tripartite approach, with each party appointing three judges, and these judges selecting the 'neutral' third of non-American and non-Iranian nationals. Since the commencing of operations in 1981, roughly 3,800 claims have been filed, and the Tribunal has issued over 600 awards totaling over US$3 billion (Iran–United States Claims Tribunal, 2008). The decisions of the Tribunal have largely been complied with, chiefly as a result of the very specific form and function of jurisdiction extended to it by the parties, and the limited range of disputes it is qualified to adjudicate.

The evolution of judicial settlement

The establishment of the world's first formal organization devoted to maintaining and promoting collective security (the League of Nations) in 1919 was part of a larger transformation in the international peace movement. This push to embed non-violent approaches to the settlement of international disputes in institutional structures also extended to adjudication, as embodied in the first truly global court – the Permanent Court of International Justice (PCIJ).

The Permanent Court of International Justice

The establishment of the PCIJ at The Hague in 1922 was a landmark event in the historical evolution of international jurisprudence. Technically, the PCIJ was not the first standing international court; the little-known Central American Court of Justice, established in 1907 by the Washington Peace Conference as part of the settlement of an ongoing conflict between Guatemala, Honduras, and El Salvador takes that honor (Merrills, 2005). However, the profile and authority ascribed to the PCIJ – based at the elaborate 'Peace Palace,' and operating under the aegis of the League of Nations – made it the first prominent example of an international standing body for the judicial redress of international disputes.

The PCIJ was most notable for its standing panel of justices, appointed for fixed terms out of a desire to craft an adjudicatory body fully independent of nation-states. Foreshadowing its successors, the PCIJ allowed states to determine the terms of the court's jurisdiction through unilateral declarations which could be amended and revised at the behest of the state. Though many states did submit to the court's compulsory jurisdiction, this arrangement allowed states to ignore the court's rulings on particularly thorny issues, such as territorial disputes. Ultimately, with the outbreak of World War II across Europe in 1940 the PCIJ was suspended; it was formally disbanded, along with the League itself, with the founding of the UN in 1946.

The International Court of Justice

Like its predecessor, the ICJ was born of a desire to further institutionalize the practice of international adjudication, and to align that practice with the existence of an international organization chartered to provide for collective security and conflict management. Unlike the PCIJ, however, the ICJ traces its origin to a treaty, the 1946 Statute of the International Court of Justice, which is subsumed within the Charter of the UN, theoretically obligating all member-states of the UN to pay heed to the Court's authority as a court of first instance with jurisdiction over virtually all areas of international law.

THE STRUCTURE OF THE COURT

The ICJ is comprised of 15 judges, appointed jointly by the UNGA and the UNSC to serve nine-year terms. No two judges from the same state can serve concurrently, and appointments are staggered such that every three years three seats are available (although reappointment is possible). Strictly speaking, judges are selected by the UNGA and UNSC with an eye to geographic and legal diversity, although the more powerful states (especially the P-5 members of the Security Council) exhibit disproportionate influence over the composition of the Court, as reflected in the fact that each has had a national representative on the Court since its establishment (Jennings, 1995). The Court also has an elaborately bureaucratic administrative staff, to aid in its remit as the final stop in international legal deliberation and opinion.

ICJ JURISDICTION

Established as the principal judicial organ of the UN, the ICJ is authorized to settle only those contentious cases involving states; NSAs are specifically excluded from submitting such petitions, though the ICJ does have additional statutory authority to render advisory opinions on legal questions referred to it by the UN and other international organizations. The jurisdiction of the ICJ relative to contentious cases is specifically elaborated in Articles 35 and 36. The first condition of ICJ jurisdiction is that a state may submit a dispute by providing explicit consent via a *'special'* (ad hoc*) agreement* (or 'compromis'), though all parties to the dispute must agree for the ICJ to adjudicate the matter. The ICJ may also attain jurisdiction in a matter via insertion of a *compromissory clause* in an international treaty; in this way, the ICJ is viewed as a source for remedy in anticipation of disputes over implementation and interpretation of a bilateral or multilateral treaty. Lastly, states may submit to the compulsory jurisdiction of the ICJ, which translates to a *declaration of willingness to consent* to ICJ rulings on any disputes with other states that have also accepted compulsory jurisdiction under similar conditions.

To the extent it infers full and mandatory consent, the term 'compulsory' is misleading. In actuality, even the compulsory jurisdiction of the ICJ is voluntary, being determined through optional clause declarations developed by each state, and typically containing reservations excluding certain types of disputes from the ICJ's jurisdiction. As of June 2008, 65 states have submitted some form of declaration recognizing the compulsory jurisdiction of the ICJ, with over 80 percent placing some form of reservation(s) on that declaration; of the P-5 states, only the United Kingdom has acknowledged the ICJ's compulsory jurisdiction (ICJ, 2008). As a result, the number of cases submitted to the ICJ since its creation has been underwhelming, with a few high-profile cases of non-compliance further undermining the ICJ's jurisdiction (see Box 10.4).

Box 10.4 The ICJ and compliance

Though a court of first instance with broad jurisdiction across a wide range of international legal disputes (including those concerning the use of armed force), since its founding the ICJ has only been consulted on average about 1.5 times per year. Some scholars have attributed the underwhelming frequency of ICJ adjudication to the varying rates of compliance with its rulings (Posner and Yoo, 2004). In this view, states are loath to submit disputes to the ICJ because its jurisdiction is far from 'compulsory' in the full sense of the term. The counter-argument holds that the spotty record of compliance with ICJ rulings is driven by the relative infrequency with which it is used, giving it a low profile and impeding its ability to assert authority (Elkind, 1984; Eyffinger, 1996).

One recent study found compliance in about two-thirds of all ICJ rulings, with varying rates of compliance associated with the source of the ICJ's jurisdiction (Ginsburg and McAdams, 2004). In the first ever contentious case decided by the ICJ (*Corfu Channel*, 1949), a ruling against Albania for damages resulting from British warships striking Albanian mines in the channel was ignored, despite Albanian acceptance of jurisdiction in the matter. ICJ rulings obtained through special agreement or 'compromis' had the highest rates of compliance (86 percent), while those associated with *compromissory clauses* within treaties had somewhat lower compliance rates (60 percent), and ICJ rulings spawned by declarations accepting its compulsory jurisdiction (despite reservations attached to such declarations) were complied with less than half the time (40 percent). The problem of compliance has been heightened by a number of high-profile cases of non-compliance, including *Anglo-Iranian Oil Company* (*United Kingdom* v. *Iran*, 1952), *Right of Passage Over Indian Territory* (*Portugal* v. *India*, 1960), *Fisheries Jurisdiction* (*UK* v. *Iceland*, 1974), *Nuclear Tests* (*New Zealand* v. *France*, 1973; *Australia* v. *France*, 1974), *United States Diplomatic and Consular Staff in Tehran* (*United States* v. *Iran*, 1980), and *Application of the Convention on the Prevention and Punishment of the Crime of Genocide* (*Bosnia-Herzegovina* v. *Serbia and Montenegro*, 1993).

Regional courts

Despite its difficulties, the establishment of the ICJ did set a precedent for institutionalization of international adjudication as a method of conflict management. The close relationship between the ICJ and UN foreshadowed additional attempts at institutionalized adjudication at the regional level, most notably in the creation of the European Court of Justice (ECJ) in Luxembourg in 1952. Other prominent examples of regional courts with compulsory jurisdiction include the Inter-American Court of Human Rights established by the OAS in 1979 to implement the American Convention on Human Rights (ACHR), and the African Court on Human and People's Rights (established by the AU in 2004 in conjunction with the Charter of the same name).

Among those regions featuring some standing institution for international adjudication, the European theater has inarguably witnessed the greatest extension of juridical authority. Designed to serve as the judicial body for disputes within the newly created European Coal and Steel Community (ECSC), the forerunner to today's EU, the ECJ remains the principal organ for juridical redress with respect to community law. Given the extensity and intensity of European integration since the founding of the ECSC, the docket of the ECJ has expanded far beyond what its architects in the Treaty of Paris envisioned.

Lacking a formal constitution, the EU (and its forerunner, the European Community, or EC) has continually added regulatory and administrative powers and member-states through treaty agreements and directives. The gradual expansion of the ECJ's remit has created numerous disputes arising from the lack of precision in individual treaties, the need for harmonization of provisions of different treaties and directives, and discord between EU institutions and the EU member-states over the implementation of Community law and policy (De Búrca and Brueschke, 2002). The backlog resulting from this expansion of legal and political authority eventually prompted the creation of the Court of First Instance (CFI) in 1989. The ECJ's long-standing functionality in upholding Community law – it receives approximately 500 new cases each year, with NSAs not infrequent petitioners to the Court – has led some to argue that tribunals such as these might serve as an effective model for reformed international courts that could similarly contribute to a robust and coherent enforcement of international law (Helfer and Slaughter, 1997).

From the standpoint of international conflict management, neither the ECJ nor other effective European courts such as the European Court of Human Rights (ECHR) represents an apt point of comparison. The vast majority of cases heard by the ECJ are in fact quasi-federal attempts to enforce member-state compliance with EU law, policy, and regulations instigated by the major institutions of the EU (particularly the European Commission). While the ECHR (established in 1950, after ratification of the European Convention for the Protection of Human Rights and Fundamental Freedoms by the Council of Europe) does receive more complaints directly from states (while also allowing, like the ECJ, petitions from NSAs and individuals), these correspond with a limited jurisdiction pertaining to individual rights as stipulated in that Convention (Van Dyk and Van Hoof, 1998). Petitions submitted by states against one another relating to disputes over territory, property, or the treatment of persons in relation to the use of deadly force are practically unknown in either instance.

Adjudication after the Cold War

The use of adjudication as an approach to managing conflicts has traditionally been shaped by a concern with upholding existing norms and rules rather than establishing new ones. This began to change in lockstep with structural changes in the international system after the Cold War. The connection between societies defined by the rule of law and the peaceful resolution of conflicts was stated strongly by the CSCE (now the OSCE) in the oft-cited Concluding Document of its Copenhagen Conference of June 1990: 'societies based on the rule of law are prerequisites for … the lasting order of peace, security, justice, and cooperation' (CSCE, 1990).

Perhaps even more important was a growing recognition of the qualitative evolution of armed conflict toward the 'new war' typology of intra-state conflicts driven by identity and unfettered by the 'laws of war' derived from and associated with inter-state warfare. The pronounced and systematic campaigns of human rights violations (in the form of war crimes, crimes against humanity, and genocide) at the heart of conflicts in the Balkans (Bosnia-Herzegovina), the Caucasus (Nagorny-Karabakh, Abkhazia, South Ossetia), and sub-Saharan Africa (Rwanda, Sierra Leone, Sudan) in the early and mid-1990s prompted a seachange in the thinking of international jurists and legal scholars (Bilder, 1992).

Tribunals in Yugoslavia and Rwanda

Whether concerning the nature of rights in armed conflict, the place of individuals relative to international legal jurisdiction, or the need for better instruments for the adjudication of international humanitarian law in order to protect those rights, the unfolding of 'new wars' sparked a dramatic revision of international law and the norms underpinning it. The first signs of this revisionism were the UNSC's creation of the International Criminal Tribunal for the former Yugoslavia (ICTY) at The Hague in May 1993 and the International Criminal Tribunal for Rwanda (ICTR) at Arusha (Tanzania) in November 1994. Introduced in response to war crimes and rampant human rights violations in intra-state conflicts in Bosnia-Herzegovina and Rwanda, these ad hoc bodies were intended to impose legal authority in circumstances where legal institutions had ceased to function, as well as to extend that authority to include the acts and rights of individuals (which the ICJ was not authorized to do). As of June 2008 the ICTY has indicted over 160 persons (convicting and sentencing 50), while the ICTR has handed down 41 judgments involving 86 accused persons; the ICTY made headlines in July 2008 with the arrest of prominent Serb political figure Radovan Karadžić, long sought for the crime of genocide.

The International Criminal Court

The experience of the two ad hoc tribunals for the conflicts in the former Yugoslavia and Rwanda reanimated long dormant calls for creating a permanent international criminal court. This reanimation brought with it calls from states and NGOs alike for the crafting of such an institution in a way that would effectively deal with violations of international humanitarian law and, by extension, remake the notion of legal personhood in international law. With mounting arguments in favor of expanding the definition of a 'legal person' beyond states to include NGOs, MNCs, and individuals, and traditional concepts linked to state sovereignty (such as diplomatic and head-of-state immunity) coming under fire, the normative landscape related to international adjudication in relation to armed conflict was changing.

To date, the most significant embodiment of these changes has been the creation of the ICC. Founded by the Rome Statute (itself established after years of diplomatic wrangling in the summer of 1998), the ICC came into effect on 1 July 2002 following the satisfaction of the minimal terms of the Statute for signatories and ratifications. Seated at The Hague, the ICC is comprised of 18 judges and a prosecutor, with an extensive multinational staff; unlike the ad hoc tribunals of the 1990s or the ICJ, it is independent of the UNSC (Bilder, 2007). Also unlike the ICJ, the ICC was intended to have stronger authority over a limited range of 'core crimes'; accordingly, the ICC has the power to prosecute three of the four crimes proposed at the Rome conference (war crimes, crimes against humanity, and genocide); the fourth crime, aggression (essentially defined as the use of force by states for reasons other than self-defense) proved exceedingly controversial and was tabled (Leonard, 2002).

As of June 2008, 106 states are parties to the ICC, and it has initiated proceedings in four situations: Darfur/Sudan, Uganda, the Democratic Republic of the Congo, and the Central African Republic. Several major military powers, including the United States, China, Russia, India, Pakistan, Iran, and Israel, have failed to ratify the Rome Statute and are not parties to the ICC. In a precedent-setting move in late July 2008, the ICC issued a case against Sudanese President Omar Hassan Ahmad Al-Bashir, the first such indictment issued against a sitting head-of-state.

Despite the hue and cry of the ICC's critics and the continued rejection of the ICC by the United States on the basis that it reflects an encroachment on US legal sovereignty, the jurisdiction of the ICC is far from universal and complete. The ICC can only exercise jurisdiction in relation to states that are parties to the Rome Statute, crimes committed within those states, or pursuant to a case referred by the UNSC (such as the Darfur/Sudan situation). As such, the ICC relies heavily on parties to it for the actual business of prosecution and for the handover of accused persons. Initially conceived of as possessing fully independent powers of prosecution, the ICC in actuality operates in accordance with the principle of 'complementarity.' The product of a brokered compromise at the Rome Conference (in part to assuage US concerns), this provision renders the one permanent international court with extensive powers of adjudication in relation to crimes directly stemming from resort to armed conflict unable to prosecute cases featuring the three core crimes enumerated above unless the relevant national court(s) is (are) unable or unwilling to do so.

How international adjudication works

International adjudication as a form of third-party conflict management can take different forms (arbitration and judicial settlement). It can be carried out by a variety of international courts and ad hoc tribunals, with procedures and rules too disparate to capture and incorporate here. With that said, several commonalities related to the incidence, timing, form, and overall effectiveness of international adjudication are evident.

Why does adjudication occur?

Why do states submit to the international adjudication of ongoing conflicts at all? Realist theory suggests that doing so would be unlikely, if not counter-productive, given that states powerful enough to engage in armed conflict are likely to have other means of influence and persuasion at their disposal. For the same reason, realists also contend that states have little incentive to consent to rulings by arbitrators or courts, whose decisions in an anarchical setting are difficult to enforce. Those of a liberal or institutionalist bent counter that international institutions influence state behavior by facilitating informational processes critical to reputation and standing in relation to international regimes (Simmons, 1999).

The empirical record shows that adjudication is hardly an unknown occurrence, but one that is growing increasingly frequent over time; over the past century, it has been most widely utilized in Latin America, though it is increasingly coming into favor in other regions and contexts. Further, compliance with the rulings of arbitrators and courts on the part of states by most estimates is surprisingly high (Lucy, 1999). One traditional explanation of the incidence of international adjudication holds that it occurs only in 'easy' cases involving relatively low-stakes scenarios (Diehl, 1996). However, more recent and comprehensive studies of adjudication as an approach to international conflict management have found that it is most often used to settle territorial disputes (Simmons, 2002).

The 'expressive theory' of adjudication

In seeking to explain the apparent paradox of a high incidence of adjudication in response to what are decidedly high-stakes situations, these studies have coalesced around the intersection of opportunity costs and domestic pressures as the primary reason for the increasing tendency of states to submit disputes to adjudication and to abide by the resulting rulings. Dubbed the 'expressive theory of adjudication,' this school of thought holds that adjudication is increasingly appealing to states who no longer wish to bear the costs of continuing the conflict and seek to reallocate resources to other pursuits, but are blocked by entrenched domestic opposition from directly engaging with their adversary to develop a settlement to the conflict (McAdams, 2005).

In light of the growing appeal of the 'expressive theory,' the increasing frequency of third party adjudication can be understood as a form of 'cheap talk' coordinating positions between and among states (Powell and Mitchell, 2007). Unable to engage in negotiation, or perhaps even to propose the idea of a direct settlement, as a result of the presence of domestic actors opposed to efforts at conflict management and resolution, the state or states in question may find it more politically feasible to propose arbitration or judicial settlement instead, using adjudication as a convenient 'cover' to justify making concessions and to alleviate domestic political pressures in the process (Allee and Huth, 2006).

Submission of an ongoing conflict to the ruling of an arbitrator or judicial settlement provides the leaders of the state(s) an attractive 'out' through the use of international organizations as means to obtain self-interested ends (Abbott and Snidal, 1998). The resort to international adjudication also allows the political leadership of the state(s) involved to transfer the 'blame' for the settlement (whatever the terms) to the adjudicator, while at least some elements of the domestic opposition are usually more likely to concede (and perhaps concede more) to an arbitrator or court than to an adversary, given the greater perceived legitimacy associated with international adjudicators and their determinations.

When does adjudication happen?

As noted previously, international adjudication differs dramatically from domestic adjudication, since the jurisdiction of international courts and arbitration panels is based largely on the consent of the parties. This arrangement begs the question of what makes adjudication occur when it does. The underlying causes for the mobilization of international adjudication vary according to the context and dynamics of the inter-state or intra-state armed conflict in which it is employed. With that said, there appear to be a few crucial variables which increase the likelihood for adjudication being employed (Sarat and Grossman, 1975).

The first of these is the *social context* in which the conflict or dispute is located. Steeped in sociological theories of social structure, this view holds that the greater the complexity, differentiation of role and task, and size and scale of a society, the more likely it will rely on formal sources of adjudication. Such a claim may be supported by the increasing frequency of international adjudication, and the proliferation of new sources (especially courts) for adjudication. Beyond the forms of social development, however, the *nature of the dispute* is crucial. When conflicts stem from interests rather than values, they prove more favorable to the positive-sum compromises of integrative bargaining, and may not require the formal imposition of binding, potentially zero-sum rulings by a third party to the extent that highly charged conflicts steeped in values do. Given this explanation for the origination of international adjudication, it stands to reason that values and identity-based 'new wars' may prove more likely to require formal adjudication than the interest-based conflicts of yesteryear. The nature of any dispute is also obviously closely correlated with the *goals of the disputants*, such that the mobilization of adjudication may be explained by very different motives depending on the strategy and time horizon of the parties to the conflict.

What forms does adjudication take?

Arbitration

As seen in the Rann of Kutch crisis, the use of arbitration as a form of international conflict management involves establishing an ad hoc tribunal through the agreement of the parties (referred to as a 'compromis'). The compromis defines the issue to be arbitrated and determines the method of selecting arbitrators, the procedures governing the tribunal, the source of funding for the arbitration, and so forth (Janis, 1992).

SINGLE-PARTY ARBITRATION

The simplest form of international adjudication is the single arbitrator. The apparent paradox of such an arrangement (how can parties to an intractable dispute come to terms on one person's suitability as an arbitrator?) is belied by the fact that the conditions for identifying an appropriate arbitrator (expertise, neutrality) are likely easier to discern and agree on than are the sources underlying an inter- or intra-state conflict. With that said, there is no guarantee that a sufficient degree of neutral expertise can be located in a single individual, which places the consideration of the parties to rely on single-party arbitration on a cost–benefit scale; each side must weigh the potential for cessation of hostilities and settlement of the conflict through employing an arbitrator with the fair prospect of a biased settlement conducted by a single arbitrator invested with extensive authority.

Whenever single-party arbitration is employed, the arbitrator is often a well-placed individual with strong official ties to the disputing parties. One of the earliest uses of international arbitration to manage an international conflict – producing the Treaty of Ghent and ending the War of 1812 between the United States and Britain – featured the adjudication of Tsar Alexander of Russia (Stuyt, 1990). It is important to remember that single-party arbitration takes place within the larger context of the iterated game of statecraft. Given the longer-term trajectory of that game, single-party arbitration (like mediation) may be facilitated and rendered more effective by such close ties as well as the presence of an overriding (self) interest on the part of the arbitrator. In the aforementioned case, the interest of Tsarist Russia in maintaining close diplomatic relations with both parties in the aftermath of the conflict fostered greater commitment from the arbitrator.

PANEL ARBITRATION

Given the perils of investing the full powers of adjudication in a single arbitrator, the use of arbitration to adjudicate international conflicts usually relies on the constitution of an arbitration panel of three (and sometimes more) arbitrators. Under the typical arrangement, each party to the conflict selects one arbitrator, and the third arbitrator (assigned to chair the panel) is selected either with the joint agreement of the disputants, the joint agreement of the initial two arbitrators, or by an independent source such as the UN Secretary-General or the president of the ICJ. At least unofficially, tripartite arbitration unfolds in accordance with normative expectations by the parties that 'their' appointees will function more like lawyers than judges in representing their interests within the context of the dispute (and the body of law governing it), while the third arbitrator (the chair) will exercise the neutrality typically associated with a presiding judge.

While the use of an arbitration panel consisting of three (or more) arbitrators is certainly more likely to provide for effective conflict management than reliance on the customary practices of diplomacy and statecraft or the continuation of armed violence, the aforementioned undercurrent of such panels renders them only a step removed from *realpolitik*. It is true, of course, that the 'appointees' to the panel are designees of the parties and not direct representatives, and furthermore they possess a degree of issue-specific as well as legal expertise in relation to the particular dispute that a direct representative (such as a foreign minister or secretary of state) likely does not. At the same time, the expectations attached to their conduct on the panel, the nebulous and potentially politicized nature of the chair selection process, and the additional onus placed on that chair to remain steadfastly unbiased all contribute significant 'noise' to such arbitration efforts. This 'noise' introduces the possibility not only for inefficiency but also bias, which reduces the likelihood of compliance.

Judicial settlement

Since it allows disputants to choose the arbitrators and limit the focus of the arbitration to a particular issue or set of issues, arbitration is used more frequently than judicial settlement. At the same time, this ad hoc arrangement invokes a greater degree of unpredictability associated with the problem of finding appropriate arbitrators able to render effective and fair rulings. The search for such expertise on a case-by-case basis is a time-consuming and costly process that retards the growth of effective jurisprudence in the realm of international conflict management. The development of such jurisprudence can only be obtained through the use of standing international courts and the existing legal framework and rules that govern them – that is, by relying on the process of judicial settlement as a means of international conflict management.

Judicial settlement involves the referral of an ongoing conflict (or the dispute on which it is based) to a permanent court. As a result, the procedures to be employed by this type of tribunal are pre-existing and embodied in governing statutes and rules; similarly, judges have already been selected and are in the employ of whatever court is to be used. Most judicial tribunals have been established to grapple with a wide range of disputes submitted by an equally wide variety of states (and, increasingly, NSAs), and will remain in existence beyond its ruling on any particular case referred to it. They are also defined by the condition of compulsory jurisdiction; that is, the submission of the parties to the court's authority in advance. Such jurisdiction at least theoretically implies that the parties submitting the matter to the court will consent to the ruling and will not withdraw from the court's jurisdiction unless that jurisdiction comes into conflict with some pre-defined conditions established by the party.

As with arbitration, judicial settlement raises a cost–benefit consideration for states and other parties to this form of adjudication. This is particularly true with regard to compulsory jurisdiction, which is a defining condition of any standing and truly independent international court. While states and other parties benefit from the ability to force other states or parties into adjudication as a 'defendant,' there is also a cost associated with the prospects of being on the receiving end of such treatment. Though the compulsory jurisdiction (as the examples of the ICJ and ICC show) associated with international courts is almost always conditional, it does pose risks to states and other legal parties in the form of court-based rulings that do not violate established pre-conditions of a court's authority, yet still turn out not to conform with the expectations or desires of the party in question. Not complying with such rulings constitutes a clear breach of international law, which in most cases incurs real (if mostly reputational) costs for any non-compliant party.

How effective is adjudication?

Not surprisingly, much of the current discourse surrounding the use of adjudication as a tool for the management of international conflicts is framed by the diametrically opposed views of idealistic proponents and realistic skeptics. Somewhere between the position of those who consider arbitration and judicial decision as the means for transforming the nature of the international system through the promotion of transnational norms, and those who cite the enduring influence of power, force, and interests as prima facie evidence of adjudication's epiphenomenal appeal lies a muted reality, in which adjudication serves as one vehicle available to overcome the obstacles to the management of international conflicts and the settlement of their underlying disputes.

The presence of impartial tribunals affords states (and increasingly other types of actors) an avenue to pursue a sub-optimal outcome that still may fall within a range of acceptability. More importantly from the standpoint of conflict management, adjudication allows the parties to avoid a return or continuation of armed violence in the process of seeking that acceptable, if sub-optimal, outcome. This is due in part to the fact that arbitrators and international courts bring significant legal and issue-area expertise to bear on any conflict setting in which they are introduced. This leads at a minimum to the revealing of additional information relevant to the dispute, in some cases even helping the parties to transcend the constraints associated with the information-poor iterated interactions that define many intra-state and inter-state conflicts.

Evidence of these functions can be found in the strong positive relationship between the use of international adjudication and the outcomes of conflicts in which it has been applied. As Table 10.2 conveys, one recent study of all forms of conflict management activity has found that while international adjudication is one of the least frequently used forms of international conflict management, when utilized it

Table 10.2 Escalation and settlement outcomes by form of conflict management

Third-party conflict management technique	Dispute escalation (%)	Peaceful settlement (%)	% of all cases
Public (diplomatic) appeals	17.2	27.6	13.1
Mediation	17.2	40.7	13.1
Observation	16.4	30.1	13.0
Intervention	13.8	30.9	5.6
Humanitarian aid	10.8	35.1	2.2
Adjudication	23.1	59.6	3.1
No management activity	32.3	32.9	70.1

Source: Adapted from Dixon, 1996.

has the highest probability of bringing about a peaceful settlement to conflict (Dixon, 1996).

Contemporary issues and debates

Why comply?

Perhaps the single greatest conundrum concerning international adjudication as an approach to conflict management is why any state would support or comply with an effective independent international legal authority to constrain its sovereignty, particularly concerning its resort to the use of force. Such self-imposed constraints seemingly contradict the vast majority of accepted views of the way in which international relations, particularly on matters of security, works (Moravcsik, 2000). Furthering this quandary is the fact that despite a number of high-profile exceptions, the surprising assertion from a generation ago that 'almost all nations observe almost all principles of international law and almost all of their obligations almost all of the time' (Henkin, 1961: 47) seems to remain more or less accurate today, even with respect to armed conflicts between states.

Traditionally, analysis of compliance in international law has focused on 'primary' compliance with international norms embodied in customary practices or international treaties, rather than 'secondary' compliance with the rulings of adjudicatory bodies (Ginsburg and McAdams, 2004). Until recently, the compliance of states and other parties with the rulings of international adjudicators were associated with a presumed correlation between adjudication and 'easy' or low-stakes conflicts. Continuing skepticism regarding the extent of secondary compliance points to the fact that international law restricts the efforts of arbitrators and courts to intervene without the consent of the parties, and only grants that jurisdiction in accordance with arrangements stipulating compliance in advance of submission of the dispute to arbitration or an international court.

However, 'secondary' compliance is increasingly important as adjudication is utilized more often and exerts greater influence on the norms and laws governing international conflicts and their management. The degree to which secondary compliance with adjudicated rulings occurs suggests that states must have some incentive to comply, or at least derive some benefit from doing so. One example of such a benefit is the reserved right to resort to international adjudication in the future, a right which is deeply rooted in the reputational effects of demonstrating a willing compliance with the ruling of an arbitrator or court.

Adjudication and statecraft

Given the rootedness of international law in the conventional practices of statecraft and the iterated nature of those practices, the orientation of states and other actors in international politics toward actions in the present that may confer benefits in the future is a major factor explaining the occurrence of, and compliance with, conflict management efforts by international adjudicators (Posner and Yoo, 2004). Indeed, this factor has led some to explain compliance with the rulings of adjudicators through the mechanism of the 'expressive theory' of adjudication introduced above. To the extent that adjudication serves as a form of inter-state signaling, as well as a means for political leaders to circumvent domestic constituencies who oppose settlement of a conflict, it stands to reason that states who utilize adjudication in this fashion are likely to comply with the rulings of the adjudicatory body they solicit. This is underscored by the fact that in the vast majority of adjudication cases, one or both parties expect that a final ruling will require concessions (Franck, 1995). In the end, high rates of compliance with the rulings of arbitrators and courts may be best explained by the fact that arbitration and judicial settlement are not employed by states or other parties seeking to 'win' in the conventional sense (relative to their adversary in the conflict), but rather as a means of surmounting internal opposition to settlement and providing useful 'political cover' in the process (Abbott and Snidal, 2000; Simmons, 1999, 2002; Allee and Huth, 2006).

Is international adjudication a threat to state sovereignty?

At both the theoretical and applied level, one of the most heated debates concerning international adjudication in relation to the management of armed conflict concerns whether arbitration and judicial settlement supports or undermines state sovereignty and the norm of non-interference. When used as a means of limiting and containing armed conflict, adjudication may represent an encroachment on the traditionally sacrosanct 'right' of states to resort to organized violence in self-defense, and almost certainly poses a challenge to the resort to force in the pursuit of interest. Not surprisingly, this point of view has most often been aired by states with large and/or active military contingents, as well as by staunch realists who contend that international adjudication represents 'an unprecedented concept … that has spread with extraordinary speed, and has not been subject to extensive debate … which risks substituting the tyranny of judges for that of governments' (Kissinger, 2001: 273).

By contrast, advocates of expanding international jurisprudence through the submission of international conflicts to adjudication point to the increasing prevalence and influence of arbitrators and courts as a reflection of inevitable (if long overdue) changes in the normative bedrock of the international system. This perspective considers the concessions made in the Rome Statute constituting the ICC as reflections of the unwelcome constraints of state sovereignty on international jurisprudence, with some pointing to the ECJ and ECHR as better models for the introduction and design of stronger international courts to supplement, if not replace, flawed institutions such as the ICJ and ICC. Such courts in turn could be used as centerpieces in upholding a 'global community of law' that would promote non-violent dispute resolution and serve as a key touchstone for the more effective management of armed conflict in the international arena.

Study questions

1   What precedent, if any, did the ruling in the Rann of Kutch dispute establish for the adjudication of international conflicts?
2   What are the defining features, advantages, and disadvantages of international adjudication in relation to inter-state and intra-state conflict?
3   What are the main examples of standing adjudicatory bodies in the contemporary international system? Which have exercised the greatest influence in advancing adjudication as a tool of conflict management, and why?

4   What is the 'expressive theory' of adjudication? Does it to help explain when adjudication of international conflicts occurs, what forms it takes, or why it is or is not effective?

5   Is the adjudication of inter-state and intra-state conflicts supportive of, or a challenge to, the concept of state sovereignty?

Suggested reading

Allee, Todd L. and Paul K. Huth. 2006. 'Legitimizing Dispute Settlement: International Legal Rulings as Domestic Political Cover,' *American Political Science Review*, 100 (2): 219–234.

Bilder, Richard B. 2007. 'Adjudication: International Arbitral Tribunals and Courts,' in I. William Zartman (ed.), *Peacemaking in International Conflict: Methods and Techniques*, revised edition. Washington, DC: USIP, pp. 195–226.

Ginsburg, Tom and Richard H. McAdams. 2004. 'Adjudicating in Anarchy: An Expressive Theory of International Dispute Resolution,' *William and Mary Law Review*, 45 (4): 1229–1339.

Helfer, Laurence and Anne-Marie Slaughter. 1997. 'Toward a Theory of Effective Supranational Adjudication,' *Yale Law Journal*, 107: 387.

Janis, Mark W. (ed.). 1992. *International Courts for the Twenty-First Century*. Dordrecht: Martin Nijhoff.

Leonard, Eric K. 2002. 'Establishing an International Criminal Court: The Emergence of a New Global Authority?' Pew Case Studies in International Affairs, no. 258. Washington, DC: Georgetown University Institute for the Study of Diplomacy.

Merrills, John G. 2005. *International Dispute Settlement*, 4th edn. Cambridge: Cambridge University Press.

Romano, Cesare P.R. 1999. 'The Proliferation of International Judicial Bodies: The Pieces of the Puzzle,' *New York University Journal of International Law and Politics*, 31: 709–751.

Stuyt, Alexander Marie. 1990. *Survey of International Arbitrations, 1794–1989*, 3rd edn. Leiden: Martinus Nijhoff.

11 A study in international adjudication
The Mapiripán massacre

This chapter depicts the adjudication of the Inter-American Court on Human Rights (IACHR) in a case involving the torture and murder of up to 49 civilians in the village of Mapiripán, Colombia in July 1997. Focusing on the context of the Colombian civil war and the details of the case and the court's ruling, this case study illustrates the prospects of using adjudication to manage intractable intra-state conflict.

Over the past quarter-century, the long-running civil war in Colombia has come to be defined by the perpetration of a succession of appalling human rights violations against civilians. Even within that context, the Mapiripán massacre of 15–20 July 1997 proved a seminal event. On 5 September 2003, the Inter-American Commission on Human Rights filed the case *Massacre of Mapiripán (Masacre de Mapiripán)* before the IACHR. Petitions from two leading NGOs accused the federal government of Colombia with complicity and support in the massacre. The IACHR's ruling against Colombia in the *Mapiripán* case has invoked both new hopes and new concerns with respect to the use of adjudication as a form of conflict management.

Background and context

Most in-depth treatments of the Colombian civil war consider the conflict's origins to be the decade of intense political violence between 1948 and 1958 known as 'la Violencia' (Leech, 1999). However, the roots of the conflict are evident in the pendulum swing of contestation between the two dominant factions defining Colombian political history since independence. The ostensible basis for this swing (discord over the extent of the powers of the state) is in actuality a product of more deep-seated ideological and cultural divides in Colombia that have played out along party lines since the establishment of the Liberal and Conservative parties in the mid-nineteenth century (Richani, 2002).

'Caudillo wars' and the 1900 civil war

The decidedly decentralized form of federalism embraced by the 'Radical Liberals' governing Colombia for most of the latter half of the nineteenth century fueled the rise of *caudillo* strongmen and their militias (opposed to the liberal policies of the government) across the countryside. The rise of direct violent challenges to federal authority and the lawlessness and disorder they spawned led to a populist-movement ('the Regeneration') seeking strong centralized control which swept the Conservatives into power in 1885. Utilizing popular support for strong central authority as a mandate, the Conservatives turned to a variety of corrupt and repressive tactics to suppress dissent and expand their political power.

With repeated accusations of electoral fraud buttressed by an economic crisis resulting from the decline of coffee prices, mounting unrest turned into full-scale civil war in 1900 (Bergquist, 1978). In a recurring theme, much of the fighting

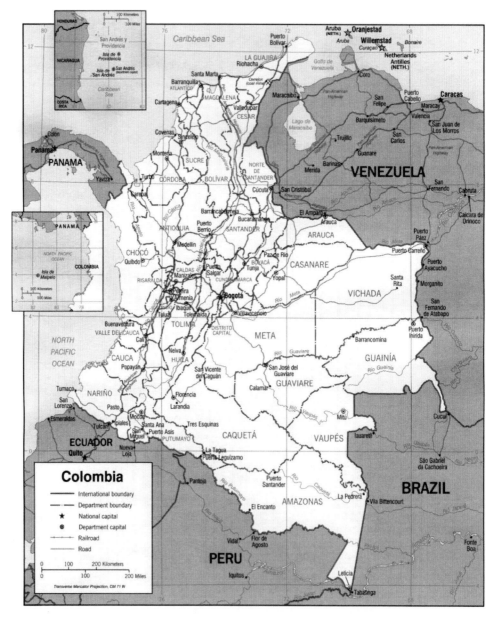

Map 11.1 Colombia (source: courtesy of Perry-Castañeda Library Collection, University of Texas-Austin).

consisted of brutal engagements between guerrilla forces and paramilitaries, with government forces intervening through mass arrests and reprisals against suspected rebels and their supporters within the civilian population. After three years of stalemate and an estimated 120,000 deaths Liberal leader Rafael Uribe capitulated, leading to the signing of the Treaty of Neerlandia in 1904, ending the war.

'The politics of civility'

For over four decades following the end of the 1900 civil war, the Colombian political system proved remarkably well-ordered. With the horrors of the 'war of a thousand days' fresh in the minds of both Liberal and Conservative elites, each side sought a 'politics of civility' (Braun, 1985: 20). The result of this coexistence, typified in the power-sharing arrangement introduced by the first post-war government (institutionalized in a 1905 constitutional amendment) was an oligarchical arrangement between the two parties. While this institutionalized power-sharing lent stability to the regime, it also fostered elitism (tinted with more than a small dose of racism and classism) within the political leadership (Bergquist, 1978). The anti-democratic attitudes inculcated by this arrangement at the top of the political system were clearly expressed by the Conservative leader, Laureano Gómez, in a 1928 address to fellow elites in Bogatá: 'Colombia has little chance of becoming a civilized nation ... the racial mixture of fanatical Spaniards, savage Indians, and primitive Negroes combined with climatic and geographic handicaps [is] fatal for Colombia' (quoted in Braun, 1985: 41).

The Gaitan era

Paradoxically, the aforementioned aura of stability faced its first test due to the economic growth of the 1920s. Market liberalization and increased exports ushered in the first significant labor activism in Colombia, generating social unrest and direct challenges to the prevailing political arrangement. The execution by police of hundreds of workers protesting company policies at the US-owned United Fruit Company plantations in the state of Magdalena in 1928 marked a turning point. Amidst the aftershocks of the event, a divided Conservative party went down in defeat at the 1930 presidential elections.

The so-called 'Banana massacre' had the end result of propelling the Liberal party leftward, a turn spearheaded by Jorge Eliecer Gaitan. Gaitan was a rising force in the party who believed that Colombia's long legacy of unrest and violence was related to the absence of labor standards and any sense of reciprocity on the part of the capitalist class (Braun, 1985). As his profile and influence grew, Gaitan began to employ an increasingly confrontational tone, raising the prospects for a return to the contentious politics of the late nineteenth century. His reliance on populist rhetoric exploiting extant class and geographic (rural/urban) divisions marked him as a threat in the eyes of both Conservative and Liberal elites, though his popularity forced the Liberal Party to name him party leader in 1947.

'La Violencia'

While campaigning for the presidency, Gaitan was assassinated on 9 April 1948. Beginning with the lynching of his assassin, a violent rampage ('*el Bogotazo*') erupted in Bogotá. The violence in Bogotá triggered smaller uprisings in other cities and rural departments. Ever-fearful of the prospects for peasant-led rebellion, the Liberal leadership (along with the Church hierarchy and the United States government) supported an intense crackdown by the arch-conservative government of Laureano Gómez under the guise of anti-communism, ushering in a decade of partisan violence ('*la Violencia*') and resulting in over 200,000 deaths and the internal displacement of an estimated one million persons (Livingstone, 2004).

In a recurring theme dating to the 'caudillo wars' of the nineteenth century, *la Violencia* was defined by a brutality, lawlessness, and banditry on par with any of the 'new wars' of the 1990s. The bulk of the violence was carried out by irregular forces of lightly armed peasants. The chief tactics employed by the leftist guerrillas and right-wing militias were rape, torture, and a variety of systematic forms of decapitation and mutilation. The main official response of the state came in the form of mass arrests and assaults on guerrillas and civilians. Unofficially, the country's political leadership engaged in a proxy war, whereby the Liberal Party (and the Colombian Communist Party) organized armed self-defense units (*bandoleros*) in the countryside to counter the infamous *chulavistas* – peasants from the staunchly Conservative district of Chulavita in Boyacá, enlisted in the national police force by the Gómez regime after dismissal of Liberal members of the force (González *et al.*, 2003).

Emergence of the National Front

Using *la Violencia* for justification, the autocratic Gómez regime suspended civil liberties, undermined the legislature and judiciary, repealed labor laws and outlawed unions, and decried Liberals and Communists as enemies of the state. The persistent violence and inability of the state to exert effective authority over the situation led to the overthrow of Gómez by a military *junta* headed by General Gustavo Rojas Pinilla in June 1953. Rojas Pinilla immediately issued an amnesty to all armed peasant groups. His decision a year later to extend the amnesty to include pro-government forces proved ill-fated, as the release of Gómez supporters triggered a return to violence.

With the peasant groups retaliating, the government launched another major offensive in the countryside (the 'War of Villarica') in 1955. Designed to crush the peasant opposition through a 'scorched earth' campaign, it precipitated the transformation of the rural armed self-defense groups into a unified front. The remaining supporters of coexistence among the moderate Conservative and Liberal elites joined forces against Pinilla, calling for a general strike which led to civil unrest and the collapse of his government in May 1957. The Conservative and Liberal elite then implemented a power-sharing agreement called the National Front. Beginning with the formation of a coalition government under Liberal Alberto Lleras Camargo in August 1958, the parties agreed to alternate four-year terms in the presidency and evenly distribute political appointments, an arrangement which lasted into the mid-1970s.

The conflict in Colombia

The politics of insurgency

Despite the National Front's emergence, the residual effects of *la Violencia* prevented a return to the status quo. The degree of brutality evident in the government response to civil unrest led much of the rural population (particularly those associated with the Liberal and Communist parties) to migrate to the uninhabited eastern departments of Meta and Caquetá. Traveling with the protection of the armed self-defense movements, in the late 1950s and early 1960s migrants cleared and worked new lands, establishing a number of 'independent republics' in a quest for autonomy. Efforts by the *campesino* to establish autonomous areas prompted violent retaliation from government forces, who seized and redistributed the landholdings associated with these areas to large landowners (González *et al.*, 2003).

This act only further isolated and radicalized the rural populace, prompting widespread mobilization for an offensive guerrilla campaign. Within such a scenario, the existence and activities of armed self-defense forces proved vital. Sharing a common point of origin in Marxist–Leninist ideology, and influenced by the successful application of such revolutionary doctrine in Cuba, these groups shared with their charges a deep frustration with mainstream politics. Given the protection they offered, the proliferation and efficacy of leftist guerrilla groups in the rural areas even after the return to civility in Bogatá marked a new stage in the Colombian civil conflict. Indeed, the early and mid-1960s was an exceedingly fertile period for insurgent activity, with the establishment of several major revolutionary guerrilla organizations including the Ejército de Liberación Nacional (ELN), the Ejército Popular de Liberación (EPL), and most notably the Fuerzas Armadas Revolucionarias de Colombia (FARC).

Timeline: Colombian civil war

April 1948	Assassination of the prominent leftist, Jorge Eliecer Gaitan, ignites riots in Bogatá.
1948–1957	Nationwide civil conflict (*la Violencia*) occurs, resulting in an estimated 200,000–300,000 deaths.
August 1950	Conservative Laureano Gómez, running unopposed, wins the presidential election.
May 1957	A military junta led by General Gustavo Rojas Pinilla overthrows Gómez; Conservative and Liberal Parties form the National Front.
1964–1966	The ELN, EPL, and FARC are established.
1968	The Liberal Restrepo government passes Law 48.
1971–1972	The revolutionary Marxist group M-19 is formed; it undertakes a series of assaults against high-profile government targets, primarily in urban areas.
1981	In response to FARC-led kidnapping campaign of drug traffickers and their families, paramilitary group MAS (Muerte a Secuestradores, or 'Death to Kidnappers') is founded in Cali. Hundreds of similar paramilitaries with cartel connections are established throughout the 1980s.
1982	Conservative President Belisario Betancur grants amnesty to guerrillas and frees political prisoners as a precursor to negotiations.

March 1984	The Betancur government and the FARC sign the Uribe Accord, establishing a cease-fire.
1985	The Patriotic Union (UP) is founded as a political wing of the FARC; it is granted recognition as a political party.
6 November 1985	An M-19 attack on the Palace of Justice kills over 100, including 12 Supreme Court justices.
August 1986	Liberal Virgilio Barco Vargas is elected President; right-wing paramilitaries step up attacks against the FARC, UP, and alleged sympathizers among civilians.
1989	M-19 suspends military operations after reaching a peace accord with the Colombian government, and begins transformation to a legal political party.
25 May 1989	Law 48 is declared unconstitutional by the Colombian Supreme Court.
Summer 1989	Liberal and UP candidates are murdered during the presidential election, reportedly on the order of drug cartels; Liberal candidate Cesar Gaviria is elected on a law and order and anti-drug platform.
February 1990	The United States announces a US$2.2 billion Andean Initiative, consisting largely of military aid to combat narco-trafficking in Colombia, Peru, and Bolivia.
May 1991	The Defense Ministry issues Order 200–05/91, expanding counter-insurgency operations.
February 1994	The Cooperatives for Surveillance and Private Security (CONVIVIR) program is launched.
August 1994	Liberal Ernesto Samper Pizano is elected president; charges of receipt of campaign funds from drug cartels ('Proceso 8000 scandal') are investigated and dropped.
April 1997	Carlos Castaño establishes an umbrella organization (Autodefensas Unidas de Colombia, AUC) to coordinate right-wing paramilitary activity. The AUC initiates a major offensive in FARC strongholds.
15–20 July 1997	The Mapiripán massacre occurs.
August 1998	Conservative Andres Pastrana Arango is elected as President and launches peace talks with guerrillas.
November 1998	Pastrana creates a demilitarized 'safe haven' for the FARC in the south-east to facilitate talks.
January 1999	Pastrana and the FARC leader Manuel 'Sureshot' Marulanda begin peace talks at El Caguan.
July 2000	Pastrana announces 'Plan Colombia,' a new initiative including more than US$1 billion in military aid and over 500 US military advisers to combat drug trafficking and production.
September 2000	Negotiations between the Pastrana government and the FARC break down.
February 2001	An emergency summit meeting between Pastrana and Marulanda marks a return to peace talks.
June 2001	A major prisoner exchange occurs; the FARC releases over 350 captives in exchange for government release of 14 guerrillas.
October 2001	The Pastrana government and the FARC sign the San Francisco Agreement, committing to further negotiations and a cease-fire. Pastrana extends the safe haven for an additional six months.
20 February 2002	The Pastrana government ends three years of negotiations after

	the FARC hijacks an aircraft. The safe haven is eliminated; the army launches a major offensive in the south after a series of guerrilla attacks. Three days later, center-left Presidential candidate Íngrid Betancourt is taken hostage by the FARC in former DMZ.
May 2002	Independent candidate Alvaro Uribe wins a first-round presidential victory, largely on promises to crack down on leftist rebels.
August 2002	FARC explosions in Bogatá moments before Uribe inauguration kill 20 people. Uribe declares a state of emergency.
November 2003	Under pressure from the Uribe government, the AUC begins disarmament.
May 2004	The captured senior FARC leader Ricardo Palmera is jailed for 35 years.
July 2004	Negotiations between the government and the AUC begin; AUC leaders address Congress.
December 2005	Preliminary negotiations between the government and the ELN begin in Cuba.
May 2006	Following a Constitutional amendment, Uribe is elected to an unprecedented second term.
November 2006	The Supreme Court investigates ties between officials from the Sucre department and paramilitaries.
December 2006	Detained paramilitary leaders withdraw from negotiations with the Uribe government.
June 2007	The government releases dozens of FARC guerrillas in an attempt to prompt reciprocation; the FARC demands the government restore the demilitarized safe haven.
September 2007	Venezuelan President Hugo Chavez offers to mediate on the prisoner swap; the Uribe government sets a deadline of 31 December 2007.
January 2008	The FARC releases two high-profile hostages, Clara Rojas and Consuelo Gonzalez. Chavez urges the United States and the EU to remove FARC from the list of terrorist organizations.
March 2008	A Colombian military incursion into Ecuador kills senior FARC rebel Raul Reyes, prompting diplomatic crisis with Ecuador and Venezuela.
May 2008	The Uribe government extradites 14 paramilitary warlords to the United States to stand trial on drug trafficking charges. The Colombian opposition decries loss of testimony in ongoing trials related to human rights violations and civil war.
May 2008	The FARC leader and founder Manuel 'Sureshot' Marulanda dies.
July 2008	The Colombian army rescues the country's highest-profile hostage, Íngrid Betancourt, along with 14 others held by the FARC.

Sources: BBC; Bergquist *et al.*, 2001; Leech, 1999.

The coca boom

Escalating poverty rates in concert with the failure of the political system to seriously address land reform proved crucial in fueling a continuing low-intensity insurgency in the countryside throughout the late 1960s and early 1970s. During the National Front years (which ended in 1974), the percentage of all Colombians below the poverty line more than doubled (from 25 percent to 50 percent), while in the rural areas over two-thirds of the population (67.5 percent) lived in absolute poverty (Keen, 1996). Among the active guerrilla forces, the FARC took particular advantage of the widespread economic downturn, consistently adding to its ranks while consolidating control in the south and east of the country.

Given the economic climate of the country, the so-called 'coca boom' of the late 1970s proved a key catalyst in escalating the conflict. The boom itself was the product of a 'perfect storm' created by the intersection of crushing poverty, high demand for cocaine in the United States and Western Europe, and the increasing density of international transit networks. The interaction of these factors prompted a massive internal migration of urban and rural poor seeking economic security to the FARC-controlled areas where much of the coca originated (Richani, 2002). This migration benefited the FARC, which was able to capitalize on increased revenue from its unofficial tax base of rural landholders requiring protection in order to modernize its arsenal and improve the conditions of its forces (Livingstone, 2004). A corresponding increase in paramilitary activity allowed the FARC to expand its strongholds in the 1980s and 1990s; whereas in 1985 the FARC controlled 173 of Colombia's 1,071 municipalities, by 1998 that number had increased to 622 (Chernick, 1998).

Rise of the paramilitaries

The early years of the coca boom featured a degree of cooperation between the drug cartels controlling production and trafficking (based in the western hubs of Medellín and Cali) and the FARC and other guerrillas active in the coca-growing regions in the south and east. However, the dramatic expansion of drug profits and reinvestment of the proceeds in legitimate enterprises such as ranching by the cartels increased their prominence and power. This placed the drug lords at odds with the guerillas, who sought to utilize drug money to foster political instability (Chernick, 2001). Accordingly, by the early 1980s another major rupture in Colombian politics and society was overlain over existing divides. The narco-traffickers used graft, corruption, and violence to increase their control and influence over the regime, while also providing support to right-wing paramilitaries engaged in frequent and bloody armed clashes with the FARC, ELN, and other leftist guerrilla forces. Meanwhile, the guerrillas initiated a kidnapping campaign targeting large landowners and their families (particularly those linked to the cartels), using ransom as a supplemental source of income (Suárez, 2000).

MAS and 'limpiar'

The kidnapping campaign employed by the leftist guerrillas incited a violent backlash from the cartels, embodied in the founding of the paramilitary MAS in Cali in

1981. The MAS provided a blueprint, as well as shorthand acronym, for the formation of hundreds of similar groups with the shared goal of *limpiar* ('cleansing') of leftists over the next decade (Tate, 2001). Given the encroachment of drug traffickers into official channels of power, these groups were often crafted with the logistical and technical support of the Colombian military. Tellingly, this nexus between the right-wing paramilitaries and the Colombian security forces was legally sanctioned; Law 48 (passed in 1968) allowed the state to organize and equip 'self-defense units' to 'fight back against organized delinquents and against armed groups operating in certain peasant regions.'

Return to 'dirty war'

Precipitated by the M-19 assault on the Palace of Justice on 6 November 1985, the paramilitaries stepped up activities with increased support from the police and armed forces. Civilian members of the UP, the political wing of the FARC established in 1985 to coordinate its negotiations with the Betancur government, constituted the newest targets for assassination by the paramilitaries. By the end of the 1980s Colombia was effectively paralyzed by crime and civil war, with little government control outside of Bogatá and a few other major administrative centers. The FARC and ELN dominated the south and east, while MAS paramilitaries and the drug cartels ruled the north and west. The pervasive links between the government and the drug cartels resulted in the frequent enlistment of active members of the police and military in the right-wing death squads (Livingstone, 2004). As a result, politically motivated killings increased from roughly 1,000 in the 1970s to an estimated 13,000 in the 1980s (Human Rights Watch, 1996).

The United States and the 'war on drugs'

Within the context of an expanding civil war, the increased involvement of the United States proved crucial. The insatiable demand for cocaine prompted a series of expansive commitments to combat the supply of illicit drugs into the United States, beginning with the Nixon Administration (Bagley, 1988). Accordingly, Colombia fell squarely within the crosshairs of the US 'war on drugs,' with that policy crusade weaving its way into the Colombian civil war.

The Andean Initiative

On the heels of a successful military intervention to overthrow and arrest Panamanian President (and former CIA operative) Manuel Noriega on the basis of alleged involvement in narco-trafficking, the George H.W. Bush Administration sought to take the US 'war on drugs' to Latin America. In February 1990 the Bush Administration launched the Andean Initiative, a US$2.2 billion aid package targeting the drug producing regions of Colombia, Peru, and Bolivia; two-thirds of the aid was earmarked for the military and police, with the remainder conditional on accepting that earmark. Though Peru and Bolivia rejected the offer, the Liberal administration of Virgilio Barco Vargas, then in the throes of a renewed offensive against the guerrillas, quickly accepted.

DIVERSION OF AID

The Andean Initiative marked the first of several major US aid packages ostensibly aimed at drug interdiction that were diverted by the Colombian government to counter-insurgency (Andreas *et al.*, 1992). In the short run, the Andean Initiative provided the necessary external military, economic, and political support to mount a renewed offensive against the FARC and other guerrilla forces. Among other things, it prompted Defense Ministry Order 200–05/91, outlining an expanded strategy against the FARC and other leftist guerrillas. Order 200–05/91 provided for the creation of up to 30 'intelligence networks' organized by the military and consisting of civilians and retired military personnel, a clear return to the spirit of Law 48 declared unconstitutional by the Colombian Supreme Court only two years prior (Leech, 1999). The order also paved the way for similar and expanded efforts such as the Cooperatives for Surveillance and Private Security (CONVIVIR) program, establishing civilian 'rural security cooperatives' to funnel intelligence on guerrilla activities to government forces and associated paramilitaries.

US RESPONSE

The Bush Administration signaled the US government's position on the matter by dispatching a military intelligence advisory team to assist in a reorganization of the Colombian security and intelligence services in the summer of 1990. This response paved the way for increasingly close ties between the military and intelligence services of each country which persist today. Under the guise of the 'war on drugs,' US policy toward Colombia has been defined by joint training exercises, arms transfers, and the commitment of large sums of economic and military aid to underwrite a highly compromised Colombian military and police force (Bergquist *et al.*, 2001). Yet US involvement in the internal affairs of Colombia transcends financial support. Like their counterparts from across Latin America, Colombian military personnel regularly receive counter-insurgency training at the United States Army's School of the Americas (SOA) in Fort Benning, Georgia; in the Colombian case, a number of graduates of the SOA have been implicated in massacres against civilians (Stokes, 2001).

'Plan Colombia'

Within the *milieu* of expanded civil war, a joint initiative called 'Plan Colombia' was introduced in 2000. First conceived by Colombian President Andrés Pastrana Arango (the candidate of the bipartisan 'Great Alliance for Change' patterned after the National Front) in 1998, Plan Colombia was initially a multifaceted plan involving a request of over US$7 billion in foreign aid to end the civil war, combat drug trafficking, and promote social and economic development. Through the efforts of the Clinton Administration, the proposal was recalibrated primarily to emphasize counter-insurgency and drug interdiction, including the use of aerial fumigation to eradicate coca crops (Holmes *et al.*, 2006). Plan Colombia was allocated US$1.3 billion in funds, 78 percent of which was earmarked for the Colombian military and police (including an initial sum of over US$800 million for fiscal year 2000), and a detachment of roughly 500 military advisers (Sweig, 2002).

Following the 2000 election, the George W. Bush Administration increased funding as well as the number of military personnel associated with the operation as part of an expanded 'Andean Counterdrug Initiative.' Along with the close military and security cooperation of Plan Colombia, the Clinton and George W. Bush Administrations have also adopted the rhetoric of their Colombian counterparts, linking the civil war to the drug trade and associating that trade almost exclusively with the activities of the FARC and other leftist guerrillas (Posada, 2001). Echoing the current Uribe government, the second Bush Administration has recast Plan Colombia as part of the 'war on terrorism,' characterizing the FARC as 'narco-terrorists' (Taylor, 2005; Isacson, 2003).

'*War without quarter*'

The convergence of these factors transformed the Colombian civil war into a veritable war without quarter, with the distinction between combatant and civilian eroded amidst a spasm of politically motivated killings, kidnappings, and massacres of civilians. With human rights violations rampant, an estimated one million Colombians were displaced from their homes in the 1990s alone (Reuters, 1998). This turn of events was punctuated by the documented involvement of numerous members of the police, military, and intelligence services in atrocities carried out by the paramilitaries (Spencer, 2001). With the siege mentality of civil war affording the military and security forces unchecked authority, such atrocities often went unpunished (Azcarate, 1999).

The complicity of the state in the activities of the paramilitaries facilitated an effective breakdown in the rule of law. Efforts to restore order such as the repeal of Law 48 by the Supreme Court and the issuance of Decree 1194 outlawing 'self-defense' groups did little to restrain the paramilitaries or the FARC, ELN, or other leftist guerrillas. Indeed, the expansion of paramilitary activity by the late 1980s and early 1990s took an even more brutal turn with the emergence of 'social cleansing' killings, in which the violence was ratcheted up by its public presentation by the right-wing squads as a campaign of moral purification. Dozens of '*sicarios*' (death squads populated by young unemployed males, typically from the urban centers) took to targeting drug users, petty thieves and criminals, homosexuals, homeless persons, and street children for assassination; during the period 1990–1994 alone there were nearly 2,000 documented cases of such 'social cleansing' (Human Rights Watch, 1996).

The AUC and the 1997–1998 counter-offensive

Despite the continued support of the Colombian government, the fractious and often undisciplined paramilitaries stood in marked contrast to the coherence of the FARC. Along with the ideological basis of the organization, this made the FARC a formidable fighting force, as was evident in a largely successful offensive aimed at expanding its geographic base (with designs on Bogatá) in the mid-1990s. In seeking to respond by similarly expanding the reach of the paramilitaries beyond their traditional geographic base, Carlos Castaño – the leader of the Autodefensas Campesinas de Córdoba y Urabá (ACCU) – established the AUC.

The first test of Castaño's strategy was a major counter-offensive, targeting the guerrilla strongholds in the south-east, beginning in 1997. This counter-offensive marked yet another departure in the Colombian civil war. Whereas the violence and lawlessness had previously been confined largely to provincial areas, after 1997 it threatened to consume the entire country. At the same time, direct clashes between the AUC and the guerrillas in the southern strongholds led to a dramatic escalation in the conflict, with an estimated 25,000 deaths in 1997 (Alape, 1998). Not surprisingly, the conflict grew even more difficult for the state to manage; when Pastrana withdrew government forces from a large tract in southern Colombia in advance of negotiations with the FARC in November 1998, the AUC interceded with a military offensive designed to derail the talks, leading to the death of 136 civilians over a four-day period.

The IACHR and the Mapiripán case

The Mapiripán massacre

The context of massive human rights violations, the absence of state authority, and the emergence of the AUC provided the backdrop for the Mapiripán massacre. A small market town with approximately 1,000 inhabitants located along the boundary of the Meta and Guaviare departments in the FARC-controlled south-east, Mapiripán was a key link in the coca economy. Over a five-day period (15–20 July 1997), approximately 100 members of the AUC kidnapped, tortured, and murdered up to 49 civilians with machetes and chainsaws, throwing their bodies in the Guaviare River.

While Castaño and the AUC claimed responsibility, the premeditation of the killings, the duration of the event, and its occurrence in a highly remote location suggested government complicity. Subsequent investigations determined that the AUC was ferried to the region on government aircraft and used an airstrip guarded by the Colombian armed forces as a base of operations, all with the organizational support of General Jaime Uscátegui and the Army's Seventh Brigade (Kirk, 2005). This complicity was confirmed by the refusal of the federal government to intervene in the massacre despite the urgent request to do so from local judge Leonardo Iván Cortés (Burt, 2000).

Establishing accountability for the Mapiripán massacre was difficult. By the late 1990s ties between the government and paramilitaries had become sufficiently institutionalized such that they had an effect even on the Colombian legal system. For example, while General Uscátegui continued to take calls from Cortés while the massacre was underway, the latter's pleas for action to the regional Superior Court went ignored. While a raft of indictments were issued for suspected participants (including dozens of AUC operatives and members of the armed forces), few arrest warrants were served. A set of furtive investigations produced convictions of 14 rank-and-file AUC participants; cases involving military personnel, including Colonel Lino Sánchez, operations chief of the Army's Twelfth Brigade, were remanded to the opaque military court system. Accused mastermind Castaño disappeared and was later presumed dead; General Uscátegui was eventually tried in 2006, but was acquitted on charges that he ordered his troops to stay away from Mapiripán while the massacre was underway.

The Trujillo precedent

Despite the paralysis in the legal system, victims advocates were determined to seek redress. They derived momentum for doing so from precedent, specifically one established by the response to a two-year campaign of premeditated political killings in the south-western town of Trujillo between 1988 and 1990. This massacre of over 100 *campesinos* by paramilitary forces and members of the Cali cartel featured the direct involvement of army officers and was based at the hacienda of a known drug trafficker. When the response of the Colombian courts proved ineffectual, Jesuit priest (Fr. Javier Giraldo) and his organization 'Justicia y Paz' appealed to the Inter-American Commission on Human Rights for assistance (Cardenas, 2002).

Enter the IACHR

A subsidiary of the OAS, the chief responsibility of the seven-member Inter-American Commission on Human Rights is oversight and enforcement of the ACHR, a binding treaty adopted in 1969 which entered into force in 1978. The Convention affords legal protection for political and civil rights (including the right to life, liberty, property, privacy, due process, equal protection, and freedom of conscience and expression) to citizens of the two dozen states of the Americas that have ratified it. In 1979 the Commission established a standing court, the IACHR, to adjudicate disputes concerning the provisions and implementation of the Convention. Although the IACHR did not directly issue a ruling in the Trujillo case, the decision to petition the Commission in the Trujillo case proved to be a critical one. The Commission's ability to marshal external legal and political pressure prompted the Colombian government to create an extra-judicial commission including non-governmental representatives to conduct an expanded investigation of the case. The subsequent investigation found the Colombian government responsible for the actions of the perpetrators and awarded damages to the families of the victims.

The Mapiripán case

The political pressure brought to bear by the Commission provided the impetus for advocacy by the independent press, citizen activists, and NGOs dissatisfied with the government's handling of the Mapiripán massacre. These efforts culminated in the lodging of a petition against the federal government of Colombia by the Corporación Colectivo de Abogados '*Jose Alvear Restrepo*' and the Center for Justice and International Law (CEJIL) on 6 October 1999. The central claim stated in the petition was that members of the Colombian armed forces had both actively and passively participated in the Mapiripán massacre. The petition requested that the Commission investigate the actions of the Colombian government with respect to the violation of several specific rights enumerated in the ACHR, including the right to life (Article 4), humane treatment (Article 5), personal liberty (Article 7), a fair trial (Article 8.1), and judicial protection (Article 25), as well as the obligation to respect all such rights required of signatories (Article 1).

After a set of hearings, the Commission declared the case admissible on 22 February 2001 (IACHR, 2005a). Following a fuller investigation of the government of Colombia's response to the accusations of the claimants, the Commission issued

Report no. 38/03 (4 March 2003), finding sufficient evidence to support the existence of systematic violations of the aforementioned articles of the American Convention by the state of Colombia. The Commission subsequently filed the case '*Massacre of Mapiripán (Masacre de Mapiripán)*' with the IACHR on 5 September 2003. In its referral, the Commission required the government of Colombia to fully comply with the Court's investigation in order to facilitate the prosecution, sentencing, and punishment of the perpetrators of the massacre. The Commission also tasked the IACHR with determining adequate compensation for the victims of the massacre and their survivors.

The outcome

Deliberations

Within a month of the filing, the IACHR Secretariat forwarded an examination of the Commission referral conducted by the President of the Court (Sergio García Ramírez of Mexico) to the Colombian government along with a request to appoint an ad hoc justice (Gustavo Zafra Roldán) to preside along with five permanent IACHR justices. Colombia's first major written response to the Court's request following a series of public hearings was an April 2004 brief outlining two preliminary objections: first, that the Commission's referral to the Court was overly preliminary and therefore in violation of Articles 50 and 51 of the Convention, and second, that it was made before full exhaustion of domestic legal process (IACHR, 2005a).

March 2005 hearing

Proceeding with the investigation, Justice Ramírez issued an order in January 2005 summoning the Commission, the claimants, and representatives of the state to a public hearing at the seat of the Court (San José, Costa Rica) on 7 March 2005. Three days prior to the hearing, designed to allow for presentation of final oral pleas regarding preliminary objections and merits, reparations, and costs of the case, the Colombian government filed an additional brief with the Court. Still maintaining that domestic remedies had not been exhausted, Colombia withdrew the first of its preliminary objections, expressed sympathy for the victims and their next of kin, and reaffirmed its respect for human rights. Most importantly, the brief contained explicit acknowledgment of responsibility for violations of Articles 4, 5, and 7 of the ACHR with respect to the events of 15–20 July 1997 in Mapiripán (CHRHL, 2006).

The 7 March 2005 hearing featured representatives from the Inter-American Commission, the Corporación Colectivo de Abogados '*José Alvear Restrepo*,' the CEJIL, and the government of Colombia. The forum provided an additional public opportunity for Colombia to restate its revised position, as well as allowing the Court to accept the admission of responsibility by the Colombian government. This procedure helped finalize the establishment of claims submitted by the petitioners, as well as allowing the Court the opportunity both to reaffirm its own competence to render a judgment and to stipulate the requirements of the Colombian government in implementing that judgment.

September 2005 hearing

Deliberation over the specific merits of the claims remained open for a six-month period. This interregnum was punctuated by public hearings featuring witness and expert testimony as well as the filings of several amicus curae ('friend of the court') briefs by legal advocacy groups. Submitted on behalf of victims and their next of kin, these briefs constituted attempts at influencing the scope of the investigation so that full disclosure of government involvement in the massacre would occur, and to ensure the Court require the Colombian government fully respect the rights of victims and mete out appropriate punishments to guilty parties (ICTJ, 2005). To some degree these attempts were successful, as the Court issued several directives during this period concerning the need for status reports from Colombia regarding related domestic legal proceedings and updated information on victims for the purpose of allocating reparations.

Judgment of the Court

On 15 September 2005, a sentencing hearing concerning the merits of the case and the determination of reparations and costs was convened in San José. The Court issued its final judgment based on the examination of all evidence submitted, finding that:

- illegal armed paramilitary groups existed in the Colombian civil war;
- the government of Colombia created self-defense groups designed to aid the armed forces in anti-subversive operations;
- the self-defense groups shifted their objectives toward paramilitary operations undermining stability, social order, and peace in the 1980s;
- relationships between paramilitaries and the armed forces existed;
- paramilitaries, drug-trafficking organizations, and the FARC competed for control of the Municipality of Mapiripán;
- members of the armed forces believed that many residents of Mapiripán were involved in subversive acts and were FARC members;
- the Colombian armed forces facilitated the transportation of 100 members of the self-defense groups to Mapiripán on 12 July 1997;
- these persons tortured and dismembered individuals they believed worked for or sympathized with the FARC on 15 July 1997;
- the paramilitary incursion in Mapiripán was an act that was carefully planned by the Colombian armed forces;
- Colombia failed to completely and efficiently investigate these acts and denied the families of victims access to the courts.

(IACHR, 2005b)

In accordance with Article 63 of the ACHR, the IACHR also declared the right of the victims' next of kin to receive reparations from the Colombian government. The Court ordered Colombia to compensate for the loss of income as well as additional payments for physical and emotional duress. The claims stipulated in the amicus curae briefs regarding the rights of victims also played an influential role in the Court's judgment. The Court directed Colombia to identify all victims' bodies and ensure an appropriate burial, to issue a public apology for the massacre and its culpability therein, to guarantee the free and safe passage of all former residents wishing to return to Mapiripán, and to continue and expand the investigation of the Mapiripán massacre so as to identify, process, and properly sanction those responsible (IACHR, 2005b).

Lessons learned

Challenging state sovereignty

The Mapiripán case establishes a significant precedent in international jurisprudence, one with particular implications for the concept of state sovereignty. The intervention of the IACHR represents a direct effort by an international court to uphold the inviolability of international human rights norms as reflected through treaty agreements. The ruling itself reflects a determination that even a grave threat to a nation-state's security posed by internal revolt and civil war does not negate the state's responsibility to ensure that human rights are protected. It also upholds the notion that the violation of such basic human rights as the right to life, humane treatment, and personal liberty cannot be attributed solely to the individuals committing those acts. Whereas Colombia's legal argument contended that the agents of the state directing the massacre were acting in an individual capacity, the Court maintained that the state was ultimately responsible for their actions.

The allocation of responsibility to the state was justified in the Court's ruling by the failure of the Colombian government to detain and sufficiently investigate the individual perpetrators after the massacre. This was presented in the ruling as an abdication of the government's responsibility to protect the residents of Mapiripán. The Court even went so far as to condemn Colombia's Law 975 (the Law of Justice and Peace) providing for amnesty and the reintegration of members of the paramilitaries in return for their contributions to the peace process, stating that no domestic law should preclude the investigation and sanctioning of those responsible for human rights violations.

As one in a succession of similar developments (such as the indictment of Augusto Pinochet in 1998, the establishment of the ICC in 2002, the trial of Slobodan Milosevic that same year, and the indictment of Sudanese President Hassan Ahmad al-Bashir in July 2008), the Mapiripán ruling constitutes an additional chink in the armor of state sovereignty. In the end, the Inter-American Commission's referral of a petition by two NGOs on behalf of the individual victims of a massacre planned and carried out by agents of a state to a standing international court is remarkable in its own right. That the Commission granted the Court the authority to direct the state in question to revisit a criminal investigation that it had already closed speaks volumes to the changing nature of legal personhood and the interpretation of rights and responsibilities in accordance with international humanitarian law. Though Colombia has yet to fully comply with the judgment (both in terms of the investigation and the extension of reparations), the ruling retains force and provides recourse should the state violate its responsibility for implementation.

Managing conflict

Aside from a potential legal precedent relative to state sovereignty, the IACHR ruling also represents an important turn in the management of intra-state conflict. The chief significance of the case from the standpoint of this volume is as an example of the use of adjudication in attempting to break the cycle of intractability in such conflicts. The petition of the Inter-American Commission and the Court suggests that directly affected parties can and do engage with external actors (in this case, an RGO and a standing international court) in attempting to contain the deleterious effects of internecine warfare when the authority of the state is compromised.

The decision to petition the Commission and the Court by individuals and NGOs in the aftermath of the Mapiripán massacre was clearly prompted by the reality that those 'deleterious effects' were systematic violations of human rights conducted with the consent and participation of the state. The Court's ruling, shaped in part by the Uribe government's own acknowledgment of Colombia's violations of several articles of the American Convention, finds pervasive evidence in support of the allegations in this particular case. More broadly, the fact that the prospects for high-profile exposure by a standing international court of the persistent links between the Colombian armed forces and the paramilitaries propelled the government to acknowledge responsibility for crimes against humanity and the state's role in sustaining and expanding the civil war clearly provides support for others in Colombia (and beyond) seeking to involve third-party adjudicators in similar circumstances.

From a conflict management standpoint, this case study of the IACHR ruling in the Mapiripán case, and the context of the Colombian civil war in which that ruling is submerged, reflects the increasing importance of the rule of law (or, more accurately, the restoration of the rule of law when it has been eroded) to the effective management of intra-state conflicts. This importance presents a clear opening for the intervention of adjudicators when the state is unwilling and/or unable to exert its political authority and legal jurisdiction toward that end. Given the complicity of agents of the state in the Colombian civil war, the rule of law in Colombia was compromised to such a degree that surrogate sources were deemed necessary. While the Mapiripán ruling has hardly fully restored the rule of law or broken the larger cycle of violence that has defined Colombian politics and society for over four decades, it does stand as an indication that the state's link to that violence and its attempts to obscure that link are no longer beyond sanction.

Study questions

1   What are the underlying political, social, and economic forces driving the Colombian civil war?
2   What role has the Colombian state played in the civil war? How has this created a climate ripe for international adjudication?
3   What role did the Trujillo case play in influencing the decision to petition the Inter-American Commission and Court?
4   On balance, do you view the IACHR's ruling in the Mapiripán case as precedent-setting? Why or why not?
5   What does this case study suggest are the main advantages and disadvantages of involving an external adjudicatory body in a protracted intra-state conflict?

Suggested reading

Bergquist, Charles W., Ricardo Peñaranda, and Gonzalo Sánchez 2001. *Violence in Colombia, 1990–2000: Waging War and Negotiating Peace*. Lanham, MD: Rowman & Littlefield.

Burt, Jo-Marie. 2000. 'The Massacre at Mapiripán,' *Colombia Journal/NACLA Report on the Americas*. New York, NY: North American Congress on Latin America.

Chernick, Mark W. 2001. 'The Dynamics of Colombia's Three-Dimensional War,' *Conflict, Security and Development*, 1: 93–100.

Livingstone, Grace. 2004. *Inside Colombia: Drugs, Democracy, and War*. New Brunswick, NJ: Rutgers University Press.

Richani, Nazih. 2002. *Systems of Violence: The Political Economy of War and Peace in Colombia*. Albany, NY: SUNY Press.

Sweig, Julia E. 2002. 'What Kind of War for Colombia?' *Foreign Affairs*, 81 (5): 122–141.

Conclusion

This chapter revisits the main questions structuring this survey of international conflict management and its major applications. It chronicles the gradual evolution of conflict management in light of the problems posed by contemporary armed conflict. The chapter also highlights a number of themes and questions raised by consideration of the major applications of conflict management featured in this book, concluding with general suggestions for enhancing the effectiveness of conflict management in the twenty-first century.

A gradual transformation

This book was launched with a fairly straightforward question. What are the major actors, approaches, and parameters characterizing international conflict management? As this comprehensive survey of contemporary conflict management shows, the basis of conflict management as a practice – not to mention how we think about it – is in a state of flux. Though not fully keeping pace with the changing security environment and the complex and largely intra-state conflicts it produces, the actors engaged in conflict management, the approaches they employ, and the boundaries that define their actions are all engaged in a gradual process of transformation.

Actors

As has been well-chronicled here, the practice of conflict management in the international realm emerged with states at the forefront. Consequently, the approaches to conflict management discussed in this book have been and remain greatly influenced by states, who often dictate when peacekeeping, mediation, peace enforcement, or adjudication will occur, how it will be provided, and what its objectives and limits are. Though the influence of state sovereignty varies across these approaches (consider the differences between peacekeeping and peace enforcement), it is a fact that states have been and will remain key actors determining the provision and effectiveness of any attempt at conflict management, either through direct involvement or the surrogacy of IGOs and RGOs. The case studies featured in this book provide copious evidence in support of this claim: three of the four profiles in conflict management were led by state-based RGOs or IGOs, while the fourth featured the intervention of an international court created by an RGO, staffed by justices from that organization's member-states, and fundamentally dependent on the willingness of the state put on trial (Colombia) to comply with its process and ruling.

The early years of the twenty-first century seem to represent a critical juncture in which conflict in the international system is increasingly transpiring without central and directive state authority, while efforts to manage that conflict remain fundamentally linked to states. However, as the discussion of peacekeeping, mediation, peace enforcement, and adjudication and the contemporary case studies profiling their application contained here also demonstrate (particularly when considered in contrast to the historical vignettes opening Chapters 4, 6, 8, and 10) conflict management practices are in fact evolving. While the end of the Cold War is better known for ushering in a 'new security environment' defined by 'new wars,' it has also come to feature expanding roles for multilateral institutions and NGOs, and cooperative arrangements between states and other actors attempting to manage contemporary security challenges and armed conflicts. Witness, for example, the nexus between the Inter-American Commission and Court and the OAS, the 'subcontracting' arrangement between the UN and the CIS (in Georgia) and Australia (in East Timor), or the efforts by the IGAD and its lead mediator Lazaro Sumbeiywo to create a 'Partner's Forum' to engage powerful states such as the United States and United Kingdom in the management of the Sudanese civil war.

As we have seen, the engagement of NSAs is often the result of the inability or unwillingness of states or intergovernmental organizations to effectively provide the public good of collective security (via conflict management) on their own. Whatever the causes or merits of this broadening of the field of actors and arrangements in the conflict management realm, they clearly signal the beginning of a transformation in the practice of international conflict management – away from conflict management as the exclusive domain and province of states, to one in which conflict management is a practice carried out by a panoply of actors.

Approaches

As was discussed in Chapter 1, efforts to manage intra-state and inter-state conflicts can be and are grouped according to the objectives of the party (or parties) providing conflict management and the means they employ when doing so. The resulting grouping of conflict management approaches by categories such as 'threat-based,' 'deterrence-based,' 'adjudicatory,' and 'accommodationist' allows for a general understanding of the underlying motivations of actors engaged in the management of international conflict, as well as the tactics associated with different motives (Bercovitch and Regan, 2004). Still, like any heuristic device, this conceptual schema is limited when pressed into application. Those limitations are brought into particularly broad relief when one considers the nature of many recent conflict management efforts.

As this theoretical and empirical assessment of contemporary conflict management shows, thinking of attempts at conflict management as entirely (or even mostly) threat-based, deterrence-based, adjudicatory, or accommodationist is shortsighted. Doing so overlooks the fact that the bulk of efforts at managing inter-state and intra-state conflict today feature multiple approaches precipitated by varying objectives and arrayed around multiple tactics (and actors). In addition, contemporary conflict management initiatives not only sometimes involve more than one actor, they also are sometimes carried out by actors with multiple or mixed motives – and in any case are frequently mid-to-long-term ventures with multiple phases and stages.

Consider the profile of the INTERFET mission in East Timor in Chapter 9. INTERFET stands as a textbook example of a peace enforcement operation, and as such represents the most distinctly coercive and threat-based approach to conflict management featured in this book. Yet clearly INTERFET was designed not only to compel the end of militia-fueled violence, but also to deter the continued interference of Indonesia in the affairs of East Timor. Further, INTERFET succeeded in its application of coercive threat power largely due to the diplomatic and political accommodations fashioned between its military commanders and their counterparts in the Indonesian armed forces. Finally, INTERFET's remit included authorization for elements of legal and political activity (such as mediating disputes between Timorese political factions, creating the conditions for humanitarian relief, and ostensibly committing to the investigation of human rights crimes), while opening the door for more extensive institutional and civil society building ventures by the UN and other outside actors in subsequent operations.

What the INTERFET example shows in this instance is the complex and uncertain picture that can be drawn with respect to the objectives and means of contemporary conflict management. A multiplicity of approaches is evident in what would seem to be a straightforward example of coercive threat-based conflict management. Surely this is due in no small part to the array of actors that were directly or indirectly involved in INTERFET (and its successor operations), and their various and changing motives and objectives. A similar degree of complexity and uncertainty also defines the other forms and applications of conflict management (peacekeeping in Georgia, mediation in Sudan, and adjudication in Colombia) profiled here. Though all of these case studies in conflict management (and the primary conflict management approach they illustrate) may hew more closely to a threat-based, deterrence-based, adjudicatory, or accommodationist model, none can be characterized exclusively. In the end, the lesson for the careful student of contemporary conflict management is not that one should abandon attempts to systematically analyze conflict management and carefully refine one's understanding of the concept; far from it. Rather, such systematic and careful analysis requires a distinct acknowledgment of the complexity and variability evident in contemporary conflict management applications that may defy easy categorization.

Parameters

As was also first noted in Chapter 1, and subsequently and repeatedly confirmed in the rest of the book, conflict management in the international arena is limited by the boundaries established by sovereignty and coercive force. In other words, it is possible for both sovereignty and coercive force to play a significant or insignificant enough role with respect to a third-party intervention that said intervention could not be considered consistent with conflict management as customarily defined. These parametric boundaries speak to the characterization of conflict management as an inherently pragmatic and centrist concept – as something falling between unrestricted warfare and peacebuilding on the larger continuum of violence in global society. Yet while the constructs of sovereignty and coercive force remain valid distinctions maintaining the outer conceptual boundaries of what can be considered conflict management, the salience of each concept relative to the specific practices of conflict management both collectively and individually is far from stable and unchanging.

In the same way that the objectives of third parties and the approaches they employ defy easy characterization, so too does the role of sovereignty and coercive force vary both across the range of conflict management techniques assessed in this volume and in particular applications of each of them. In thinking about the major approaches to international conflict in their entirety, sovereignty is strongest with respect to the 'traditional' peacekeeping operations discussed and profiled in Chapters 4 and 5, and weakest in relation to peace enforcement, which assigned a 'right' to NSAs to use coercive force against states. Mediation and adjudication fall somewhere in between those poles, with the latter approach and its impingement on state sovereignty by international courts and tribunals relatively less constrained by sovereignty than the former.

Such characterizations are borne out by the wide berth between the highly constrained UNOMIG operation in Georgia and the extensive authority ascribed to INTERFET in East Timor, or the attempts at expanding international jurisprudence in international humanitarian law reflected in the Mapiripán case versus the arduous attempts by IGAD mediators to bring together official representatives of the Khartoum government and the south Sudanese rebels along with representatives of other interested states. The same kind of variability that is evident across conflict management approaches with regard to the importance of sovereignty is also apparent with regard to coercive force. While clearly force was most central to the INTERFET operation, as a backdrop to the UNOMIG deployment in Georgia (and more directly through the surrogate interposition of the CIS-PKF) it played a nominally important (if in the abstract) role. Conversely, the IGAD mediation of the Sudanese civil war and the IACHR adjudication of the Mapiripán massacre carried with them little evident possibility of a resort to force.

In considering the importance of sovereignty and force in light of particular approaches to conflict management, a micro-level analysis facilitated by in-depth case studies shows that even discrete applications of conflict management practices contain a significant degree of variation in the importance of each. This is especially true when time and context are taken into account. The deference of INTERFET commanders to their Indonesian counterparts and the self-imposed restraint associated with the application of force changed as militia activity persisted, and as INTERFET personnel came to appreciate the connections between members and officers of the TNI and the pro-Jakarta militias, and the way that nexus sustained the devastation wrought by the militias. On the other hand, the scope and activity of the UNOMIG deployment largely receded over the lifespan of the operation. Continuing violations of the ceasefire and direct challenges to UNOMIG's mandate by the warring factions in and around Abkhazia actually resulted in periodic *disengagements* by UN personnel from the most contested areas – suggesting a persistent if not increasing emphasis on sovereignty and the commitment to avoiding the use of force.

Similarly variable dynamics played out in the IGAD mediation and in the IACHR's handling of the Mapiripán case, particularly related to sovereignty as a limiting condition for conflict management activities. Whereas in the former instance Sumbeiywo's adoption of a more directive and manipulative mediation style can clearly be understood as a break from a pattern of deference to the parties to the conflict, in the latter the interminable investigation of the initial claim and the priority placed on the government of Colombia's preliminary objections stood in stark contrast to the strikingly direct (and directive) tenor of the ruling against

Colombia. In the end, as is true with respect to both actors and activities, conflict management in the international system is going through an important (if gradual) transformation in terms of the effects of major constructs such as sovereignty and coercion. While such constructs retain their importance in helping us to distinguish how conflict management is unique and distinct from fundamentally different forms of activity within the broader expanse of conflict and security (such as war and peace), it would be a mistake to say that these constructs apply equally to different conflict management techniques or even consistently within specific applications of any one of those techniques.

Key themes, recurring questions

This concluding chapter also provides an opportunity to reflect on the specific themes and questions raised by this book's consideration of each of the four major applications of conflict management. Surely there is much to be said for an integrative and synthetic approach to the concept of conflict management, such as the preceding consideration of the gradual transformation of the practice of conflict management. At the same time, we would be remiss in not also reflecting on some of the 'big picture' themes and questions highlighted in this contemporary assessment of several specific translations of conflict management.

Peacekeeping: is peacekeeping an anachronism?

Traditional peacekeeping is a reactive phenomenon that has as much to do with the parties to and context of a particular conflict as it does with the actors providing peacekeeping or any larger agenda for promoting peace. Peacekeeping operations reflect, and are themselves reflections of, an international system which is fundamentally oriented around state sovereignty, and in which questions of security, war, and peace are predicated on states and their authority. This is borne out by the contingency of such operations on obtaining the consent of the parties, as well as their overriding goal of remaining neutral and impartial with respect to the political situation underlying the conflict and in carrying out mandated responsibilities. However, in light of the changing nature of both conflict and security in the contemporary international system, the possibility exists that this emphasis on consent, impartiality, neutrality, and non-coercive ROE make peacekeeping deficient, if not anachronistic.

Obtaining consent for peacekeeping from the combatants of many contemporary conflicts is problematic since in many situations no legitimately recognized source or sources for providing it exists or can be identified. Considering the degree to which many of the specific conflicts profiled in this book (and the idealized type of conflict they represent) are oriented around the marshalling of organized violence in an intra-state struggle for political, social, and economic power and standing, it stands to reason that this scenario is increasingly the rule rather than the exception. With a multiplicity of actors engaged in a struggle for control of the machinery of state and the sovereignty and legitimacy associated with it, a strict adherence to consent may unduly impede or restrict the provision of a necessary peace operation.

Likewise, impartiality and neutrality are likely to be difficult to maintain in intra-state conflicts. This is particularly true for conflicts resembling the 'new war' typology in which various factions are engaged in intense conflicts launched and encouraged by identity politics and fueled by absolute and relative deprivation. Deploying a lightly armed military force with the authority to use deadly force only in self-defense within such settings is almost certain to prove insufficient for protecting civilians and containing violence, while also potentially jeopardizing the safety and security of the peacekeepers themselves. In an international system where state sovereignty remains paramount, while intra-state conflicts are waged over, against, without regard to, or in the absence of the state are commonplace, peacekeeping is forced to confront these and other thorny dilemmas raised by the gradual erosion of state sovereignty.

Mediation: demonstrating commitment, avoiding capture

The requisite of impartiality requires mediators to convey commitment without capturing and dominating the conflict management process. This difficult balance between commitment and capture renders mediation more of an art than a science. The commitment of a third-party mediator (defined as the maintenance of a necessary and significant level of effort and intensity aimed at managing and eventually resolving an intra-state conflict) is absolutely essential to the successful employment of mediation as a tool of conflict management. Mediation without sincere and significant commitment to conflict management and resolution for its own sake is tantamount to failed mediation; the lack of (real or perceived) credibility that flows from half-hearted mediation almost ensures that mediation efforts will go for naught.

At the same time, mediators must steadfastly avoid capturing the negotiations (such that the necessary effort and intensity put into mediation becomes diverted to the mediator's interests and agenda rather than toward the identification of an effective and acceptable solution). Overzealous and domineering mediators generally wind up pursuing, and producing, self-interested and forced 'solutions' that serve the interests of mediators more than the interests of the combatants. As is the case with weak and desultory efforts at mediation, the capture of the conflict management process by the mediator generally has undesirable consequences. These include leaving the sources of the conflict unaltered, or worse, introducing new disputes and resentments among the parties. Either situation translates into the unintended outcome of a conflict setting this is fundamentally unaltered, and thus prone to recurrence.

Peace enforcement: resolving the consent conundrum

The multiplicity of issues surrounding peace enforcement has generated a great deal of concern with how peace enforcement might be made more effective in the pursuit of its explicit objectives, while not abrogating the norm of non-interference or becoming a rhetorical smokescreen for the pursuit of *realpolitik* by powerful states. At the heart of this concern lies a conundrum posed by the issue of consent – namely, that those conflicts seemingly most in need of extensive operations of an enforcement character are also those where consent for third-party intervention is most elusive.

Given the costs, risks, and controversy associated with peace enforcement, even the mention of such operations has typically engendered heated debates and elicited great reservations on the part of potential contributors or other concerned parties. Due to the convergence of these factors, the debate over peace enforcement often reverts to the default position; that is, to a position where obtaining some form of consent is crucial in order for the operation to proceed. Yet as was discussed in Chapter 8, consent for third-party intervention is nearly impossible to secure from any 'legitimate' political authority in many contemporary conflicts, since those conflicts are contested in part over who possesses that legitimacy. This problem is greatly magnified when the form of intervention in question is peace enforcement, in which third parties are authorized to use coercive military force to carry out some measure of social re-engineering (by introducing and enforcing 'peace' where it does not entail).

One attempt to circumvent this conundrum, prompted by a sustained interest on the part of the UN and the international community in carrying out such expansive forms of peace operations, is the introduction of the notion of 'imperfect consent.' First articulated in 'An Agenda for Peace' and again in the Brahimi Report, this concept explicitly acknowledges that the objective of enforcing cease-fires and peace settlements where they have failed, or restoring the conditions of peace where they are absent, carries with it the burden that at least some of the combatants wish to continue engaging in violence. At the same time, advocates of 'imperfect consent' also maintain that it is possible to obtain at least some degree of consent from the parties with respect to the operation despite the lack of 'ripeness' or a mutually hurting stalemate.

The manner in which the concept of imperfect consent has been elaborated holds out hope that despite the prospects for spoilers resulting from the limited range and hold of consent, the applicability of consent could somehow be salvaged for peace enforcement operations – making them more palatable not only for the parties to the conflict, but to potential contributors. Yet as specific applications of peace enforcement (such as INTERFET in East Timor) show, in continuing to make the case for a renewed and expanded role for the UN in responding to intra-state conflicts, the securing of consent in any meaningful sense of the term remains a major obstacle. If attained at all, 'consent' may itself prove fleeting, in turn leading to major complications for the implementation of an operation by blurring the major qualitative distinctions between peace enforcement and other forms of conflict management.

Adjudication: how independent should adjudicators be?

Conventional wisdom holds that the effective functioning of standing courts and arbitration panels in adjudicating international conflicts is closely related to (if not entirely dependent on) the independence of the adjudicating body. This precondition is clearly related to the fact that most advocates for international adjudication base their vision of jurisprudence in international law on analogies drawn from the domestic sphere, where arbitrators and courts possess almost unlimited powers of compulsory jurisdiction. The fact that arbitrators and judges in the vast majority of domestic legal systems serve fixed terms, and are appointed or elected through fixed rules rather than at the whims of the parties to a dispute or through a pre-arranged formula for national representation, helps to maintain the impartiality, and by extension the credibility of such tribunals. In extending this argument to its logical conclusion, the inability to attain a similar degree of jurisdiction in the international arena – or even to establish standing procedures for the selection and service of adjudicators – means that arbitrators and courts will continually fall victim to accusations of politicization. By extension, their legitimacy and ability to advance the cause of international jurisprudence is likely to suffer in the process.

A significant point often overlooked in this conventional wisdom is the possibility that more independence may actually work against the effectiveness of an adjudicatory body in the international legal context. Lacking the deep and entrenched normative, institutional, political, and cultural ties that define domestic legal systems, international courts typically function as prominent but solitary institutions without the benefit of an extensive backing in case law, an established legislative body, or an effective mechanism for enforcement. Particularly in entrenched international conflicts, the introduction of a powerful third party such as a court or arbitrator that possesses a distinct and independent agenda, but lacks grounding in a coherent, hierarchical, and unified legal system may lead to suspicion and reticence on behalf of the parties to the dispute.

One recent and high-profile expression of this opposition to the expansion of international adjudication on these very grounds is the vocal opposition to the creation of the ICC in its present form, as expressed by China, Iran, Israel, Russia, and especially the United States. In the United States opposition both to the ICC and the concept of international jurisprudence has in recent years reverted to the recurring theme of suspicion toward international law, particularly an international law in which independent adjudicatory powers are evident. This theme, broadly evident throughout American history, is emblematized in the depiction of the ICC by former Undersecretary of State and US Ambassador to the UN John Bolton, who referred to the Court as 'an organization that runs contrary to fundamental American precepts and basic Constitutional principles of popular sovereignty, checks and balances, and national independence' (Bolton, 2003).

Managing 'new wars'

The second major question advanced in this book concerns the effectiveness of the major approaches to conflict management in responding to contemporary conflicts. The multifaceted security challenges and 'new wars' of the late twentieth and early twenty-first century, such as those in Georgia, Sudan, East Timor, and Colombia (to name just a few) underscore the importance of this question. Defined by the involvement of weak or compromised states, fueled by clashing identities, NSAs, and transnational networks, rife with human rights violations and humanitarian suffering, and taking place mostly within states and societies rather than across or between them, the complexity, volatility, and stakes associated with most post-Cold War conflicts are exceedingly high. Are practices such as peacekeeping, mediation, peace enforcement, and adjudication sufficient responses to the challenges posed by contemporary armed conflicts?

Challenges for conflict management

The 'broadening and deepening' of the security studies field, and the relationship of that effort to the redefinition of the concept of security, makes it clear where the point of origin of most 'new war' theorizing lies. The possibility of shifting the security referent from states to individuals or the international system (or both) allows one to consider how best to manage the effects that armed conflict has on these alternative referents. Likewise, (re)defining security threats to include not just military, but also political, economic, environmental, and societal dimensions raises the prospect that armed conflict originates from a wide variety of sources, is carried out using an equally wide variety of means and tactics, and is advanced in pursuit of a disparate set of objectives.

As the core of 'new war' theorizing indicates, the diminished authority of the state, weak and incomplete mechanisms of political representation, and a loss of confidence in the ability and willingness of the state to respond to public concerns (especially those related to violence, lawlessness, and economic scarcity) are all key factors shaping and advancing conflict today. While the effects of these changes are not system-wide, they are assuredly system-induced. In addition to serving as triggers of conflict, these dynamics tend to reinforce such conflicts in a 'negative spiral of incivility' (Kaldor, 2000). Such features are common enough aspects of public life in conflict-torn and conflict-prone societies today that they have direct implications for international conflict management.

Intervening in internal conflict

Perhaps the foremost challenge for contemporary conflict management is the reality that most armed conflicts today feature violence which occurs entirely within the boundaries of a state (or former state). As was discussed in Chapter 3, 'new wars' typically unfold at least in part around an effort by sub-state actors and NSAs to contest, hijack, or weaken the authority of the state. In an abstract sense, contemporary conflicts that approximate the 'new war' model are waged against the concept of the state itself. The internal character of most contemporary conflicts makes external intervention by a third party – always a risky proposition – decidedly riskier. The lack of familiarity with the issues, actors, and society in which the conflict occurs on the part of the third party further compounds this risk.

It is important to remember that most of the rules and practices of international conflict management flow from a state-centric approach to security and international order oriented at managing conflicts between, rather than within, nation-states. In concert with the fact that most third-party conflict managers are either states or member-state-based international organizations, the challenges facing third-party intervention for the purpose of conflict management are many and varied. Among these, the traditional focus of conflict management on obtaining consent from the parties to a conflict is most directly affected. In intra-state conflicts defined by a violent contest over political authority, the institutions and authority of the state are likely to be either so compromised or so contested that no effective source for providing that consent may be evident.

Identity as the source of conflict

Similarly, another recurring feature of international conflict management efforts – the effort to remain, or at least appear, impartial to the parties to the conflict – may be impossible to achieve in contemporary conflicts. Considering the intensity and nature of the grievances at the heart of many contemporary conflicts (rooted in deep-seated and hard-wired identities) it is more likely that third parties will be subjected to accusations of partiality by the various warring factions, irrespective of the nature or intent of their actions. Further compounding the difficulty of cultivating impartiality is that the origins of many contemporary conflicts, in particular identity politics, as well as the war profiteering rampant within them, creates a dynamic where the main objective of the warring parties is continuation of the conflict. To the extent that the 'target' of conflict management is the instability and insecurity associated with conflict (as discussed in Chapter 1), as well as any actors who wish to perpetuate that instability and insecurity, the dynamics of 'new wars' would seem to set conflict managers and combatants on a direct collision course.

'Networked' warfare

The complex interdependence associated with globalization provides not only the catalyst for 'new wars,' but also its sustaining force. Multifaceted cross-border networks built around political elites, security forces and recruits, legal and illicit entrepreneurs, and transnational diasporas linked by religious, ethnic, linguistic, or national identity constitute the social basis for, as well as the centripetal forces driving, 'new wars.' Such networks are complex, opaque, and in the end essential sources for supplying the necessary arms, equipment, combatants, and especially funds. Their densely transnational character effectively exploits the permeable boundaries (literal and otherwise) of weak states and their equally weak security and law enforcement apparatus.

Accordingly, a critical challenge facing contemporary conflict management is the need to identify the tactics and secure the resources needed to manage conflicts laced with transnational dimensions, including the presence of broad and complex networks to sustain and reinforce them. With the rules and processes of conflict management decidedly state-centric, marshaling and applying the necessary breadth of available resources to counter wars that themselves are at least partially globalized in nature is an obviously daunting proposition. Failing that, the relatively easy flow of weapons, money, and people into and out of conflict zones poses a direct obstacle to any peacekeeping, mediation, peace enforcement, or adjudication effort.

Economic underpinnings

Many contemporary conflicts are fueled by diminished confidence in the institutions of the state and an associated weakening of national affiliation. These dynamics have the ancillary effect of propelling individuals to other sources for the provision of public goods (especially, but not only, security) as well as social and psychological reinforcement. Typically, these surrogates are sub-state groups which lack institutional representation or official political power, but who possess a profound degree of legitimacy rooted in group identity. The claim to political power at the heart of 'new wars' is therefore based on the labels associated with group identity rather than the institutional legitimacy associated with the machinery of the state.

The challenges of economic development and scarcity evident in many weak states greatly exacerbate this trend. Given the economic roots of 'new wars,' it should not come as a surprise that the vast majority of contemporary conflicts occur either in developing countries or those experiencing transitions from planned economies (Duffield, 2001). In such societies, state institutions have long underperformed in addressing short-term economic needs and providing for long-term economic prospects, while external pressure from donor states, international lending agencies, and the like have typically magnified economic problems stemming from scarcity and inequality. The economic underpinnings of contemporary conflict pose direct and major challenges to effective conflict management, given the overtly political and institutional focus of the concept and its various translations.

The way forward

In briefly returning to a general consideration of the concept of conflict management in all its various translations, several key considerations for enhancing the effectiveness of conflict management as a practice are evident.

Resource access and mobilization

The effectiveness of the management of contemporary conflicts by third parties is closely related to the ability of third parties to successfully marshal available resources in support of whatever approach to conflict management is being employed. Marshaling sufficient resources and using them effectively can persuade involved parties of the merits of conflict management – and by extension, the merits of terminating the conflict. These resources can be, and often are, material in nature, but they can be symbolic as well. In this light, the prestige of the actor(s) involved as third parties is important. Actors with higher profiles are likely to have access not only to more material 'carrots' and 'sticks,' but are also likely to have the capacity to appeal directly to domestic and international constituencies to build up support for their efforts.

Flexibility

Successful conflict management efforts also require a significant degree of flexibility on the part of the conflict manager. This flexibility stems in large part from a sophisticated understanding of the conflict setting and principals. Such understanding requires a nuanced grasp of the historical, political, and cultural grievances that lie at the heart of the conflict, the attitudes of the combatants, and the dynamic context in which the conflict is unfolding. Access to reliable information is critical to attaining the needed level of understanding about the conflict itself, and the parties to it. The ability to draw upon an available reserve of information about the parties and the conflict itself is crucial in formulating – and revising – an effective response to the conflict and its underlying concerns, concerns which may materialize (sometimes in new translations) during the conflict management operation.

Receptive political context

In many cases the success or failure of conflict management has little to do with the third party per se, but rather the values, attitudes, and behaviors of the parties to the conflict itself and the larger context enveloping the conflict. Regardless of what form of conflict management is employed, conflict management is more likely to succeed when there are recognizable and authoritative leaders associated with each party to the conflict. Such leaders are accepted as legitimate representatives by a significant constituency and as such can deliver on promises and agreements. If they are drawn from the mainstream of their respective political communities, they provide the third party with a reliable source of information, and beyond that can confer significant legitimacy and political capital upon third parties engaged in conflict management simply by virtue of working with them. Conversely, conflicts that feature parties with competing leaders and factions (such as the various splinter paramilitaries that defined the landscape in Northern Ireland in the years leading up to the Good Friday Accords) are exceedingly difficult to manage. Effective conflict management is therefore very much contingent on the absence of 'spoilers,' and by extension is likely to work when actors or segments of a political community committed to continuing the violence are either absent or effectively contained.

External reinforcement

Few, if any, instances of conflict management in the international arena have generated effective containment of a conflict without some kind of significant and sustained reinforcement. Rather, conflict management by definition usually leads only to a temporary and limited 'victory,' in the form of a settlement that is in actuality situated within the larger continuum between unrestrained warfare on the one hand, and reconciliation and peace on the other. At best, conflict management can fashion what Gabriella Blum (2007) has called 'islands of agreement' in a larger sea of conflict; a temporary space in which violence can abate and the political process be afforded space to operate. It would seem that our understanding of and expectations for conflict management should be tailored with this fundamental defining feature of international conflict management in mind.

Bibliography

Abbott, Kenneth W. and Duncan Snidal. 1998. 'Why States Act Through Formal International Organizations,' *Journal of Conflict Resolution*, 42 (1): 3–32.

Abi Saab, G. 1978. *The United Nations Operation in the Congo, 1960–1964*. Oxford: Oxford University Press.

Adar, Korwa G. 2000. 'Conflict Resolution in a Turbulent Region: The Case of the Intergovernmental Authority on Development (IGAD) in Sudan,' *African Journal of Conflict Resolution*, 1 (2): 39–66.

Alape, Arturo. 1998. 'The Possibilities for Peace,' *NACLA Report on the Americas*, 31 (5): 36.

Aldrich, George H. 1996. *The Jurisprudence of the Iran–United States Claims Tribunal*. New York, NY: Oxford University Press.

Alker, Hayward R. Jr, James Bennett, and Dwain Medford. 1980. 'Generalized Precedent Logics for Resolving Insecurity Dilemmas,' *International Interactions*, 7 (2): 165–206.

Allee, Todd L. and Paul K. Huth. 2006. 'Legitimizing Dispute Settlement: International Legal Rulings as Domestic Political Cover,' *American Political Science Review*, 100 (2): 219–234.

Alter, Karen. 2003. 'Do International Courts Enhance Compliance with International Law?' *Review of Asian and Pacific Studies*, 25: 51–77.

Andreas, Peter R., Eva Bertram, Morris Blachman, and Kenneth Sharpe. 1992. 'Dead End Drug Wars,' *Foreign Policy*, 85: 106–128.

Ashley, Richard. 1981. 'Political Realism and Human Interests,' *International Studies Quarterly*, 25 (2): 204–236.

Azar, Edward E. 1990. *The Management of Protracted Social Conflict: Theory and Cases*. Aldershot: Dartmouth.

Azcarate, Camilo A. 1999. 'Psychosocial Dynamics of the Armed Conflict in Colombia,' *Online Journal of Peace and Conflict Resolution*, 2 (1). Available at: www.trinstitute.org/ojpcr/2_1columbia.htm.

Bagley, Bruce M. 1988. 'Colombia and the War on Drugs,' *Foreign Affairs*, 67 (1): 70–92.

Baldwin, David A. 1997. 'The Concept of Security,' *Review of International Studies*, 23 (1): 5–26.

Baldwin, David A. 1980. 'Interdependence and Power: A Conceptual Analysis,' *International Organization*, 34 (4): 471–506.

Barash, David P. and Charles P. Webel. 2008. *Peace and Conflict Studies*, 2nd edn. Thousand Oaks, CA: Sage Publications.

Barber, Benjamin R. 1996. *Jihad vs. McWorld: How Globalism and Tribalism Are Re-Shaping the World*. New York, NY: Ballantine.

Baylis, John. 2001. 'International and Global Security in the Post-Cold War Era,' in J. Baylis and S. Smith (eds.), *The Globalization of World Politics*, 2nd edn. Oxford: Oxford University Press, pp. 254–276.

Beauvais, Joel C. 2001. 'Benevolent Despotism: A Critique of UN State-Building in East Timor,' *New York University Journal of International Law and Politics*, 33 (4): 1101–1078.

Bellamy, Alex J. and Paul D. Williams. 2005. 'Who's Keeping the Peace? Regionalization and Contemporary Peace Operations,' *International Security*, 29 (4): 157–195.

Bellamy, Alex J., Paul D. Williams, and Stuart Griffin. 2004. *Understanding Peacekeeping*. London: Polity.

Benson, Kevin C.M. and Christopher B. Thrash. 1996. 'Declaring Victory: Planning Exit Strategies for Peace Operations,' *Parameters*, 26: 69–80.

Bercovitch, Jacob and Scott Sigmund Gartner. 2006. 'Is There Method in the Madness of Mediation? Some Lessons for Mediators from Quantitative Studies of Mediation,' *International Interactions*, 32 (4): 329–354.

Bercovitch, Jacob. 2005. 'Mediation in the Most Resistant Cases,' in C. Crocker, F.O. Hampson and P. Aall (eds.), *Grasping the Nettle: Analyzing Cases of Intractable Conflict*. Washington, DC: USIP, pp. 99–122.

Bercovitch, Jacob. 2004. 'International Mediation and Intractable Conflict,' in Guy Burgess and Heidi Burgess (eds.), *Beyond Intractability*. Boulder, CO: Conflict Research Consortium.

Bercovitch, Jacob. 1996. 'Understanding Mediation's Role in Preventative Diplomacy,' *Negotiation Journal*, 12 (3): 241–258.

Bercovitch, Jacob. 1986. 'International Mediation: A Study of Incidence, Strategies, and Conditions of Successful Outcomes,' *Cooperation and Conflict*, 21: 155–168.

Bercovitch, Jacob. 1984. *Social Conflicts and Third Parties: Strategies of Conflict Resolution*. Boulder, CO: Westview Press.

Bercovitch, Jacob and Patrick Regan. 2004. 'Mediation and International Conflict Management: A Review and Analysis,' in Zeev Maoz, Alex Mintz, T. Clifton Morgan, Glenn Palmer, and Richard J. Stoll (eds.), *Multiple Paths to Knowledge in International Relations*. Lanham, MD: Lexington, pp. 249–272.

Bercovitch, Jacob and Patrick M. Regan. 1999. 'The Structure of International Conflict Management: An Analysis of the Effects of Intractability and Mediation,' *International Journal of Peace Sciences*, 4 (1).

Bercovitch, Jacob and Jeffrey Z. Rubin. 1992. *Mediation in International Relations: Multiple Approaches to Conflict Management*. New York, NY: Macmillan/St. Martin's Press.

Bercovitch, Jacob, J. Theodore Anagnoson, and Donnette L. Wille. 1991. 'Some Conceptual Issues and Empirical Trends in the Study of Successful Mediation in International Relations,' *Journal of Peace Research*, 28 (1): 7–17.

Berdal, Mats. 2003. 'How "New" Are "New Wars"? Global Economic Change and the Study of Civil War,' *Global Governance*, 9 (4): 477–502.

Bergquist, Charles W. 1978. *Coffee and Conflict in Colombia*. Durham, NC: Duke University Press.

Bergquist, Charles W., Ricardo Peñaranda, and Sánchez G. Gonzalo 2001. *Violence in Colombia, 1990–2000: Waging War and Negotiating Peace*. Lanham, MD: Rowman & Littlefield.

Berman, Eric and Katie E. Sams. 2000. *Peacekeeping in Africa: Capabilities and Culpabilities*. Geneva: United Nations Publications.

Berman, Ilan. 2005. 'The New Battleground: The Caucasus and Central Asia,' *The Washington Quarterly* (Winter): 55–66.

Betts, Wendy. 1999. 'Third Party Mediation: An Obstacle to Peace in Nagorno Karabakh,' *SAIS Review*, 19 (2): 161–183.

Bilder, Richard B. 2007. 'Adjudication: International Arbitral Tribunals and Courts,' in I. William Zartman (ed.), *Peacemaking in International Conflict: Methods and Techniques*, revised edition. Washington, DC: USIP, pp. 195–226.

Bilder, Richard B. 1992. 'International Law in the "New World Order": Some Preliminary Reflections,' *Florida State University Journal of Transnational Law and Policy*, 1: 1–21.

Bilder, Richard B. 1989. 'International Third-Party Dispute Settlement,' *Denver Journal of International Law and Policy*, 17: 471–503.

Billings-Yun, Melanie. 1983. 'Korean War Aims,' Case number C14–82–484. Cambridge, MA: Kennedy School of Government, Harvard University.

Birgisson, Karl. 1993. 'United Nations Peacekeeping Forces in Cyprus,' in W.J. Durch (ed.), *The Evolution of UN Peacekeeping: Case Studies and Comparative Analysis*. New York, NY: St. Martin's Press, pp. 218–236.

Bloomfield, David. 1998. 'Case Study: Northern Ireland,' in Ben Harris *et al.* (eds.), *Democracy and Deep-Rooted Conflict: Options for Negotiators*, International Institute for Democracy and Electoral Assistance.

Blum, Gabriella. 2007. *Islands of Agreement: Managing Enduring Armed Rivalries*. Cambridge, MA: Harvard University Press.

Bolton, John R. 2003. 'American Justice and the International Criminal Court,' Remarks by the Undersecretary of State for Arms Control and International Security at the American Enterprise Institute, 3 November. Available at: www.state.gov/t/us/rm/25818.htm (accessed 16 July 2008).

Boulden, Jane. 2001. *Peace Enforcement: The United Nations Experience in Congo, Somalia, and Bosnia*. Westport, CT: Praeger.

Boutros-Ghali, Boutros. 1995. 'Supplement to an Agenda for Peace,' Position paper of the Secretary-General on the occasion of the Fiftieth Anniversary of the UN. In Boutros Boutros-Ghali, *Agenda for Peace*, 2nd edn. New York, NY: United Nations, pp. 5–38.

Boutros-Ghali, Boutros. 1992a. 'Empowering the United Nations,' *Foreign Affairs*, 71 (5): 89–103.

Boutros-Ghali, Boutros. 1992b. 'An Agenda for Peace.' New York, NY: United Nations. Available at: www.un.org/Docs/SG/agpeace.html (accessed 19 July 2007).

Booth, Ken. 2005. *Critical Security Studies and World Politics*. Boulder, CO: Lynne Rienner.

Booth, Ken. 1997. 'Security and Self: Reflections of a Fallen Realist,' in Keith Krause and Michael Williams (eds.), *Critical Security Studies*. Minneapolis, MN: University of Minnesota Press.

Booth, Ken. 1991. *New Thinking About Strategy and International Security*. London: Harper-Collins.

Brahimi, Lakdar. 2000. 'Report of the Panel on United Nations Peace Operations,' A/55/305-S/2000/809, 21 August. Available at: www.un.org/peace/reports/peace_operations/docs/a_55_305.pdf (accessed 8 January 2008).

Braun, Herbert. 1985. *The Assassination of Gaitan: Public Life and Urban Violence in Colombia*. Madison, WI: University of Wisconsin Press.

Brecher, Michael and Jonathan Wilkenfeld. 2000. *A Study of Crisis*. Ann Arbor, MI: University of Michigan Press.

British Broadcasting Corporation. 2008. 'UN Gives Timorese Police Control,' 4 February. Available at: http://news.bbc.co.uk/2/hi/asia-pacific/7226393.stm (accessed 6 February 2008).

British Broadcasting Corporation. 1998. 'Millions dead in Sudan civil war,' 11 December. Available at: http://news.bbc.co.uk/2/hi/africa/232803.stm (accessed 2 June 2007).

Brown, Michael (ed.). 1996. *The International Dimensions of Internal Conflict*. Cambridge, MA: MIT Press.

Brown, Seyom. 1998. 'World Interests and the Changing Dimensions of Security,' in Michael T. Klare and Yogesh Chandrani (eds.), *World Security: Challenges for a New Century*, 3rd edn. New York, NY: St. Martin's Press.

Brownlie, Ian. 1999. *Principles of Public International Law*. New York, NY: Oxford University Press.

Bulterman, Mielle K. and Martin Kuijer. 1996. *Compliance with Judgments of International Courts*. The Hague: Martinus Nijhoff.

Burt, Jo-Marie. 2000. 'The Massacre at Mapiripán,' *Colombia Journal/NACLA Report on the Americas*. New York: North American Congress on Latin America. Available at: www.colombiajournal.org/colombia6.htm (accessed 18 July 2008).

Burton, John and Frank Dukes. 1990. *Conflict: Practices in Management, Settlement and Resolution*. New York, NY: St. Martin's Press.

Butler, William E. 1992. 'The Hague Permanent Court of Arbitration,' in Mark W. Janis (ed.), *International Courts for the Twenty-First Century*. Leiden: Martinus Nijhoff, pp. 43–53.

Butterworth, Robert Lyle. 1978. 'Do Conflict Managers Matter?' *International Studies Quarterly*, 22: 195–214.

Buzan, Barry. 1991. *People, States, and Fear: The National Security Problem in International Relations*, 2nd edn. Boulder, CO: Lynne Rienner.

Buzan, Barry and Richard Little. 2000. *International Systems in World History: Remaking the Study of International Relations*. Oxford: Oxford University Press.

Buzan, Barry and Ole Wæver. 2003. *Regions and Powers: The Structure of International Power*. Cambridge: Cambridge University Press.

Buzan, Barry, Ole Wæver, and Jaap de Wilde. 1998. *Security: A New Framework for Analysis*. Boulder, CO: Lynne Rienner.

Cardenas, Maria Christina. 2002. 'Colombia's Peace Process: The Contentious Search for Peace,' *Florida Journal of International Law*, 15: 273–297.

Carnevale, Peter J. and Dean G. Pruitt. 1992. 'Negotiation and Mediation,' *Annual Review of Psychology*, 43: 531–582.

Carr, Edward Hallett. 1939. *The Twenty Years Crisis, 1919–1939: An Introduction to the Study of International Relations*. London: Macmillan.

Carter, Jimmy. 1982. *Keeping Faith*. New York, NY: Bantam Books.

C.A.S.E. Collective. 2006. 'Critical Approaches to Security in Europe: A Networked Manifesto,' *Security Dialogue*, 37 (4): 443–487.

Center for Human Rights and Humanitarian Law (CHRHL). 2006. 'Mapiripán v. Colombia,' *Human Rights Brief*, 13 (29): 4–6.

Center for Political and International Studies (CPIS). 1995. *Operations Involving the Use of Armed Forces in the CIS*. Moscow: Center for Political and International Studies.

Chernick, Mark W. 2001. 'The Dynamics of Colombia's Three-Dimensional War,' *Conflict, Security and Development*, 1: 93–100.

Chernick, Mark W. 1998. 'The Paramilitarization of the War in Colombia,' *NACLA Report on the Americas*, 31: 28–33.

Chesterman, Simon. 2004. *You, the People: The United Nations, Transnational Administration, and State-Building*. Oxford: Oxford University Press.

Chesterman, Simon. 2001. *East Timor in Transition: From Conflict Prevention to State-Building*. New York, NY: International Peace Academy, Project on Transitional Administrations.

Chopra, Jarat. 2000. 'The UN's Kingdom of East Timor,' *Survival*, 42 (3): 27–39.

Chopra, Jarat and Thomas G. Weiss. 1995. 'Prospects for Containing Conflict in the Former Second World,' *Security Studies*, 4 (3): 552–583.

Chufrin, Gennady (ed.). 2001. *The Security of the Caspian Sea Region*. Oxford: Oxford University Press.

Claude, Inis L. 1984. *Swords into Ploughshares: The Problems and Progress of International Organization*. New York, NY: McGraw Hill.

Clausewitz, Carl von. 1976. *On War*, edited and translated by M. Howard and P. Paret. Princeton, NJ: Princeton University Press.

Coleman, Katharina P. 2007. *International Organizations and Peace Enforcement: The Politics of International Legitimacy*. Cambridge: Cambridge University Press.

Collier, John and Vaughan Lowe. 1999. *The Settlement of Disputes in International Law: Institutions and Procedures*. New York, NY: Oxford University Press.

Conference on Security and Cooperation in Europe (CSCE). 1990. 'Concluding Document of the CSCE Copenhagen Conference on the Human Dimension, June 29, 1990,' *International Legal Materials*, 29: 1305–1306.

Cosgrove, Major General P.J., AC, MC. 2000. 'The ANZAC lecture at Georgetown University, Tuesday 4 April 2000,' *Journal of the Australian Naval Institute*, 26 (2): 9.

Cotton, James. 1999. 'Peacekeeping in East Timor: An Australian Policy Departure,' *Australian Journal of International Affairs*, 53 (3): 237–246.

Coufoudakis, Van. 1976. 'United Nations Peacekeeping, Peacemaking, and the Cyprus Question,' *The Western Political Quarterly*, 29 (3): 457–473.

Crawford, Neta. 1991. 'Once and Future Security Studies,' *Security Studies*, 1 (2): 283–316.

Crigler, T. Frank. 1993. 'The Peace Enforcement Dilemma,' *Joint Forces Quarterly*, (Autumn): 64–70.

Crocker, C.A., F.O. Hampson, and P. Aall. 2001. 'Is More Better? The Pros and Cons of Multiparty Mediation,' in C.A. Crocker, F.O. Hampson, and P. Aall (eds.), *Turbulent Peace: The Challenges of Managing International Conflict*. Washington, DC: USIP, pp. 497–513.

Crocker, C.A., F.O. Hampson, and P. Aall (eds.). 1999. *Herding Cats: Multiparty Mediation in a Complex World*. Washington, DC: USIP.

Dale, Catherine. 1993. 'Turmoil in Abkhazia: Russian Responses,' *RFE/RL Research Report*, 2 (34).

De Búrca, Gráinne and Jason D. Brueschke (eds.). 2002. *The European Court of Justice*. New York, NY: Oxford University Press.

De Visscher, Charles. 1956. 'Reflections on the Present Prospects of International Adjudication,' *The American Journal of International Law*, 50 (3): 467–474.

de Waal, Alex. 2007. 'Sudan: International Dimensions to the State and Its Crisis,' Social Science Research Council Occasional Paper no. 3. Crisis States Research Centre, London School of Economics.

de Waal, Alex and A.H. Abdelsalam. 2004. 'Islam, State Power and Jihad in Sudan,' in Alex de Waal (ed.), *Islamism and Its Enemies in the Horn of Africa*. London: Hurst.

Dee, Moreen. 2001. 'Coalitions of the Willing and Humanitarian Intervention: Australia's Involvement with INTERFET,' *International Peacekeeping*, 8 (3): 1–20.

Deng, Francis M. 1999. 'Sudan Peace Prospects at a Cross-roads: An Overview,' Special paper prepared for the US Institute of Peace Consultation on the Sudan Project. Washington, DC: USIP.

Department of Peacekeeping Operations. 2008. *United Nations Peacekeeping Operations: Principles and Guidelines*. New York, NY: United Nations.

Department of Peacekeeping Operations. 2007a. 'Monthly Summary of Contributors to UN Peacekeeping Operations' (September). Available at: www.un.org/Depts/dpko/dpko/contributors.

Department of Peacekeeping Operations. 2007b. 'Completed Peacekeeping Missions: United Nations Operation in the Congo.' Available at: www.un.org/Depts/DPKO/Missions/onuc.htm (accessed 14 June 2007).

Deudney, Daniel. 1990. 'The Case Against Linking Environmental Degradation and National Security,' *Millennium: Journal of International Studies*, 19 (3): 461–476.

Dickens, David. 2001. 'The United Nations in East Timor: Intervention at the Military Operational Level,' *Contemporary Southeast Asia*, 23 (2): 213–232.

Diehl, Paul F. 1994. *International Peacekeeping*. Baltimore, MD: Johns Hopkins University Press.

Dixon, William J. 1996. 'Third-Party Techniques for Preventing Conflict Escalation and Promoting Peaceful Settlement,' *International Organization*, 50 (4): 653–681.

Doyle, Michael W. 1983a. 'Kant, Liberal Legacies, and Foreign Affairs,' *Philosophy and Public Affairs*, 12 (3): 205–235.

Doyle, Michael W. 1983b. 'Kant, Liberal Legacies, and Foreign Affairs, Part 2,' *Philosophy and Public Affairs*, 12 (4): 323–353.

Doyle, Michael W. and Nicholas Sambanis. 2006. *Making War and Building Peace: United Nations Peace Operations*. Princeton, NJ: Princeton University Press.

Druckman, Daniel. 1994. 'Nationalism, Patriotism, and Group Loyalty: A Social Psychological Perspective,' *Mershon International Studies Review*, 38 (1): 43–68.

Druckman, Daniel and Christopher Mitchell (eds.). 1995. *Flexibility in International Negotiation and Mediation*. The Annals of the American Academy of Political and Social Science, vol. 542. Thousand Oaks, CA: Sage.

Duffield, Mark. 2001. *Global Governance and the New Wars: The Merging of Development and Security*. London: Zed Books.

Duffield, Mark. 1999. 'Globalization and War Economies: Promoting Order or the Return of History?' *Fletcher Forum of World Affairs*, 23 (2): 21–38.

Dupont, Alan. 2000. 'ASEAN's Response to the East Timor Crisis,' *Australian Journal of International Affairs*, 54 (2): 163–170.

Durch, William J. (ed.). 1993. *The Evolution of UN Peacekeeping: Case Studies and Comparative Analysis*. New York, NY: St. Martin's Press.

Eck, Kristine, Bethany Lacina, and Magnus Öberg. 2008. 'Civil Conflict in the Contemporary World,' in Magnus Öberg and Kaare Ström (eds.), *Resources, Governance Structures, and Civil Conflict*. London: Routledge, pp. 23–42.

Economist, The. 2003. 'A Moment of Truth – The Caucasus,' 29 November.

el-Affendi, Abdelwahab. 2001. 'The Impasse in the IGAD Peace Process for Sudan: The Limits of Regional Peacemaking?' *African Affairs*, 100: 581–599.

El-Bettahani, Atta. 2006. 'A Complex Web: Politics and Conflict in Sudan,' in *Peace by Piece: Addressing Sudan's Conflicts*, Accord: An International Review of Peace Initiatives (no. 18). London: Conciliation Resources.

Elkind, Jerome B. 1984. *Non-Appearance Before the International Court of Justice: Functional and Comparative Analysis*. The Hague: Martinus Nijhoff.

el-Mukhtar Hussein, Mohamed. 2006. 'Negotiating Peace: the Road to Naivasha,' in *Peace by Piece: Addressing Sudan's Conflicts*, Accord: An International Review of Peace Initiatives (no. 18). London: Conciliation Resources.

Eriksson, Mikael and Peter Wallensteen. 2004. 'Armed Conflict, 1989–2003,' *Journal of Peace Research*, 41 (5): 625–636.

Eyffinger, Arthur. 1996. *The International Court of Justice, 1946–1996*. The Hague: Kluwer Law International.

Fairbanks, Charles. 2004. 'Georgia's Rose Revolution,' *Journal of Democracy*, 15 (2): 110–124.

Falk, Richard A. 1971. 'The Relevance of Political Context to the Nature and Functioning of International Law: An Intermediate View,' in Karl Deutsch and Stanley Hoffmann (eds.), *The Relevance of International Law*. Cambridge, MA: Schenkman.

Fearon, James D. and David D. Laitin. 2003. 'Ethnicity, Insurgency, and Civil War,' *American Political Science Review*, 97 (1): 75–90.

Fisher, Richard. 1981. *Improving Compliance with International Law*. Charlottesville, VA: University of Virginia Press.

Fortna, Virginia Page. 2004. 'Does Peacekeeping Keep Peace? International Intervention and the Duration of Peace After Civil War,' *International Studies Quarterly*, 48 (2): 269–292.

Franck, Thomas M. 1995. *Fairness in International Law and Institutions*. New York, NY: Oxford University Press.

Freedman, Lawrence. 1998. 'International Security: Changing Targets,' *Foreign Policy*, 110: 48–63.

Friedman, Thomas L. 2007. *The World is Flat: A Brief History of the Twenty-First Century*. New York, NY: Picador/Farrar, Straus, and Giroux.

Fukuyama, Francis. 1989. 'The End of History?' *The National Interest*, 16: 3–16.

Fuller, Elizabeth. 1994. 'The Transcaucasus: War, Turmoil, Economic Collapse,' *RFE/RL Research Report*, 3 (1).

Fuller, Lon L. and Kenneth I. Winston. 1978. 'The Forms and Limits of Adjudication,' *Harvard Law Review*, 92 (2): 353–409.

Gallie, Walter Bryce. 1956. 'Essentially Contested Concepts,' *Proceedings of the Aristotelian Society*, 56: 167–198.

Gartner, Scott Sigmund and Jacob Bercovitch. 2006. 'Overcoming Obstacles to Peace: The Contribution of Mediation to Short-lived Conflict Settlements,' *International Studies Quarterly*, 50 (4): 819–840.

Gelashvili, Sophie. 2001. 'The Georgian–Abkhazian Conflict: Lost Momentum for Establishing Accountability?' in Albrecht Schnabel (ed.), *Southeast European Security: Threats, Responses, Challenges*. Hauppage, NY: Nova Publishers, pp. 193–204.

Ghosn, Faten, Glenn Palmer, and Stuart Bremer. 2004. 'The MID3 Data Set, 1993–2001: Procedures, Coding Rules, and Description.' *Conflict Management and Peace Science*, 21: 133–154.

Ginsburg, Tom and Richard H. McAdams. 2004. 'Adjudicating in Anarchy: An Expressive Theory of International Dispute Resolution,' *William and Mary Law Review*, 45 (4): 1229–1339.

Goldenberg, Suzanne. 1994. *Pride of Small Nations: The Caucasus and Post-Soviet Disorder*. London: Zed Books.

González, F.E., I. Bolívar and T. Vázquez. 2003. *Violencia Política en Colombia: De la. Nación Fragmentada a la Construcción del Estado*. Bogotá: CINEP.

Gordon, D. Stuart and F.H. Toase (eds.). 2001. *Aspects of Peacekeeping*. London: Routledge.

Goulding, Marrack. 2003. *Peacemonger*. Baltimore, MD: Johns Hopkins University Press.

Goulding, Marrack. 1993. 'The Evolution of United Nations Peacekeeping,' *International Affairs*, 69 (3): 451–465.

Gray, Christine and Benedict Kingsbury. 1993. 'Developments in Dispute Settlement,' in *The British Year Book of International Law, 1992*, vol. 63. New York, NY: Oxford University Press, pp. 97–134.

Gray, Colin S. 2005. *Another Bloody Century: Future Warfare*. London: Weidenfeld & Nicolson.

Greig, Michael J. 2005. 'Stepping into the Fray: When Do Mediators Mediate?' *American Journal of Political Science*, 49 (2): 249–266.

Haas, Ernst B. 1993. 'Collective Conflict Management: Evidence for a New World Order?' in Thomas G. Weiss (ed.) *Collective Security in a Changing World*, Boulder, CO: Lynne Reinner.

Haas, Ernst B. 1983. 'Regime Decay: Conflict Management and International Organizations, 1945–1981,' *International Organization*, 37 (2): 189–256.

Hall, Jonathan, Erik Melander, and Magnus Öberg. 2006. *The 'New Wars' Debate Revisited: An Empirical Evaluation of the Atrociousness of 'New Wars.'* Uppsala Peace Research Papers no. 9. Uppsala: Department of Peace and Conflict Research, Uppsala University.

Harbom, Lotta and Peter Wallensteen. 2007. 'Armed Conflict 1989–2006,' *Journal of Peace Research*, 44 (5): 623–634.

Harding, Jeremy. 1994. *Small Wars, Small Mercies: Journeys in Africa's Disputed Nations*. London: Penguin.

Haysom, Nicholas. 2006. 'Reflecting on the IGAD Peace Process,' in *Peace by Piece: Addressing Sudan's Conflicts*, Accord: An International Review of Peace Initiatives (no. 18). London: Conciliation Resources.

Hegre, Håvard, 2004. 'The Duration and Termination of Civil War,' *Journal of Peace Research*, 41 (3): 243–252.

Heldt, Birger. 2008. 'Trends from 1948 to 2005: How to View the Relation Between the United Nations and Non-UN Entities,' in Donald C.F. Daniel, Patricia Taft, and Sharon Wiharta (eds.), *Peace Operations: Trends, Progress, and Prospects*. Washington, DC: Georgetown University Press.

Heldt, Birger. 1999. 'Domestic Politics, Absolute Deprivation, and the Use of Armed Force in Interstate Territorial Disputes, 1950–1990,' *Journal of Conflict Resolution*, 43 (4): 451–478.

Heldt, Birger and Peter Wallensteen. 2005. *Peacekeeping Operations: Global Patterns of Intervention and Success, 1948–2004*, Research Report no. 2. Stockholm: Folke Bernadotte Academy.

Helfer, Laurence and Anne-Marie Slaughter. 2005. 'Why States Create International Tribunals: A Response to Professors Posner and Yoo,' *California Law Review*, 93: 1–58.

Helfer, Laurence and Anne-Marie Slaughter. 1997. 'Toward a Theory of Effective Supranational Adjudication,' *Yale Law Journal*, 107: 387.

Henderson, Errol and J. David Singer. 2002. 'New Wars and Rumors of New Wars,' *International Interactions*, 28 (2): 165–190.

Henkin, Louis. 1961. *How Nations Behave*. New Haven, CT: Yale University Press.

Hettne, Björn and Fredrik Söderbaum. 2005. 'Intervening in Complex Humanitarian Emergencies: The Role of Regional Cooperation,' *The European Journal of Development Research*, 17 (3): 449–461.

Holmes, Jennifer S., Sheila Amin Gutiérrez de Piñeres, and Kevin M. Curtin. 2006. 'Drugs, Violence and Development in Colombia: A Department Level Analysis,' *Latin American Politics and Society*, 48 (3): 157–185.

Holsti, Kalevi. 1996. *The State, War, and the State of War*. Cambridge: Cambridge University Press.

Homer-Dixon, Thomas. 1999. *Environment, Scarcity, and Violence*. Princeton, NJ: Princeton University Press.

Honeyman, Christopher and Nita Yawanarajah. 2003. 'Mediation,' in Guy Burgess and Heidi Burgess (eds.), *Beyond Intractability*. Boulder, CO: Conflict Research Consortium.

Human Rights Watch. 1996. *Colombia's Killer Networks: The Military–Paramilitary Partnership and the United States*. New York, NY: Human Rights Watch.

Human Security Centre. 2008. 'Human Security Brief 2007.' Human Security Centre, Simon Fraser University. Available at: www.humansecuritybrief.info.

Hunter, Shireen. 1994. *The Transcaucasus in Transition*. Washington, DC: Center for Strategic and International Studies.

Huntington, Samuel P. 1996. *The Clash of Civilizations and the Remaking of World Order*. New York, NY: Simon & Schuster.

Huysmans, Jef. 1998. 'Security! What Do You Mean? From Concept to Thick Signifier,' *European Journal of International Relations*, 4 (2): 226–255.

Huysmans, Jef. 1995. 'Migrants as a Security Problem: Dangers of "Securitising" Societal Issues,' in Robert Miles and Dietrich Thranhardt (eds.), *Migration and European Integration: The Dynamics of Inclusion and Exclusion*. London: Pinter.

Ikenberry, G. John. 2001. *After Victory: Institutions, Strategic Restraint, and the Rebuilding of Order After Major Wars*. Princeton, NJ: Princeton University Press.

Institute for Security Studies. 2004. *The Sudan–IGAD Peace Process: Signposts for the Way Forward*, African Security Analysis Program, Occasional Paper no. 86.

Inter-American Court on Human Rights (IACHR). 2005a. *Case of the 'Mapiripán Massacre' v. Colombia: Preliminary Objections*. Judgment of 7 March 2005. Series C No. 122. Available at: www.corteidh.or.cr/casos.cfm (accessed 29 August 2008).

Inter-American Court on Human Rights (IACHR). 2005b. *Case of the 'Mapiripán Massacre' v. Colombia: Merits, Reparations and Costs*. Judgment of 15 September 2005. Series C No. 134. Available at: www.corteidh.or.cr/casos.cfm (accessed 29 August 2008).

Intergovernmental Authority for Development (IGAD). 2002. IGAD Secretariat on Peace in the Sudan (Machakos Protocol), 20 July.

International Center for Transitional Justice (ICTJ). 2005. Summary of amicus brief on the Mapiripán Massacre. Submitted to the Inter-American Court of Human Rights, 5 May. Available at: http://ictj.org/en/where/region2/514.html (accessed 21 August 2008).

International Court of Justice. 2008. 'Declarations Recognizing the Jurisdiction of the Court as Compulsory.' Available at: www.icj-cij.org/jurisdiction/index.php?p1=5&p2=1&p3=3 (accessed 13 June 2008).

International Crisis Group. 2004. 'Bringing peace to EU's "new neighbours"' *The European Voice*, 19 May. Available at: www.crisisgroup.org/home/index.cfm?id=2769&l=1 (accessed 11 November 2007).

Iran–United States Claims Tribunal. 2008. 'The Iran–U.S. Claims Tribunal: Background Information.' Available at: www.iusct.org (accessed 11 July 2008).

Isacson, Adam. 2003. 'Washington's "New War" in Colombia: The War on Drugs Meets the War on Terror,' *NACLA Report on the Americas*, 36 (5): 13.

Jakobsen, Peter Viggo. 1996. 'National Interest, Humanitarianism, or CNN: What Triggers UN Peace Enforcement after the Cold War?' *Journal of Peace Research*, 33 (2): 205–215.

James, Alan. 1990. *Peacekeeping in International Politics*. New York, NY: St. Martin's Press.

Janis, Mark W. (ed.). 1992. *International Courts for the Twenty-First Century*. Dordrecht: Martin Nijhoff.

Jennings, Robert. 1995. 'The International Court of Justice After Fifty Years,' *American Journal of International Law*, 89: 493–505.

Jervis, Robert. 1978. 'Cooperation Under the Security Dilemma,' *World Politics*, 30 (2): 167–214.

Jervis, Robert. 1976. *Perception and Misperception in International Politics*. Princeton, NJ: Princeton University Press.

Johnston, Nicola. 2001. 'Peace Support Operations,' in *Inclusive Security, Sustainable Peace: A Toolkit for Advocacy and Action*. Denver, CO: Hunt Alternatives Fund.

Jung, Dietrich (ed.). 2003. *Shadow Globalization, Ethnic Conflicts, and New Wars*. London: Routledge.

Kakabadze, Irakli. 1997. 'Russian Troops in Abkhazia: Peacekeeping or Keeping Both Pieces,' *Perspectives on Central Asia*, 2 (6).

Kaldor, Mary. 2000. *Cosmopolitanism and Organised Violence*. Paper prepared for Conference 'Conceiving Cosmopolitanism,' 27–29 April, Warwick.

Kaldor, Mary. 1999. *New and Old Wars: Organized Violence in a Global Era*. Stanford, CA: Stanford University Press.

Kalyvas, Stathis N. 2001. '"New" and "Old" Civil Wars – A Valid Distinction?' *World Politics*, 54 (1): 99–108.

Kaplan, Robert D. 1994. 'The Coming Anarchy,' *Atlantic Monthly*, 273 (2): 44–76.

Karns, Margaret P. and Karen A. Mingst. 2001. 'Peacekeeping and the Changing Role of the United Nations: Four Dilemmas,' in Ramesh Thakur and Albrecht Schnabel (eds.), *United Nations Peacekeeping Operations: Ad Hoc Missions, Permanent Engagement*. Tokyo: United Nations University Press, pp. 215–237.

Karns, Margaret P. and Karen A. Mingst. 1998. 'The Evolution of United Nations Peacekeeping and Peacemaking: Lessons from the Past and Challenges for the Future,' in M.T. Klare and Y. Chandrani (eds.), *World Security: Challenges for a New Century*, 3rd edn. New York, NY: St. Martin's Press, pp. 200–228.

Katzenstein, Peter J. 1996. *The Culture of National Security: Norms and Identity in World Politics*. New York, NY: Columbia University Press.

Keen, Benjamin. 1996. *A History of Latin America*. Boston, MA: Houghton Mifflin.

Kelsen, Hans. 1943. 'Compulsory Adjudication of International Disputes,' *The American Journal of International Law*, 37 (3): 397–406.

Keohane, Robert. 1989. *International Institutions and State Power*. Boulder, CO: Westview Press.

Keohane, Robert and Joseph S. Nye. 2001. *Power and Interdependence*, 3rd edn. New York, NY: Longman.

Ker-Lindsey, James. 2006. 'The UN Force in Cyprus After the 2004 Reunification Referendum,' *International Peacekeeping*, 13 (3): 410–421.

Kirk, Robin. 2005. 'The Lessons of Mapiripán,' *Transforming Anthropology*, 13 (2): 116–118.

Kissinger, Henry. 2001. *Does America Need a Foreign Policy? Toward a Diplomacy for the 21st Century*. New York, NY: Simon & Schuster.

Krause, Keith and Michael C. Williams (eds.). 1997. *Critical Security Studies*. Minneapolis, MN: University of Minnesota Press.

Krause, Keith and Michael C. Williams. 1996. 'Broadening the Agenda of Security Studies: Politics and Methods,' *Mershon International Studies Review*, 40 (2): 229–254.

Krieger, Heike (ed.). 1997. *East Timor and the International Community*. Cambridge: Cambridge University Press.

Kritz, Neil J. 2007. 'The Rule of Law in Conflict Management,' in C. Crocker, F. Hampson, and P. Aall (eds.), *Leashing the Dogs of War: Conflict Management in a Divided World*. Washington, DC: USIP, pp. 401–424.

Kuklick, Bruce. 2006. *Blind Oracles: Intellectuals and War from Kennan to Kissinger*. Princeton, NJ: Princeton University Press.

Kupchan, Charles A. and Clifford A. Kupchan. 1991. 'Concerts, Collective Security, and the Future of Europe,' *International Security*, 16 (1): 114–161.

Kydd, Andrew H. 2006. 'When Can Mediators Build Trust?' *American Political Science Review*, 100 (3): 449–462.

Lacina, Bethany Ann. 2006. 'Explaining the Severity of Civil War,' *Journal of Conflict Resolution*, 50 (2): 276–289.

Lacina, Bethany. 2004. 'From Side Show to Centre Stage: Civil Conflict after the Cold War,' *Security Dialogue*, 35 (2): 191–205.

Lacina, Bethany Ann and Nils Petter Gleditsch. 2005. 'Monitoring Trends in Global Combat: A New Dataset of Battle Deaths,' *European Journal of Population*, 21: 145–165.

Lacina, Bethany Ann, Nils Petter Gleditsch, and Bruce M. Russett. 2006. 'The Declining Risk of Death in Battle,' *International Studies Quarterly*, 50 (3): 673–680.

Leech, Garry. 1999. 'Special Report: Fifty Years of Violence,' *Colombia Report*. New York, NY: Information Network of the Americas.

Leonard, Eric K. 2002. 'Establishing an International Criminal Court: The Emergence of a New Global Authority?' Pew Case Studies in International Affairs, No. 258. Washington, DC: Georgetown University Institute for the Study of Diplomacy.

Levy, Jack S. 1988. 'Domestic Politics and War,' *Journal of Interdisciplinary History*, 18 (3): 653–673.

Livingston, Steven. 1997. 'Clarifying the CNN Effect: An Examination of Media Effects According to Type of Military Intervention.' Joan Shorenstein Center on the Press, Politics, and Public Policy, John F. Kennedy School of Government, Harvard University.

Livingstone, Grace. 2004. *Inside Colombia: Drugs, Democracy, and War*. New Brunswick, NJ: Rutgers University Press.

Lucy, William. 1999. *Understanding and Explaining Adjudication*. New York, NY: Oxford University Press, 1999.

Lynch, Dov. 2006. *Why Georgia Matters*, Chaillot Paper no. 86. Paris: Institute for Security Studies.

Lynch, Dov. 2004. *Engaging Eurasia's Separatist States*. Washington, DC: USIP.

Lynch, Dov. 1998. *The Conflict in Abkhazia: Russian Peacekeeping Dilemmas*. London: Chatham House Discussion Paper no. 77.

McAdams, Richard H. 2005. 'The Expressive Power of Adjudication,' *University of Illinois Law Review*, 5: 1043–1121.

MacFarlane, S. Neil and Albrecht Schnabel. 1995. 'The Russian Approach to Peacekeeping,' *International Journal*, 50 (2): 294–324.

MacFarlane, S. Neil, Larry Minear, and Stephen D. Shenfield. 1996. *Armed Conflict in Georgia: A Case Study in Humanitarian Action and Peacekeeping*, Occasional Paper no. 21. Thomas J. Watson Jr. Institute for International Studies, Brown University.

McIntosh, David D. 1998. 'The Muscular Mediator: Richard Holbrooke and the Dayton Peace Conference,' Working Paper 98–1. Harvard Program on Negotiation.

Mack, Andrew. 2005. *Human Security Report 2005*. New York, NY: Oxford University Press.

Mackinlay, John and Jarat Chopra. 1992. 'Second Generation Multinational Operations,' *The Washington Quarterly*, 15 (3): 116–120.

McLaughlin, Abraham. 2005. 'Africa's Peace-Seekers: Lazaro Sumbeiywo,' *Christian Science Monitor*, 12 September. Available at: http://www.csmonitor.com/2005/0912/p01s04-woaf.html?s=spworld .

Mangone, Gerard J. 1954. *A Short History of International Organization*. New York, NY: McGraw-Hill.

Mann, Michael. 1993. *The Sources of Social Power: Volume 2, The Rise of Classes and Nation States 1760–1914*. Cambridge: Cambridge University Press.

Marks, Edward. 1995. 'Dynamics of Peacekeeping in Georgia,' *Strategic Forum*, Institute for National Strategic Studies, no. 45 (September). Washington, DC: National Defense University.

Marshall, Monty G. and Ted Robert Gurr. 2005. *Peace and Conflict, 2005: A Global Survey of Armed Conflicts, Self-Determination Movements, and Democracy*. College Park, MD: Center for International Development and Conflict Management, University of Maryland.

Martin, Harriet. 2006. *Kings of Peace, Pawns of War: The Untold Story of Peacemaking*. London: Continuum Publishing.

Martin, Ian. 2001. *Self-Determination in East Timor: The United Nations, the Ballot, and the International Intervention*. Boulder, CO: Lynne Rienner.

Matthews, Jessica Tuchman. 1989. 'Redefining Security,' *Foreign Affairs*, 68 (2): 162–177.

Mearsheimer, John J. 1990. 'Back to the Future: Instability in Europe After the Cold War,' *International Security*, 15 (1): 5–56.

Merrills, John G. 2005. *International Dispute Settlement*, 4th edn. Cambridge: Cambridge University Press.

Minorities at Risk Project. 2005. College Park, MD: Center for International Development and Conflict Management. Available at: www.cidcm.umd.edu/mar.

Mirbagheri, Fari. 1998. *Cyprus and International Peacemaking, 1964–1986*. London: Routledge.

Moore, Christopher W. 2003. *The Mediation Process: Practical Strategies for Resolving Conflict*, 3rd edn. San Francisco, CA: Jossey-Bass.

Moravcsik, Andrew. 2000. 'The Origins of Human Rights Regimes: Democratic Delegation in Postwar Europe,' *International Organization*, 54 (2): 217–252.

Morgenthau, Hans J. 1948. *Politics Among Nations: The Struggle for Power and Peace*. New York, NY: Alfred A. Knopf.

Morgenthau, Hans J. 1946. *Scientific Man vs. Power Politics*. Chicago, IL: University of Chicago Press.

Morris, Justin and Hilaire McCoubrey. 1999. 'Regional Peacekeeping in the Post-Cold War Era,' *International Peacekeeping*, 6 (2): 129–151.

Morrison, Alex. 1999. *Peacekeeping by Proxy*. Cornwallis Park, NS: Canadian Peacekeeping Press.

Mueller, John. 2004. *The Remnants of War*. Ithaca, NY: Cornell University Press.

Mueller, John. 1989. *Retreat from Doomsday: The Obsolescence of Major War*. New York, NY: Basic Books.

Münkler, Herfried. 2004. *The New Wars*. London: Polity.

National Institute for Dispute Resolution (NIDR). 1992. *A Conversation on Peacemaking with Jimmy Carter*. Washington, DC: National Institute for Dispute Resolution. Fifth National Conference on Peacemaking and Conflict Resolution in Charlotte, NC, 7 June 1991. Available at: www.pbs.org/wgbh/amex/carter/peopleevents/e_peace.html.

Newman, Edward. 2004. 'The "New Wars" Debate: A Historical Perspective is Needed,' *Security Dialogue*, 35 (2): 173–189.

Nichols, Jim. 2008. *Armenia, Azerbaijan, and Georgia: Political Developments and Implications for U.S. Interests*. Congressional Research Service Report, June.

Norwegian Refugee Council. 1995. *Survey on Internally Displaced People in Georgia*. Tbilisi: Norwegian Refugee Council.

O'Neill, John Terence and Nicholas Rees. 2005. *United Nations Peacekeeping in the Post-Cold War Era*. London: Routledge.

Paris, Roland. 2001. 'Human Security: Paradigm Shift or Hot Air?' *International Security*, 26 (2): 87–102.

Pavri, Tinaz. 1997. 'Help or Hindrance: Third Parties in the Indo-Pakistani Conflict,' *Negotiation Journal*, 13 (4): 369–388.

Phillips, David L. 2004. *Stability, Security, and Sovereignty in the Republic of Georgia*. Rapid Response Conflict Prevention Assessment, Center for Preventative Action. Washington, DC: Council on Foreign Relations.

Posada, Eduardo. 2001. *Civil War? The Language of Conflict in Colombia*. Bogotá: Fundación Ideas para la Paz. Available at: www.ideaspaz.org/publicaciones/download/guerra_civil_english.pdf (accessed 17 August 2008).

Posner, Eric A. and John C. Yoo. 2004. 'A Theory of International Adjudication,' John M. Olin Law and Economics Working Paper, no. 206 (2nd series). University of Chicago School of Law (February).

Powell, Emilia Justyna and Sara McLaughlin Mitchell. 2007. 'The International Court of Justice and the World's Three Legal Systems,' *The Journal of Politics*, 69 (2): 397–415.

Powell, Walter W. 1990. 'Neither Market Nor Hierarchy: Network Forms of Organization,' *Research in Organizational Behavior*, 12: 295–336.

Prendergast, John and David Mozersky. 2004. 'Love Thy Neighbor: Regional Intervention in Sudan's Civil War,' *Harvard International Review*, 26 (1): 70–74.

Princen, Thomas. 1994. 'Joseph Elder: Quiet Peacemaking in a Civil War' in Deborah Kolb *et al.* (eds.), *When Talk Works: Profiles of Mediators*. San Francisco, CA: Jossey-Bass.

Princen, Thomas. 1992. *Intermediaries in International Conflict*. Princeton, NJ: Princeton University Press.

Pruitt, Dean G. 1997. 'Ripeness Theory and the Oslo Talks,' *International Negotiation*, 2 (2): 237–250.

Regan, Patrick M. and Allan C. Stam III. 2000. 'In the Nick of Time: Conflict Management, Mediation Timing, and the Duration of Interstate Disputes,' *International Studies Quarterly*, 44 (2): 239–260.

Reuters. 1998. 'Colombia War Displaces 241,312 People in 1998,' (29 November).

Rice, Edward E. 1988. *Wars of the Third Kind: Conflict in Underdeveloped Countries*. Berkeley, CA: University of California Press.

Richani, Nazih. 2002. *Systems of Violence: The Political Economy of War and Peace in Colombia*. Albany, NY: SUNY Press.

Richardson, Lewis. 1960. *Statistics of Deadly Quarrels*. Pittsburgh, PA: Boxwood Press.

Rieff, David. 1994. 'The Illusions of Peacekeeping,' *World Policy Journal*, 11 (3): 1–18.

Rikhye, Indar Jit. 2000. *The Politics and Practice of United Nations Peacekeeping: Past, Present and Future*. Cornwallis Park, NS: Canadian Peacekeeping Press.

Roberts, Adam. 1995. 'From San Francisco to Sarajevo: The UN and the Use of Force,' *Survival*, 37 (4): 7–28.

Robertson, Commodore B.D. 2000. 'Not Learning the Lessons of Operation Stabilise,' *Journal of the Australian Naval Institute*, 26 (2): 11.

Robinson, Geoffrey. 2001. 'People's War: Militias in East Timor and Indonesia,' *South East Asia Research*, 9 (3): 271–318.

Romano, Cesare P.R. 1999. 'The Proliferation of International Judicial Bodies: The Pieces of the Puzzle,' *New York University Journal of International Law and Politics*, 31: 709–751.

Rose, Gideon. 1998. 'The Exit Strategy Delusion,' *Foreign Affairs*, January/February: 56–67.

Rosner, Gabriella. 1965. 'The International Military Force Idea: A Look at Modern History,' in Joel Larus (ed.), *From Collective Security to Preventative Diplomacy*. New York, NY: Wiley, pp. 445–456.

Ryan, Alan. 2000. *Primary Responsibilities and Primary Risks: Australian Defence Force Participation in the International Force, East Timor*. Canberra: Land Warfare Studies Centre.

Sarat, Austin and Joel B. Grossman. 1975. 'Courts and Conflict Resolution: Problems in the Mobilization of Adjudication,' *American Political Science Review*, 69 (4): 1200–1217.

Schmidl, Erwin A. (ed.). 2000. *Peace Operations Between War and Peace*. London: Routledge.

Schreuer, Christoph. 1993. 'The Waning of the Sovereign State: Towards a New Paradigm for International Law?' *European Journal of International Law*, 4: 447–471.

Schrodt, Philip A., Ömür Yilmaz, and Deborah J. Gerner. 2003. 'Evaluating "Ripeness" and "Hurting Stalemate" in Mediated International Conflicts: An Event Data Study of the Middle East, Balkans, and West Africa,' paper delivered at the Annual Meeting of the International Studies Association, Portland, OR.

Sharma, Surya Prakesh. 1997. *Territorial Acquisition, Disputes, and International Law*. Leiden: Martinus Nijhoff Publishers.

Shashenkov, Maxim. 1995. 'Russian Peacekeeping in the "Near Abroad,"' *Survival*, 36 (3): 47–48.

Shaw, Martin, 1999. 'War and Globality: The Role and Character of War in the Global Transition,' in Ho-Won Jeong (ed.), *The New Agenda for Peace Research*. Aldershot: Ashgate, pp. 61–80.

Shaw, Martin. 1994. *Global Society and International Relations: Sociological Concepts and Political Perspectives*. Cambridge: Polity.

Sheehan, Michael. 2008. 'The Changing Character of War,' in John Baylis, Steve Smith, and Patricia Owens (eds.), *The Globalization of World Politics: An Introduction to International Relations*, 4th edn. New York, NY: Oxford University Press.

Sheehan, Michael. 2005. *International Security: An Analytical Survey*. Boulder, CO: Lynne Rienner.

Shenfield, Stephen. 1995. 'Armed Conflict in Eastern Europe and the former Soviet Union,' in Thomas G. Weiss (ed.), *The United Nations and Civil Wars*. Boulder, CO: Lynne Rienner, pp. 31–48.

Simmons, Beth A. 2002. 'Capacity, Commitment, and Compliance: International Institutions and Territorial Disputes,' *Journal of Conflict Resolution*, 46 (6): 829–856.

Simmons, Beth A. 1999. 'See You In "Court"? The Appeal to Quasi-Judicial Legal Processes in the Settlement of Territorial Disputes,' in Paul F. Diehl (ed.), *A Roadmap to War: Territorial Dimensions of International Conflict*. Nashville, TN: Vanderbilt University Press, pp. 205–237.

Simmons, Beth A. 1998. 'Compliance with International Agreements,' *Annual Review of Political Science*, 1: 75–93.

Simmons, Beth A. and Lisa L. Martin. 2002. 'International Organizations and Institutions,' in Walter Carlsnaes, Thomas Risse, and Beth A. Simmons (eds.), *Handbook of International Relations*. Thousand Oaks, CA: Sage, pp. 192–211.

Simmons, Mark and Peter Dixon. 2006. 'Introduction,' in *Peace by Piece: Addressing Sudan's Conflicts*, Accord: An International Review of Peace Initiatives (no. 18). London: Conciliation Resources.

Singer, J. David and Melvin Small. 1972. *The Wages of War 1816–1965: A Statistical Handbook*. New York, NY: Wiley.

Slider, Darrell. 1985. 'Crisis and Response in Soviet Nationality Policy: The Case of Abkhazia,' *Central Asian* Survey, 4 (4): 51–68.

Smith, Michael G. (with Moreen Dee). 2003. *Peacekeeping in East Timor: The Path to Independence*. Boulder, CO: Lynne Rienner.

Smith, Michael G. and Moreen Dee. 2006. 'East Timor,' in William J. Durch (ed.), *Twenty-First Century Peace Operations*. Washington, DC: USIP, pp. 389–466.

Snow, Donald M., 1996. *Uncivil Wars: International Security and the New Internal Conflicts*. Boulder, CO: Lynne Rienner.

Socor, Vladimir. 2006. *Eurasia Insight*, 20 November.

Spangler, Brad. 2003a. 'Problem-Solving Mediation,' in Guy Burgess and Heidi Burgess (eds.), *Beyond Intractability*. Boulder, CO: Conflict Research Consortium.

Spangler, Brad. 2003b. 'Adjudication,' in Guy Burgess and Heidi Burgess (eds.), *Beyond Intractability*. Boulder, CO: Conflict Research Consortium. Available at: www.beyondintractability.org/essay/adjudication (accessed 17 July 2008).

Spencer, David. 2001. 'Colombia's Paramilitaries: Criminals or Political Force?' Strategic Studies Institute, U.S. Army War College Working Paper (December).

Stein, Janice Gross. 2001. 'Image, Identity, and the Resolution of Violent Conflict,' in C.A. Crocker, F.O. Hampson, and P. Aall (eds.), *Turbulent Peace: The Challenges of Managing International Conflict*. Washington, DC: USIP, pp. 189–208.

Stepanova, Ekaterina. 2008. *SIPRI Yearbook 2008: Armaments, Disarmament and International Security*. Oxford: Oxford University Press.

Stiglitz, Joseph E. 2002. *Globalization and Its Discontents*. New York, NY: W.W. Norton.

Stokes, Doug. 2001. 'Better Lead Than Bread? A Critical Analysis of the US's Plan Colombia,' *Civil Wars*, 4 (2): 59–78.

Stuyt, Alexander Marie. 1990. *Survey of International Arbitrations, 1794–1989*, 3rd edn. Leiden: Martinus Nijhoff.

Suárez, Alfredo Rangel. 2000. 'Parasites and Predators: Guerrillas and the Insurrection Economy of Colombia,' *Journal of International Affairs*, 53 (2): 577–601.

Suhrke, Astri. 2001. 'Peacekeepers as Nation-Builders: Dilemmas of the UN in East Timor,' *International Peacekeeping*, 8 (4): 1–20.

Sumbeiywo, Lazaro. 2006. 'The Mediator's Perspective: An Interview with General Lazaro Sumbeiywo,' in *Peace by Piece: Addressing Sudan's Conflicts*, Accord: An International Review of Peace Initiatives (no. 18). London: Conciliation Resources.

Suny, Ronald. 1988. *The Making of the Georgian Nation*. Bloomington, IN: Indiana University Press.

Sweig, Julia E. 2002. 'What Kind of War for Colombia?' *Foreign Affairs*, 81 (5): 122–141.

Talman, Stefan. 2002. 'Impediments to Peacekeeping: The Case of Cyprus,' in Harvey Langholtz, Boris Kondoch, and Alan Wells (eds.), *International Peacekeeping: The Yearbook of International Peace Operations*, Vol. 8, Leiden: Martinus Nijhoff, pp. 33–63.

Tate, Winifred. 2001. 'Paramilitaries in Colombia,' *Brown Journal of World Affairs*, 8 (1): 163–175.

Taylor, Steven L. 2005. 'When Wars Collide: The War on Drugs and the Global War on Terror,' *Strategic Insights*, 4 (6): 15.

Thakur, Ramesh. 2006. *The United Nations, Peace and Security: From Collective Security to the Responsibility to Protect*. Cambridge: Cambridge University Press.

Thakur, Ramesh and Albrecht Schnabel (eds.). 2001. *United Nations Peacekeeping Operations: Ad Hoc Missions, Permanent Engagement*. Tokyo: United Nations University Press.

Theodorides, John. 1982. 'The United Nations Peacekeeping Force in Cyprus (UNFICYP),' *International and Comparative Law Quarterly*, 31: 765–783.

Touval, Saadia. 1995. 'Mediator's Flexibility and the U.N. Security Council,' *Annals of the American Academy of Political and Social Science*, Vol. 542 (*Flexibility in International Negotiation and Mediation*). Sage, pp. 202–212.

Touval, Saadia. 1992. 'The Superpowers as Mediators,' in Jacob Bercovitch and Jeffrey Z. Rubin (eds.), *Mediation in International Relations: Multiple Approaches to Conflict Management*. New York, NY: Macmillan/St. Martin's Press.

Touval, Saadia. 1982. *The Peace Brokers*. Princeton, NJ: Princeton University Press.

Touval, Saadia and I. William Zartman. 2001. 'International Mediation in the Post-Cold War

Era,' in C.A. Crocker, F.O. Hampson, and P. Aall (eds.), *Turbulent Peace: The Challenges of Managing International Conflict*. Washington, DC: USIP, pp. 427–443.

Traub, James. 2000. 'Inventing East Timor,' *Foreign Affairs*, 79 (4): 74–89.

Ullman, Richard. 1983. 'Redefining Security,' *International Security*, 8 (1): 129–153.

United Nations. 2007a. 'UNOMIG: United Nations Observer Mission in Georgia – Background.' Department of Peacekeeping Operations. Available at: www.un.org/Depts/dpko/missions/unomig/background.html (accessed 21 June 2008).

United Nations. 2007b. 'Report of the Secretary-General on the Situation in Abkhazia, Georgia,' Security Council, S/2007/15, 11 January.

United Nations. 2003. 'Somalia – UNOSOM I Background.' Department of Peacekeeping Operations. Available at: www.un.org/Depts/dpko/dpko/co_mission/unosom1backgr2.html (accessed 17 July 2007).

United Nations. 1999a. 'Report of the Secretary-General pursuant to General Assembly Resolution 53/55: The Fall of Srebrenica.'

United Nations. 1999b. 'Report of the Security Council Mission to Jakarta and Dili, 14 September 1999.' Available at: www.un.org/peace/etimor99/9926220E.htm (accessed 12 November 2007).

United Nations. 1999c. 'Resolution 1264 (1999),' S/RES/1264, 15 September. Available at: http://daccessdds.un.org/doc/UNDOC/GEN/N99/264/81/PDF/N9926481.pdf (accessed 14 November 2007).

United Nations. 1996. *The Blue Helmets. A Review of United Nations Peace-Keeping*, 3rd edn. New York: United Nations Publications.

United Nations. 1994. 'Consolidated Interagency Appeal for the Caucasus, 1 April 1994–31 March 1995.' Office of the High Commissioner for Human Rights. Geneva: United Nations.

United Nations. 1980. *Report of the Independent Commission on International Development Issues, North–South: A Programme for Survival*, Brandt Commission. London: Pan Books.

United Nations. 1961. UN Document S/PV.941, 20 February.

United Nations. 1960a. UN Document S/PV.873, para. 28, 13 July.

United Nations. 1960b. UN Document S/4417, 6 August.

United Nations. 1960c. General Assembly Resolution 1474 (ES-IV), 20 September.

United States Department of State. 2003. 'Fact Sheet: Intergovernmental Authority on Development.' Bureau of Political–Military Affairs, Washington, DC. Available at: www.state.gov/t/pm/rls/fs/22517.htm (accessed 4 June 2007).

Untawale, Mukund. 1974. 'The Kutch–Sind Dispute: A Case Study in International Arbitration,' *The International and Comparative Law Quarterly*, 23 (4): 818–839.

Uppsala Conflict Data Program. 2008. UCDP Database. Available at: www.ucdp.uu.se/database.

Urquhart, Brian. 1994. *Hammarskjold*. New York, NY: W.W. Norton & Co.

Urquhart, Brian. 1990. 'Beyond the Sheriff's Posse,' *Survival*, 32 (3): 196–205.

van Creveld, Martin. 1991. *The Transformation of War*. New York, NY: Free Press.

Van Dyk, Peter and G.J.H. Van Hoof. 1998. *Theory and Practice of the European Convention on Human Rights*, 3rd edn. Boston, MA: Kluwer.

Von Hippel, Karin and Michael Clarke. 1999. 'Something Must Be Done,' *The World Today*, March: 4–7.

Wæver, Ole. 1995. 'Securitization and Desecuritization,' in Ronnie Lipschutz (ed.), *On Security*. New York, NY: Columbia University Press.

Walker, R.B.J. 1997. 'The Subject of Security,' in Keith Krause and Michael Williams (eds.), *Critical Security Studies*. Minneapolis, MN: University of Minnesota Press, pp. 61–81.

Wall, James A. Jr, John B. Stark, and Rhetta L. Standifer. 2001. 'Mediation: A Current Review and Theory Development,' *Journal of Conflict Resolution*, 45 (3): 370–391.

Wallenstein, Peter and Karin Axell. 1995. 'Armed Conflict at the End of the Cold War, 1989–93', *Journal of Peace Research*, 30 (3): 331–346.

Walt, Stephen. 1991. 'The Renaissance of Security Studies,' *International Studies Quarterly*, 35 (2): 211–239.

Walt, Stephen. 1987. *The Origins of Alliances*. Ithaca, NY: Cornell University Press.

Walt, Stephen. 1985. 'Alliance Formation and the Balance of World Power,' *International Security*, 9 (4): 3–43.

Waltz, Kenneth N. 1979. *Theory of International Politics*. Reading, MA: Addison-Wesley.

Wells, Alan. 2008. *International Peacekeeping: The Yearbook of International Peace Operations*, Vol. 13. Leiden: Brill.

Werner, Suzanne and Amy Yuen. 2005. 'Making and Keeping Peace,' *International Organization*, 59 (2): 261–292.

West, Deborah L. 2006. *The Sudan: Saving Lives, Sustaining Peace*, Belfer-WPF Report no. 42, Program on Intrastate Conflict.

Wetter, J. Gillis. 1971. 'The Rann of Kutch Arbitration,' *The American Journal of International Law*, 65 (2): 346–357.

Wilkenfeld, Jonathan, Kathleen J. Young, David M. Quinn, and Victor Asal. 2005. *Mediating International Crises*. London: Routledge.

Woodward, Peter. 2006. 'Peacemaking in Sudan,' in Oliver Furley and Roy May (eds.), *Ending Africa's Wars: Progressing to Peace*. London: Ashgate, pp. 167–178.

Woodward, Peter. 2004. 'Somalia and Sudan: A Tale of Two Peace Processes,' *The Round Table: The Commonwealth Journal of International Affairs*, 93 (375): 469–481.

Wright, Quincy. 1968. 'War: The Study of War,' in David L. Sills (ed.), *International Encyclopedia of the Social Sciences*, Vol. 16. New York, NY: Macmillan/Free Press, 453–468.

Wyn Jones, Richard. 2001. *Critical Theory and World Politics*. Boulder, CO: Lynne Rienner.

Wyn Jones, Richard. 1996. 'Travel without Maps: Thinking About Security After the Cold War,' in M. Jane Davis (ed.), *Security Issues in the Post-Cold War World*. Cheltenham: Edward Elgar, pp. 196–218.

Yoo, John. 1999. 'Globalism and the Constitution: Treaties, Non Self-Execution, and the Original Understanding,' *Columbia Law Review*, 99: 1955.

Young, John. 2005. 'Sudan: A Flawed Peace Process Leading to a Flawed Peace,' *Review of African Political Economy*, 32 (103): 99–113.

Young, Oran R. 1972. 'Intermediaries: Additional Thoughts on Third Parties,' *Journal of Conflict Resolution*, 16 (1): 51–65.

Young, Oran R. 1967. *The Intermediaries: Third Parties in International Crises*. Princeton, NJ: Princeton University Press.

Zartman, I. William. 2008. 'Introduction: Toward the Resolution of International Conflicts,' in I. William Zartman (ed.), *Peacemaking in International Conflict: Methods and Techniques*, revised edition. Washington, DC: USIP, pp. 3–22.

Zartman, I. William. 2003. 'Ripeness,' in Guy Burgess and Heidi Burgess (eds.), *Beyond Intractability*. Boulder, CO: Conflict Research Consortium

Zartman, I. William. 2000. 'Ripeness: The Hurting Stalemate and Beyond,' in Paul C. Stern and Daniel Druckman (eds.), *International Conflict Resolution After the Cold War*. Washington, DC: National Academy Press.

Zartman, I. William. 1995. 'Systems of World Order and Regional Conflict Reduction,' in I. William Zartman and Victor A. Kremenyuk (eds.), *Cooperative Security: Reducing Third World Wars*. Syracuse, NY: Syracuse University Press.

Zartman, I. William (ed.). 1994. *International Multilateral Negotiation. Approaches to the Management of Complexity*. San Francisco, CA: Jossey-Bass.

Zartman, I. William. 1991. 'The Structure of Negotiation,' in Victor A. Kremenyuk (ed.), *International Negotiation*. San Francisco, CA: Jossey-Bass, pp. 65–77.

Zartman, I. William and Maureen R. Berman. 1982. *The Practical Negotiator*. New Haven, CT: Yale University Press.

Zartman, I. William and Saadia Touval. 2007. 'International Mediation,' in C. Crocker, F.

Hampson, and P. Aall (eds.) *Leashing the Dogs of War: Conflict Management in a Divided World*. Washington, DC: USIP, pp. 437–454.

Zartman, I. William and Saadia Touval. 1992. 'Mediation: The Role of Third Party Diplomacy and Informal Peacemaking,' in Sheryl J. Brown and Kimber J. Schraub (eds.), *Resolving Third World Conflicts*. Washington, DC: USIP.

Zartman, I. William and Saadia Touval. 1985. 'International Mediation: Conflict Resolution and Power Politics,' *Journal of Social Issues*, 41 (2): 27–45.

Index